DATE DUE

JY 30 '98			

DEMCO 38-296

Shadows of Vietnam

Shadows of Vietnam

of

Vietnam

Lyndon Johnson's Wars

Frank E. Vandiver

Texas A&M University Press
College Station

ce: LBJ reviewing troops, October, 1966.
R. Okamoto; courtesy LBJ Library Collection

The paper used in this book meets the minimum requirements
of the American National Standard for Permanence
of Paper for Printed Library Materials, Z39.48-1984.
Binding materials have been chosen for durability.

∞

Library of Congress Cataloging-in-Publication Data

Vandiver, Frank Everson, 1925–
    Shadows of Vietnam : Lyndon Johnson's wars / Frank E. Vandiver.
    p.   cm.—
    Includes bibliographical references and index.
    ISBN 0-89096-747-4
        1. Vietnamese Conflict, 1961–1975—United States.   2. United
States—Politics and government—1963–1969.   3. Johnson, Lyndon
B. (Lyndon Baines), 1908–1973.   I. Title.   II. Series.
    DS558.V38   1997   96-50121
    959.704'3373—dc21   CIP

For my wife,

Renée,

who helped, encouraged,

and kept faith

against the odds.

And for Sara and John Lindsey,

whose help goes beyond

mere thanks.

contents

illustrations

preface

Why another book on Lyndon Johnson and his wars?

Defeated American war presidents have been few, but those few have not fared well in memory. Jefferson Davis, perhaps the most thoroughly defeated American president, is scarcely given a loser's mite on history's roll. Harry Truman is excoriated, still, for "losing" China. John F. Kennedy keenly felt the sting of the debacle at the Bay of Pigs. Lyndon Johnson, who, like Woodrow Wilson, did not want to be a war president, will always be judged against the weight of Vietnam, the shadow that overspreads his term in office.

Everything about LBJ's career should have made him a good war president—tough, seasoned in various political wars, a shrewd assessor of people, skilled in suasion, a consummate conniver, he had the gumption for the job. And yet he somehow failed to use America's power effectively against North Vietnam. Why?

In this book I try to find an answer through a biographical study of a president embroiled in a baffling war he came to hate, a man adrift in martial matters that seemed to work in a miasma beyond the "art of the possible." In trying to present Johnson's own perspective on Vietnam decisions and realities, I am following my own idea of the biographer's task—to get close enough to the subject for empathy. I do not suggest that empathy is approval, only that it can lead to an understanding of pressures and motives. This is a methodology I followed in my biographies of Stonewall Jackson and John J. Pershing. In both those books I attempted to let the reader see through the eyes of the subjects, to feel what they felt, to grasp their problems and understand why they did what they did.

So, with Lyndon Johnson I am concerned with what he did and how he did it, but most of all with motivation. I am interested in Johnson's motives because they often shaped his actions. Certainly I do not argue that good motives forgive bad deeds. I do argue, though, that motives can elucidate how people interpret facts and act upon them, and are vital in assessing character.

An eight-year look at motives, precedents and pressures, deeds and reasons, leads me to a personal view of Johnson as commander in chief.

acknowledgments

Let me begin by thanking my wife, Renée; my daughters, Nita Brata and Nancy Wahl, and my son, Frank (all of whom have long endured the vagaries of a writing father); my stepsons, Joseph, Timothy, Patrick, and Arthur Carmody III; and my stepdaughters, Virginia and Mary Carmody, Renée Mathews, and Helen Stroud, for their willing ears, sharp eyes, and constant encouragement over eight years of writing. Without them, this task would have been infinitely harder and much longer. Furthermore, without the aid, comfort, and willing help of many others, this task would never have been finished.

No author writes alone, and I am grateful far beyond thanks to the legions who have helped me follow Lyndon Johnson through the mazes of Washington and Vietnam. Mrs. Lady Bird Johnson offered time and encouragement from the start; her insights, contacts, and, most of all, her interest, smoothed my path immeasurably. My debt to her is lasting. So, too, is my debt to the marvelously helpful staff of the Lyndon Baines Johnson Library in Austin, Texas. Director Harry Middleton offered not only cooperation but his own fresh insights. Ted Gittinger, head of the library's Oral History Section, provided steady encouragement and guided me through his voluminous files with skill and wit and let me bask in a lasting friendship. David Humphreys, longtime head of the library's Manuscripts Division, shortened the pathway through an infinity of material with customary courtesy and humor. Phillip Scott of the Photographic Division made looking for photographs a real pleasure. Indeed, the entire staff of that splendid library helped beyond the call of duty, and thanks seem puny in return.

Don Wilson and David Alsobrook of the George Bush Library, College Station, Texas, cordially helped in finding elusive sources.

Many other libraries opened doors and collections and offered guidance and inspiration. Chief among these were the Carl Albert Collection of the University of Oklahoma Library; the John F. Kennedy Library; the Richard Russell Collection, University of Georgia Library; the Manuscripts Division, Library of Congress; the University of Texas Library; the New York Public Library; the U.S. Army Military History Institute at Carlisle Barracks, Pennsylvania (where special help came from the prodigiously learned Dr. Richard Sommers). Deep thanks go to the able director and energetic staff of the Sterling C. Evans Library at Texas A&M University. Everyone there showed patience beyond common in arranging interlibrary loans, checking references, helping research assistants, and doing myriad chores in support of this project.

Two research assistants did most of the digging for this book. In 1989 and 1990, Julie Mote, a Texas A&M student, worked with me on interviews and conducted several on her own, for which I offer deep thanks. From 1991 until 1994, Edith Anderson Wakefield, a history graduate student at Texas A&M, took up the trail. Her historical training and determination gave her work a special dimension that broadened the scope of the book. I am indebted for her diligence in pursuit of people, materials, and ideas, and for her unfailing good humor.

I am especially indebted to the many people who gave their time in personal interviews. Without their cooperation, this book simply could not have been written. Copies of their interviews are in my possession, along with their permissions to quote. They each deserve personal thanks and they should not be held responsible for my conclusions. They are: the late George W. Ball; Ben Barnes, Austin, Texas; the late McGeorge Bundy; William P. Bundy, Princeton, New Jersey; Liz Carpenter, Austin, Texas; George A. Carver, Jr., Washington, D.C.; George Christian, Austin, Texas; Clark Clifford, Washington, D.C.; Sheldon Cohen, Washington, D.C.; the late Gov. John Connally; the late William Colby; the late Sir Alec Douglas-Home; Daniel Ellsberg; the late Sen. J. William Fulbright; Gen. Andrew J. Goodpaster, Washington, D.C.; Dr. Henry Graff, New York City (to whom I am also indebted for a copy of his important book, *The Tuesday Cabinet*); Richard M. Helms, Washington, D.C.; Tom Johnson, Atlanta, Georgia (who took invaluable notes at White House meetings); Luci Baines Johnson, Austin, Texas; Gordon Jones; Robert W. Komer, Washington, D.C.; Lt. Gen. Victor H. Krulak, San Diego, California; the late Gen. Curtis E. LeMay; Robert S. McNamara, Washington, D.C.; Adm. Thomas H. Moorer, Washington, D.C.; Paul Nitze, Washington, D.C.; Douglas Pike, Lubbock, Texas; Charlotte Rhodes, Dripping Springs, Texas; Sen. and Mrs. Charles S. Robb, Washington, D.C.; the late Dean Rusk (who started me off well); Adm. Ulysses

S. Grant Sharp, San Diego, California; Neil Sheehan, Washington, D.C.; Hon. Cyrus R. Vance, New York City; Gen. Volney Warner, Washington, D.C.; Paul Warnke, Washington, D.C.; the late Ralph Yarborough.

I thank William C. Gibbons for a copy of his essential *The U.S. Government and the Vietnam War* and for helpful hints and direction. I am deeply indebted to Ralph Newman of Chicago for invaluable contacts. Thanks, too, to Henry Schandler for a copy is his pioneering book, *The Unmaking of a President: Lyndon Johnson and Vietnam*. Dr. Walter Rostow and Dr. Elspeth Rostow, of the University of Texas, Austin, provided not only invaluable material but also invaluable insights and guidance for which I offer warm thanks. My gratitude goes to Dr. and Mrs. Emory Thomas, Athens, Georgia, for arranging a meeting with Dean Rusk and for their delightful hospitality during the visit. Special acknowledgment must be made to Mae Dean and Bert Wheeler, College Station, not only for warm friendship but also for essential help.

Adequate ways to thank Jack Valenti of Washington, D.C., and Hollywood, California, defy me—he listened, cajoled, stood special example, and read beyond any call of friendship. I hope he likes the finished project.

My dear friends Diana and Bill Hobby, Jr., have my affectionate gratitude for admirable tolerance and encouragement. Bill did yeoman service in reading an earlier draft of this book.

Let me thank, too, all those scholars in the Vietnam field who did the vital early research that made this book so much easier.

Four splendid secretaries contributed more to this work than they will ever know. Suffice to say that without the help of Ms. Andi Wilson, Lincoln, Nebraska; Mrs. Debbie Riley, College Station, Texas; Mrs. Leslie Knight, Bellingham, Washington (whose cordial encouragement came warmly and often); and Ms. Sarah Harris, Harlingen, Texas, this book probably would be strewn, still, across my office floor.

I've been fortunate to have had the help of superior graduate students in a series of military biography seminars at Texas A&M over the past few years, and I thank them all.

Let me say, finally, that I am indebted to the Texas A&M University Press for faith, hope, and charity.

Shadows of Vietnam

chapter

"That Damn Little Pissant Country"

A bout six o'clock on the evening of November 22, 1963, the presidential plane landed at Andrews Air Force Base outside Washington. Lyndon Johnson asked his staff to wait until Jacqueline Kennedy had deplaned with John F. Kennedy's body. In a few minutes the new president and First Lady walked down a waiting ramp into the blinding glare of camera lights and power. Johnson stepped up to a microphone, a chill wind whipping his trousers, and unfolded a prepared statement—to which he had added a last line—and began to speak: "This is a sad time for all people. We have suffered a loss that cannot be weighed. For me, it is a deep personal tragedy. I know that the world shares the sorrow that Mrs. Kennedy and her family bear. I will do my best. That is all I can do. I ask for your help—and God's."[1]

Then he called for the presidential military aide, Maj. Gen. Chester V. Clifton, and asked for three meetings as soon as possible after arrival—one with the cabinet (which had to be postponed because most members, en route to Japan, had turned back on hearing of the assassination), one with Defense Secretary Robert McNamara and National Security Advisor McGeorge Bundy, and a bipartisan meeting with congressional leaders. So began an administration.

Lyndon Johnson, with his appreciation of history, knew that he came to the office of the presidency with more usable experience than any other politician in American history.

He looked back on an early interest in campus politics at Southwest Texas State Teachers College in San Marcos where he had gloried in campaigning. That interest propelled him to Washington in 1931 as secretary to Texas Democratic congressman Richard Kleberg (owner of the famed King Ranch), and a few months there made him an adept congressional maneuverer. That talent, plus energetic cultivation of Democratic leaders, brought LBJ to Franklin D. Roosevelt's notice and the president made him the Texas state administrator of the National Youth Administration. Encouraged by success in a tough federal post, LBJ ran for Congress in 1937, won, and held his seat until 1948—his tenure interrupted only by a World War II stint in the U.S. Navy, where he received the silver star for valor during a brief exposure to combat. The medal became one of his most treasured awards.

He remembered disappointments. LBJ lost a 1941 U.S. senate race to Texas's anti–New Deal governor W. Lee "Pappy" O'Daniel. But he searched the ashes and learned the mechanics of close elections in this campaign and never lost again. In fact, his lesson in narrow margins helped him turn apparent defeat in the 1948 senate race into an 87-vote victory—a victory that earned him the nickname "Landslide Lyndon." From that thin beginning, he went on to become an effective senator and served as a member of the Armed Services Committee, where he worked for greater American military power.

Popular with colleagues because he "did his homework," LBJ became Democratic whip in 1951, and, at age 44, the youngest Senate minority leader ever. As majority leader in 1955, he set new records for effectiveness as a whirlwind "wheeler-dealer."

Why did he succeed? Tall, thinnish, awkward, sometimes brash and blustering with his loud Texas drawl, he had, to those who looked closely, some of FDR's suasion to him—a breezy air that pulled people into the sweep of his big hands and into his rhetoric and held them enthralled. Even those who did not find him charming usually had a grudging admiration for his bumptious enthusiasm. By 1960 Lyndon Johnson ranked as one of the two or three most powerful leaders in the country.

That power came as much from style as substance. Congress gave him polish, ardor gave him eloquence, a desire for change gave him strength, but a lady gave him greatness.

While in Austin on congressional business in September, 1934, Johnson met Claudia Alta Taylor from Karnak, Texas—a bright, winning, dark-haired girl called "Lady Bird" (she was given the name at age two by a nurse who said she looked "as pretty as a lady bird"), freshly graduated from the University of Texas. At first turned down when he asked her for a date, Johnson persisted. He bombarded her with phone calls, letters, and telegrams from Washington just to make sure she remembered him. Two months later he went to Texas, proposed, and was accepted. "Sometimes," Lady Bird observed, "Lyndon simply takes your breath away."[2]

They were a wonderful blend together. Both were outgoing, talkative, and charming; both had manners and respect for people and place; both were participants in the depression that so badly stunted the American dream; both were young and vigorously devoted to Texas and their country and to making things better wherever they went. Lyndon's zest sometimes turned his hopes to fancy, but Lady Bird kept him grounded with a keen, oft-hidden, analytic mind that saw behind a lot of things—and saw in him things that only time would show the world.

Aggressively independent at times, often too certain in conceits, LBJ rarely strayed far from Lady Bird's left hand. They talked a lot because they listened to each other—he never had a better, more honest sounding board, and he knew it. She was smaller than he was physically but she did not lack for courage. She told him what she thought, sometimes bluntly, often subtly—with acceptable alternatives tucked in as she went. Lyndon might sometimes be crude and cunning in political need, other times arrogant or bullying. Lady Bird often felt swamped as though she was "suddenly onstage for a part I never rehearsed."[3] But their years together forged a oneness that surprised many and impressed most; their ambitions, like their feelings, hopes, and fears, fused their love into a special partnership of friends.

Their partnership had survived through tough times—but could it stand the pressure-cooker life in the White House?

Johnson knew a good deal about global problems. President Kennedy had gone to unusual lengths to keep him informed, to give substance to a job that John Nance Garner saw as not "worth a bucket of warm spit."[4] As things worked out, LBJ had been JFK's "outside man," sent to far parts of the globe on fact-finding, reinforcing, or ceremonial missions. Lady Bird went along on most of those trips where her gracious manner charmed foreign hosts and her sharp eye helped LBJ cut through diplomatic veneer. One of their most interesting visits had been to Vietnam. That visit left LBJ uneasy about American prospects in Southeast Asia although his conviction that American commitments to the Saigon government should be kept was unshaken. Vietnam kept bothering Johnson as he listened to national security briefings and reports from the Joint Chiefs of Staff.

FITTING INTO OFFICE

Eyes and emotions fixed on confirming continuity, LBJ's first meetings really were briefings on world conditions and means of meeting people. He knew all of his predecessor's cabinet, all the White House staff, most of the higher-level workers in the departments, but he wanted to see the cabinet members close up, to judge their willingness to work with him. They should know he wanted them to stay; he did, not only because of the country's need, but also because they were JFK's men.

That last point is noteworthy. Critics have argued that he should have asked all the JFK cabinet and staff to resign, but it never seems seriously to have crossed his mind. On the surface, it does look as though he should have ensconced his own people in such sensitive secretaryships as state, defense, treasury, commerce—every working department. Rumors persisted that those from JFK's realm who stayed, did so more for vengeance than support. These rumors were stoked by a press unstrung by the end of Camelot and angry at the coming of a boorish Texan with pretensions to prominence. A few cabinet members may have guessed that he needed their suave entrée to government, their imprimatur for stability.

There is no doubt that LBJ came to office scared—despite his exterior placidity. But he never felt he needed legitimizing when he asked cabinet and staff to stick with him. He thought of continuity, yes, but he acted mainly from a decent sense that he "wanted to treat President Kennedy's people the way I would have expected him to treat mine." That deep-seated decency probably stemmed, too, from the guilt survivors often feel. In LBJ's case it made him a trustee for JFK: "He knew when he selected me as his running mate that I would be the man required to carry on if anything happened to him. I did what I believed he would have wanted me to do."[5]

Johnson had considerable respect for the cabinet members—thought them dedicated patriots, able, hard-working, honest. They were, all in all, a distinguished group. He believed the toughest posts for the immediate crises were in especially trustworthy hands.

Secretary of State Dean Rusk's cotton-soft accent branded him a Georgian; his quick, piercing eyes looking out of a rounded face, showed a quick mind and wit. Years of diplomacy, considerable war service, and legendary patience made him unusually successful. Background and experience would bind him to the president, would make him one of the most trusted deciders—and Rusk had not really been among JFK's inner circle.

Johnson held Robert McNamara, the secretary of defense, almost in awe. When he met McNamara upon returning to Washington from Dallas, LBJ gave him a touch of the "treatment" so many came to know. If he ever tried to quit, LBJ threatened to send police to bring him back. McNamara had been one of the so-called Whiz Kids, had been at Ford Motor company when Kennedy charmed him into government. He brought new ideas of organization and management to the Byzantine Defense Department. Johnson thought McNamara "carried more information around in his head than the average encyclopedia."[6] Respect tinged with a dash of inferiority led the president to a nickname trick remindful of Huey Long: he branded McNamara the man with the "Stay-Comb" hair.

Johnson began with an experienced cabinet that served him with growing admiration, even affection. So, too, the staff, again dimming rumors of bloodletting between "Kennedy men" and "Johnson men."[7]

As for Johnson, himself, his agenda had been fixed by his predecessor. Kennedy had been trying to get a series of important bills through Congress that touched on foreign aid, civil rights, tax reduction, higher minimum wages, and Medicare. In the last months of Kennedy's administration, legislation had piled up in a crucial logjam. Congress simply would not act; intense pressure had failed to move anything. Now Johnson, using his considerable powers of congressional persuasion, pressing the obvious need for bipartisan unity, and playing in natural sympathies, threw himself into the battle. He had a passion for the telephone—he probably used it more effectively than any president before or since—and called friends and foes alike to battle for JFK. An example: He phoned his old friend and political opposite, Sen. Everett M. Dirksen of Illinois, to say that partisan politics had no place in the immediate crisis and to ask him to lead his party behind a program to show the continuing power of Congress, of the administration, and especially of the United States. Johnson could hear heavy breathing, could imagine that big, craggy face, the curling gray locks afly, and then he heard the deep, nearly dulcet tones of one of the greatest senatorial orators: "Well, Mr. President, you know I will."[8]

Domestic issues were so urgent, so close to LBJ's heart that they naturally came first to his mind, while Vietnam lurked in the background—green, ominous, and alien.

INHERITING A SHAMBLES

Not until two days after Kennedy's death did LBJ fully pick up the mantle of commander in chief.[9] On November 24, still working out of vice-presidential quarters in the Executive Office Building, he summoned Dean Rusk,

Robert McNamara, Undersecretary of State George Ball, Central Intelligence Agency (CIA) Director John McCone, McGeorge Bundy, and the U.S. ambassador to South Vietnam, Henry Cabot Lodge.

This first Vietnam meeting had instructive overtones; it shows the kind of information LBJ thought he needed. McCone covered the latest intelligence; Rusk, of course, the world view; McNamara, the military situation; Ball offered his own vision of European matters, especially those pertaining to the North American Treaty Organization (NATO). Ambassador Lodge, who had recently returned from Saigon to brief JFK and then attended his funeral, offered an appreciation of current problems and possibilities in Vietnam.

There were interesting tensions running the cast. The shadow of another assassination hung over the room—just three weeks before JFK's death, South Vietnamese president Ngo Dinh Diem had been murdered in a governmental spasm. Indications were that the American government had at least condoned, if not actively participated, in the coup. Diem's increasingly Mandarin-like isolation in his Saigon palace, his inability to resolve the growing uprising of Buddhist monks who often immolated themselves before television cameras, the alarming rise in power of Diem's brother, Ngo Dinh Nhu and his glamorous but arrogant wife—whom many considered the model for the Dragon Lady character in Milton Caniff's comic strips "Terry and the Pirates" and "Steve Canyon"—were rumored causes of the overthrow. Other rumors hinted that an accommodation might soon be made between Diem and Ho Chi Minh! But the real reason was that most American officials in Vietnam and Washington had lost faith in Diem and his regime as effective war administrators. In sum, the puppet's strings were fraying.

No doubt Diem had defects. Arrogant and aloof, he rarely left his palace and had completely lost touch with his people. He also connived at the greed of some of his generals and officials. And, in William Colby's words, "he was not overly impressed with the idea of total democracy either." In short, Diem seemed hardly a model for Americans. But he had some virtues. Alone among Vietnamese leaders, Diem had credibility as a sound, anti-Communist nationalist of long standing. In the earlier years of the war against the VC and the North Vietnamese regulars seeping south to help foment revolt, Diem had fought back grimly, developed a useful "strategic hamlet" plan, and sustained morale in an unformed, fragmented country.

Some ascribed Diem's decline to increased U.S. involvement: the more aid America offered, the more complicated Diem's situation became. He did not want to win against the Communists by losing to the Americans. He and his brother tried for some kind of accommodation—but they were simply too un-Western. Diem had to go.

It is possible that some of the men at that first Vietnam meeting under-estimated Johnson, or at least underestimated his knowledge of Vietnam's condition.[10]

What the new president wanted was information. He sat back and let the others talk, whirling his glasses and fixing a hard stare at each speaker with steady eyes that seemed somehow never to blink. His questions showed him a canny listener.

Lodge, cloaked always in the starched, creased look of the proper Boston Brahmin, remained unruffled. An old-line Republican of prominence, he had accepted JFK's invitation to diplomacy as destiny's reward. Typically, Lodge began his first meeting with President Johnson with a crisply optimistic overview of his domain.

He had been in favor of any kind of change in the South Vietnamese government—had certainly acquiesced in the coup—and felt that the military leaders who now controlled the state would revitalize the war effort, attack corruption, and reform administration throughout the nation.

Skeptical, LBJ asked for the CIA's views. They were discouraging. Since the coup, McCone reported, Viet Cong (VC) attacks had increased and seemed likely to continue. He had alarming things to say about the new government: the leaders were disorganized, they were not working with civilian officials, and they were likely to fight among themselves. He doubted that a stable South Vietnamese government could be created in any reasonable time, and concluded with a gloomy truth: "As long as the Ho Chi Minh trail was open and supplies and convoys of people could come pouring in there without interruption, we couldn't say things were so good."[11]

All of this brought back disquieting memories for LBJ. He and Lady Bird had met Diem on their Asian trip in 1961, and had mixed feelings about him. Lady Bird assessed him as able "to cover his ground and be real tough, like a thug, a strong man," but was not sure "that he was a *good* man—in a gentlemanly sense."[12] Johnson remembered his own impressions of Diem as a pudgy, short, self-satisfied man who worried about money and whether or not he ought to take more American aid, but who was tough and passionately anti-Communist. After handing Diem a letter from JFK offering more aid, Johnson told the press that Diem ranked as "the Churchill of the decade . . . in the vanguard of those leaders who stand for freedom."[13]

When the Johnsons resumed their Far Eastern tour, Stanley Karnow, one of the news media veterans accompanying them, asked if LBJ had really meant his astounding comparison of Diem to Churchill. "Shit," came a Texas drawl, "Diem's the only boy we got out there."[14] Johnson worried that too many Americans put too much emphasis on creating a Vietnam in America's image[15]—an act of stupidity that ignored Vietnam's history and heritage. He firmly believed that Diem's assassination had bad portents. At least there had been a semblance of government to work with—in his wake came disaster.

After listening to various reports during the meeting, Johnson suddenly whirled on Lodge and announced that he had some "serious misgivings" about American actions in Vietnam. Stories of persistent dissension in the Saigon mission added to those misgivings. The troubles must end. The president bluntly ordered Lodge to develop and manage a strong team; he promised Lodge Washington's backing. Johnson added that he would personally pick some members of Lodge's new team, with the understanding that the primary objective would be to support the South Vietnamese government. Lodge now had enlarged authority along with full responsibility for what happened out there.[16]

Mac Bundy watched the meeting with a growing appreciation for his new boss. There was a point to the whole affair that Lodge's hauteur might have blurred, a point Bundy grasped quickly. Johnson thought Lodge a "soft man" who needed stiffening. The president wanted the ambassador to know that his new chief was not weak, was not going to lose the war, and that "neither was Cabot Lodge."[17] Johnson believed, as had JFK, in the domino theory—feared that if one democracy fell to communism, so would others. He wanted the word out to Lodge and everyone else holding office that the United States would stick by the Vietnamese.

Johnson followed the meeting by approving National Security Action Memorandum (NSAM) 273, addressed to government officers responsible for defense and diplomatic affairs:

> It remains the central objective of the United States in South Vietnam to assist the people and Government of that country to win their contest against the externally directed and supported communist conspiracy. The test of all U.S. decisions and actions in this area should be the effectiveness of their contribution to this purpose.[18]

All officials were reminded of a White House statement of October 2, 1963, which stated the goal of bringing advisors back from Vietnam. That, too, remained policy. Showing the president's disgust at infighting, the memo added that

> all senior officers of the government will move energetically to insure the full unity of support for established U.S. policy in South Vietnam. Both in Washington and in the field, it is essential that the government

be unified. It is of particular importance that express or implied criticism of officers of other branches be assiduously avoided in all contacts with the Vietnamese government and with the press.

Finally, the memorandum asked for coherent plans covering U.S. support of South Vietnamese secret operations against the north and into Laos. Johnson had known about "covert actions" helping South Vietnam, vaguely disliked them, and now was ordering them himself because all information pointed to their importance.

Johnson noted that the memorandum was "my first important decision on Vietnam."[19]

The more he thought about Vietnam, the more LBJ became convinced that his determination had to be made plain to the world. John Kennedy's funeral offered a macabre opportunity to talk to a good many foreign leaders, hear their views, and explain his intent to stand firm everywhere, especially in Vietnam. Several heads of state were coming; those who could not were sending high-level representatives. President Charles de Gaulle personally would represent France, and Soviet deputy premier Anastas Mikoyan— he liked to call himself a poor Armenian rug merchant—would stand in for Chairman Nikita S. Khrushchev, who had sternly challenged JFK's mettle in Vienna. Johnson looked forward to meeting his colleagues and sizing them up with his own special skill.

On Monday, November 25, he greeted the tall, imperious de Gaulle. The French president mouthed elaborate sympathies for America's loss, talked of the historic friendship between France and the United States, praised JFK, and said the French people basked in the assurance of American aid in war. That last almost brought a Texas jeer—LBJ had heard just a few hours before that "Le Grand Charles" had told the U.S. Ambassador that he could not count on the Americans in any European war because they were late to the last two conflicts and had only gotten into World War II because of Pearl Harbor! At the moment an advocate of holding on in Indochina, de Gaulle would soon switch positions—an action that surprised LBJ not at all. They were not friends.[20]

Mikoyan, a survivor, brought the toughness of an original Bolshevik to a job of mixed objectives—he dabbled in foreign trade, diplomacy, and domestic affairs and sat close to Khrushchev in Moscow's councils. Listening intently to LBJ's assurances that the United States sought peace and that his administration would work to continue policies begun by Kennedy, Mikoyan reciprocated with pleasure, but his dark eyes flashed (was it humor?) when Johnson complained about Fidel Castro's Cuban ventures in Latin American subversion. It was ironic, Mikoyan thought, that so small a country could subvert anyone, especially a big power. He knew Castro had no such designs. Johnson had seen intelligence reports of Cuban intrigue across the hemisphere—and knew that Mikoyan knew he had. "It was a cat and mouse game," and the Russian envoy noted that the American president played it well. Mikoyan got the message that the United States would not let subversion continue and that it would honor its worldwide commitments.[21]

Convinced by these conversations that the world needed even clearer signals of America's sticking power, LBJ addressed a joint session of Congress on November 27, 1963. "In this age when there can be no losers in peace and no victors in war," the president said, "we must recognize the obligation to match material strength with national restraint." He went on to pledge that the United States would keep its commitments "from South Vietnam to West Berlin."[22]

Politics has its foibles, complexities, quirks and frustrations, all of which brought out Johnson's artistry in compromise. Politics, to him, was rational and had an ethic of its own. Diplomacy, though, seemed a collection of mysteries tended by a priesthood—and it bothered him. Most harrowing of all were the daily lists of dead that came to audit diplomacy's failure in Vietnam.

As he examined America's twisting path to Indochina, Johnson may have been disheartened. He remembered Senate briefings and had listened in cabinet and National Security Council (NSC) meetings as the Kennedy administration followed Eisenhower's hortatory urgings to hold Laos and Vietnam. Johnson had watched American involvement escalate beyond a small Military Assistance Advisory Group (MAAG) in July 1959, to more than 16,000 men in November, 1963.[23]

Information. LBJ consumed it like a sponge. He needed to know facts, figures, and, most of all, people as the bases for Vietnam decisions. He probed for these ingredients and found himself engulfed in memos, words, newspaper clips, TV sound bites, opinions, promises, curses, regrets—all apparently pointing one way. Victory, or simply the survival of a free South Vietnam, depended on vastly expanded aid, not just in guns, planes, and helicopters, but in men, blood, and treasure from America. That implacable fact rimmed the edges of all the president's worries. Eisenhower had thought men might be needed; Kennedy listened but had fended off decision. As Lyndon Johnson searched files and memories for a strategy, plans, and ideas, he realized that all the missions that had gone and come; all the reports from the Bundys, McNamaras, and trusted soldiers like Gen. Maxwell D. Taylor; and on-the-spot assessments from men like Gen. Paul D. Harkins, head of the Military Assistance Command, Vietnam (MACV), told a tale of gloom and tried to make it shine.

The president tried again toward the end of 1963 to get a grip on what had happened, what might happen, and what to do in Vietnam. He asked Secretary McNamara to stop there en route from a NATO meeting to take a hard look at conditions and put his thoughts in writing. McNamara made an overnight visit—December 19–20—which enabled him to produce one of his masterful overviews of things seen and unseen for the president, Rusk, McCone, and a few other White House advisors.

"The situation is very disturbing," McNamara said. "Current trends, unless reversed in the next 2–3 months, will lead to neutralization at best and more likely to a Communist-controlled state." Yet he was convinced that something deeper than military weakness eroded South Vietnam.

"The new government," he emphasized, "is the greatest source of concern. It is indecisive and drifting. Although [Gen. Duong Van "Big"] Minh states that he, rather than the Committee of Generals, is making decisions, it is not clear that this is actually so." Nobody really knew who was doing what in Saigon, certainly not the American officials, who were leaderless, ignorant, and drifting. Results were predictable: VC inroads were seen everywhere, "with the best guess being that the situation has in fact been deteriorating in the countryside since July to a far greater extent than we realized because of our undue dependence on distorted Vietnamese reporting."[24]

Lodge, General Harkins, and General Minh all expected improvement in January. But a government by committee, especially one made up of multiple prima donnas with virtually no governmental experience, could hardly escape disaster. McNamara had no "quick fix" recommendations, and concluded, in a kind of wistful whimper, that "we should watch the situation very carefully, running scared, hoping for the best, but preparing for more forceful moves if the situation does not show early signs of improvement."[25]

McNamara's report confirmed everything LBJ had heard about Southeast Asia. Laos might fall to the Communists any day, and South Vietnam's government might collapse overnight. Clearly American policy there sagged from a shambles toward a catastrophe. President Johnson knew he would, sooner or later, have to decide whether the United States got farther in or got out.

For Lyndon Johnson at the end of 1963, any decision might affect the election of 1964.[26] He wanted to run and he wanted to win. The question was, would the war in that "damn little pissant country"[27] blow up into an election disaster and smash his whole campaign?

chapter
TWO

A Tough Campaigning Year, 1964

Campaigning mobilized all of LBJ's juices. He loved stump speaking, charging into crowds, and "pressing the flesh," nearly drowning in the waves of affection and energy sweeping through him. These feelings touched him sentimentally, struck his deep-running love for people and his need to be needed.

A lot of people wondered why he accepted the second spot on JFK's ticket; many had pushed him for the presidency back in 1960 and felt shortchanged. Most of Johnson's congressional cronies and colleagues thought he might be president, and many were certain he would. Among the believers had been President Dwight D. Eisenhower. Clearly, Johnson's psyche pushed him to it. His current caretaker status, though, stunted him into being JFK's lingering surrogate. The election of 1964 could free him, making him president in his "own right." Teddy Roosevelt had looked on the presidency as a "bully pulpit" and used it to spread his views widely. Johnson did a good deal of that in his first months in office, using Teddy's method of bringing groups to the White House, talking to all kinds of gatherings, and using modern media for national coverage.

Elections in the post–World War II era were increasingly things of radio and television images, statements tuned down to sound bites, and commercials crafted by public relations people who make truth from fantasy and great men from small. Johnson had pioneered new kinds of politicking in Texas: He first used the helicopter to reach far stretches of the state, swooping down on ranches and towns and asking for votes. In the upcoming campaign he planned to blend all kinds of exposure to present an image of responsible leadership. Campaign? Yes, he certainly would, as would Sen. Hubert H. Humphrey, his running mate, but all the while he would push Kennedy's liberal programs for the people and tend all the tokens of government.

Disturbed by Vietnam, Johnson stressed a "steady on course" policy there and his hope for a solution. He received providential help from his Republican opponent, Barry M. Goldwater, a former senate colleague from Arizona. At Knoxville, Tennessee, in August, Goldwater staked out just about the most outrageous ground any politician could imagine: He assaulted public power in the United States, attacked the poverty and Medicare programs, said he would abolish social security, declared that the eastern seaboard should be sliced from the rest of the country, and fulminated dangerously against Communism.[1] A kind of dazed and uneasy jubilation ran through the White House. Goldwater seemed to be giving the election away, which worried Johnson and some of his old campaigners. Things looked *too* good.

A MATTER OF DAU TRANH

Vietnam kept interfering.

Not much information leaked to South Vietnamese or U.S. sources about goings-on in North Vietnam (NVN). Clearly, VC aggression increased early in 1964. Viet Cong units attacked not only South Vietnamese troops but also U.S. advisors early in the year. They attacked at different places and showed better discipline and weapons. These actions reflected interesting changes in Hanoi.

First, to those with an understanding of "People's War," they showed a shift in military *dau tranh* (struggle). An argument in Hanoi over the proper course of the war had hurt Gen. Vo Nguyen Giap. He wanted to consolidate Communist control of North Vietnam and then work subtly against the south. Although a national hero, his views were rejected by Ho Chi Minh, who branded Giap a "revisionist" and shunted him aside. Management of North Vietnamese strategy was given to Giap's rival, Gen. Nguyen Chi Thanh. A good deal of North Vietnam's mind change stemmed from the chaotic situation in Saigon.[2]

There is a possibility that Ho Chi Minh may have agreed to Thanh's strategic ideas as a way of stunting Giap's growing personality cult, because Giap kept the title of defense minister. This apparently honorary job left all logistical and administrative support efforts in the south in Giap's hands. With characteristic energy, he began a massive program of upgrading VC arms and equipment. Giap sent Chinese Communist (Chicom) 75mm recoilless rifles, U.S. .50-caliber machine guns on Chicom mounts, 90mm rocket launchers, and mortars to the VC. He made a giant improvement when he issued the VC many 7.62mm Chicom AK-47 rifles and machine guns.[3]

Better arms and equipment for the VC came at a tenuous time in Saigon. Big Minh's government hardly merited the name, although the general had tried to infuse order into his country's confusion. Increasing U.S. aid had strengthened him, morale rose in his army, and a semblance of progress glossed the surface, but waves of ill luck engulfed Minh's administration. Buddhist and Catholic unrest rose again, restive university students cried for reforms, and splintered political parties demanded more spoils for helping topple Diem. Well-armed and efficient VC incursions threatened Minh's wobbling structure.

TWO CAMPAIGNS FOR THE COMMANDER IN CHIEF

In late January, 1964, Gen. Nguyen Khanh toppled Minh's junta. Nothing about this blow struck the United States as favorable. First, the U.S. intelligence network failed to give any warning of an impending coup. If that were not disquieting enough, General Khanh, a flamboyant, French-trained officer of varying loyalties, enraged Buddhists, Catholics, and various splinter parties by appearing to be turning back to Diem's discredited henchmen. Although he established a new three-man junta, Khanh soon announced a government charter that would give him powers rivaling those of Charles de Gaulle. American officials were galled, students were appalled, and Khanh backed down. Still, he was the only man holding Saigon's reins. Ambassador Lodge decided to be optimistic about the new Vietnam, optimistic in peculiarly Western terms: "We have everything we need in Vietnam . . . our side knows how to do it. We have the means with which to do it. We simply need to do it. This requires a tough and ruthless commander. Perhaps Khanh is it."[4]

Khanh was not it. The kind of turmoil LBJ had feared following Diem's death happened again. Governments would come and go in Saigon for more than a year—each one spending more men, treasure, thought, and time on staying in office than on fighting the war, which faded into an oddly remote limbo.[5]

Worst of all from LBJ's standpoint, no coordinated plan seemed to exist for success in Vietnam. For that matter, no one seemed to know what the

U.S. objective was out there, NSAM 273 notwithstanding. Johnson alone seems to have known what he wanted: to save South Vietnam without starting World War III.[6]

As he looked over the masses of reports from people who went over to assess things, the president could see that objectives seemed to change. From some came thoughts of defeating the North, or the VC, in the field; even leading war proponent Bob McNamara seemed to shift his view in March, 1964: "We seek an independent non-Communist South Vietnam. We do not require that it serve as a Western base or as a member of a Western Alliance."[7]

For that matter, the word objective itself lacked precise definition. Defense of Vietnam constituted only part of the U.S. problem: If Vietnam fell, most authorities believed the rest of Southeast Asia would be sucked into the Communist orbit. So Southeast Asia had to be included in the objective question.

Aware of the danger lurking in these uncertainties, Johnson plunged into the election campaign. The many targets of opportunity offered by Goldwater almost choked the Democratic camp. Former vice president Richard Nixon, campaigning for the senator, tried to take advantage of LBJ's frequent assertion that he "sought no wider war." That, said Nixon, indicated Johnson would leave Vietnam if he won the election. Johnson thus became the "peace candidate!" All he had to do was promise not to be reckless but to be firm.[8]

Through what seemed to some Americans an excessively long year in Vietnam, President Johnson displayed uncommon, if not astounding, restraint. A long-standing crisis in Panama flared and tested his determination. In January, rioting broke out and U.S. troops took casualties. Johnson permitted return fire and held firm to U.S. commitments. He pushed for renegotiation of relations. Fidel Castro, possibly with Soviet prodding, tested Johnson's mettle in February by threatening to cut off the water to Guantanamo Naval Base. Again, the president held firm. He frustrated the Cubans by building a desalinization plant and eliminating Cuban jobs at the base.[9] North Vietnam also pushed him harder, testing him during the turbulence of election.

Vastly increased VC activity harassed Americans and Army of the Republic of Vietnam (ARVN) units across the south. During the first week of February, the VC pushed an offensive northwest of Saigon and in the Mekong Delta. On the third, the enemy hit a U.S. advisory compound far north at Kontum. Johnson refused to react. A VC bomb exploded in a popular American Saigon haunt, the Kinh-Do Theater, on February 7; three Americans were killed, and 50 wounded. Fuming, the Joint Chiefs repeated a proposal for an escalating series of attacks against North Vietnam. Johnson still held back.

Actually, he reacted—but not publicly. Throughout his early days in the White House, Vietnam lurked at the edge of his consciousness. Too many events kept it there. If some thought the president missed the significance of things in Asia, they were wrong. "He was not so stupid," Mac Bundy said, "that he didn't know that he was pushing his problem ahead of him. And he knew that it was going to be there as a great big nuisance."[10]

Some of his aides worried, too, that increased Vietnam responses ought to involve Congress. Johnson, the consummate congressional persuader, kept the leadership of both houses in touch with Vietnam, aware of what the provocations were and the impending possibilities. But, again showing caution, he did not ask for a declaration of war.

Politics had much to do with Johnson's caution throughout the year when North Vietnamese provocations seemed to demand response. For Johnson, though, there were considerations beyond the election that held him back. He did not relish restraint; he had a large streak of frontier Texas in him that dictated beating bullies.

One of the things that cramps a president is that so much seems to depend on his every decision. No president has the luxury of being insulted or goaded. And Johnson had another tether on him—he understood politics better than most, but military affairs were terra incognita. He admired and respected Robert McNamara, that quintessential corporate manager, because he fitted his business ken into martial matters. But military thinking had few tangents to political thinking. Johnson knew many military men of all ranks, had seen them before various congressional committees and had played their game of overestimates for years. He respected most military for their skill at trying to encircle him.[11] But generals in command were a different breed. It was hard to negotiate with them. They had immediate needs and nothing to trade, so none of the usual deals could be made.

Did LBJ, like Georges Clemenceau, think that war was too important to be left to the generals? The varying answers are interesting. Jack Valenti did not believe that LBJ "ever thought generals were all that great. He had a strong skeptic factor about how smart generals were." According to McGeorge Bundy, "He was careful with the generals, he had an experience with them that they were powerful. . . . Enough [knowledge] to know them; enough to care. Enough to regard them as second-rate politicians . . . not all of them."[12] Clearly Johnson appreciated military men, but he was not a member of their clan. He heard them and they him, but the words they spoke meant different things to the different listeners.

Part of his problem lay with his secretary of defense and the way war business was conducted. McNamara made himself the funnel through which military opinion reached the president. The chairman of the Joint Chiefs of Staff, Gen. Maxwell Taylor, attended certain meetings—and by personality, sheer will, and great experience, won attention. Mainly though, the chiefs of the armed services worked through Taylor, who in turn worked through McNamara. If the chiefs differed over Vietnam policy—and they often did— they sent their views up through channels. More importantly, they usually received policy decisions down the same route, filtered through McNamara.[13]

As president, LBJ learned of clandestine operations CIA agents had been conducting with and for the South Vietnamese. Most of these focused on planting groups of saboteurs or assassins along the northern coast. They were to infiltrate, collect intelligence, eliminate selected nuisances, blow up bridges, and disrupt communications.

In January, Johnson had approved an extension of something called Operation Plan (OPLAN) 34A, which expanded covert action to include support of South Vietnamese navy raids along the North's coastline. These raids were combined more closely with intelligence gathering efforts made by the U.S. Navy since 1962—the De Soto patrol program.[14] Under cover of routine cruises, specially equipped ships collected electronic intelligence (ELINT) in the Tonkin Gulf area, between Hainan Island and the coast of North Vietnam. So far, none of these patrols had encountered trouble, had been carefully hidden from the American press, Congress, even high government officials—but not from the North Vietnamese.

Like most Americans, LBJ had a vague distaste for "dirty tricks," but Secretary McNamara included some of these kinds of activities in the twelve recommendations he presented to Johnson and to the National Security Council in March, 1964, after he and General Taylor took another look at Vietnam. McNamara reviewed the situation carefully, described the shaky political climate in Saigon, suggested reiterating U.S. determination to stick by South Vietnam "for as long as it takes," while emphasizing support for Khanh's government, announcing assistance in increasing South Vietnamese forces by 50,000 men, and at the same time promising aid in reorganizing district and hamlet pacification programs. Some effort ought to be made, said the secretary, to help South Vietnam create "an offensive guerrilla force," and he also recommended $5 million to $10 million for upgrading South Vietnamese military equipment. He urged continuation of U-2 flights beyond Vietnamese borders and permission for "hot pursuit" operations into Laos for "border control"—although only with Laotian government approval. McNamara's last recommendation was deceptively bland: "Prepare immediately to be in a position on 72 hours' notice to initiate . . . Laotian and Cambodian 'Border Control' actions . . . and . . . 'Retaliatory Actions' against North Vietnam, and to be in a position on 30 days' notice to initiate . . . 'Graduated Overt Military Pressure' against North Vietnam." All these recommendations were dangerously aggressive, but McNamara thought that "if the Khanh Government can stay in power and the . . . actions can be carried out rapidly . . . the situation in South Vietnam can be significantly improved in the next four to six months." First, of course, the deterioration of everything in South Vietnam had to stop—which might be achieved by the proposed measures.[15]

Lost in the general discussion were three important comments about "other actions considered but rejected": possible return of U.S. dependents; the possibility of sending in a U.S. combat unit to "secure the Saigon Area;" and the possibility of the U.S. simply taking command of the war. McNamara stressed that all three of these options had been ruled out "for the time being."

Much discussion followed, and "no one opposed any of the military recommendations."[16] The Joint Chiefs of Staff wondered if the suggested actions would be enough. They urged immediate attacks against North Vietnam, perhaps even encouragement of President Khanh's recent bombast about invading the north.[17] Some of Johnson's key advisors squelched that with the thought that South Vietnam's political and military weaknesses would hardly sustain increased war. A real and constant deterrent hung over every discussion of harder war: would China and Russia enter? Both were supplying the north with all kinds of equipment, even with advisors of their own. At what point would they come to the full aid of their ally and perhaps widen the war?

If approved, McNamara's measures could bring strong reaction. But reaction might be delayed or minimized by gradual application of pressure. McNamara clearly believed that to do nothing would finish the South Vietnamese.

All these actions were, of course, potentially disastrous, but Johnson approved all of them, while at the same time forbidding anything more.[18]

Johnson's toughest test of both firmness and discretion came at an unusual place and an unexpected time. And the test came partly because of the secret operations that so worried him.

PUZZLE IN THE TONKIN GULF

USS *Maddox,* a World War II–type destroyer doing antisubmarine duty, had age but some grace and a lot of years left. Commander Herbert L. Ogier ran a tight ship with a good crew. Not one of the modernized destroyers, the 376½-foot *Maddox* boasted an unusual number of guns—six 5-inchers and four 3-inchers.

Veterans are alike in any service—they sense things before the brass knows they're going to happen. The old salts' interest piqued as *Maddox* prepared to sail from Japan. Several strange packages arrived, then the destroyer division Commander John J. Herrick (a Navy captain with the temporary rank of commodore) and his staff were piped aboard. A second class photographer's mate came, too, weighted down with cameras and all kinds of telescopes. *Maddox* cleared port alone—the other ships of Destroyer Division 192 remained in port at Yokosuka. Things got even more spooky in Taiwan. At Keelung Naval Base, *Maddox* sidled up to another destroyer from which a crane lifted a huge, gray, boxlike cubicle and set it down between *Maddox*'s stacks. Most crewmen recognized the communications van (COMVAN) structure and now knew something of their mission: They were destined for a De Soto patrol, with some extra added. But where?

The crew would have been surprised and more apprehensive had they known about Herrick's briefing for the cruise. He thought there might be trouble ahead when he learned that the Joint Chiefs had warned Adm. Thomas Moorer, commander in chief of the Pacific Fleet (CINCPACFLT), that the U.S. "has stepped up assistance to RVN" and also that the American media was widely circulating rumors of attacks on North Vietnam. Herrick's superiors in Taiwan dismissed his worries with a breezy "don't sweat the North Vietnamese."[19]

A close look at the beginning of *Maddox*'s adventure shows strange differences from other De Soto patrols: Clocks were set on a different time and there were to be no radio or radar signals transmitted. Ogier's route seemed elusive, too, a long way around to the Tonkin Gulf, apparently on a course for the Philippines. By July 30, *Maddox* had curved around the eastern and southern shores of Hainan Island.

Any of the off-watch crewmen who bothered to look at the Gulf would have been touched by the beauty of its water. Busy with sampans and other small boats, the blue expanse spouted limestone shafts here and there; to the west the mountains of Vietnam rode on the horizon, peaks softened in misty clouds, and a sense of ineffable peace hung in the air. But it was a sea of war. Vietnam's enemies had come often across the Gulf. *Maddox*'s presence on a De Soto patrol in the wake of the 34A operation must have seemed to Hanoi's officials yet another try by another foe—this time the Yankees and their South Vietnamese lackeys.

On August 2, Herrick and Ogier received an attack warning from the COMVAN crew, activated their new air search radar, and sent a sensitive message to VAdm. Roy L. Johnson, Seventh Fleet Commander: "Consider continuance of patrol presents unacceptable risk." The admiral's answer came two hours later: continue the patrol, with such minor course changes as necessary. But, after Herrick's alerts, the aircraft carrier USS *Ticonderoga* armed a jet and kept it ready to go. Since *Maddox* was about 150 miles north of Yankee Station, the jet should arrive within fifteen minutes if help was needed.

Sunday turned into a fine, slightly hazy day, water rippling and blue as the destroyer followed a roughly northeasterly compass heading. At about 2 P.M. three small, fast, apparently hostile craft approached through a barrage of junks.

Maddox turned east for open sea and stepped up speed as Ogier's clipped voice came over the intercom to say that radar had spotted high-speed craft approaching, and that *Maddox* would fight, if necessary for its right to be in international waters. He did not add that radio traffic reported a North Vietnamese attack order. At 2:30 P.M. the intercom blared again: "General Quarters, General Quarters. This is not a drill!" Not long after, an uncoded flash message went to *Ticonderoga*: "Am being approached by high speed craft with apparent intention of torpedo attack. Intend to open fire if necessary."[20]

North Vietnamese torpedo boats closed and *Maddox* opened fire just after 3 P.M. with both the 5- and 3-inchers. The torpedo boats kept coming. They launched several "fish" (which were evaded), fired heavy machine guns, and finally turned for the coast, one apparently damaged. *Maddox* took one enemy bullet. Planes from *Ticonderoga*—a flight of four A-7 Crusaders commanded by Comd. James B. Stockdale—put one of the fleeing boats out of action and damaged another.[21]

Early Sunday morning, August 2, 1964, Washington time, a surprised duty officer in the White House Situation Room followed established orders and sent a message to the president's bedroom announcing the attack and reporting no casualties or damage.

It was bad timing, indeed, for the election. Johnson, who thought privately that Hanoi might have believed the *Maddox* had been supporting a South Vietnamese 34A raid, realized that he would have to make some response but stuck to restraint. He gathered several key advisors later in the morning—Rusk and George Ball from State, deputy defense secretary Cyrus Vance, Gen. Earle G. "Bus" Wheeler, chairman of the Joint Chiefs of Staff (he took the post when Gen. Taylor became Ambassador to South Vietnam in July 1964), "and several experts in technical intelligence." After a briefing, they all shared LBJ's feeling that Hanoi might have misjudged the situation. No retaliation was ordered.

Johnson tempered restraint with resolution. The Navy would continue its Tonkin Gulf patrols, adding another destroyer with adequate air cover.

Although "we would give Hanoi the benefit of the doubt," the United States sent a stiff diplomatic protest, declaring that American ships always travel the seas freely and would so continue. Let there be "no misapprehension as to the grave consequences which would inevitably result from any further unprovoked offensive military action against United States forces."[22]

Restraint became strained two days later. During the night of August 4, the *Maddox*, with a companion destroyer, USS *C. Turner Joy*, was fighting a heavy Gulf thunderstorm when the National Security Agency (NSA) flashed Captain Herrick that a radio intercept indicated a possible PT boat attack. At 8:35 P.M. radars spotted three high-speed craft thirty miles out; both U.S. ships went to General Quarters. About an hour later all hell erupted. Radarmen reported contact here, there, nearly everywhere, and sonar reported some twenty torpedoes coming toward the U.S. ships. Pilots flying air cover from the *Ticonderoga* saw no North Vietnamese boats or torpedo wakes—but bad weather and darkness blurred vision.

First word of this second engagement reached Washington about midmorning on August 4. As it happened, a National Security Council meeting to discuss conditions in Cyprus had been called for noon. Secretary of the Treasury Douglas Dillon attended, along with Attorney General Robert Kennedy, George Ball, CIA director John McCone, U.S. Information Agency (USIA) director Carl Rowan, and the director of emergency planning, Edward A. McDermott. Held up by a phone call, Johnson arrived late, as did Rusk, McNamara, air force chief of staff Gen. Curtis LeMay, and Mac Bundy. Just as the president arrived, so did Cyrus Vance. Cyprus faded into the background as everyone focused on the Tonkin Gulf.

McNamara provided the latest news and Rusk said that he and the secretary of defense were working on response options. All agreed that the second attack could not be ignored.

In the afternoon an intercepted North Vietnamese radio message boasted of attacking two "enemy airplanes." Another to North Vietnam's PT boat headquarters, reported an "enemy vessel" had been hit.[23] On the basis of a clear North Vietnamese attack, Johnson approved an air strike as punishment.

Almost on the heels of those confirming reports—and before orders had been cut at the Pentagon—came a suggestion from *Maddox* urging caution in evaluating the second attack. Commodore Herrick had doubts about what had happened: an electrical storm might have confused an overeager sonar operator; the dark excitement might have conjured visions. Herrick confessed he had not seen any enemy vessels or torpedo wakes.

The jumbled reports created enough doubt for the president to hold up action. McNamara was told to "go and find out what it's about."[24] Johnson planned a television broadcast for evening prime time, but he delayed it. Mac Bundy, recalling those hectic hours, said that "by his standards he took extraordinary care to make sure that the first reports were checked again by his most reliable subordinates."[25]

McNamara, harassed and also confused, bypassed the Joint Chiefs of Staff (JCS) and called Adm. Ulysses S. Grant Sharp, the commander in chief, Pacific (CINCPAC), in Honolulu. Sharp checked up and down his line of communication with *Maddox, Ticonderoga* and other ships in the area; he checked, too, with his intelligence people. From the first, Sharp told McNamara there had been two attacks and urged, as he did to the JCS, "immediate punitive air strikes against North Vietnam." While he checked further, McNamara kept after him—"must have called me sixteen times." The secretary of defense put it clearly: No action could be ordered "unless we were damned sure that the attacks had taken place."[26] Sharp and Admiral Moorer, after sifting the muddled recollections of participants in a night sea action, all radio intelligence, plus what was known at the Navy's Pentagon war center, FLAGPLOT, concluded there had been a second attack.[27]

All the dithering calls showed how nervous McNamara was; he knew that Johnson's next actions required accurate information. He reported back to the president that there had been a second attack and urged a strong response.

Johnson convened the NSC a second time at around six in the evening, covered the news since the last gathering, and said he had given final authorization to hit North Vietnam. At 7 P.M., he met the congressional leadership at the White House.

All along the president had worried about the need to get congressional backing for U.S. actions in Vietnam, several times musing to his staff that he might have to "go to the Hill." William Bundy at State had been working on various drafts of a congressional resolution authorizing military and other action in Vietnam. Johnson knew there had been various drafts, but sometime in July he scuttled the whole project—told Bundy to put it away, there was no reason for it.[28] There had been a reason on August 2, after the first attack—but LBJ let it pass. Now he guessed the North Vietnamese were testing him in ways to influence the American people, and possibly the election. If the United States failed to stand up for its ships at sea he would confirm Goldwater's worst accusations of cowardice.[29]

Johnson eluded most acquaintances, even friends. He had a frightening prescience at times, caught nuances, understood things in Lincoln's way of country drollery. He knew Congress best. Its members were like tokens on a checkerboard of power that had once been his special keep; he knew their needs, their egos, and their boasted love of country. And he knew he would have their approval to sustain the national honor.

Nine senators and seven congressmen listened intently as the president recounted the Tonkin Gulf incidents, sharing with them a statement he would read to the American people later that night outlining "limited" retaliatory air strikes against the PT boat bases. One senator thought the wording might be stronger, but LBJ said that "we want them [the North Vietnamese] to know we are not going to take it lying down . . . but we are not going to destroy their cities and we hope we can prepare them for the course we will follow." He told them, then, that he needed their support; that he recalled Truman's problems with his response to the North Korean attack, absent congressional approval. Constitutionally, the president ranked as the commander in chief, but over the years Congress had shown increasing uneasiness with executive wars. Johnson wanted no such trouble.

General discussion ran favorably to the president's plans. Secretary Rusk thought it important to emphasize that "we are *not* doing this as a pretext for a larger war."[30] Everyone in the room knew that some U.S. military actions had supported South Vietnamese operations, but only on a severely restricted basis.

They also knew that the president expected further involvement and wanted congressional approval. Senator Bourke Hickenlooper of Iowa, ranking Republican on the Foreign Relations Committee, felt no doubt that LBJ had the authority to order military action. "It is my own personal feeling that it is up to the President to prepare the kind and type of resolution he believes would be proper. It is up to Congress to see whether they will pass it or not. I have no doubt in my mind that concrete action would be taken."

Johnson said he thought that, too, but "I wanted the advice of each of you and wanted to consult with you." Then he polled the leadership and got unanimous support for the bombing and the resolution.

Senator J. William Fulbright of Arkansas, chairman of the Foreign Relations Committee, declared flatly, "I will support it." Speaker of the House John McCormack of Massachusetts, said Congress would present a united front.[31]

Next, LBJ sought to reach Senator Goldwater. At a little past 10 P.M. Goldwater listened to all that had happened and was planned and agreed without qualm. And Johnson had adroitly removed the Tonkin Gulf issue from the campaign!

Timing his speech to the nation became an acute question. Johnson decided that he would talk after the first U.S. planes were on the way to North Vietnam. A little before midnight he went before White House cameras and addressed the nation. "Repeated acts of violence against the armed forces of the United States," Johnson said solemnly, "must be met not only with alert defense, but with positive reply. That reply is being given as I speak to you tonight." Sixty-four carrier aircraft hit torpedo boat bases and an oil storage area on August 5. They destroyed eight boats, damaged twenty-one others and left oil smoke billowing up to fourteen thousand feet.[32]

Rusk and George Ball collaborated with Senate Foreign Relations Committee members to produce a resolution giving the commander in chief authority to "repel any armed attack" against U.S. forces and "to prevent further aggression." In addition, the resolution said the U.S. "is . . . prepared, as the president determines, to take all necessary steps, including the use of armed force, to assist any member or protocol state of the Southeast Asia Collective Defense Treaty requesting assistance in defense of its freedom."[33]

McNamara, Rusk, and General Wheeler testified before a joint meeting of the Senate Foreign Relations and Armed Services Committees on Thursday, August 6, and won a combined vote of 31-1—the single dissenter being Sen. Wayne Morse of Oregon, a former law professor who branded the resolution an "unconstitutional, pre-dated declaration of war." That same day, the House Foreign Affairs Committee voted 29-0 in favor; the House Armed Services Committee did not bother to meet.

In fact, the House did not debate the resolution because nobody opposed it. Senators talked about it in some depth. Fulbright, full of prestige and good sense, served as one of the sponsors, along with Hickenlooper of the Foreign Relations Committee, Richard Russell of Georgia, and Leverett Saltonstall of Massachusetts and a member of the Armed Services Committee.

John Sherman Cooper of Kentucky had some pertinent questions for Fulbright. "Looking ahead, if the President decided that it was necessary to use such force as could lead into war, we will give that authority by this resolution?"

"That is the way I would interpret it," Fulbright answered. "If . . . we thought the approval should be withdrawn, it could be withdrawn by concurrent resolution." Like Johnson, Fulbright hoped for no wider war, but the authority lay in the resolution.

A rush of patriotic rhetoric swept Congress, with Sen. Frank Church saying that "there is a time to question the route of the flag, and there is a time to rally around it, lest it be routed. This is time for the latter course, and in our pursuit of it, a time for all of us to unify."[34]

Privately, Fulbright told Rusk that the resolution was the best of its kind he had ever seen, and he wanted quick, unanimous senate passage.[35] He nearly got his wish.

On Friday, August 7, after forty minutes of talking, the House approved the resolution by a vote of 416-0. Arguments in the Senate that had dragged through Wednesday, Thursday, and Friday morning, came to an end at 1:15 P.M. with a favorable vote of 88-2. Those opposing were Morse and Sen. Ernest Gruening of Alaska.

Although he was pleased, the president realized that with the authority went vastly increased responsibility: Vietnam had become Lyndon Johnson's war.

A WAR FOR THE PEOPLE

The Democrats had the high ground. They could fight the election by counterpunching: let Goldwater talk, then hit back with calm reason couched in polished packages. Bill Moyers, Jack Valenti, Richard Goodwin, Larry O'Brien, and Clark Clifford engineered one ad—it showed an exploding H-bomb in the background that slowly eroded an image of a pretty little girl holding a daisy—that LBJ ordered off the air. But victory came almost inevitably to "the peace candidate." It wasn't a landslide, but rather an avalanche that topped almost anything in American political history. Johnson swept forty-four states and the District of Columbia, and collected 42,995,259 popular votes to Goldwater's 27,204,571, which translated into a 486-52 electoral vote margin.

Johnson told the nation that for him the victory "was a mandate for unity," for an end to hatred and division, and he would work to make it so.[36]

With a power base beyond his best hopes, he changed the White House into a command post for reforms at home and abroad.

Not that he thought of it that way; he did think of what kind of people he had to work on different programs. Some of the White House staff were Kennedy holdovers—he was proud of the number who stayed—and some were his own people, many of them long associates from senatorial and vice-presidential days. He needed good aides because he planned a fast, hard rush at Congress with programs going beyond JFK's to reform the nation. He had sketched out something of the crusade he had in mind to Jack Valenti and others hours after becoming president. In a way he planned a war, a war on the status quo, on hubris and complacency, a war for the people. He had a tremendously infectious enthusiasm when his rhetoric matched his passion and, in those early hours, he laid out tasks that would absorb hours beyond days, energy beyond human endurance, and the patience of a clutch of saints.

He focused, in those moments of waking vision, on his country and its people; he talked little about Vietnam. Looking back, Valenti thought Johnson felt the war would yield to reason. He was convinced LBJ "really believed that if he applied his total intellect and concentration to a problem and if there was any alternative possible, he would find a way to an agreement."[37] His charge for Kennedy's program blasted the logjam and bills came to his desk for signature—bills for college facilities and for vocational, Indian, and general manpower training. Throughout 1964 the push continued and Johnson signed an amazing number of important laws. In his mind the most vital were the Civil Rights Act, which Kennedy had tried for, and the War on Poverty, which sprang from Johnson's remembrance of ragged, hungry students in his Cotulla, Texas, classroom.

Much of it happened by telephone, as Johnson used an old technique of vote tallying and then calling the "uncertains" or "nos" and applying suasion by sheer force of personality. Sir Alec Douglas-Home, British prime minister, made an Oval Office visit early in 1964 and observed LBJ in action. "He was on the telephone. . . . I said, shall I go?" Douglas-Home recalled.

"Oh, no," came the urgent response, and Johnson pulled him back in his chair.

The prime minister listened for twenty-five minutes as the president worked on a recalcitrant senator. "I don't know what the issue was," Douglas-Home recalled, "but I would have voted for it!"[38]

Through most of that early legislative blitz, Vietnam remained on a back burner. Deliberately. Skillful management and manipulation kept Vietnam muffled through the election. Unfortunately, not even a political chef as skilled as LBJ was could keep a lid on the pressure cooker that was about to explode onto the nation's front pages.

PLEIKU: WHERE IT STARTED

"We're going to die. We're all going to die," an American voice screamed into a darkness streaked with mortar explosions. Rifles and automatic weapons joined in and echoed across the U.S. base at Pleiku in Vietnam's central highlands.

A remote market town normally frequented by mountain folk, Pleiku had acquired importance as a staging point for ARVN patrols against Communist infiltrators from Laos and Cambodia. American advisors and Special Forces troops were stationed some three miles away at a heavily protected camp near a U.S. transport and helicopter airstrip. South Vietnamese and American troops guarding the planes and runways were utterly surprised when shooting began about two o'clock on the cold Sunday morning of February 7, 1965. By dawn, nine Americans were dead and more than 120 wounded. Sixteen helicopters and six fixed-wing planes were destroyed. A new dimension had come to the Vietnam War.[39]

Not only did the Pleiku attacks stand as the worst aimed at Americans so far, but they were carefully coordinated, bravely delivered, and devastatingly surprising. They also came at an especially tender time: They caught a U.S. fact-finding mission in Saigon, and Soviet chairman Aleksei N. Kosygin in Hanoi.

Several attacks on U.S. personnel and installations showed a growing problem since the Tonkin Gulf troubles. When the Viet Cong attacked a U.S. air base at Bien Hoa on November 1, 1964, destroying five planes and damaging several others, the Joint Chiefs of Staff—along with the U.S. ambassador, Gen. Maxwell Taylor—urged air strikes against North Vietnam. Johnson refused for several reasons: the election days away, hesitant to hit the North Vietnamese lest China and Russia come to their aid, possible retaliation against American dependents, and doubts about the stability of the South Vietnamese government. Dean Rusk and Robert McNamara shared the president's caution.[40]

On Christmas Eve, 1964, a bomb shattered the Brinks Hotel, a U.S. officer's billet in downtown Saigon, killing two Americans and wounding fifty-eight others. Furious, General Taylor again urged air attacks in the north. Still, the president refused. So fragile seemed the government of South Vietnam, that any kind of counterstrike might finish America's tottering ally. Information coming to the White House painted a decaying picture of the Vietnam situation. Johnson began to doubt that air strikes alone would suffice.

Little had gone well for the South Vietnamese after President Ngo Dinh Diem's assassination in November, 1963. The ARVN's field operations against the VC languished, and General Taylor's assignment to Saigon had not had the expected result of shoring up the government. Now the Pleiku attack caught special attention. Johnson's fact-finding group, led by McGeorge Bundy, reached Saigon just days before the VC struck, and Pleiku cemented a Bundy opinion given to Johnson in late January: he and McNamara were "pretty well convinced that our current policy can lead only to disastrous defeat."[41] When Bundy first heard about Pleiku, he called the White House Situation Room from Saigon and talked with Deputy Defense Secretary Cyrus Vance. Go ahead with air strikes, Bundy urged, adding that Taylor, Gen. William C. Westmoreland, the MACV commander, and others agreed.

Tension and edginess had sparked Bundy's conversations at the U.S. military headquarters in Saigon, where everyone felt that the VC had thrown a gauntlet. The same mood, more accented, charged the Situation Room. This crisis might well force a reluctant Lyndon Johnson to a decision. The president knew what he wanted to do, had a "gut feeling" about Far Eastern policy, but he nursed a nagging insecurity about his military intuition.

Options were narrowing. Sticking by the South Vietnamese had become a point of American honor, but it was a point blurred by debates about how much more was needed to sustain South Vietnam's independence and the U.S. posture in southeast Asia. American prestige could best be preserved by convincing the North Vietnamese they could not conquer the south. But Johnson had a growing conviction that to achieve even that smaller objective he had "no acceptable option but to intensify our effort. . . ."[42] There was a possibility that he had allowed the options to narrow without realizing what had happened.

While the president delayed coming to grips with Vietnam through late 1964, he did authorize a "working group" of national security advisors, chaired by Assistant Secretary of State for Far Eastern Affairs William P. Bundy, to study future Vietnam actions.[43] By the end of November, 1964, this group proposed a two-phased program of escalating, graduated pressure against North Vietnam—the first phase would include resumption of intelligence-gathering De Soto patrols along the North Vietnamese coastline together with armed reconnaissance along the Laotian corridor, and the second phase would involve mounting air strikes to force North Vietnam to seek peace.

Johnson, increasingly feeling that "our forces deserved the support that air strikes against the source of aggression would represent," chafed at increasing VC incursions.[44] Time also bothered him. How long could the United States stay its hand without losing face in Asia? Answers varied, but Undersecretary of State George Ball's was the only voice urging disengagement, urging simply dumping the war. Ball had urged that position from the beginning, despite the mounting cries for action. "Once on the tiger's back," he would argue, "we cannot be sure of picking the place to dismount." Escalation would beget escalation he said, because "once you get one of those things [a bombing program] going, it's like getting a little alcohol; you're going to get a taste for more."[45]

Johnson listened to George Ball; that great bear of a man had iron integrity and a willingness to be counted. And the president knew the odds in the scales of intervention—the course would be long and difficult. General Taylor confessed in early January, 1965, that "we are presently on a losing track and must risk a change," and McGeorge Bundy argued that, despite everything the United States had done, the VC saw America's failure to exert its full power in the war zone as evidence of unwillingness to take risks.[46]

Now came Pleiku on February 7, the latest instance of growing enemy boldness. This particular VC attack loomed larger than others because Soviet chairman Aleksei Kosygin had reached Hanoi on February 6, 1965, where he told a cheering crowd that his country would "not remain indifferent" to "acts of war" committed against North Vietnam. Kosygin's publicized visit had caused another American avoidance of risk—the delay of a De Soto patrol. Forbearance seemed the better part of bombast, and might convince Kosygin to try peacemaking.[47] Yet failure to react would show the United States as weak while an American attack would give the North Vietnamese an excuse to ask for massive military aid.[48]

This sticky situation led Johnson to call a meeting of Vietnam advisors in the Cabinet Room at 7:45 P.M. on February 6. Vice President Humphrey, McNamara, and his able deputy Vance were at the meeting. So, too, were Gen. Earle Wheeler and George Ball, who represented a sick Dean Rusk. Bill Bundy attended, along with Treasury Secretary Douglas Dillon, Carl Rowan from the USIA, and Marshall Carter from the CIA. House Speaker John McCormack and Sen. Mike Mansfield represented Congress. They talked for seventy-five minutes, but from the beginning everyone present could tell that Pleiku had struck a presidential nerve; LBJ was mad.

"I've gone far enough," the president grumped loudly. "I've had enough of this."[49] Surely the time had come to punish the enemy. He reported that Mac Bundy, General Taylor, and General Westmoreland in Saigon had recommended reprisal. He glanced around the table and saw general agreement, but got a mild surprise from George Ball's indirect opposition.

That wily maneuverer saw the drift of the meeting as it began. "Faced with a unanimous view," he remembered later, "I saw no option but to go along, although I did try one filibustering tactic, countering McNamara's insistence on immediate bombing with the argument that we should at least postpone the action until after Kosygin . . . had left the country."[50] Senator Mansfield liked this approach, as did Hubert Humphrey. Llewellyn Thompson, former ambassador to Moscow, suggested that the Russians would probably think the United States deliberately chose the bombing moment to humiliate the Soviet Union.

McNamara rushed in to sweep aside dissent. American power had to be used in immediate reaction to the Viet Cong attack, he argued with his usual fervor. Ball noted at the time that "it was the quintessential McNamara."[51]

Johnson wanted action. "We have kept our gun over the mantle and our shells in the cupboard for a long time now," said Johnson. "And what was the result? They are killing our men while they sleep in the night. I can't ask our American soldiers out there to continue to fight with one hand tied behind their backs." Maybe a swift and fierce reaction to Pleiku would convince Hanoi's leaders, not only of U.S. power, but also of U.S. determination. Johnson acknowledged Mansfield's worries about China and Russia, but thought that since neither seemed to be trying for peace, their feelings need not be too carefully considered. Johnson doubted either wanted direct involvement—intelligence sources indicated that China would intervene only if North Vietnam were invaded or about to lose. Humphrey's objection irritated the president as a kind of internal disloyalty—once the president's mind was made up, he resented opposition—and the vice president disappeared from Vietnam discussions for a time.[52]

Johnson activated an already-devised retaliatory bombing program code-named Flaming Dart by ordering four selected targets hit in North Vietnam. He also directed the swift evacuation of American dependents from the south. Within fourteen hours, U.S. carrier aircraft and South Vietnamese planes hit one of the targets, enemy barracks and staging areas at Dong Hoi, north of the Demilitarized Zone (DMZ) that divided the Vietnams at the seventeenth parallel. Bad weather protected the other three targets and gave the great U.S. countermove *opéra bouffe* overtones.[53]

Tuned to public opinion, Johnson made a statement the next day emphasizing that "we seek no wider war. Whether or not this course can be maintained lies with the North Vietnamese aggressors." Close reading shows this statement to be both reassuring and admonitory. There might be wider war if the enemy would have it so.[54] Evidence that the enemy either willed it or did not understand the American position soon followed: On February 10, a VC attack killed twenty-three Americans and wounded twenty-one others at Qui Nhon.

Another Flaming Dart response struck the Chanh Hoa barracks just north of the seventeenth parallel, and both U.S. and Vietnamese air force planes hit a base at Chap Le. Anyone listening for changes in administration rhetoric would have noticed that these attacks were not billed as reprisals. They instead were announced as air operations in response to "further direct provocations by the Hanoi regime." The words "air operations" and "response" instead of "retaliation" signaled a clear change in the U.S. Vietnam program,[55] although the president stressed that there had been no basic shift in the U.S. position.

It seemed hardly noticeable when, on February 13, Johnson approved "a program of measured and limited air action jointly with GVN [the government of South Vietnam] against selected military targets in the DRV [North Vietnam]." This program—code named Rolling Thunder—involved more or less constant air strikes north of the DMZ and would last more than three years.[56]

By the time the president authorized Rolling Thunder, he had pretty well come to the conclusion that strong ground forces would be needed to protect U.S. air bases and prop up the ARVN. The idea was not new. Almost from the beginning of U.S. involvement, some thought focused on possible future troop needs.[57] No one wanted to send troops beyond those needed for the military assistance program, but after 1961 increasing numbers of Americans had joined the advisor ranks. By the time LBJ became president some 16,000 U.S. troops were in South Vietnam.[58]

Continued deterioration of the South Vietnamese government kept the prospect of American ground commitment alive as the "morale building" bombing effort failed to strengthen things in Southeast Asia. Yet serious questions surrounded the possibility. Not all military men were certain that U.S. troops could function well in Southeast Asia—climate, culture, and race were all uncertain factors. General Maxwell Taylor wondered if Caucasian troops could be effective. It seemed a strange worry, but it surfaced when Taylor heard that General Westmoreland, on February 22, 1965, had asked for two Marine battalions to protect the important U.S. airfield at Da Nang. Taylor opposed sending troops and he seems to have been scrambling for reasons to keep them out. Taylor and others feared that one deployment would lead to others with widening missions until the United States found itself in a ground war in Asia. Generations of military and civilian thinkers since Alfred Thayer Mahan preached the horrors of just such a conflict, and Taylor dreaded the prospect.[59]

Taylor thought sending troops to support the eroding Saigon administration made little sense. A weak government there would relax and let the United States run the war if large numbers of American combat soldiers arrived. Far better, Taylor thought, to wait and see if the ruling generals could mount effective efforts at pacification in the backcountry, if they could create a nation in the post-Diem chaos. But opposition, he could sense, grew less useful as presidential advisors and the Joint Chiefs concentrated on how many troops were needed in Vietnam.[60] Even Taylor wavered as Rolling Thunder failed to produce positive reaction from Hanoi; he began to think firmer, heavier raids were essential to prop up the Saigon regime.[61]

In any event, President Johnson formally approved sending two Marine battalions to Da Nang on February 26. Pleiku had spawned a lengthening cord of U.S. attachment to South Vietnam.

THE DECISION PROCESS

The decision to react to the Pleiku attack ranks as one of the most important ones Johnson made about Vietnam. Some might argue that decision was made too hastily and without careful consideration. Nothing could have been further from the facts. Long months of presidential agonizing preceded

Johnson's post-Pleiku orders. He commissioned various studies by the Defense and State Department staffs offering different courses of action. The president's mind remained open, although several members of his inner circle thought he was offered increasingly narrowed options.

To some extent, LBJ limited his own opportunities by trying for a strong military position before making peace overtures. Ball kept urging an end to the South Vietnam embroglio through negotiation,[62] as did Mike Mansfield and a few others. Johnson listened, always carefully, but in the months after his election in 1964 he came increasingly to a fighting stance. Personality had a lot to do with the course he finally chose. He did not want to "cut and run," to suffer the same emasculation President Harry S. Truman did in the wake of "losing" China. Doris Kearns, a biographer who interviewed Johnson frequently, heard him confirm those feelings. If he lost Vietnam, he said, Americans would say "that I was a coward. An unmanly man. A man without a spine."[63]

How did he make Vietnam decisions? "Very carefully," in the words of Jack Valenti. "I do not want to be the president who started World War III," Johnson often said, nor did he want to kill civilians by indiscriminate bombing. His decision-making had a "disarmingly simple" look to Walt Rostow, who succeeded Mac Bundy as LBJ's National Security Advisor. "It was a very orderly process of very reluctant decision. . . . He would call together a meeting to take the next step. Everyone would be heard, he would go away to think about it, and have another meeting. It was very orderly. Then he would have his outside consultants. . . . Then he would go away and think about it and kick the dog. It was a hell of a tough kind of decision."[64]

War decisions were always Johnson's hardest. His background, experiences, and mentors had taught the power of suasion in winning consensus. In martial decisions consensus often weakened the outcome. Napoleon, after all, finally avoided councils of war as pulpits for timidity. Johnson consistently sought consensus in congressional support for actions in Vietnam. Some in his inner circle thought that he tried too hard for consensus in military matters. A few believed he subordinated Vietnam decisions to his Great Society programs, others that he always based war decisions solely on military and diplomatic grounds. Some complained that he deliberated too long, and others said that he filtered information carefully, made a decision, and expected everyone to carry it out instantly.[65]

Johnson did all of these things to some degree. His main concern, always, centered on information. The president consumed data voraciously and remembered it. He worked his advisors hard; Mac Bundy, Taylor, McNamara, Rusk, George Ball—he badgered all of them for plans and critiques of plans.

The president read the documents coming to him, often as he combed through his "night reading," and marked significant passages—occasionally to the surprise, sometimes to the chagrin, of the senders. Differing views on Vietnam policies always earned a presidential probe for usable alternatives, which is one of the reasons he kept George Ball at hand—not as house critic but as a trusty voice of opposition[66]—and kept "looking for the offbeat."[67] Some students of his presidency question whether Johnson listened closely enough to his generals, question whether he really heard them save through McNamara's mind.[68]

Johnson's decision-making style differed greatly from Kennedy's; it was less personal and more structured. But in Vietnam matters he held to a close circle. Occasionally the whole cabinet would be informed of war measures, but usually Mac Bundy, McNamara, Rusk, Ball, Bill Moyers, McCone, and sometimes Bus Wheeler and Valenti, were the confidantes. Presidents fear leaks of sensitive information, and Johnson clearly felt that the more closely held the secrets, the better kept. He slowly groped toward a program of more orderly discussion with a few people and by early 1967 came to a deep reliance on his Tuesday lunch meetings. In the early stages of understanding an issue he might seem hesitant or unsure—and he was. He always wanted good homework done and he prodded everyone to look ahead.[69]

The presidency tied him down in difficult ways. In earlier careers he could touch people, look them in the eye, and get a personal feel for opinions and deceits. He might have gone to Vietnam and tested the ground and the people; he might even have found a way to meet Ho Chi Minh—he always believed that if they could sit together, some deal would emerge. That deep need for personal engagement led him to listen to people just back from Vietnam—eyewitnesses had the credibility of presence.

A look at the post-Pleiku decisions gives a fair view of how the president operated. When Mac Bundy and others of his fact-finding group (including Gen. Andrew J. Goodpaster, assistant to the Joint Chiefs chairman, and John T. McNaughton, assistant secretary of defense) returned from Saigon and gave LBJ a report on the situation right after Pleiku, he read it with care—with the October, 1964, report from William Bundy's study group, and with other plans for further U.S. involvement fresh in memory.[70]

Pleiku's vulnerability seemed to Mac Bundy and his team a symptom of the paralysis creeping across South Vietnam. "Without new U.S. action defeat appears inevitable, probably not in a matter of weeks or perhaps even months. . . . There is still time to turn [it] around, but not much," Bundy said. He stressed that American prestige was on the line in Vietnam and made getting out almost impossible. "There is no way of unloading the burden on the Vietnamese themselves," he thought, and added, significantly, that "there is no way of negotiating ourselves out of Vietnam which offers any serious promise at present. . . ."[71] About the best hope lay in a program of "*sustained reprisal* against North Vietnam—a policy in which air and naval action against the North is justified by and related to the whole Viet Cong campaign of violence and terror in the South."[72]

Johnson might have been permitted a moment of ironic amusement as he read an assessment and a program strangely similar to ones offered earlier by CINCPAC headquarters and the Joint Chiefs of Staff. Those proposals, proffered by the military, had been violently opposed by McNamara and Rusk and hardly condoned by Mac Bundy. But, philosophically, the president recognized that "the situation had changed and that our actions would have to change too."[73]

A little before ten o'clock in the morning on February 8, Johnson convened most of the National Security Council to talk about Bundy's new recommendations. As he looked around the big table and along the walls in the Cabinet Room, the president saw Ball (Rusk was ill), Ambassador Thompson, "that other Bundy" (Bill), and Leonard Unger from State; McNamara, Vance, and McNaughton from Defense; Secretary Dillon from Treasury; Bus Wheeler and Andy Goodpaster from the Joint Chiefs; Director John McCone of the CIA; Carl Rowan of the USIA; David Bell and William Gaud from the Agency for International Development (AID); Mac Bundy, and some White House aides. Everyone present had either seen Mac Bundy's report or knew its main thrusts—and the president wanted its contents kept confidential. As LBJ went around the room he found unanimous support for sustained reprisals against North Vietnam. A few present differed over how the plan should be implemented. Wheeler and Goodpaster urged an intensive program from the start; others cautioned gradualism.

Shortly after the session began, the president welcomed Speaker McCormack to the group, along with Gerald R. Ford from the House and Mike Mansfield and Everett Dirksen from the Senate. Everyone heard McNamara on the results of recent air strikes. Ball discussed diplomatic maneuvering at the UN and with the Russians in the wake of Pleiku. Then Johnson rehearsed his months of assessing reports and recommendations and enemy action. Flagrant actions against American men and bases demanded reaction—but he stressed that reaction came not to isolated cases but to a "whole pattern of aggression and terrorism," and reflected only an extension of existing policy. He promised action, but added that U.S. responses would be "temperate and careful." America's objective, he explained was to deter the North Vietnamese, deny them victory, and convince them to "leave South Vietnam alone."

Ambassador Taylor received word late that same day about Johnson's decision to initiate "continuing action" against the enemy.[74] At the moment it seemed a small, incremental escalation, but it marked Johnson's real commitment to war in Vietnam.[75]

Portentous decisions came after Pleiku. Those that followed were logical extensions of the ones made in February. And they would be made in roughly the same way. In some of them military opinion would be directly sought by the president, sometimes not. But all of them show a commander in chief taking his job seriously—one who moved slowly toward escalation, and then only after he pondered all the portents for the future.[76]

THREE

Command Post for a Two-Front War

Once it had been Camelot, a castle high and shining in the air, a keep of dreams and hopes and promises for a place worthy of love and service. Once it had been JFK's house. Now it was not, although some familiar faces still roamed the halls and tended governmental tokens. Some faces were gone with the shattered dream and new ones came with a new president. Old White House hands could feel the differences in the atmosphere, differences in pace and measure, in manner and in grace. Transition times are hard, but never harder than following a tragic death. The public wondered about the change because it fanned old rumors of trouble between JFK and LBJ. Had they been allies only on the surface? Was it true that the easterners clustering in Camelot sneered almost openly at the Texas twang and country manner so much the mark of Johnson?

There had been some of that, some snobbery of place and style, but less than gossip fancied. Sometimes Vice President Johnson sensed the snickers but he masked reaction out of loyalty to a president he admired and liked. JFK in turn admired the Texan's professional work with congress and also liked him.[1]

Most of the transitional unease came from grief, real and deep and quenching. Although rumors linger, memories are clear. Johnson asked members of the cabinet to stay. Many did, and they came to admire their new boss and to fit his personal ways of working. Johnson took some familiarizing for the cabinet and White House staffers who had little or no acquaintance with him. Stories came with him about his Texas manner, his storytelling and his jibes at associates—stories somehow remindful of Lincoln and Truman. News folk liked to enlarge on him, make his foibles match his bulk, paint him large and egregious; but they had trouble doing so because, as president, he had a different self to find.

His early months in office—during the time he considered himself a trustee for JFK—showed his skill in legislative maneuver, in getting an amazing number of important bills through Congress. That time, too, showed him to be patient and crafty as he waited for his own election. To anyone looking closely at the White House itself, that adjusting time revealed organizational changes to fit a leader accustomed to hands-on suasion and direct pressure of power.

WARRIORS FOR THE GREAT SOCIETY

Often the White House served as the nexus of various powers and frequently served as the commander in chief's headquarters. In recent times it had known war tensions as JFK struggled with the Bay of Pigs fiasco, troubles in Berlin, the Cuban missile crisis, and nagging irk in Vietnam. It knew the tension of combat again almost as soon as Johnson took up residence. Within a few weeks he had declared war on poverty and commanded a massive effort against that ancient enemy of mankind. Each president finds personal ways of waging war, but Johnson faced an unusual challenge in commanding two different wars—one in Asia and one at home.

In his first months as custodian of JFK's programs, Johnson learned much about command functions. Congressional relations he understood, all the avenues of political maneuver; he understood, too, that things had changed, and he worked to make the switch from Senate majority leader to president. Recognizing that as chief executive he must propose legislation and push for its passage, must oversee congressional doings while at the same time managing the pesky war in Southeast Asia, he chose his people carefully, his eyes focused on capability and on loyalty.

There were some of JFK's people whose domestic political talents Johnson admired and wanted to keep as representatives on the Hill. Some cabinet members would be first-line warriors in the poverty conflict: Anthony Celebrezze, secretary of health, education and welfare; Henry Fowler, secretary of the treasury; and Orville Freeman, secretary of agriculture. Among the staff, LBJ wanted very much to keep Kenneth O'Donnell, an able, wise, detail man. For a time O'Donnell stayed with Johnson, but memories were too tender and he finally drifted into Robert Kennedy's camp.

Johnson tagged Jack Valenti early as a man to keep handy. The precision of arrangements during JFK's Texas trip, the splendid crowds thronging Houston's streets on November 21, the hitchless dinner in honor of Congressman Albert Thomas, at which the president addressed a truly overflow crowd—none of these things surprised LBJ. Valenti, who, with partner Weldon Weekley, ran a highly successful advertising agency, had considerable Houston and Texas influence.

A short man, he never seemed so, overcoming brevity in height with energy, with that clear-eyed force of character that wins trust and admiration. Quick witted and worded, he surveyed scenes and people and could encapsulate them pithily for a busy president. Most important, he was loyal.

Valenti, who also served as a kind of personal aide, probably had the most direct contact with LBJ—his constantly at the president's beck and call, almost from the moment LBJ asked him to arrange things to move to Washington and the White House. Nominally the appointments secretary, Valenti's role defied description and so caused much speculation in the press. He was the insider's insider, a confidante's confidante, a too-close-for-comfort man, a Texas adman come too far uptown. Closeness begat envy and malignity, all of which could hardly surprise a Harvard M.B.A. and a votary of British history who saw his role in high perspective.

Things were done in the White House by a small, dedicated staff of secretaries who handled correspondence, prepared endless documents, took notes, dictation, made phone calls, and helped Jack Valenti juggle appointments. Juanita Roberts headed the list: zealous, a furiously competent organizer, facilitator, doer, and persuader, she worked the president's office with efficiency and style. A long time cohort, she had been with Johnson since his Senate days and traded on her seniority, Valenti noted, "to keep her place in the hierarchy." She irritated some staff people because she kept an almost martial mien and manner. The White House staff soon labeled her—on tough days—"Colonel Roberts," which reflected her actual Women's Army Corps rank. And she kept everything for posterity—much like Dorothy Territo in Lady Bird's service. Once, during LBJ's vice-presidential days, Bill Moyers (another fixture in the Johnson entourage), sent the "colonel" a package containing chicken bones and a note saying "the vice-president just ate and I thought you might want these for the archives."[2] There is no record that Roberts smiled.

She had her "insistencies," irked and commanded, but kept things running with consummate professionalism. Her work in the hectic first days ranked beyond praise and she kept it up. But not without help.[3]

White House business came in torrents, sometimes in tsunamis and typhoons. The kind of staff LBJ had during his Senate or vice-presidential days simply could not keep up. Aiding in management of the whelm of people, calls, and papers, was Marie Fehmer, nearly Johnson's personal secretary—a woman of patience, tact, and charm. Jack Valenti loved her because "she *was* sweet beyond all possibility. She *was* soft and feminine and invariably gentle-tempered." More than that, she kept secrets.[4] Victoria "Vicki" McCammon, quick, witty, and pretty, joined the burgeoning office routine; the president leaned on her and took her with him on trips to the ranch. Yolanda Boozer completed the senior-level secretarial staff with humor and zest, enjoying her role as an exemplary Mexican American close to LBJ.[5]

No sketch of the White House mechanism would come close to a full diagram without mention of the legion of telephone ladies who fielded the incoming and aided the outgoing voices. White House phones are operational twenty-four hours a day and rarely are there delays or mishaps in transmission. Johnson taxed the formidable ingenuity of the White House phone corps. More than any predecessor, he cherished the phone. He kept one handy in every room, including the bathroom, and in his cars, helicopters, and planes. He wanted his close staff no farther away than a phone. He lived by the phone, figuratively and literally. Stories of his phone fetish are legion and have been mentioned before. They are not a diversion in any discussion of his lifestyle and his house. Essential though they were to a man who worked in words for deeds, phones did sometimes cause embarrassment to the president. Most people who came to see him wanted his full attention, and many were flustered and wounded at sharing their time with various people and varied concerns.

Staffers got used to it or learned to tolerate fragmented attention. Close aides and those shaping vital issues of the War on Poverty and the war in Vietnam shared direct access to the commander in chief and enjoyed closer listening.

Most other staff members who came to work for the new president had qualities Johnson needed. Many of them had served him long enough to be cronies, some were recent additions to his staff, but all shared his informal zeal and roughhewn western patriotism.

Presidential aides worked in the West Wing of the White House, whereas Mrs. Johnson's staff used the East Wing and some offices in the Old Executive Office Building. Soon after the Johnsons moved in, the White House changed to their tempos and plans.

Johnson had a vision of America long bubbling in his blood. Things he did, programs he pushed from early congressional days under FDR to later senatorial days under Truman and Eisenhower, were aimed at reelection but also at helping poor and underdeveloped communities. In the 1930s LBJ taught school in Depression-wracked Cotulla, Texas. As a teacher, Johnson struggled against the apathy that poverty makes to involve parents in the future of their children and the school. He learned that Cotulla parents "had about the same hopes for their children that bankers do."[6]

Those hopes amid no little human wastage touched a kinship in Johnson's memory, a kinship to his own youth. The Johnsons were poor; they lived in a dogtrot house without electricity or indoor plumbing; they struggled sometimes for food and, as children came, struggled to send them to a one-room school in Johnson City. Sam Johnson, LBJ's father, had ambitions beyond his grasp and took solace, sometimes, in drink. When he did, he often squandered his money. Living high one year, impoverished the next, proved hard on LBJ's mother, on him, and on his brother and sisters. Hard living sometimes made his parents hard, which often confused young Lyndon about the difference between love and punishment. His early years made him a lifelong enemy of squalid hardscrabble. His Cotulla students fueled an urge to do something about people in need—an urge that never left him and grew stronger with his own success.[7]

Lots of things bothered him, but poverty seemed almost a negation of the democratic spirit. John Kenneth Galbraith's assessment of the "affluent society" in the 1950s hit home with Johnson. Galbraith had aptly assessed a serious defect in affluence: "the arithmetic of modern politics," he wrote, "makes it tempting to overlook the very poor." He added that "modern liberal politicians" ignored them because they were an "inarticulate minority." Those words challenged Johnson.[8]

A surprisingly determined Johnson told Congress in March, 1965, "I never thought . . . that I . . . might have the chance to help the sons and daughters of those students [in Cotulla] and to help people like them all over this country. But now I do have that chance—and I'll let you in on a secret: I mean to use it."[9] And he did.

He brought Walter Heller, chairman of the Council of Economic Advisors, and Kermit Gordon, director of the Bureau of the Budget, to the LBJ Ranch on the Pedernales River, near Stonewall, Texas, during the Christmas holidays in 1963. The president knew the nation was still benumbed, in shock, but he guessed action to be shock's best treatment. Heller had inspired Johnson in his first days as president with a question: did he want the Council of Economic Advisors to plan an attack on poverty? Most people, Heller said, had no idea of poverty's pervasiveness; some writers and some government officials had glimmerings. President Kennedy had approved planning a program, but no specifics were given and the question lingered. Johnson caught the high potential in that question. For just a moment—with JFK still lying in state and the country holding its breath—opportunities coalesced: there was an obvious need, a willingness to do something positive, and the president had the power to act. Johnson told Heller to "push ahead full tilt."

So the planners came and worked in a small, green frame building not far from the main ranch house. During one of their tinkering sessions, the president dropped in on Heller, Gordon, Jack Valenti, and Bill Moyers. The place looked like a political conniver's den: the small kitchen table was strewn with papers, coffee cups, and an overstuffed ashtray; layers of smoke hung in the dull air. Johnson surveyed the scene and caught a whimsical thought as he looked out the window at some Herefords grazing noisily outside. "It struck me," he later noted, "that . . . perhaps the setting, with scholars and government officials sitting around a kitchen table on a ranch far from an urban center, was not inappropriate for the drafting of a new program that would touch the lives of city and country dwellers alike."[10]

Think big, the president said. In America's vulnerable moment really big things could be done—and they would probably cost money. Out of those ranch meetings came a name: the War on Poverty. That set the stage, gave a framework for effort, and triggered energies in many places.

Everyone at the ranch thought the Poverty War should be handled by a separate agency, commanded by a tough, visionary leader untrammelled by caution and unfazed by change. Well schooled in bureaucratic bumf, the president avoided creating a committee; an executive office appeared instead, with Sargent Shriver as director. Johnson's clear support gave energy to the project, and his blessing gave it life. His blessing came in his first State of the Union address on January 8, 1964.

"This administration today, here and now, declares unconditional war on poverty in America," LBJ told Congress. He urged an attack on its causes, rather than simply its consequences. Members greeted Johnson's different war variously; there was much sentiment running to help LBJ, to work with him to move on past the assassination, to focus attention on the future. But one of his proposals, the Economic Opportunity Act, offered a tempting target for Republicans in an election year. Not only did it fan old Republican furies of rampant liberal spending, but it seemed almost tailored for

Republicans to win southern Democratic help in opposition. Rumor had it, along with some of the press, that economic opportunity as designed in the bill would only benefit African Americans. Untrue, of course, since at least "four out of every five families . . . living in poverty in the United States were white."

Peter Frelinguysen, a wealthy New Jerseyan and ranking Republican on the vital House Education and Labor Committee, kicked off the contest by damning LBJ's whole program as silly. After all, he said, "This country has been engaged in fighting poverty since it was founded."[11]

Johnson expected heavy weather in Congress. He pulled Larry O'Brien in for close conniving on getting the bill through.

Outgoing, amazingly easy with people, O'Brien had been a Massachusetts public relations executive when JFK caught his eye. O'Brien thought he could do good things for the country and had joined Kennedy's team. He, like others of the Camelot team, felt the awful crush of Kennedy's loss, but responded to Johnson's call for help.

As a leader of Kennedy's congressional liaison team, O'Brien studied Congress carefully. He came to know and be known by almost everyone on the Hill. Popular and winning, he and his henchman, Dick Donahue, made a specialty of doing favors for various congressmen. They were liked, but were they effective? Thomas "Tip" O'Neill, veteran Massachusetts congressman destined for the speakership, thought not. "They weren't . . . effective at their job, which was to help get the president's legislation through Congress. Other than the Manpower bill, there wasn't much Kennedy legislation that actually passed during his shortened term in office. . . . it took the political skills of Lyndon Johnson to make it happen."[12]

Johnson's personality and suasion made the difference. O'Brien and others became increasingly effective as they worked under LBJ's amazing rubric of activity. Jack Valenti understood something about the president that other White House staffers soon came to appreciate—his "all-pervading eye for detail."[13] That penchant, communicated to his congressional liaison people, made the difference between mere presence and persuasion. Larry O'Brien, once attuned to precision, became formidable in assessing congressional whims and ways and nearly legendary in snatching victory out of chaos.

O'Brien, Valenti, Moyers, Walter Jenkins, Douglas Cater and Joseph A. Califano Jr., with others, pushed the domestic legislative drive. They were opposites in almost every way, but they shared a firm devotion to getting things done.

Moyers ranked as the phenomenal young man of the group. He had come to White House prominence with Vice President Johnson. John Kennedy's youthful specialists, the "Whiz Kids," swept White House halls and systems with the arrogance of saviors. Even among that self-justifying group of hard-nosed realists who projected a dazzling virility of mind and body, the earnest Baptist minister from Texas more than held his own. Almost welcomed to the Harvard, Rhodes scholar, eastern establishment fold, Moyers nearly fitted that new generation who were dedicated to JFK's promise to "get America moving again" toward a destiny all the young men somehow knew. They were the new visionaries, quick-minded patriots intolerant of old ways and old men, so they were often fooled. But not by their own ranks—and they took to Moyers.

He did have a deep strain of biblicality in him, but, as some of the Whizzers guessed, much of it burned away in White House heat. Earnestness, heightened by innocence, never left him. Politicians envied his straight in the eye style, and the president liked his obvious loyalty.

For his part, Moyers admired Johnson's fulminating passion, his tenacity in getting JFK's program through Congress, his dogged defense of underdogs, and his inflexible dedication to civil rights. Some things about Johnson, though, seem to have affronted something in Moyers that led him, finally, to a small rebellion against his leader—a rebellion that would cast him from the halls of power to a periphery of frustration. A close presidential advisor admired Moyers for resisting a Johnsonian immolation. "One of Moyers' great skills," Clark Clifford later remarked, "was his ability to transmit accurately the President's mood, while subtly detaching himself from what he was conveying." Clifford admitted that a tinge of dissimulation might be involved: "Some of his colleagues in the Johnson White House may have thought Moyers was not always completely loyal to his chief, but I felt he served the President all the better by retaining a degree of independence of thought."[14]

"A degree of independence" worked for a while, especially in Moyer's early days as a special assistant to the president, but hampered him when he became press secretary. For a time, though, he rode high in handsome invulnerability, hard to see, tough to touch, and rock hard in a fight. Valenti, who liked him, knew part of the reason for his success: "Early in the LBJ years he did what every durable bureaucrat and power-gatherer does—he installed friends and colleagues in damn near every nook and cranny of the government so that he was the most knowledgeable and best informed of all the aides in the West Wing."[15]

In July, 1965, Califano joined Johnson's domestic team. A special assistant to McNamara at defense, he caught Mac Bundy's and Moyers's attention with deft work in Cuba, Panama, and the Dominican Republic. They thought his Latin American experience would be a help to the White House, not only in policy making but also in finding good people for various niches in the government. Califano wanted the job when it was offered in November, 1964, but McNamara did not want him to leave. A determined LBJ got him in July, 1965, when a major shuffle of White House staffers opened a slot for a manager of domestic legislative programs and crises. McNamara saw this assignment as vital and agreed. Califano brought zest, enthusiasm, energy, and good ideas with him. Legislation flowed after him as visions became plans and plans became realities—he was LBJ's kind of man.[16]

There were others. Alabaman Douglas Cater worked educational realms for the president, and did needed things throughout LBJ's administration. A gifted correspondent for the small but influential *Reporter* magazine, Cater knew LBJ from old—and he had long chronicled government problems. Johnson admired him and wanted him on his staff. But Cater came hard. Enjoying his reportorial independence, he resisted a mere invitation. The president gave him the "treatment." He invited Cater to the White House for a swim, along with Moyers and Valenti. All of them, naked as jaybirds, gathered at the presidential pool. Flustered or not, Cater wallowed with the rest as he heard an unusual proposition. "You've been writing a long time about what was wrong with how the government was run," Johnson said, paddling away, "now I'm giving you a chance to put your theories to work. Come on in and help run the country instead of writing about it." So splashy an approach proved hard to resist—and LBJ kept up the attack. It took time and it taxed the swimmers, but when they wearily climbed from the pool, Cater had joined up. Neither he nor the president nor the educational community regretted his decision.[17]

Speech writing has always ranked high among the tasks on Pennsylvania Avenue. LBJ had a splendid corps of wordsmiths at his call. Horace "Buzz" Busby had long been a Johnson favorite and fitted his boss' ways perfectly. Quick, with a fine mind and gifted pen, Buzz served well but kept something of himself aloof—just enough to intrigue a boss who wanted everything a man could give. A casual, he came and went at the White House, sometimes drifting off to his own business and then coming back full time, enjoying Johnson's constant admiration. Richard Goodwin, who wrote most of three great Johnson orations, had an uncommon gift for words. An admiring Jack Valenti described Goodwin as "a prickly chap. At his worst, he was as lovable as a sullen porcupine; at his best, incandescent and possibly a near-genius in the field. For when Goodwin is collaborating with his muses, he is the most skilled living practitioner of an arcane and dying art form, the political speech."[18]

Bob Hardesty and Will Sparks had quick words for prosaic moments that elevated Johnson's casual Rose Garden comments to something beyond the ordinary.

Four aides served on all White House fronts—domestic, foreign, and war. Jack Valenti did any duty needed.

Walter Jenkins, long-term Johnson friend, ally, aide, confidante, helper, and manager of things unmanageable, came as close to being a chief of staff as ever existed in LBJ's White House. They went back a ways together—Jenkins had worked for Johnson since the congressional days of 1939. Time and problems and long conversations built a special trust between the two. As their ties grew closer, LBJ gave Jenkins the most important charge of all: he made Jenkins treasurer of the Johnson family corporation. Observers and reporters were puzzled by Jenkins's exact White House duties—he did just about anything and everything. Whatever the president most needed, Jenkins somehow discerned and produced. Mainly he listened to his boss and took shorthand notes that translated into actions done by a corps of followers.

Above all things, this chunky, shambling, graying, warmly kind man knew Lyndon Johnson. He felt and reflected the president's moods and attitudes, and he treated young comers with more than courtesy—he treated them to wisdom in Washington's ways. None in the corps attending to presidential whims earned more affection and respect than Walter Jenkins. And when fatigue dogged him and scandal wrecked his life and he left the White House, true collegial grief followed his sad trek back to Texas.[19]

Jenkins's eleven months in the White House helped set a tone of high capacity in the staff and he left that legacy behind.

Another long-term henchman of LBJ's filled out the ranks of the all-front White House corps. Marvin Watson had, over the years, earned Johnson's complete confidence. When he became appointments secretary, Watson had power beyond most on the staff: his to manage the presidential calendar, his the gift of presence to endless circlers of the flame. Watson's wizardry protected LBJ's energies and attention by funneling those the president needed to see into the Oval Office, while keeping swarms of others, if not happy, at least sure they had executive attention. He had an essential gift of saying no in ways that stuck—even to the monumental egos that flocked to the executive Mansion. He was, in Valenti's perceptive eye, the president's "sumbitch." Yet he projected no ogre's manner. Gentle, kind, always concerned with the families of fellow staffers, Watson got mixed reviews from the press. Rigid, some called him, a man of little political sensitivity, a kind of mindless flunky for his hero LBJ, a man who roamed congressional halls without purpose. Those who wrote him off as a neanderthal helped fashion a Watsonian image that cloaked shrewd managerial skills. A conservative

Texas Democrat, Watson worked Congress diligently in support of liberal programs that sometimes galled his conscience.

To George Reedy went the often nasty chore of dealing with the press after Pierre Salinger decamped in March, 1964. He knew his boss well after years of campaigning with LBJ and had come to have mixed feelings about him. A Jekyll-and-Hyde he surely seemed, "'a magnificent, inspiring leader'" at one moment, "'an insufferable bastard'" the next.[20] Reedy, himself, had some Jekyll-Hyde qualities. Bearlike in his own conceits, he hid behind a special relationship with Johnson. Years, he thought, tenured him in favor. After all, he knew how to get along with the press, how to offer little in the guise of much, how to talk endlessly in deep background, how to expound on Johnson's methods and motion. As keeper of the Johnson mysteries, Reedy had considerable clout, and he liked it. That his clout did not necessarily translate into admiration may have missed him, but what he had seemed enough.

Propulsion to the White House staff changed Reedy's relationship to his boss and his job. Reporters now wanted quick fixes on presidential doings, not lengthy seminars on the ways of the world. Sudden, hard news probably frightened Reedy; it certainly befuddled him. He did not quite know how to deal with a press conference that pilloried the president or demanded some kind of printable statement from the press secretary.

Increasingly uncomfortable in a growing sense of irrelevance, this hulking, rumpled man sulked and resented himself, his job, and the president. As press relations eroded—which they did in 1965 and 1966—Johnson came to an acute discomfort with his longtime friend. Something would have to be done about the press secretaryship.

This diverse, zestful, enthralled group constituted the main body of Johnson's domestic shock troops. Theirs the challenge to wage a war against complacency, to realize Johnson's vision of—the phrase was Dick Goodwin's—"the Great Society." Theirs the challenge, too, to survive a leader whose awesome energy charged the war they waged. The president pushed them, cajoled, berated, bullied, charmed, and goaded them because, more than anyone else, he realized that time might turn against them, against the special chance they had to make "a more perfect Union." So it was that the people who battled for LBJ's dream suffered, endured, gloried, and made a difference.

WARRIORS FOR SOUTH VIETNAM

While LBJ gathered a leadership team for his War on Poverty, he worked with an inherited headquarters apparatus already engaged in the Vietnam imbroglio. It, too, consisted of people noted for skill and dedication, a group that surely matched the talent of the Great Society's campaigners. Chief among the martial leaders were Secretaries Rusk and McNamara, CIA director McCone, and the president's national security advisor, McGeorge Bundy. Statutory members of the National Security Council also shared in war management.

Johnson trusted Dean Rusk in a way that came from a link of place, time, and circumstance. Rusk's life had been different from LBJ's, his career entirely so, but there were tangents in their backgrounds that made these men, who had grown up as poor southerners, natural friends. If LBJ's Texas twang did not quite meld with Rusk's soft Georgia drawl, their words blended into common understanding. Rusk would recall, fondly, that he and LBJ often caught each other's unspoken thoughts. Asked once if he liked Johnson, Rusk turned, smiling at his questioner, and said "Like him? I loved him; we talked the same language."[21]

Like Lyndon Johnson, Dean Rusk had struggled for an education; unlike Johnson, Rusk had an international bent that led to a successful bid for a Rhodes scholarship from Davidson College, North Carolina, to Oxford University in 1931. At St. John's College he felt the power of an old democracy. Rusk won friends at Oxford and in Germany because he had empathy for things foreign and southern manners that smoothed Yankee brashness.

Back from Oxford to a Depression-ridden America, Rusk happily accepted a faculty position at Mills College in California. Although he knew nothing about it when he took the job, he quickly grew to appreciate this strong, liberal arts–oriented women's college. Rising swiftly, he became dean of the faculty at age 29—while studying law at Berkeley, courting his future wife, and teaching full time. This hectic rushing was not new to him; he had put himself through Davidson on the same rigid program of work and study. Presbyterian upbringing in rural Georgia required full commitment as a matter of duty.

Duty pretty much summed up Rusk's way of doing things. He had kept an army reserve commission since his Davidson days, and when war came, he moved into another of duty's places. First a staffer in Washington, he was later attached to Gen. Joseph W. "Vinegar Joe" Stilwell's entourage in the China-Burma-India theater. There, Rusk saw hard war close up, worked at smoothing relations between the Chinese and British, helped send some supplies to Vietnamese nationalist Ho Chi Minh's guerrillas fighting the Japanese, and came home already marked as a "comer" in international policy matters. That landed him a job in the "Abe Lincoln Brigade," the War Department Operations Division. Among its leaders were three other

Rhodes scholars. Their assignment: plan the postwar world! From these heady realms, Rusk moved into the State Department under Secretary George Marshall. After a stint on the UN desk, Rusk became deputy undersecretary of state for Dean Acheson. Later, amidst McCarthyite attacks against State, Rusk volunteered to take a demotion to the hottest seat in the department—assistant secretary for Far Eastern affairs—just in time for the Korean crisis. Near the end of the Truman administration, Rusk accepted the presidency of the Rockefeller Foundation. For eight years, 1952–1960, Rusk held what Harry Truman called "the best job in America."

Apparently an abrupt jump of career track, the switch fitted Rusk's pattern. The foundation's stated aim to "serve the well-being of mankind" won his utter devotion and never did he work with greater zest or confidence. Even there he had to fight McCarthyism, which he did with firmness and honesty. There, too, he had a chance to marvel at the successes a private foundation can make in complex world environments. They were lessons not forgotten.

To everyone's surprise, John Kennedy named Rusk his secretary of state in 1960. Why? Kennedy didn't even know the man! But JFK kept him on because Rusk's cool self-effacement intrigued the new president. As crises tested the whole administration, Rusk kept looking good. Critics argued that he lacked charisma, was too nice, wouldn't fight for his views, and let power pass to Defense. All of those charges had specks of truth—yet, somehow, that tall, balding figure stayed at hand with his wise counsel and the kind of honesty growing increasingly rare in public men.

President Johnson, who had grown to respect Rusk's professionalism at State during his vice-presidential days, took special comfort in Rusk's agreeing to stay.

The president also took comfort in the continued service of Rusk's gifted undersecretary.

George Ball had an outsider's background. Law at Northwestern University, admission to the Illinois bar, dogged patriotism, and interest in international monetary matters took him to a counsel's job with the Treasury Department in 1933. Two years of that sent him back to private practice in Chicago. Lured to working with the Lend-Lease Administration in 1942, Ball got a crash course in Allied politics. During 1944–1945, as a director of the U.S. Strategic Bombing Survey, he became convinced of the inutility of aerial bombardment—a conviction that lasted. Law practice after the war went well for him; a big man with an impressively large head crowned with curling locks, Ball looked good before the bar. He had principle and guts enough to defend Henry A. Wallace from Sen. Joseph R. McCarthy's Subcommittee on Investigation of the Government Operations in 1951. A fervent believer in Adlai E. Stevenson, Ball supported his two failed campaigns, and so, when Kennedy won the nomination, cherished small hope of serving the new government.

Never an office seeker, Ball knew his own worth. He had better qualifications than anyone to be undersecretary of state for economic affairs, but grew depressed when he heard that a prominent Republican would get the post. "I was not happy," he later confessed, even though "I had few illusions regarding my chances." Lesser posts were proffered and refused. Friends went to work on the president. Senator J. William Fulbright visited Kennedy and said too many Republicans were going in the new cabinet, and Ken Galbraith added that Ball was the right choice. On January 10, 1961, Dean Rusk called with the news: Ball would have the economic affairs slot.[22]

Correct in self-assessment, Ball did well with world economic imbroglios, understood the arcane business of global finance, and, more than that, got on splendidly with his boss. Increasingly Rusk turned to Ball for his cool, knowledgeable, and wittily presented opinions. In November, 1961, Ball became undersecretary of state, a post in which he developed a unique partnership with Rusk that gave him power beyond his office. "Dean Rusk had told me early in our relationship," Ball recalled, "the President was as entitled to my views as his—a magnanimity that has haunted me ever since." The haunt came from doubt of equal generosity.[23]

Later, when LBJ considered various candidates for the Saigon ambassadorship and Ball's name surfaced, Jack Valenti opposed him. "I regarded George Ball as too valuable a man to position so far away. I felt Ball was a wise counselor of the president and he ought to stay where that counsel could be heard and heeded," Valenti wrote later.[24]

Had Ball known of this at the time, he doubtless would have been relieved. Europe had been his interest and remained so, even as Vietnam crowded his mind. Ball had doubts about Vietnam policy almost from the start. A lonesome naysayer for a time, Ball never wavered, keeping the respect of his boss and his president in one of the finest examples of loyal disagreement in American history.

Robert McNamara won LBJ's dazzled admiration during the vice-presidential period. McNamara's "Stay-Comb" calm earned LBJ's deeper admiration as the Vietnam mess gradually intruded on world attention. Early presidential confidence in the former Ford executive grew with experience. McNamara's awing knowledge, his crisply tolled statistics, and his staccato rejection of squashy opposition impressed an embattled president whose own mind absorbed data like a sponge. Johnson listened to McNamara, trusted his judgment, and wanted him at every world crisis meeting. If he noticed that the expanding energy of the defense secretary encroached on Dean Rusk's turf, he did nothing to check it—save to keep a special closeness to Rusk that prevented his total extinction. The president served as a buffer between these two diversely remarkable men.

A San Franciscan with a Cal B.A., McNamara had taken a step toward success with a Harvard M.B.A. in 1939, and his swiftness with numbers won him a spot on the Harvard faculty. From there he moved to the Army Air Forces in 1943, and caught Robert Lovett's eye. Lovett tagged him as a man to watch. The war over, McNamara moved on to Ford Motors and began a quick rise to controller, assistant general manager, vice president and general manager, and, in 1960, at age forty-five, company president. Yet he was more than president, in a sense, because the company had restructured itself around McNamara and his system of cost analysis management/production.

When Kennedy's headhunters approached, McNamara rejected Treasury and accepted Defense because it offered the kind of power he liked. He arrived in Washington a week later fully equipped with a grasp of his problems and an agenda for solutions. He and the young president hit it off so well that McNamara and his wife, Margaret, were soon fixtures in Camelot's society.[25]

Many watchers of the McNamara phenomenon saw him as an oddly passionless man, coldly honed to his stats and his job. But they missed a quality he hid carefully beneath that slicked down, unflappable drive for power: He yearned to be loyal to someone or something that would release a deep-struck passion of his heart. Jobs fulfilled him partially, but John Kennedy caught the whole of his hope and all of his devotion. Although he hit the Defense Department running, he shared in the administration's bumbling of the Bay of Pigs business and it smarted. He regretted not having better served JFK, and learned from the experience.

Devastated by Kennedy's assassination, McNamara wondered about his ability to serve under Johnson, but soon found that he could give the complicated Texan the same loyalty he had given JFK. It was a loyalty that kept him in government and one that LBJ reciprocated.

Although the president admired and relied on McNamara, he was a difficult man to like. Not that McNamara cared much about being liked; his own competence elevated him above emotion in a certitude of worth. Practice of organizational dynamics at Ford demystified the Pentagon labyrinth for McNamara. His Whiz Kids laid their statistical grids on arcane military logistics and soon proved predicted waste and bumbling. McNamara shrewdly deployed his "number crunchers" in middle-management levels of the Defense Department—and hence dominated policy and procedure making. By his energy and the energy of his henchmen, McNamara put his personal stamp on the government's largest business structure. At last it seemed that civilian management knew all about defense planning and spending, could balance the two, and could assure rational war decisions.

Success came from McNamara's almost uncanny skill in spreading ability throughout his domain. David Halberstam hit the mark when he later detected an "old boy" look to Defense.[26] Even so, he had to concede it was a thinner, suppler bureaucracy.

Interestingly, McNamara did not pick all of his subordinates or associates but he did deploy them to his taste. Consider the case of Cyrus Vance.[27]

Vance, a West Virginian from Stonewall Jackson's hometown, Clarksburg, attended Kent School, received B.A. and LL.B. degrees from Yale, served in the navy during World War II, settled into a New York City law practice and, from there, moved to public service.[28] Kennedy's scouts had asked Vance if he'd like to be in government; he said yes, as secretary of the navy. McNamara approved him, but installed him as Defense's general counsel in 1961. That launched him. As secretary of the army in 1962–63, Vance did such sound work that McNamara made him his deputy in 1964.

A quiet, impressive man who gave off quiet, impressive energy, Vance set standards for every office he held. Vance muffled tough brilliance in the unfailing courtesy of an old-line southern lawyer; those he met across cases knew his iron honesty and his rock-hard mind. Durable under stress and loyal to friends and causes, "Spider" Vance seemed the ideal public servant— and, somehow, strangely more.

What of the professional military? Were they part of the Vietnam decision-making process? Yes, in a way. LBJ had some discomfort with them, perhaps from distance, or perhaps from his penchant for following proper channels.

Channels worked this way: McNamara would receive the views of the Joint Chiefs of Staff from the chairman, Gen. Earle Wheeler. When necessary—and as rarely as possible—Wheeler would participate in decision-making meetings. Most people liked Bus Wheeler, a charming, self-effacing soldier, sharp in mind and persuasive, but quiet. Courteous always, he lacked some of the service chiefs' sharp rhetoric. No one could imagine Bus using Air Force chief of staff Gen. Curtis LeMay's hyperbole, for instance, or envision him quitting in a fit of pique. Some might have thought Wheeler more a go-along-to-get-along man than a hard-hewn trooper, but that missed an important Wheeler skill. He knew that effectiveness came with trust. More than anything, he wanted the service chief's to be heard; whining or shouting or imperious demands would muffle them, so he adjusted his personal self to the ways of the moment.

The chiefs trusted Wheeler much more than his predecessor, Gen. Maxwell Taylor, who they thought pushed himself and his agenda without letting their views seep through to the president. Wheeler also gained credibility with McNamara's band of bean counters because, for one thing, he looked more like a scholar than a shoot-em-up horse soldier. A receding hairline pushed his dark-rimmed glasses out from his face, magnified his eyes, and gave him either a curious or owl-eyed look that lent him a kind of questing dignity. He also spoke and wrote well, keeping a civilian manner that took him a little out of the military niche. A lot about Vietnam worried Bus Wheeler and the group he chaired, and he struggled against a rising tide of civilian management as he tried to push sound military options. But, when overruled, he publicly supported his bosses.

Sometimes, surely, he wanted to cheer George Ball's lonesome lament for the future, but, though obviously uncomfortable, he did not directly oppose McNamara's efforts to intervene. Slowly he found himself, like LBJ, trapped in a shrinking web of options. A smart, sensitive, dutiful man, Wheeler spoke out early with honest doubts of quick victory. But his warnings paled in the glare of McNamara's daunting optimism. Seeing clearly the trend of things, good soldier Wheeler, in the end, could not buck the system. Frustration finally led him to devise a system of his own, which did his country great disservice.

John McCone of the CIA held an odd spot in Johnson's entourage. A Republican arch conservative and man of corporate money (some said a war profiteer), McCone had a Catholic convert's zealotry against Reds everywhere and had dragooned the CIA into a massive organism for cleansing America of its enemies—whom he could identify easily enough. A bit shorter than JFK, his white hair immaculately clipped and combed, his long, rather handsome face strengthened by glasses that emphasized a probing glance, McCone avoided strutting by simply being right. And he had a quality vital in any public servant: he told his boss the harder truths.

Why Kennedy appointed him as Allen Dulles's replacement no one in the liberal camp could guess—they regarded McCone's appointment as an astounding disaster. And, from their standpoint, they were right. But, despite his hard-nosed view of the world, McCone had real doubts about success in Vietnam. As he voiced those views, Johnson grew uneasy with him. They could never be friends—too much political sludge gurgled between them; their personalities clashed almost by definition. McCone would not stay long, but for a time he worked hard and sometimes effectively.[29]

While State and Defense had highly visible roles in making U.S. policy toward Vietnam, Johnson and key White House staff members made fundamental war policy. Johnson sought all kinds of advice, always, but he never shirked his duty as commander in chief. Military views were usually expressed through McNamara's machine-gun phrases, and he heard diplomatic views from Rusk, Ball, and some others. But he turned first—and usually last—to McGeorge Bundy for information, implications, strategy, tactics, and an overall Vietnam perspective.

Mac Bundy generated almost no neutral feelings. In some ways he seemed a permanent fixture in the White House, an impression coming surely from his own certitude in action. There were special facets to him. He looked, somehow, to be in a hurry even when he was quiet. His dark-rimmed glasses accented high and sharp cheek bones, and his dark hair added youth to the scarcely contained speed that seethed within his body. Bundy came in a tight package—compact, neither too tall nor too short, with a quick walk, an easy manner, and a precise mind. Some would say that he had small tolerance for fools or contrary ideas. There was truth to that, in a sense—not from arrogance but rather from sureness and history. He often seemed serious, but a hardy humor ran near the surface and sometimes softened his pointed wit. He had the kind of imprimatur that lineage lent.

Born in 1919, Mac Bundy grew up in a rowdy, happy, highly competitive family. His mother, Katherine Lawrence Putnam—daughter of Augustus Lowell and sister of Amy, the poet—had a nimble, voracious mind and carried it over into parenting. Her children felt and soon shared her confidence in the rightness of things; she played energetic games with them, engaged their minds and taught them her world view. "Mother," said daughter Harriet later, "never forgot for a minute that she was a Lowell. . . . For her, things were black and white. It's an outlook that descends directly from the Puritans and we all have it. But Mac has it more than the rest of us."[30]

Henry L. Stimson had long employed Bundy's father and became the son's hero. Austere, gracious in a remote way, impeccable in honor and manners, superb in details, Stimson adhered to the highest personal standards. Mac Bundy absorbed those standards.

Groton and Yale, a prestige appointment as a Harvard Junior Fellow, and a Harvard deanship at age thirty-nine prepared Bundy for Stimson's kind of career. He had friends and made enemies, but mainly he served his presidents with the zeal and honesty long bred into his blood. Lyndon Johnson, his diametric opposite, trusted and respected him, and came, sometimes, to a curious kind of closeness.

These were the White House warriors supporting South Vietnam. Theirs the task to suggest the strategy, manage the tactics, and juggle the logistics of a faraway conflict growing daily in size and puzzlement. Theirs to persuade a doubtful commander in chief to stick to a dubious course. Theirs to keep believing against reality that what they thought was right truly was.

chapter
FOUR

Vietnam as
Virtual Reality

nformation about Vietnam came to the White House in restless doses. Presidential fact finders trooped in steadily, reporters filed endless reams of copy about "Saigon, USA," and the various television sets crowding the Oval Office revealed Vietnam in baffling richness on every newscast. A morning report briefed the president on the CIA's appreciation of things in the world, especially things in Vietnam.

Facts, figures, speculations, charts, maps, pictures, and fantasies about Vietnam, north and south, almost satiated Lyndon Johnson's hunger for data—but not quite. How reliable was the information? Information did not necessarily equate with intelligence in the geopolitical sense. How to separate fact from fiction?

Johnson's love of raw data scared veteran intelligence types, who never wanted amateurs poring over unanalyzed field reports. Hundreds of bits of information could overwhelm an untutored mind with minutiae beyond comprehension. Besides, the professionals would lose some importance if everybody got in the act. But Johnson dogged the teletypes in the White House, the televisions, the newspapers; most of all, he dogged his national security advisor for a digest of intelligence before the CIA's daily dosage arrived. He delighted in hearing McCone, or someone else from the Agency, building up to a point. Then, just at the crucial moment, the president would jump in and anticipate it with a throwaway line showing how his tentacles encircled the globe. As William Colby noted, "there was a terrible tendency to be first with something, and Johnson wasn't about to be second on anything."[1]

By and large, though, Johnson respected his intelligence people. He simply shared their own doubts about the information coming from Vietnam.

With military activity increasing after Pleiku, Johnson came more and more into the role of commander in chief. He had discomforts about it, but guessed that what experience had not taught him, he would learn soon enough. How well he learned would depend on his teachers. Bob McNamara served as Johnson's prime military source, and the way he ran the Defense Department tended to push the president's military views into predetermined paths.

McNamara's style had much merit. It preserved the channels important to him and to Johnson, while keeping a clutter of military views from the Oval Office and from presidential ears. Unfortunately, it muted divergent opinions.[2] Previous chief executives had lamented their isolation, and LBJ felt a growing remoteness with each month he spent in office. He fought against the easy practice of telling the boss only the good news; he struggled to hear opposing ideas, but once a decision had been made, he resisted second-guessing. Still, he regularly sought different opinions. His congressional experience had made him expert in sifting, sorting, and coagulating all kinds of diverse views from official and subofficial sources. Dissonance, of course, was the essence of politics, but not of administration. Trying to be a good administrator trapped the president in the channels chain.

As Senate majority leader he had learned to plan a campaign, probe for a middle ground, herd his senatorial voters, and then deliver his strength at the moment of victory. War had a dynamics that confounded this old political wisdom, especially the war in Vietnam. There, several wars raged in different times and places, with different rules and realities. The differing views of the soldiers who waged these various conflicts would have taught Johnson more about war than his closed channels of contact. More than he guessed, LBJ needed to hear the babble from the battlefield.

SAIGON'S WAR

In the 1950s Saigon had a sleepy French provincial look to it. Handsome villas dotted its residential district, its wide, tree-lined streets were barely disturbed by traffic, and over it hung the scents of the tropics—jasmine, bougainvillea, mimosa. Sidewalk cafes brought fleeting thoughts of Paris, but not its pace of life. Saigon seemed settled into lethargic doldrums. There had been times of high excitement in this ancient capital city of Cochin China, but years of French colonial rule, years of ease, and years of peace had made a place of strange content. That same seeming satisfaction spread across the southern part of Vietnam, with provincial towns lazing in the setting sun of France's empire.

The French left after the disaster at Dien Bien Phu, their departure jolting this old colony into uncommon worry about the future. What did Ho Chi Minh mean for South Vietnam? He boasted several colors—Vietnamese patriot, nationalist revolutionary, and Communist reformer—and showed different faces to east and west. Many Vietnamese guessed him to be a Communist with designs on all of Vietnam, designs likely to make great changes in ancient ways of living. Many were scared of Ho, and under the temporary arrangement of dividing Vietnam into northern and southern parts, lots of people from Ho's north went south. Saigon grew with these early refugees, and when Ngo Dinh Diem made his capital there, the small, sleepy city awoke to a teeming future.

In the 1960s Saigon had shifted into a kind of hectic decadence. John Kennedy reluctantly came to the realization there was a war in southern Vietnam and sent advisors in to help the ARVN. Their numbers multiplied as the war intensified. Like the American Civil War after the middle of 1862, the conflict in Vietnam became a "war against—": against the Communists, against the Viet Cong and their henchmen, against evil in all its forms. It also became a war against civilians—against "dinks" or "slopes," as Vietnamese were called—a development greatly disturbing to Saigon's often persecuted Chinese population crowded into the exotic Cholon district.

Racism touched the whole of America's war effort in Vietnam, but it hardly caused alarm because racism ran rampant on both sides. The North Vietnamese looked down on their southern brethren, even aided the VC with puristic contempt. To the surprise of most of LBJ's advisors, Asia did not look on the Vietnam conflict as a racial war. Carl Rowan investigated this problem and found that the farther one got from the scene of action, the more racism intruded.[3] Racism hung a constant backdrop over Saigon as stages, choruses, and casts came and went. And, in the nature of backdrops, racism eluded much notice.

Backdrops can, now and then, change the scenery. In Vietnam, generalized racism altered the American grasp of Vietnamese culture. Culture is hard to define—harder still to understand—but vital to any allied relationship. Culture, too, can be a loaded word. In war, culture's fancies seem either irrelevant or troublesome.

• • •

Saigon—despite the corruptions of war and money, the different morality of the bar girls and the "Cowboys" who ran them and the awe-inspiring black market, and the scooters, motorcycles, and cars belching smoke and fogging the air—still kept enclaves of older, prouder cultures. American GIs are quick to learn how welcome they are in faraway places. Fathers and others who had been in earlier conflicts could offer insights about women: about the easy kinds and the tougher, about the ones available and those off limits to soldiers. But such advice seemed hardly necessary in Saigon's steamy clime. American money made life easy for those who had it—which posed a problem for South Vietnam's economy.

Traditionally low prices soared and Vietnamese piasters became almost worthless. A currency black market drove inflation in a dizzying whirl that ate into American dollars. Vietnamese efforts to control inflation by regulating exchange rates failed. American efforts to stabilize the situation by issuing GI scrip also failed. Stanley Karnow, who was on the scene, described new and various ways that "the United States was . . . bilked." These included "imaginative 'irregularities,' as the euphemism went, such as fake invoices for supplies that were never delivered." Consider the matter of cement, for instance. "At one point . . . American investigators estimated that the amount of cement earmarked for Vietnam in a single year could have paved over the entire country."

These symptoms of a sick economic structure eddied in all directions. Theft ran rampant. Past exchanges and U.S. warehouses were fat targets that yielded mountains of cigarettes, hose, hair spray, liquor, and other civilian luxuries, along with arms, ammunition, helmets, flak jackets—almost any military item. Entire shipments of such things as office equipment, furniture, machinery vanished—all available for repurchase on the streets of Saigon.[4]

Millions in cash vanished as waste became the order of business. American officials soon adapted in order to get on with the war. Karnow, increasingly amazed at streets teeming with American goods, jokingly commented to a high-level American civilian, "The way we're squandering money here, we could probably buy off the Vietcong at five hundred dollars a head."

"We've staffed it," came the reply. "Twenty-five hundred dollars a head."[5]

With waste came corruption—at every level and in every way. Petty administrators skimmed their budgets; higher administrators did the same; cabinet members took most of what was left.

COMES THE REVOLUTION

General Duong Van "Big" Minh's government wobbled from the start. Spawned by a coup, it courted a similar fate. For nearly three months Minh and his generals tried to stabilize South Vietnam. Despite good intentions, the junta lacked experience in political and governmental realms. Too much time lapsed in efforts to plan programs and develop courses of action. Minh, handsome, big, and introspective, lacked any sort of zeal. He much preferred raising orchids to raising revolution.

Some good ideas were advanced, but the government languished in Byzantine layers of administration. The Military Revolutionary Council (MRC), consisting of twelve generals with Minh at the top, paired with a civilian cabinet of fifteen, presided over by a prime minister who had served as Diem's vice president. The generals were in competition, and the civilians acted like mandarins. Although the prime minster had vast administrative experience, he managed a marvelous coil of inaction. Among the generals were a few who grasped the need for urgent change. Although the Americans had not participated openly in the coup, they had done a lot more than condone it, and their continued help depended on swift stabilization of South Vietnam's political, economic, and military scenery.[6]

Minh's minions were caught at the top of a rolling ball of revolution—faced with the almost unmanageable task of staying ahead of the forces it had unleashed.[7] They tried mightily to channel their country's future toward the strangeness of democracy and the steadiness of patriotism. Mass releases of political prisoners, students, priests, and Buddhist bonzes returned large numbers of former dissidents to the streets. Arbitrary arrests—one of the worst offenses of the Diem era—were banned, freedom of religion and opinion were proclaimed, and overtures were offered to the important Hoa Hao and Cao Dai sects.[8]

Over all these efforts hung an economic cloud caused by the stoppage of American aid during the uncertainty of the precoup days. Financial problems combined with ritualistic administration by the prime minister to worsen the inflation crisis. Still, some hoped the government could muddle to success. Like Diem in his later days, many of Minh's men missed the signs of changing weather in Washington. After JFK's death, Johnson demanded unity on the Saigon front, but doubted—deep in himself—that Big Minh's generals could hold things together.

Johnson tried to help them. Just before Christmas, 1963, he sent McNamara on one of his whirlwind visits to size up the situation in South Vietnam. Shaken by his fresh view of the Saigon scene, the secretary of defense reported much worry to the president and other White House insiders. The South Vietnamese government lay in a state of oddly fuzzy paralysis. Generalized weakness sapped not only military energy but even the simple urge toward making everyday decisions. Minh's administration struck McNamara as "indecisive and drifting." He added that "Neither [Minh] nor the Committee are experienced in political administration and so far they show little talent for it."[9] Government by an indecisive committee seemed in place and conjured visions of a nightmare wrapped in despair.

Viet Cong activities increased heavily in the months following Diem's downfall. Nguyen Huu Tho, head of the VC's parent organization, the National Liberation Front (NLF), could scarcely believe the Americans had connived to destroy one of the strongest Communist enemies. The coup was, he remarked, "a gift from Heaven for us."[10] McNamara admitted his uncertainty about VC action because of mixed reporting systems in South Vietnam, but he ventured a guess that "the situation has . . . been deteriorating to a far greater extent than we realized. . . . The Viet Cong now control very high proportions of the people in certain key provinces, particularly those directly south and west of Saigon."[11]

Infiltration from the north continued through parts of Laos and Cambodia, along the Mekong River from Cambodia, and from sea routes at the tip of the Delta region. McNamara urged deployment of more ARVN forces in the most threatened areas, but doubted the MRC could organize the effort. The secretary of defense suggested cross-border operations in Laos to halt infiltration, but thought them too venturesome for the weak government in Saigon. The requirements were awesomely basic. "Our first need," McNamara confessed, "would be immediate U-2 mapping of the whole Laos and Cambodian border." He had ordered this mapping done immediately, since important "sabotage and psychological operations [planned] against North Vietnam" also required a sound grasp of the ground.[12]

To make matters worse, America's house had not come to order in Saigon. Johnson's fears about the so-called country team were all too perceptive. Always defensive about U.S. efforts in Vietnam, McNamara confessed problems not only at the embassy in Saigon, but with various American efforts throughout the country. Nobody seemed to get organized. Various budget requests wandered in from various organizations to the Office of Management, so no clear picture emerged of what expenditures were or what they were likely to be in military and pacification areas. Aware that LBJ lacked confidence in Ambassador Lodge, McNamara tried a soft indictment: "Lodge has virtually no official contact with Harkins. Lodge sends in reports with major military implications without showing them to Harkins, and does not show Harkins important incoming traffic. My impression is that Lodge simply does not know how to conduct a coordinated administration. This has of course been stressed to him by Dean Rusk and myself (and also by John McCone), and I do not think he is consciously rejecting our advice; he has just operated as a loner all his life and cannot readily change now." [13]

The MRC managed to ignore American problems in the weeks after coming to power, weeks in which Big Minh and his generals basked in a false calm they mistook for generalized satisfaction across their beleaguered land. "We were inspired by the spontaneous outburst of friendship toward us," General Tran Van Don recalled, and were too euphoric to see themselves as they were seen—lax, confused, and unctuously indecisive.[14] While they basked, their country crumbled and their Yankee ally fumed. Internal chaos at last made an impression on one member of the junta—Gen. Nguyen Khanh. On January 30, 1964, he arrested most of the MRC generals and took charge of the government.

Khanh apparently did his deed out of frustration with colleagues who talked, planned, congratulated each other, and did nothing. He had been a former chief of the general staff under Diem and cherished a lingering affection for his lost leader. William Colby had thought Khanh might take over earlier, probably spoiling for revenge. The tip-off for Colby was Khanh's goatee—a wispy little one that sprouted in the days after Diem's death. It marked a promise of some kind, a promise defined clearly when Khanh took over and promptly had Diem's and Nhu's assassin shot.[15]

Ever the pragmatist, Johnson, suspicious of hopes for Khanh and skeptical of much good coming from the political revolving door in Saigon, nonetheless knew the United States had only a few weak reeds to prop. Khanh, for the moment, looked like the best of them.

Johnson felt stuck with Khanh. Who else? Not that Khanh's actions earned confidence. Some of his coup confederates were radical generals who cherished ambitions of their own, so he began in a cesspool of mistrust. But Khanh had a cunning to match his ambition—he realized that the Johnson administration feared the possible neutralization of South Vietnam almost more than defeat. Neutralization would result in Ho Chi Minh sharing the government, probably most of it, in time; neutralism would mean the defeat of U.S. efforts to sustain the south's thin nationalism. Khanh talked of theoretical neutralism, implicated some of Minh's old junta, and managed to win Lodge's support. Stanley Karnow noted the ambassador's misrationalization of all U.S. problems in Vietnam as a management imbroglio.[16]

The United States tried to put a serene face on the crinkling map of its client state. While VC inroads continued in the back country, while strategic hamlets dissolved or eroded, while provincial efforts to build up protective forces went unaided and ignored, the country that America sought to save shrank in the minds of most to the cramped confines of Saigon.

Dazed with the haphazard run of governments through Saigon in 1964, the American public and the world were treated to an equally confusing kaleidoscope of U.S. generals, ambassadors, civilian leaders, and entrepreneurs during those uncertain months of survival in that fractured, puzzling land.

SAIGON'S AMERICANS

Prestige counts in diplomacy, so a lot of money and effort went into fashioning the American presence in Saigon. The embassy building—older and in the French colonial mode—had a bigness to suit American pretensions. Other Yankee compounds going up around Saigon were built to show America had permanent interests. As the number of U.S. personnel increased, so too did the official superstructure to sustain them. With each new group of military advisors came a civilian contingent as well: civil servants to staff the offices, and semiofficial people to support volunteer activities in the backcountry. By early 1964, Americans were a common element of Saigon's population.

All of this meant that the United States ambassador presided over a large number of soldiers and civilians whom LBJ expected Henry Cabot Lodge to organize into a working team pushing a cohesive U.S. policy. But, as McNamara had reported just before Christmas, 1963, Lodge had not welded his people into anything like a team. He had, in fact, let various of his responsibilities wander off into small enclaves of self-interest. Worst of all, a mutual distrust developed between the civilian and military elements of the U.S. mission.

General Paul Harkins, the U.S. military commander at the time, bulked large on the Saigon scene not only because of his rank and job, but also because of his irritating independence of civilians. He seems to have been especially jealous of Lodge, which may have stemmed from shared school days at Boston Latin. At any rate, Harkins and Lodge missed cooperation by wide margins for reasons beyond mere personalities. Lodge felt—with LBJ's tough talk in November, 1963, still ringing in his ears—that as ambassador he had the mission and the power to shape up the American effort in Vietnam. Harkins, on the other hand, had specific orders giving him control over all American military affairs—orders written for him by his old friend and mentor, Gen. Maxwell Taylor.[17] Lodge and Harkins had opposite views on Ngo Dinh Diem: Harkins pro, Lodge con. The general believed in sustaining an ally who had been propped up for years; the ambassador believed all good had been squeezed from Diem's regime.

Harkins, in David Halberstam's apt phrase, "was a man of compelling mediocrity" whose career confirmed all premises of the Peter principle. In

Saigon at Taylor's bidding and despite JFK's doubts,[18] Paul Donald Harkins had all the trappings for success—from West Point to George Patton's staff to a well-connected social life and a wife who gossiped, listened, and told him the trending of things. He escaped being merely a stuffed tunic by being earnest. Short on real combat experience, long on staff work and logistical planning, he floated upward with his mentors.[19]

Military matters in old Cochin China were always complicated, and Harkins learned soon after arriving in Vietnam in February, 1962, that time and reality ran differently in the mysterious East. More than that, the new MACV commander brought no knowledge of Asia with him and had no time to adjust—he inherited something from the earlier MAAG people, but not much that seemed useful to him.

Maxwell Taylor had told him to get out to Vietnam and report that good things were happening. Obviously Taylor wanted JFK's White House unworried about Vietnam. Harkins kept that point clearly in view.

The general muzzled critical subordinates with a revealing personal boast: "I am an optimist, and I am not going to allow my staff to be pessimistic."[20] David Halberstam noted that "the Saigon command soon reflected Harkins's views, with a flabby, foolish confidence."[21] Surprisingly, for a time, things seemed to be working well.

Taylor, as JFK's special advisor for military affairs, had watched as the president's options narrowed. An early advocate of strong troop support for Diem's regime, the general had seen his 1961 recommendation for an eight thousand-man "logistical task force" in South Vietnam first attacked and then only partly endorsed by Kennedy.[22] He worried about the future and felt that the South Vietnamese had needed an infusion of U.S. troops to shore up morale. Conditions were a bit different when he persuaded JFK to appoint Harkins to the MACV command, but Taylor's concerns remained constant. Without continued commitment, America's Southeast Asia effort would likely fizzle—an unacceptable alternative. When he became chairman of the Joint Chiefs of Staff in late 1961, Taylor was able to push his own agenda with considerable chance of success.

In a way, he was the consummate civilian general—personable, articulate, holder of all the correctly punched tickets, favored of the favored, author, officer, and gentleman. It is hard now to see him clearly because mythic clouds and honors shroud the athletic figure and smiling face so often seen on camera. He achieved near icon status in what may now be called the "Old Army." Reasons are a bit elusive while his figure remains so large.

Perhaps key to understanding Taylor is his loyalty to the U.S. Army. A combat hero in World War II and an influence in Korea, he agonized as the army sought new missions and meaning in the Atomic Age. Vietnam offered an opportunity for another expeditionary force and Taylor pushed to have it happen. Yet, as he moved from army chief of staff to special military advisor to the president to chairman of the Joint Chiefs of Staff, responsibility opened his vision. While still hopeful for the army, he grew cautious when JFK fixed him with a dubious eye and asked for his best advice. Johnson had harder eyes and harder demands and expected honest answers from the chairman—as did Robert McNamara, who deferred somewhat to Taylor's repute as he tried to run the war in Vietnam according to Euclid by computer.[23]

When Taylor encouraged Harkins to take the new MACV command in February, 1962, the challenges looked fairly light. American commitment remained small, although JFK had allowed an increase in the number of American advisors from 3,205 in December, 1961, to 9,000 by the end of 1962. Well trained, these advisors often were combat veterans of World War II and Korea, many of them highly trained in counterinsurgency warfare. Rowdy and daring, irregulars—not really Taylor's types—they did all kinds of duty. "Special Forces units conducted Civic Action programs among the primitive Montagnards of the Central Highlands," according to one account, while "Marine and Air Force helicopter pilots dropped detachments of ARVN troops into battle zones deep in the swamplands, and picked up the dead and wounded after engagements." Americans helped Vietnamese trainees on field missions, often fighting alongside them.[24]

General Harkins had really no idea what advisors did. Like all officers, he had some book learning about counterinsurgency and must have known of young President Kennedy's curious fascination with irregular warfare, but there is no indication that Harkins made himself a student of these new and unconventional methods. He did do his best to see that advisors served diligently within strict military limits.

His blinkered eyes showed everything going well in 1962. Positive action reports came from various places, but had he known his command better, Harkins would have realized that these areas were peaceful ones without many Viet Cong. Without much direct enemy contact, all kinds of fantasies were legitimate and in those early days the misleading system of body counting began. Soon, weekly reports on enemy casualties became a running index of success. Any sound statistician would have asked brutal questions about methodology. However, none did—either because none were out there or because no one really cared. At any rate, in keeping with Harkins's galloping optimism, body counts inflated with every visitor from Washington.

One of MACV's main missions centered on making the ARVN a force formidable enough to defeat VC units in the field. Harkins had no doubt that the efficiency of ARVN organizations grew with each week of advising, and he boasted such progress that thought was given to bringing some Americans home in 1963. The reasons were obvious to any student of U.S. logistics and tactics: airborne firepower made ARVN units masters of field and forest, and helicopters gave a traditional land army amazing capacity for fast delivery of well-armed elements almost anywhere. Happily for Harkins and Taylor, summer operations in 1962 proved almost every claim of coming victory and, for the first time in anyone's memory, the ARVN seized the war's initiative. This was heady and comforting grist for Saigon's daily briefings, and for several enchanted weeks fantasy assumed an odd reality.

New weapons usually hold only a small advantage for a short time in war, and by the end of 1962 the VC were back on the attack. They learned to hide from the helicopters or shoot them down with small-arms fire. But the ARVN's morale remained high as it focused on the wrong objective: main-force enemy units. The VC had a few division-like organizations, but they relied mainly on battalion- or company-size cadres that roamed at night, frightened villagers into acquiescence, and then vanished with the dawn. The ARVN focus on big units came from their American advisors, but some Vietnamese officers had the vision to resist American demands that they copy U.S. military structure.[25] Big units for big war did not fit the insurgency situation in the hills and on the plains of the Republic of Vietnam. Forced to conform to American requirements, ARVN troops increasingly relied on U.S. air and artillery support—and often avoided contact with the VC. It was probably just as well, considering the dismal showing made by the ARVN 7th Division in two encounters, one in October, 1962, the other in January, 1963.

In the first engagement, parts of the division on a routine sweep in the Delta flushed some enemy who made a stand. The resulting firefight consumed a highly touted Vietnamese Ranger platoon. Lieutenant Colonel John Paul Vann, U.S. advisor to the 7th Division, made an uncommon fuss about the terrible performance of allied officers and troops.

Almost immediately, the 7th got into trouble again, this time at the small village of Ap Bac in the Mekong Delta, not fifty miles from Saigon. Intelligence reported a VC battalion in or near the village, and the 7th responded with two regular battalions, two Civil Guard battalions, and a company of M113 armored personnel carriers (APCs), all supported with helicopters and artillery—a manpower advantage of nearly 10 to 1, with enough firepower to smash a whole division. Confronted with so much force, the VC might well have decamped or surrendered. No such luck. Without air or artillery help, 350 guerrillas—armed mainly with rifles and one 60mm mortar—fought all day, drummed by thousands of rounds of small-arms ammunition, and 600 artillery shells, plus napalm, bombs, and rockets from some thirteen planes and five UH-1 Huey gunships. They lost eighteen killed, had thirty-nine wounded, and vanished in the night. The Seventh Division took about 180 casualties (including three Americans dead), lost five helicopters (not all to enemy fire), and earned fulminating damnation from Lieutenant Colonel Vann, who called it "a miserable fucking performance, just like it always is." Vann blamed much of the ARVN timidity on President Diem, who had told his generals to avoid casualties and save their men for anticoup work in Saigon![26]

With the avalanche of criticism from the 7th Division's advisors accepted by middle commanders and sent on to MACV, the stage seemed set for reappraisal of the whole advisor program—certainly for a hard look at South Vietnam's devotion to its own salvation. To virtually no one's amazement, General Harkins managed to find evidence of victory in all the accounts of disaster. After all, he said, the 7th Division took the village of Ap Bac—the objective—and that, in anyone's understanding of conventional war, constituted success. Admiral Harry D. Felt, CINCPAC, swept into Saigon two days after the battle, heard headquarters comments and rapped reporters who were filing doubtful stories—Ap Bac was a win and the reporters were aiding the enemy. To a particularly critical Peter Arnett of the Associated Press, Felt said, "Get on the team."[27]

That kind of sensitivity reflected not only Harkins's unwavering obedience to General Taylor's demand for good tidings, it reflected, too, MACV's and CINCPAC's worry that all service records and previous military programs would be subjected to civilian review in McNamara's Pentagon—a horror to be avoided at virtually any stretch of fact or fiction.

All this added another dimension to the results of Ap Bac: a serious rift between MACV and newsmen sent to cover the war. Until that extreme example of victory conjured from ashes, the press corps had been relatively sympathetic to American efforts. Many reporters thought Diem an unlikely ally, but, nonetheless, understood and supported U.S. policies in that faraway, embattled place. Harkins's myopia, compounded by Felt's uncritical acceptance of the "official" version of truth, finally shattered the newsmen's faith in MACV's reports on the war. Historian William Hammond says that "Ap Bac and the controversy surrounding it marked a divide in the history of U.S. relations with the news media in South Vietnam. . . . After it, correspondents became convinced that they were being lied to and withdrew, embittered, into their own community."[28]

Nothing could have been worse for the American people. As the conflict between the military and the media made its own kind of news, puzzling questions of reality in Asia disturbed the U.S. body politic—and the White House. And nothing more clearly shows that LBJ needed to hear the dissonance coming from men like Vann—but Vann could not get his complaints heard above MACV; he was thwarted in being debriefed in the Pentagon and finally resigned from the army in disgust.[29]

There is what amounts to a counterfactual opinion offered by some commentators on the episode at Ap Bac. William Colby suggests there were some reservations about Vann's assessment. The ARVN, after all, were "under the gun not to get heavy casualties from their side. Sun Tzu says that the way you fight is you always leave the guy a way out. . . . Remember our advisors were over there for a year. . . . They [the ARVN] are there for ten years, twenty years. They look at it from a different time perspective: this thing is going on for a long time; you don't go out and get killed in 15 minutes in the war because you're forgotten a month later." Colby's long-term Asian experience lends interest to his thoughts on timing.[30] Others, however, thought Ap Bac reinvigorated the VC.[31]

A natural soldier, unhappy and bored in civilian traces, Vann got back to Vietnam as a member of the AID team in Saigon. This agency had a large and growing mission in Vietnam, and directed its efforts toward just the kinds of things Vann understood and championed: political warfare and pacification.

This large organization ranked as one of the most important U.S. enterprises anywhere in the world because it channeled the spending of most foreign aid dollars. A spawn of the Kennedy years, AID evolved as an umbrella organization from several earlier bureaucracies. In his first foreign aid message to Congress, Kennedy stressed the need for unified efforts.[32] As things worked out, AID seemed the brainchild of economic theorists and took an independent road; it reported to the president, with a kind of vague obligation for policy consultation with the secretary of state. The agency skirmished with most other government offices because its work crossed everybody's. Especially delicate relations sometimes existed between AID and the CIA, since both supported a variety of covert efforts—CIA usually pushing paramilitary actions in different places and AID pushing pacification and civil enhancement efforts that sometimes required armed support.

AID's writ ran strongly because of efficiency and success.[33] Its officers were usually assigned as part of the country team in embassies where American development efforts were underway. Nearly fifteen hundred AID people were in Saigon by late 1963,[34] and the administrator for Vietnam sat on the ambassador's staff. The organization's efficiency reflected badly on Hawkins's waffling MACV.[35]

John Richardson became the CIA head in Saigon and completed the ambassador's country team, but was soon sacrificed by Lodge.[36]

With the coming of the generals, with JFK's anger over Diem's assassination, with Kennedy's own assassination in a matter of days, with LBJ as president of the United States, a sea change rolled across Vietnam. Lodge resigned to go home and seek the Republican presidential nomination (his early meetings with Johnson clearly shrank his satrap's status), Harkins left, and Richardson was gone. Johnson thus had to create an entirely new South Vietnam team.

He moved quickly. Several good people volunteered for the ambassadorship, including Bobby Kennedy, but Johnson picked the quintessentially civilian general, Maxwell Taylor, for the job, with veteran diplomat U. Alexis Johnson as his deputy. The president hoped to appease congressional hawks with Taylor's assignment, but he knew the ambassador secretly shared his hope of containing the war. General William Childs Westmoreland moved up from his deputy's slot to take command of MACV. Taylor had long been his mentor, and LBJ expected the two to work well together.

As one veteran reporter remarked, "Never before in history had such a distinguished array of talent been assigned to cope with a conflict that was not being directly conducted by the United States."[37] That looked to be true enough for the moment—but Vietnam's sea still heaved toward realities new and different.

chapter FIVE

"What Can We Do in Vietnam if We Can't Clean Up the Dominican Republic?"

L yndon Johnson looked forward to weekends. They sometimes brought a chance for a brief break in the daily pressure, or maybe an opportunity to get away to the presidential retreat at Camp David in Maryland. Saturday, April 24, 1965, seemed to have all kinds of good potential. A routine visit to the White House Situation Room around eight in the morning brought LBJ up to date on Vietnam and after breakfast he called Bob McNamara and Bill Moyers, met with some of his staff, and worked on getting ready for a festive afternoon. No matter what, he had to concede this day to Luci.

Luci was to be crowned Queen of the Azalea Festival in Norfolk, and that event came ahead of everything else—even affairs of state! She had gone ahead to do whatever about-to-be-queens do. The president and Lady Bird, with Lynda and her escort, Lt. (jg) Bernie Rosenbach, and White House secretary Vicki McCammon, made ready to follow Luci. At about 1:30 they all climbed aboard *Air Force One*, a giant DC-6, and flew to Norfolk.

Ceremonies began when the president took his place. A happy half-hour program highlighted the events of the day and built up to the climax: Luci came forward and the President of the United States held up her crown and gently put it on her head. He said some appropriate words and bragged that Luci had "been my queen for a long time." Luci then spoke briefly and the family gathered for a picture session—after which mother, daddy, sister, and escort left Luci to her royal duties and headed for Camp David.[1]

In the mountains, remote and made especially private by every security method, the Camp boasted modern conveniences amid rustic elegance. Arriving about 5:20 P.M. the president's party found the Valentis already on hand, and their daughter, Courtenay, welcomed her "Uncle LBJ" happily. The Valentis, along with Lieutenant Rosenbach and Mr. and Mrs. Wally Hopkins (friends from the Norfolk festival), gathered with the family in the living room. At six o'clock LBJ returned a call from Tom Mann, recently promoted to undersecretary of state for economic affairs from assistant secretary for inter-American affairs. There were troubles to the south.

As he listened to Mann reading a cable from the U.S. Embassy in the Dominican Republic, Johnson must have had a sense of déjà vu; recent problems with Panama and Guantanamo Bay were still raw in his memory. Clearly, though, the problems in the Dominican Republic were larger than the others. A coup had apparently been launched against a shaky government, and gunfire could be heard in the capital city. The main radio station had been lost to dissident army officers and retaken. Johnson listened calmly; rumors had persisted for months about another *golpe* in Santo Domingo, but action came sooner than expected. In fact, Dean Rusk had just recalled Ambassador W. Tapley Bennett home for an update. The safety of Americans was LBJ's only immediate concern. Did Mann think the United States should do anything? Not at the moment, but he promised to report developments.

There were all kinds of options if things got worse in Santo Domingo. If the situation deteriorated, the United States could rely on some tattered fringes of international law to send in troops to protect American nationals, or it could ask the Organization of American States (OAS) to intervene with such force as might be mustered, all the time using every ounce of diplomatic bluster available to the "Colossus to the North." But pushing the North American macho image was just what LBJ did not want to do—he would seek some kind of consensus.

At four on Sunday, LBJ and Lady Bird and the three Valentis boarded a helicopter for Washington. They reached the White House at about 5:15 P.M. Things had gone from bad to worse in Santo Domingo. Nervous President Donald Reid y Cabral had resigned; rebels favoring former president Juan Bosch had taken the presidential palace and installed a puppet to hold office for their absent hero. That propelled more officers into the cauldron, since most of the military men thought Bosch weak and probably pro-Communist. The Dominican air force joined the fray, bombing and strafing the palace on Sunday afternoon.

The Dominican Republic was not unknown to Johnson. In February, 1963, he, as vice president, had represented the United States at Bosch's presidential inauguration. Intelligent and pleasant, Bosch, first properly elected Dominican president since the dictator Rafael Trujillo, was a man teeming with idealism, but to Johnson's practiced eye the new president had little substance to him.[2] Bosch, ousted by a coup d'état in September, 1963, seemed hardly the man to back as president in the current Dominican upheaval.

In the series of Dominican crisis meetings that dominated White House gatherings through the rest of April and into May, LBJ heard increasingly unfavorable opinions of Bosch. Unfortunately, the other players seemed scarcely better. Johnson was faced with a situation not unlike that in Vietnam: the choice of whom to support would boil down to the least of the evils and would, in the final analysis, lie outside U.S. hands.

Recent news was not comforting. The spreading battlefield was peopled with small bands of rebels, each pursuing vague aims of their own. Guns and machetes taken from government arsenals and police stations had been issued with wild indiscretion to almost anybody who held out an eager hand. Innocent civilians fell in growing numbers as Santo Domingo teetered toward anarchy. Americans in that battered place were in real danger.

From the start, LBJ made it clear that the United States was not supporting anybody and would not meddle in Dominican politics. While someone other than Bosch might make a better head of a stable government, he would be acceptable if properly elected.[3]

Johnson and his advisors decided that for the moment they would monitor the situation, wait for reports, and be prepared for further action.

DETERIORATION

By Monday morning, April 26, the Dominican situation had deteriorated radically. Tom Mann called LBJ at 9:35 A.M. with word from the U.S. embassy—the switchboard was clogged with calls from terrified Americans who wanted to be rescued. The president asked Mac Bundy, Rusk, McNamara, and George Ball to come to the White House at about 12:30 P.M. Fifteen minutes into the conference, Tom Mann, Jack Vaughn (Mann's replacement as assistant secretary of state for inter-American affairs), and Ambassador

Bennett arrived. The meeting, with a shifting cast, went on until almost two o'clock, plagued by a lack of information.[4]

Johnson, though, had already decided that things might have to be done to protect Americans, and from Camp David he had directed elements of the Atlantic Fleet to stand out of sight off Santo Domingo in case there was a need for evacuation. State had already alerted the U.S. embassy to be prepared to evacuate American nationals and others who wanted out. The embassy was to ask for a protective cease-fire for a double reason: to cover removing civilians and, perhaps, to help cool off the loyalists and rebels. On Monday the embassy began telling Americans to gather the next morning at the Embajador Hotel—a great, modern, touristy monolith—for extraction; many non-Americans were also included. Both sides in the fighting agreed to the U.S. request for a cease-fire.

Everything began well on the twenty-seventh; evacuees had been registering through the night and into the morning. By evening, though, fighting had intensified and spread to different parts of Santo Domingo. Embassies began to come under fire; El Salvador's was looted.[5]

President Johnson grew increasingly concerned on Tuesday. Talking with Tom Mann a little after seven in the morning, LBJ learned of the continued killing. Clearly the safety of Americans—indeed of everyone—rested on some quick resolution of the crisis.

Realizing that commitment of Marines might be necessary to protect the evacuation process, LBJ decided to brief the congressional leadership at the White House. Senate majority leader Mike Mansfield arrived with Russell Long (George Smathers came later), and Speaker McCormack came with Carl Albert and Hale Boggs. The president told them the Dominican story up to that moment, then mentioned the possibility of sending in the Marines. The safety of Americans was everyone's paramount concern, and he met general approval of what had been done.[6]

Johnson spoke carefully of events in the island nation during a short afternoon press conference, and he continued to monitor the situation closely. That night, at a party honoring retiring CIA chief John McCone, Johnson talked about the crisis with several members of the intelligence community, including incoming CIA boss Adm. William F. Raborn, famed for building the first nuclear submarine. How many Communists were playing the Dominican game? That question plagued Johnson and the varying answers he got plagued him even more. Some thought there were many Castro-type Reds on the scene. Others believed that Communists numbered fewer than a hundred. No consensus emerged.

Some of the murk cleared the next morning. While fighting sputtered on,

Radio Santo Domingo reported, about midmorning, that regular forces had constructed a new governing junta and taken power. Although a military threesome, this group proclaimed its desire for peace and intent to prepare for free elections—a first step toward resolution of the crisis. One of the junta's first acts was to contact Ambassador Bennett and ask for twelve hundred U.S. Marines to restore order. In reporting this startling event, Bennett said he had given the junta no encouragement because, "I do not believe [the] situation justifies such action at this time."[7] But he made the realist's suggestion: get ready, just in case things disintegrated.

ACTION

With things momentarily calm in Santo Domingo, Johnson turned his attention to entirely different problems in Vietnam. At 4:45 Wednesday afternoon, the twenty-eighth, he gathered Rusk, McNamara, Ball, Mac Bundy, and Bill Moyers in his little lounge off the Oval Office. While they were talking, someone entered quietly and handed the president a top-priority message from Bennett.[8] Everything had changed. Civil authority had collapsed and the chief of the Dominican national police told the ambassador that he could not protect the evacuation route to the port of Haina. American lives were in real jeopardy: the AID office had been ransacked, and the embassy and four hundred evacuees near the Embajador Hotel were under sniper fire. Bennett advised sending in the Marines.

Johnson told his advisors they must not sit by and wait for American deaths. All agreed, although they were acutely aware that sending in Marines would stir up a hornet's nest in Latin America—it would conjure up old memories of a previous leatherneck visit to the Dominican Republic from 1916 to 1924. The president turned to Rusk and said, "Mr. Secretary, I want you to get all the Latin American Ambassadors on the phone. Get your people to touch all bases. Get in touch with the OAS. Tell them the decision I am making and urge them to have an immediate meeting." Then he asked McNamara to alert the Marines—they were in a spot for quick action, the secretary reported. To Moyers: Invite the congressional leaders to the White House immediately.

Always comfortable with his Capitol Hill friends, Johnson met them at about 7:30 in the evening. He asked Rusk to cover recent events in the Dominican Republic and Ambassador Bennett's views. McNamara outlined a plan already in place to handle the situation. The president said he was about to make a news announcement of his intent to send Marines to protect American nationals. He met general approval but some members hoped for substantial OAS support in the coming days.[9]

Rusk's report of many requests from OAS members to help get their nationals safely away brought much satisfaction.[10] At about 8:45 the president taped an address to the nation (the National Broadcasting Corporation carried it live), in which he reviewed the crisis, announced that four hundred Marines had gone ashore without trouble, and he called on both sides to make peace.[11]

Television is a difficult challenge for old-line, hands-on politicians. Johnson loved people, and when he talked to crowds he could test the reception, could warm up his words or chill them off, according to the waves of reaction that washed over him. But television put a terrible barrier between him and America. Press secretaries tried to help bridge the chasm, and Jack Valenti, among the most articulate of men, agonized as Johnson froze before the cameras. Valenti wanted him to throw his script away, depart from the podium, and simply be himself. But the relentless tube, the lights, the awful void, pushed Johnson behind his glasses, behind teleprompters, shrank his bulking frame, and drained his natural juices into a daunting dullness.[12]

That quenching sometimes drove the president to excesses as he sought some understanding beyond the camera. That April night, as he tried to describe the Dominican problem and what his government had done, he talked of the shooting, the unrest, the uncertainty of everything there. The round eye stared silently back. He felt, somehow, that more should be said about the need for U.S. troops; the commitment had to be explained beyond the mere recitation of events. So he expanded on his theme of a Communist threat and described scenes of horror, of "headless bodies lying in the streets of Santo Domingo," of lurid deeds demanding redress.[13]

In the swift aftermath of LBJ's remarks, critics pooh-poohed his mangled corpses and he got mad. His veracity questioned, Johnson turned to Tap Bennett: "For God's sake, see if you can find some headless bodies."

Undaunted, the ambassador produced some gruesome pictures in proof.[14]

Meanwhile, Rusk and Ball had gone to work contacting representatives of the OAS. They soon discovered it would be impossible to schedule a meeting before Thursday morning. Rusk, Ball, and others at State made careful preparations for that gathering. They expected opposition but wanted to turn it at least to acquiescence if not outright support.

Johnson, too, prepared for opposition—but information coming to him later in the evening strengthened his belief in firm action. Bennett caught the president's attention with one paragraph in a late cable:

All indications point to the fact that if present efforts of forces loyal to the government fail, power will be assumed by groups clearly identified with the Communist party. If the situation described above comes to pass, my own recommendation and of the Country Team is that we should intervene to prevent another Cuba from arising out of the ashes of this uncontrollable situation.[15]

All along, Johnson had worried about Castro's influence in the Dominican crisis. These worries were fanned by several conversations with FBI director J. Edgar Hoover, who knew most of Johnson's alarm buttons. By phone and in person, Hoover offered varying numbers of Communist agents identified in Santo Domingo. At a White House function just the day before, Hoover had "expressed his deep concern for the communistic [sic] activities in this hemisphere as well as affecting the Vietnamese war situation."[16]

Not all of LBJ's advisors were sold on the Red menace. George Ball noted that the numbers were ludicrous: first fifty-three, then seventy-seven. Rusk had doubts of his own and wanted the president to soft-peddle Communists in his comments "until . . . we knew more accurately the extent of Communist participation."[17]

"Somewhat heated," is Rusk's genteel description of the OAS meeting that began at nine in the morning on April 29. Ellsworth Bunker, the U.S. representative, threaded a sticky course through knee-jerk reactions about heavy-handed Yankee doings. Bunker kept calm, pushed the need for concerted action, and said American intentions were purely humanitarian: the evacuation of innocent civilians of various nations, and the provision of urgently needed food and medicines. Debate ran long and acrid as recriminations were heaped on the United States. Bunker managed to prevent overt condemnation. Despite the continuing crisis, any kind of official OAS reaction seemed hours away, and might be hampered by news that LBJ had ordered fifteen hundred more Marines to Santo Domingo Thursday afternoon.

Reports that day gave some hope that the situation in Santo Domingo might be containable. George Ball phoned the president optimistically in the afternoon. The new junta seemed to be mopping up and thought they could handle it without U.S. intervention.[18] Ambassador Bennett, though, had no doubt of the need for more Marines—the small force already on hand likely could not handle any increase in duties and was showing some signs of wear.[19]

The president kept close to the situation all Thursday afternoon. He talked

with Admiral Raborn, who still worried about Communists and with senators Mansfield and Dirksen. Most of all, he wanted to keep the press on his
side, and had instructed Ball to keep correspondents informed, along with
both congressional houses. He took his own counsel and talked about the
Dominican situation during a press walk around the White House lawn.[20]

Late afternoon brought confusing information; intelligence still lagged
behind rumor and intrigue. Too many people thought too many different
things and, slowly, Johnson got fed up. He stuck to proper channels while
they seemed useful, but they were not producing enough hard data. So he
began to act on his own. "Godamnit," he railed at Raborn, "send fifty of
your people out there. I want them in every town."[21] The CIA director got
the message and the agents went.

Like all presidents in difficulty, LBJ began to shorten his lines. He took
almost total control of the Dominican crisis—became, in George Ball's
phrase, "the Dominican desk officer."[22] In this role the president noted that
formal diplomacy had merit, but ground too slowly, and sometimes whole
dimensions of problems were sifted out. He turned out of channels to an
old friend with special connections—Abe Fortas. Fortas had done presidential chores before with dispatch and with uncommon secrecy.[23]

Lawyer Fortas, smooth, and well mannered, had a short man's brimming
energy. Soon to be nominated by LBJ to the U.S. Supreme Court, Fortas
had an insider's comfortable cunning. More than his legal and conniving
backgrounds would serve him in LBJ's current task: he had been undersecretary of the interior in FDR's time and had worked closely with Puerto
Rico's Gov. Luis Muñoz-Marín, who, in turn, was a close friend of Juan
Bosch's. Bosch's position remained crucial in everything happening in Santo
Domingo.

Fortas accepted the president's request that he talk to Bosch. Fortas,
though, did not share LBJ's belief in heavy Communist infiltration of the
Dominican Republic. Approving evacuation of endangered civilians, he
opposed outright U.S. intervention. With Fortas in the picture, the Dominican situation took on a new energy.

Meanwhile, LBJ pushed ahead with other efforts. On Thursday he called
Valenti, Moyers, Mac Bundy, Rusk, McNamara, Admiral Raborn, and Tom
Mann to a 7:40 P.M. meeting in the Cabinet Room. They were joined twenty
minutes later by JCS chairman Gen. Earle Wheeler, deputy CIA director
Richard Helms, Jack Vaughn, and some others.

The president bored in on the Communist problem and Raborn obliged.
The CIA agreed with Ambassador Bennett that as many as fifteen hundred
armed Communists were fighting in Santo Domingo. Raborn guessed there

were as many as four thousand in all of the Dominican Republic, but reminded his listeners that their small numbers were compensated by their organization. If the fighting fragmented into small groups, Communists could easily take over the revolution and install their own administration.

As he listened, Johnson came to a firm conclusion: "with most of the moderate leaders in hiding or asylum, the Communist leadership had the keys to what Lenin once called 'the commanding heights' of power in the Dominican Republic. Of that there is no doubt in my mind."[24] What U.S. forces could be used to prevent another Cuba? That question bothered the JCS: U.S. strength was spread thin from Vietnam around the globe. But Wheeler and McNamara reported part of the 82d Airborne Division was en route from Fort Bragg, North Carolina, to Ramey Air Force Base in Puerto Rico. Johnson ordered them on to Santo Domingo. The meeting ended a little after nine, with Johnson calling another at eleven to iron out details.

George Ball and a civilian analyst from the CIA joined the previous cast of advisors when they reconvened. McNamara confirmed that the airborne troops were going to Santo Domingo. Ball, who thought Communist numbers ludicrously inflated, mused that "our increasing pouring in of troops was wildly disproportionate," a kind of "Texan overkill."[25] But Johnson had his own view on numbers. Fearing a continued bloodbath, he asked a Marine general the numbers needed to control the Dominican crisis; the general said five thousand Marines could settle things. Obviously reflecting his anguish about numbers in Vietnam, Johnson told his advisors that he would "send 25,000, so we can get in there faster and we can get out faster."[26] When he had listened enough, the president looked around the cabinet table, fixing each man with those steady, careful eyes. "Do you agree?" they seemed to ask. The eyes, the chin, the awing figure made it hard to say no. Johnson recalled with satisfaction that everyone united "in deciding that action was required if the citizens of the Dominican Republic were not to fall under the control of a small Communist minority and lose control over their own political destiny."[27]

One of Bennett's suggestions received considerable attention at this later conference—the idea of putting U.S. troops in between warring factions. This translated into the concept of an "international security zone," which the OAS suggested in a resolution passed that night. Such a zone would cordon off the danger area and sustain the cease-fire requested by the OAS. This idea met unanimous approval.

While military initiatives were being approved, diplomatic efforts were not ignored. The United States would focus on protecting nationals and on seeking an interim government to keep order until a free national election could be held in the Dominican Republic. One other important move that night came as a result of Abe Fortas's suggestions and George Ball's support: it involved recalling Ball's old friend John Bartlow Martin, JFK's ambassador to the Dominican Republic, to active duty. He was asked to rekindle his old contacts, assess the situation, and give the president a new perspective.[28] Martin agreed, but he harbored the old misgivings about—and little empathy for—Bosch.

If some of Johnson's advisors did seek to corral his Communist imaginings, they failed to appreciate how firm were his convictions. There was much of Davy Crockett in LBJ—once decided he was right, he went ahead with gusto. He acted with that same certitude and strength in his congressional dealings on commanding ground well known to him. In recent meetings his ideas about quick reaction with massive strength were instinctive and sound. He saw clearly, too, that continuing diplomacy would have a better chance of success as military operations proceeded. Vietnam had taught him a lot.

CONSOLIDATION

Skillful operations by U.S. forces under Lt. Gen. Bruce Palmer, Jr., contained the rebellion within Santo Domingo. That proved the key military move. Problems remained, especially involving disarming the city, but by containing the rebels, U.S. forces soon controlled the country.[29]

A lot depended on how soon the OAS could get together on what to do. The resolution calling for a security zone helped, but firmer steps were needed. As long as the United States acted alone, it took hot criticism from Bosch's supporters for conspiring against his return.[30]

Martin, working under Fortas's general direction, tried to get Bosch to accept a restrained democracy for his country. Martin's ten hours of confabulation with Bosch through May 2 and 3 convinced him that Bosch, to use an LBJ term, exuded penny-ante megalomania. In telegraphic exasperation, Martin wired Washington that Bosch "is completely out of touch with reality" in his support of the rebels.

The challenge for the United States was to keep Bosch constructively involved but physically out of the Dominican Republic. So formidable did that chore appear, that Fortas finally went to Puerto Rico for personal negotiations. There he thought he won Bosch's agreement to support a compromise presidential candidate and a coalition government.

When the arrangement collapsed, Johnson shoved other players into the game.[31] He sent Mac Bundy and Cy Vance, along with Tom Mann and Jack Vaughn, south to "have a try." An important thing about this mission: The fact that these trusted men went showed much progress had been made in controlling the chaotic situation in Santo Domingo. By mid-May LBJ saw that things were stabilizing in the Dominican Republic. Perhaps, moderation could at last prevail in the search for a political solution.

As it happened, the new team worked under difficulties unknown to them. They were hampered and confused about their reasons for being in the Dominican Republic. Mac Bundy thought he was there because "the President wanted me out of town," whereas Vance was there because LBJ "trusted him." As it worked out, Vance negotiated with the generals and Bundy negotiated with the rebels. In time, Bundy fastened onto a man who had been mayor of Santo Domingo as a possible rallying figure (the CIA fingered him as "dangerous"), and Vance struggled to find someone solid in the government ranks.[32] Both of them hung a lot of their rhetoric on Bosch, whom they thought should come back. This stuck in LBJ's and Rusk's craws, and their prejudices were reinforced by Tom Mann's loud demand for assurances against Communists in an interim government. Before any serious rift developed between the president and his deputies, however, the OAS intervened.[33]

Ellsworth Bunker, well liked by his OAS colleagues, had kept pushing and at last prevailed. On April 30, José Mora, OAS secretary general, reached Santo Domingo to show the various flags. Then, during the first week of June, a special three-man OAS commission arrived to sort out the various rump governments and proposed solutions. Bunker served as the kingpin and major doer of the triumvirate.

An OAS-sponsored Inter-American Peace Force arrived in June, bolstering the twenty-eight thousand U.S. troops already there and helping stabilize the situation. By midyear, all sides had grudgingly accepted a provisional government, amnesty, and free elections. Widely respected García Godoy headed the provisional government to preside over elections nine months hence.

In June, 1966, Joaquin Balaguer, a popular moderate, received a clear election majority and became president of a country at peace and happy with itself. All foreign troops were gone by the end of September.

How had this happened? Largely because LBJ stuck to his own ideas and did what he thought had to be done. Military moves were vital and General Palmer summarizes them succinctly: "The U.S./OAS intervention in the Dominican Republic . . . provides a good example of how to use the time element to maximum advantage. We exploited the great political, military, and psychological advantages of intervening quickly in strength, and we withdrew our intervention forces as soon as conditions permitted and in any event before they wore out their welcome."[34]

Johnson's decisiveness in this whole episode impressed most observers. Cy Vance thought Johnson clearly displayed his command manner in the Dominican crisis, as did Mac Bundy.[35] The president's usual method of finding as many facts as possible, thinking them through, and then taking decisive action worked almost to perfection in the days of the April, 1965, crisis and beyond. And in the Dominican Republic itself, Johnson's image changed dramatically from big Yankee bully to national savior—and he is still fondly remembered there.

Critics did clamor about LBJ's impetuousness in leading a reckless anti-Communist cavalry charge in the Dominican Republic. Senator Fulbright, who conducted some disturbing Foreign Relations Committee hearings about the Dominican crisis in July, burned all bridges to the White House by saying that Johnson's motives were not humanitarian; rather, the president linked the United States with a "corrupt and reactionary military oligarchy" to block a grossly exaggerated Communist threat in Hispaniola; moreover, Fulbright alleged that treaty obligations forbade U.S. intervention in any country of the Americas. Another senator commented on the credibility strain that the Dominican business put on the White House: "If we know the President was impetuous in the Dominican Republic and exaggerated the situation there to the point of falsifying it, how can we trust him anywhere else?" Others in Congress quietly agreed.[36]

Most, though, felt good in retrospect. Rusk had positive memories: "I have no regrets about the United States' role in the Dominican crisis. The outcome reflects what we were working for. The Dominican people emerged with an elected president, a constitutional democracy, and a stable government. . . ."[37]

Even the sometimes acerbic George Ball remembered with sympathy: "Viewed in retrospect, the exaggerated Dominican reaction did little harm. Though it stirred up liberal outrage at the time, such outrage was largely a conditioned reflex; no one could seriously argue that Bosch's return would have made anything but a bigger mess. Our intervention left few permanent scars and . . . produced a relatively benign result."[38]

As for Johnson, he had his firm convictions. When historian Henry Graff, working as a kind of official scribe for the White House, asked him his ideas on the Dominican crisis, LBJ boasted. Reminding Graff that Ambassador Bennett had been under fire in the U.S. embassy, the president explained in measured tones: "So I sent in the Marines. And we took out 5,641 people from forty-six nations—without even a sprained ankle. . . . Some of them were [Harold] Wilson's people, some of them [Lester] Pearson's, some of them de Gaulle's. . . . If I hadn't acted, Castro would have had them all.

Now they call me an interventionist and they say that I should have called the OAS. . . . Why, anybody smart enough to pour piss out of a boot knows the OAS isn't going to send in any Marines."[39]

Two years later, at a Latin American conference in Uruguay, Johnson said that intervening in the Dominican Republic was the deed he was proudest of: "The only thing I would do different if I had it to do over again, would be to go in an hour earlier." [40]

How could Lyndon Johnson be so effective in the Dominican Republic and not in Vietnam? Largely because the Dominican crisis came on his watch, all of its drama played out before him, and its problems were essentially political. He had his hands more firmly on the power tokens, knew how to use them, and was able to work without fear of nuclear holocaust. He dealt with the Dominican crisis as he wanted to deal with Vietnam—but there he controlled fewer of the players on a stage that brinked the third world war.

chapter

SIX

"Welcome to the Gallant Marines"

Monday morning, March 8, 1965. A fine, clear day, added to the holiday atmosphere as an enthusiastic crowd gathered along the beach at Da Nang to watch the arrival of the first U.S. combat units in South Vietnam. The Vietnamese had seen a good many Yankee uniforms in the previous few years as advisors came in a growing stream, but two battalions of the vaunted U.S. Marine Corps were coming, which surely meant an important shift in the tempo of the war. Odd-looking landing craft slid close on the sand and thirty-five hundred Marines in full battle gear rushed toward the crowd and were dazed by their greetings. A huge poster dominated the beach: "Welcome to the Gallant Marines." Lots of pretty, smiling, Vietnamese girls stood in the sand and hung garlands of flowers on the leathernecks as they sloshed ashore. So much for the horrors of war.[1]

Why were the Marines arriving? Why had the U.S. expanded its military presence in Vietnam beyond the twenty-five thousand advisors already there?[2] The landing, a great military and propaganda success, at least for the South Vietnamese, resulted from a tangled cluster of causes. General Westmoreland had asked for troops to protect the U.S. air base growing at Da Nang. Security worried him. As air operations increased within South

Vietnam and against the north, air bases would likely come under VC attack, especially one isolated in the uncertain I Corps area, barely a hundred miles south of the DMZ. Westmoreland thought that U.S. forces would provide more enthused security than ARVN troops.

While Vietnamese cheered the arrival of the Marines, there were some critics back home who saw them as the first ripple of a fateful tidal wave that might sweep the United States into war on the Asian mainland. LBJ had nevertheless approved this first infusion of American combat forces—but not without much discussion.

The debate had been bitter enough at times—bitter and deep, often disturbing, but thorough, a debate to rip away tact and reveal emotions, prejudices, fancies, and facts. It had been LBJ's doing, a burrowing for hints below the surface that cut through to the trending of things. It began, coincidentally, with the debate following the battering of Pleiku and ran on long beyond the beginning of Rolling Thunder.

From the outset, discussions about future U.S. plans were shaped by conditions in Vietnam—so committed had America become to its faltering ally that options were thinning dramatically. And this happened despite depressing evidence that increased commitment had little chance of success. Omens had never really been especially good. Back in September, 1963, the JCS had played an elaborate war game with teams made up of Mac Bundy, John McNaughton, Bus Wheeler, Curtis LeMay, Max Taylor, John McCone, and others taking the American and North Vietnamese sides. Sigma I, as the game was known, produced deflating results: More than a half million U.S. troops would be needed to achieve what passed for victory. These unpleasant conclusions were conveniently ignored until a year later, when virtually the same cast (minus McNamara) tried again in Sigma II, this time focusing on what kind of wreckage the coming air operations would wreak in the north. Results were again infernally negative: North Vietnam could continue the war even if every significant target was mauled. Again, the unwelcome results were rejected.[3]

Rejection, though, reflected frustration, not indifference. The players were puzzled that, somehow, their conception of things varied so much from war gaming. And that frustration touched most Vietnam planners. By the end of 1964 and the beginning of 1965, a fuddling miasma settled over LBJ's top secretaries. Vietnam routine became an acute problem. As realities continually shifted there, returning visitors from that unhappy land (too many officials made the trip) brought back rumors, stories, and facts that shaped changing slices of Southeast Asian truth, slices that kept recutting the pattern of the war. Increasingly uncertain of America's best course, the advice

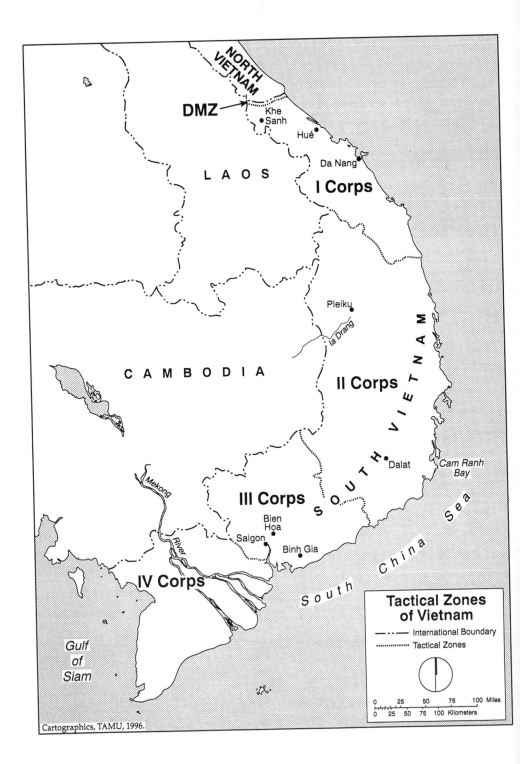

NORTH VIETNAM

DMZ

Khe Sanh

Hué

Da Nang

LAOS

I Corps

Pleiku

Ia Drang

CAMBODIA

II Corps

SOUTH VIETNAM

Dalat

Cam Ranh Bay

Mekong

III Corps

Bien Hoa

Saigon

Binh Gia

River

South China Sea

IV Corps

Gulf of Siam

South

Tactical Zones of Vietnam

— ·· — International Boundary

············· Tactical Zones

| 0 | 25 | 50 | 75 | 100 Miles |
| 0 | 25 | 50 | 75 | 100 Kilometers |

Cartographics, TAMU, 1996.

that LBJ's advisors gave to their embattled boss wobbled between wishful thinking and fright.

Rusk believed staunchly that the south could be preserved by escalating pressure on the north; McNamara, despite warlike public pronouncements, began to waffle in private presentations to the commander in chief as his own moral dilemma expanded into an agonized split between belief and will.[4] Mac Bundy, late in 1964, remained fixed on the original objective of preserving South Vietnam's existence at whatever cost. The JCS, divided between such outright "hawks" (a term coming to have both emotional and descriptive connotations) as Curtis LeMay and Marine Maj. Gen. Victor Krulak and softer thinkers like Bus Wheeler himself (though not a "dove" in the coming parlance), rallied behind stronger war as the traditional way of winning. Hawkish views in this case were loudly echoed by the CINCPAC, Admiral Sharp.[5]

Johnson had his own deep qualms that were of a worrisome sameness to those of his counselors. But when he probed and prodded, he heard few voices raised in caution.

"AN UNMISTAKABLE SMELL OF ESCALATION IN THE AIR"

Never enthusiastic about military choices in Vietnam, George Ball came, at last, to a personal Rubicon: he felt compelled to speak out before events themselves "carried us deeply into the Slough of Despond called Vietnam."[6] Team player ever, Ball decided to test his fears on his boss, Dean Rusk, along with McNamara and Mac Bundy.

Late in September, 1964, working after hours at home, he began dictating his thoughts into a tape recorder. The more he put down, however, the farther he realized he was straying from the conventional wisdom. Holding his views close, he asked trusted aides to type up his thoughts. On October 5, he had revised and finished a remarkable appraisal of the entire Vietnam imbroglio that ran to sixty-seven pages. Writing with grace, customary wit, and deep world understanding, Ball also wrote with prescience and acute appreciation of U.S. and Vietnamese differences in style, thought, and reaction. His manuscript, "How Valid Are the Assumptions Underlying Our Viet-Nam Policies?" aimed at calling everything into question and at putting Vietnam into foreign policy perspective. Aware that this document would attract wild media coverage, Ball classified it Top Secret, made five copies, put two of them in his safe, and had Rusk's, McNamara's, and Bundy's hand delivered.

His colleagues could guess the main thrust of his message—they knew Ball had always wanted America to avoid a war on Asia's mainland. But they were stunned by the detailed, insightful analysis he offered, one that addressed virtually every expected contingency in cogent detail. Ball knew the nation was approaching a dismal crossroads; it could still escape from Vietnam but the chances were dwindling. He sensed "an unmistakable smell of escalation in the air" as he sent off his plea for reason.[7] Reason's writ ran thin those days among Washington's higher heads.

Why? Because most could only see reason in the course toward fuller involvement. Those who visited South Vietnam came back convinced that it teetered toward collapse. General Khanh's government reeled under his overreaching ambitions and inability to work with a civilian administrative structure. The cast of characters expanded as Khanh's problems with his prime minister, Dr. Nguyen Xuan Oanh, increased when that amiable, pro-American, and much harried bureaucrat called—with U.S. approval—for an increased South Vietnamese draft. The call sparked riots among students and Buddhists, and the generals sloughed away from Oanh. Khanh, who had doubted the wisdom of his sharing power with a Harvard-educated economist, took over, promising to restore civilian rule as soon as things settled down. No one believed him, least of all Ambassador Taylor, who watched in mounting frustration as South Vietnam self-destructed.

Max Taylor, whose sense of reality expanded that winter amidst his ambassadorial troubles, deplored all the feckless power playing. He reported to Washington that "we need two or three months to get any sort of government going that has any chance of maintaining order."[8] No sooner had he deplored the Saigon merry-go-round than it took another turn.

In mid-September, a group of irked officers—either just out or about to be out of their jobs—turned on Khanh. A new man entered the cast, Air Vice Marshal Nguyen Cao Ky, head of the air force. Young, personable, and energetic, Ky fancied flamboyant, deep purple jumpsuits (so did his glamorous wife, who may have seen herself a younger Madame Nhu) and, projecting a Pattonesque image, he even carried ivory-handled pistols! No one could guess, really, which way Ky would jump in the coup, but he wound up siding with Khanh, and the air force's added weight ended the uprising. Still, winner though he seemed, Khanh lost prestige simply because the coup occurred.

It is hard to judge Ky's role in all this; he disguised his plans behind a broad, confident smile, a thin moustache, and a boyish exuberance that easily masked ambition or uncertainty.[9] He and some of his younger colleagues watched as Khanh tried to resurrect a civilian government. Craving power, Khanh could never really let go the reins of government, and so selected some nearly senile sycophants to sit in various offices. One of them, octogenarian Phan Khac Suu, the new chief of state, revealed more of himself than he guessed in a formal mandarin gown. Prime Minister Tran Van Huong, still in his early sixties, a schoolteacher and former Saigon mayor, had a charming, ruddy face framed by short white hair; he looked the part of a leader but lacked the talent and pretty well characterized the whole administration as he described himself to Stanley Karnow: "I am completely tranquil, as I must be to have faith in this country's future. You know, we Asians are fatalistic. I believe in providential assistance."[10]

This tranquil man faced nothing but turbulence for three months and finally declared martial law—which fanned renewed plotting by Khanh and his followers, including Ky. Nothing traveled faster in Saigon than coup rumors, and soon the city seethed.

It happened that Ambassador Taylor had just returned from Washington and a tough meeting with LBJ on December 1, 1964. He had forwarded an action program to the president, who liked it. Taylor urged three points: avoid negotiating with the North Vietnamese until they were "hurting"; make Hanoi pay an enormous price for every victory; and keep the southern government in front of the fighting and possible negotiations. He urged a two-phased military program, not unlike the Bundy plan: In the first phase, perhaps to last a month or two, expand U.S. operations and launch reprisal raids; in the second phase, start a gradual but systematic bombing of North Vietnam combined with generally increased pressure.

When they met, LBJ talked through the suggestions with Taylor and indicated he would not go for increased attacks against the north until he felt certain everything possible had been done for the south. If Taylor wanted his bombing scheme, he had to shore up South Vietnam's leaders. The general pressed the president for something positive to take back to Saigon, some promise of military action to encourage the flimsy administration. He finally got a statement to use: LBJ said that the United States was "prepared to consider" direct military pressure against Hanoi once the Saigon government firmed up. The ambassador knew that LBJ had made a fundamental shift in mind when he issued that statement—even a conditional commitment to bomb the north put the United States farther into Vietnam than ever before.

Whatever elation Taylor felt soon sank under a barrage of LBJ's frustration. The general listened throughout that tense White House session as the president fumed about the revolving door in Saigon's presidential palace. Oanh's fall, Huong's faltering and hints at another circuit of the southern governmental maze infuriated Johnson. Stop the nonsense, LBJ declaimed, and then exploded, "I'm getting sick and tired of this coup shit."[11] The ambassador got the message.

Almost on touching down at Saigon's Ton Son Nhut Airport a few days later, Taylor caught the swirling whiffs of intrigue. Wasting no time conveying LBJ's feelings, he met with President Phan Khac Suu, and Prime Minister Huong, then concentrated on the generals. How best to get their attention? Taylor turned to his protégé, Westy, for help. General Westmoreland offered to do whatever Taylor thought was needed. Would Westy and his splendid lady, Kitsy, open their imposing villa to the generals for dinner? Gladly. Kitsy invited Taylor, and generals Khanh, Ky, Tran Van Don, and a few others to their home on the evening of December 8, 1964.

It promised to be a memorable moment in Washington-Saigon relations. The Vietnamese, many of them connoisseurs of the best French cuisine, found themselves treated to a lavish American steak dinner. The red wine had the proper bouquet, everyone enjoyed the food and company, and relaxed toward a sated satisfaction. Suddenly the mood shifted as Taylor began an unexpected monologue.[12] In a rising tone of preachment, he announced that teetering southern governments "dismayed the staunchest friends of South Vietnam," and if they continued, America's support might soften.[13]

Taylor, afloat on his rising energy, warmed to his subject. Focusing on Khanh and Ky, he launched into a pedantic sermon about not using the army for political purposes. To close listener General Don, Taylor overdid it. "He made it clear in a rather condescending way that the United States was losing its patience at so many coups and other changes in our political framework. To me, he sounded like a schoolmaster lecturing a class of errant students."[14]

The guests left "apparently chastened,"[15] but resentful of Taylor's domineering airs. "Taylor was a splendid soldier," Don noted, but he seemed almost too soldierly—he "tended to be a little too blunt and forthright to function as a diplomat." And Taylor's domineering manner dulled the impact of his words. Scarcely two weeks later, on December 20, Khanh and his friends harassed Huong and arrested several generals, newsmen, "dissident" politicos, and various members of the High Council, which they replaced with the Armed Forces Council as the main governmental body in the capital—Khanh as its head. The tranquil Huong stayed in place.

Taylor seethed. He invited the "young Turks"—Ky, Gen. Nguyen Van Thieu, Gen. Nguyen Chanh Thi, and Adm. Chung Tan Cang—to his office on December 21. There, the ambassador lashed the four younger officers "in blunt soldierly language." Why hadn't they remembered his words at the Westmoreland dinner? Instead they had now made a "real mess" of everything. Arguments waxed hot but without result, except, recalled General Don, "to bring Unites [sic] States–Vietnamese relations almost to the breaking point."

Taylor worked himself into a considerable rage overnight and the next day phoned Khanh. "You understand English, do you?" he raged. "That night at Westmoreland's house, I made it clear to all of you that the United States is no longer willing to tolerate any attempts to destabilize the situation." Khanh, pretending to have missed some of the diatribe, asked would Taylor repeat his points? Taylor did, unaware that Khanh was carefully taping every syllable. The ambassador had made a colossal blunder: He had made the foursome lose face, and then had repeated the affront to Khanh.

Khanh did not miss his chance. Armed with the offending tape, he told the *New York Herald Tribune*'s Saigon correspondent that Taylor was meddling in Vietnamese affairs. Taylor's damage can only be assessed in colonial context. Full panoplied with powers, he acted like a viceroy. That gave Khanh a chance to boast his devotion to independence, even from America— a theme that played well in Saigon. Khanh said he might expel Taylor, who reacted with a suggestion that Khanh resign and leave the country. Finally, the two tried to patch together a working relationship—but not for long.[16]

Over the next few months, Taylor's problems mounted in direct ratio to Saigon's. Chaos in the capital encouraged increased VC activity; more and more villages were hit, their chiefs killed or intimidated, and government influence ebbed. Intelligence confirmed that VC units of up to division strength were in the field by the end of 1964. By December, allied estimates gave the VC an army of roughly fifty-five thousand well-trained, experienced troops efficiently organized and well led. Two battalions of this regenerated army laid a careful ambush in the rubber plantation country east of Saigon. Relentless, the VC sucked government troops into battle near Binh Gia on December 31; a two-battalion VC ambush destroyed two elite ARVN battalions (casualties ran to more than five hundred officers and men) and mauled armored units trying to relieve them. Binh Gia ranked among the worst South Vietnamese defeats in a shattering winter.

Results were predictable: Desertions multiplied from demoralized government forces, and recruiting slowed to a trickle. Bad as that news was, the worst came with confirmation that, for the first time, a North Vietnamese main-force unit had entered the fray by attacking Dak To. Southern troops might have done better had they had more air support. But with most of South Vietnam's air force on "coup alert," defeats multiplied and morale nearly collapsed. "Hanoi is extremely confident," confessed William P. Bundy, "they see Vietnam falling into their laps in the fairly near future."[17]

Stepped-up enemy action began to convince Westmoreland that Gen. Vo Nguyen Giap's forces were about to move to the general offensive phase of national liberation war within the next few months—and he predicted South Vietnam's forces could not stem the tide.

Such unravelling caused a scramble of conflicting reactions in Washington and Saigon. George Ball, in his lengthy October demurrer, had hit on a most sensitive point when he asked, "Should we move toward escalation because of the weakness of the governmental base in Saigon; or can we risk escalation without a secure base and run the risk that our position may at any time be undermined?" Even Max Taylor doubted the wisdom of heavier involvement just because the South Vietnamese government was sliding toward ruin.[18] On the other hand, the Joint Chiefs of Staff urged heavy bombing of the north to provide South Vietnam the "relief and psychological boost" needed to stay alive.[19] A poll of the JCS would have shown Gen. Curtis LeMay baffled by the south-before-north dictum. "I never understood this argument. . . . And my point was that we're never going to have any stability in the south unless you went north."[20]

High hopes and predictions aside, bombing failed. Even some of its loudest proponents defected and whispered that they secretly expected failure all along. Rolling Thunder, hesitantly applied and awkwardly managed, worked against itself. Instead of sparking a southern national resurgence, bombing put more iron in northern determination. As for the south, American bombing brought in more Americans, more goods, more sophisticated equipment—and, most of all, more reliance on the Yankees every day. Out of this came an odd, unhealthy co-dependence: the more South Vietnam needed America, the more desperately America reciprocated. As one Saigon official told Stanley Karnow, "Our big advantage over the Americans is that they want to win the war more than we do."[21]

Ball had forecast the whole dismal denouement in his October memo to Rusk, Bundy, and McNamara. When the initial bombing campaign failed to convince Hanoi to stop harassing the south, increased bombing would trigger a natural reaction. He predicted each side would turn to the warfare "best adapted to its resources." The north, with vastly more soldiers, would commit masses of men to the war while U.S. efforts would hover between air escalation and, finally, committing ground forces to stem the enemy rush. Mounting casualties, doubtful South Vietnamese enthusiasm, and rising world resentment would put the United States "in the position of France in the early 1950s" and earn the same political results.

Ambassador Taylor wanted to win the war, but he became increasingly impatient and frustrated. He still believed bombing would do some good, especially if pursued vigorously. But he came to a healthy admiration for the enemy. North Vietnam's powers of recuperation amazed him, and he thought U.S. troops should not be committed in open war against northern regulars.[22] Surely, there were times, in the dark hours in his handsome quarters—away from the teletypes, staff reports, aides, and South Vietnamese—when Maxwell Taylor thought the United States should throw in the towel. And he began to see a way to do it, an ingenious way, one that really might have worked had it not gone against the growing warp toward war in Washington. For the moment, though, he tried resisting U.S. troop deployments—despite his old search for a new army role.

Rolling Thunder changed Taylor's hopes. When the bombing failed to dim Hanoi's ardor or significantly slow the flow of supplies to the south, and when Westy requested security troops for expanded air bases and LBJ sent in the Marines, Taylor and others (especially John McNaughton, Bob McNamara's aide) lost their first skirmish against ground commitment.

THE ELUSIVE OLIVE BRANCH

President Johnson and the whole administration downplayed the Vietnam game with adroit dissembling.[23] The U.S. bombing campaign engaged widening media attention. Alarmist TV newscasts hinted at a growing war. Johnson "lampooned the 'crisis' tones of the television broadcasters, the long faces, and the grim talk of big, black limousines assembled for weighty policymaking." He put attack and riposte in good Texas parlance: "They woke us up in the middle of the night, and we woke them up in the middle of the night. Then they did it again, and we did it again." An apparently unworried LBJ calmed the country.[24]

But Johnson worried constantly. Some advisors may have thought that he had been partly hoodwinked into approving Rolling Thunder by military men who failed to tell him about needed airfields and land installations—and so he was inching toward land war unknowingly.[25] But LBJ must have known. Although he had little professional military know-how, his years in politics had equipped him with antennae tuned especially to feelings, hints, and human signals. He knew all too clearly that his options were narrowing because of a process that worked to suck more Americans into Vietnam. No matter where he looked, relief seemed unlikely. The new year brought increasing demands for help for an ally almost beyond resuscitation, and the president reluctantly inched closer to essential war decisions.

He fought for other roads to follow. He pushed hard on the diplomatic front. He wanted peace and he wanted everyone to know he wanted peace—Americans, allies, nonaligned nations, and whoever might be counted among the enemy. There had been some efforts to make secret contact with Hanoi through unofficial channels. Blair Seaborn, Canadian representative to the

International Control Commission, had visited Hanoi in June, 1964, and found no interest in negotiations. U Thant, UN secretary general, visited LBJ and others in the administration. Thant thought the Americans wanted him to try for some kind of diplomatic contact in Asia (his initiative happened to coincide with Nikita Khrushchev's urging Hanoi toward negotiations) and had gone away to work—but nothing helpful was heard from him.[26]

Johnson knew there were skeptics aplenty about America wanting peace, but he knew with the certainty of a canny mover of men that intent could be proved by deeds. And who ranked as the most prominent doer of deeds? The president. So Johnson prepared to take up the cudgels by showing the world some of America's hopes for a future filled with the benefits that would flow from an end to killing. He wanted the right stage—a serious setting, a podium worthy of what had to be said—so he accepted an invitation from Milton Eisenhower (Ike's brother), president of Johns Hopkins University, to address faculty, students, and the public at the Baltimore campus.

Johnson had several scenes to paint in this address—but so did some of his White House staff. Johnson saw it as a platform for outlining a peace program that Hanoi might accept. Others, such as Mac Bundy (who pushed his boss to give a full public picture of Vietnam),[27] saw it as a chance to let the American people in on some Vietnam realities, including future actions. More than that, it came at a moment of heightened world interest in Vietnam: Rolling Thunder made international headlines and, in mid-March at a meeting in Belgrade, leaders of seventeen nonaligned nations appealed to North and South Vietnam and the United States for peace talks unburdened by preconditions.

Dean Rusk, at a NSC meeting in Washington on April 2, 1965, welcomed this initiative and urged a "serious, restrained, and positive" U.S. response. Ambassador Taylor, home for consultations, agreed, and so did LBJ. The Baltimore speech offered a splendid showcase for a wide-ranging reply. Several speech writers—mainly Richard Goodwin—helped the president craft a discourse with wide appeal. Despite its various burdens, the Johns Hopkins address had interest, punch, and a special kind of generosity to indulge America's sentimentalism.

Mac Bundy suggested LBJ defang the highly independent columnist Walter Lippmann by giving him an advance copy. The president invited Lippmann to the White House on April 6, showed him the speech, and said he was doing what Lippmann had often advocated: offering a carrot and a stick to Hanoi. As he talked about what he would propose, LBJ grew excited, waved his arms as he surveyed enemy actions, and finally almost shouted his feelings: "I'm not going to pull up my pants and run out of Vietnam. . . . You say to negotiate, but there's nobody over there to negotiate with. So the only thing there is to do is hang on."[28] Yet that is not all that he thought. His complex and nimble mind saw through obstacles, around corners, and into possibilities unguessed. He would stay, but he had a vision beyond staying, a vision in keeping with something deep in his heart.

THE BALTIMORE SPEECH

A packed auditorium waited for President Johnson on Wednesday, April 7, 1965, at Johns Hopkins. When Dr. Eisenhower escorted LBJ, Lady Bird, and Lynda on stage, the huge crowd rose and cheered. Bright lights flooded the hall as television cameras focused on the stage party. Eisenhower introduced the President of the United States, after which a solemn LBJ walked to the podium. He had no notes, but the teleprompter flashed his speech up in front of him as he surveyed his listeners. He would talk to them about a theme growing deeply in his mind—an offshoot of a concept voiced by Woodrow Wilson in 1917: peace without conquest.

What would constitute a just peace in Asia? Johnson offered his ideas: the United States would "not be defeated," he warned, or "withdraw, either openly or under the cloak of a meaningless agreement." America would hold to its purpose of a sovereign South Vietnam "securely guaranteed and able to shape its own relationships to all others—free from outside interference—tied to no alliance—a military base for no other country. . . . And we remain ready, with this purpose, for unconditional discussions."

Then the president did the thing he did best: He looked ahead to a vision of an Asia beyond war, of Asians, like Americans, needing help toward a greater society. He explained that "These countries of Southeast Asia are homes for millions of impoverished people. Each day these people rise at dawn and struggle through until the night to wrestle existence from the soil. They are often wracked by disease, plagued by hunger and death comes at the early age of 40."

That wrong needed righting, needed a massive effort from all humankind. His voice fervent, LBJ laid out the first step: All the countries of Southeast Asia should band together "in a greatly expanded cooperative effort for development." This was the LBJ of the reforming heart, the man who wanted things better everywhere, and when he talked of the things in his heart he carried conviction and people believed. Lady Bird and Lynda, Milton Eisenhower, the whole audience bent to hear a true believer make an offer in altruism much like the Marshall Plan.

Johnson urged a huge development program aimed at the Mekong Delta, "on a scale to dwarf even our own TVA," to transform that rich agricultural area into one of the world's super granaries. He called upon North Vietnam to "take its place in the common effort just as soon as peaceful cooperation is possible. . . . And I would hope that all other industrialized countries, including the Soviet Union, will join us in this effort to replace despair with hope, and terror with progress.[29]

This bold initiative deserved better than its fate. LBJ—that complicated mix of duplicity and altruism—got worked up in his words, meant what he said, yet also hoped to charm home critics and bribe the North Vietnamese. His speech became a prime target for carpers who branded it a dissembler's masterpiece. About the only people who accepted LBJ's remarks at face value were members of his vast television audience—the public he wanted to reach and convince. One leading historian of the Vietnam conflict assessed the Baltimore speech with sympathy for LBJ but not for American sincerity:

> The President was unquestionably sincere in his desire for peace, but the spring 1965 initiatives were designed primarily to silence domestic and international critics rather than to set in motion determined efforts to find a peace settlement. Despite Johnson's offer to participate in "unconditional discussions," the United States had no real desire to begin serious negotiations at a time when its bargaining position was so weak. . . . The President made clear . . . that the United States would not compromise its fundamental objective of an independent South Vietnam, which, by implication, meant a non-Communist South Vietnam. And administration officials were certain that the North Vietnamese would not negotiate on this basis.[30]

This account enjoys much hindsight. Some administration officials, it is true, deplored American negotiations while South Vietnam sagged on the ropes. Rusk and Senator Fulbright, chairman of the Senate Foreign Relations Committee, both doubted the chances of an acceptable deal coming from a position of obvious weakness.[31]

And there is truth to the idea that various elements of government—including the presidency—opposed a quick, sell-out peace. But to say that Johnson played a game with peace feelers is simply wrong. Early efforts by Blair Seaborn, for example, had much administration support. As Rusk later recollected: "Throughout Seaborn's travels American policy could have gone either way. We were building up our forces but reluctantly; we wanted a negotiated end to the war."

The president, during his flight back to Washington after his Baltimore speech, hoped fervently that peace talks might soon start, and told Bill Moyers that "old Ho can't turn me down." And yet, deep in his heart, LBJ thought the chances slim to none for negotiations. Not long afterward, he told some of his staff, "If I were Ho Chi Minh, I would never negotiate."[32] North Vietnamese prime minister Pham Van Dong's insistence on ending the bombing and creating a neutral coalition government in Saigon before negotiations could start hardly surprised LBJ—although he lamented acutely his inability to sit face to face with Uncle Ho.

More than that, he worried about the widening war and about whether South Vietnam really ought to be saved.

As the "smell of escalation" rose in February and March, 1965, and became nearly a stench in April and May, George Ball's lonely battle waxed fervent and undaunted. His cautionary position took a severe hit from VC guerrillas on March 29, 1965, when they bombed the U.S. embassy in Saigon. Demands for more Americans in South Vietnam deluged the White House. The president had been sifting various requests ever since he allowed the Marines to land at Da Nang. Westy wanted more troops for more airfields as Rolling Thunder droned on. Six weeks of bombing had produced no peace negotiations and little evidence of slowing the flow of supplies from north to south—but the heavy infrastructure necessary to sustain the campaign grew apace. The best military estimates supported the need for more men, and LBJ pondered whether to send them and, if so, how many?

Ball knew of the myriad irritations strewn over South Vietnam by the VC and increasing numbers of North Vietnamese Army (NVA) regulars. The obvious buildup of hostile units threatened not only the Saigon government but also the whole fabric of civil life across the country. Assassination proved one of the most effective VC programs: From 1952 to early 1965, more than six thousand South Vietnamese civilians were slain—many of them important village and provincial administrators. In 1964 alone, more than four hundred officials were killed and another twelve hundred kidnapped. As demoralization and disorganization began to creep across parts of South Vietnam, it became more and more difficult to find new leaders. All of this contributed directly to the dysfunction of the southern government, weakened it, and drove many southerners to think of accommodation with the north.[33] While Ball saw these symptoms as reasons for disengagement, most U.S. authorities saw them as reasons for increasing America's involvement in the war.

Johnson simply saw them as pressure points in the decision-making process.

Most American presidents are more shapees than shapers of their office. Johnson, accustomed to congressional facets of power, learned quickly the frustrations of being chief executive and came to wear the presidency like a yoke. He did make differences, but with oxlike speed—and always in front of the camera's unwinking eye. Often the differences he made angered people, confused and distracted them, made them doubt his candor and his mind. The office offered LBJ a wondrous opportunity to make America better. It also mired him in Vietnam's quicksand. No unmixed blessings seemed to come with a war president's job.

Wars had to be amenable to some political rules: If you had a big political problem that needed minimizing, then you minimized it, downplayed it, declared its dimensions, and worked it from there. Vietnam would stay manageable. The president's pledge not to expand the war but to contain it within Vietnam's boundaries, to minimize its human and material costs, would be kept. But as it grew larger, it bumped up against the bounds of that promise. How to handle that? By sticking to the dimensions of the promise and not changing the description of the conflict. There were those on the White House staff who agreed with this kind of artful dodging and there were those who didn't. As for LBJ, there was no problem. And yet this "bitch of a war"[34] kept seeping out beyond definitions and beliefs like a topsy-turvy horror movie.

Finally, LBJ decided to act on his own. In early March he called Gen. Harold K. Johnson, army chief of staff, to breakfast in the White House family quarters. The general, a tough, feisty, intellectual soldier known widely as "H. K." had his own strong views, but followed orders. He listened as his commander in chief ticked off frustrations about Vietnam. Calls came for more men; Rolling Thunder disappointed. Irritated by all kinds of whirling opinions, the president ordered the general to go to Vietnam and come back with some answers that made sense, with a program that promised progress. Breakfast finished, LBJ took the general downstairs in the elevator. He leaned over H. K., and poked him in the chest to emphasize his words: "You get things bubbling, General."[35] The general departed for Saigon on March 5, 1965.

Once there, he sank into the cocoon of military bureaucracy at MACV headquarters. Westmoreland had spawned a large staff, replete with myriad briefers all adept with charts, statistics, and martial jargon. General Johnson, though, had long experience in the briefing labyrinths, and he listened with a practiced, skeptical ear. Westy, as it happened, had some optimism. With the dry season at hand, VC actions waned because of greater ARVN mobility. Bombing the north had, indeed, boosted southern morale—but Westy guessed that familiarity would breed less effect. Halting the bombing would be disastrous, he thought. Pressed, he confessed his real worries about heavy VC concentrations in the northern provinces (I Corps Zone) and their plans to capture most of the central highlands. There, rumor had it, they intended to put a capital of their own and launch a drive toward the coast to bisect the south. Westy summed it all up succinctly:

> It would take about a year . . . to increase the ARVN to approximately 650,000 men, enough to counter the growing VC strength if not the North Vietnamese reinforcements. Meanwhile, the VC's demonstration . . . that he was ready to move into Mao Tse-tung's Phase Three, the big unit war; his concentration in the I Corps Zone and the highlands; and the possibility of large-scale North Vietnamese intervention made it obvious that the advent of the rainy season . . . only about two months away, would precipitate a crisis. Because the rainy season interfered with air support, it was always the enemy's best time for major operations.[36]

General Johnson then announced that he was there as the president's representative, and that LBJ "asked me to come and tell you that I came with a blank check. What do you need to win the war?"[37]

Westy and his staff were astounded, but COMUSMACV gave a measured answer. He had believed from the start, he said, that bombing the north would produce no real results without military successes in the south—and he still believed that. With a weak ARVN in the throes of expanding, Westy saw "no solution . . . other than to put our own finger in the dike."[38]

Johnson consoled Westy with the assurance that the president shared COMUSMACV's feelings about bombing alone being a dubious weapon and was considering sending more ground troops to South Vietnam. Happy at that news, Westy pressed the army chief of staff to recommend an international force to interdict infiltrators along the DMZ and the assignment of an army division to defend the highlands or some important air bases. Westy really wanted the division, plus a brigade he'd already requested, as well as another Marine battalion for Da Nang.

A DELUSION OF NUMBERS

General Johnson headed back for Washington with a clearer picture of the Vietnam situation. After listening to Westy and his staffers, to ideas from the Vietnamese Joint General Staff, and to Ambassador Taylor and others of the country team, the general compiled a list of twenty-one recommendations for LBJ's consideration. Clearly most influenced by COMUSMACV, Johnson essentially ignored Taylor's ideas and proposed sending a full U.S. division to Vietnam, where it could be used to protect bases or to deter enemy incursions into the central highlands. As he outlined his proposals during a secret session with LBJ in mid-March, the general predicted that sustaining South Vietnam would require five years and at least five hundred thousand men. The president, shaken, listened and remembered.

However, the president soon heard from Westmoreland that one division would not be enough—he wanted three divisions, one of them composed of allied forces. What did McNamara think? The defense secretary supported the assignment of one division and agreed with Westy's request to let the men he already had take on combat missions. The president then made the significant move of approving combat missions—and thus changed the whole face of the war.

This decision came in the midst of agonizing over troop and division numbers, in the midst of an approaching total reassessment of America's commitment to South Vietnam—and LBJ did not tell the public what he had done. This major policy shift brought consternation and condemnation when word of it leaked, and it added to doubts about the government's credibility.[39] Mac Bundy thought the president erred in hiding the changes in war policy and later came to think that doing so reflected a serious lack of leadership. "One of the functions of the Commander in Chief is to lead the people. He [LBJ] was just passing a bill a day and didn't want any trouble. He didn't want to explain the war—there wasn't any war. There was no change, there was only a change in what policy required."[40] Others in LBJ's inner circle disagreed with this apparent deception, too, but Rusk felt that the president had made less of a policy shift than "a change in detail. The basic policy remained unchanged. . . . I had no problem with U.S. forces protecting air bases." And, with a combat infantryman's understanding, Rusk also said that "even in a defensive role, troops have to patrol aggressively and take on anyone trying to shoot at them." He didn't push the president to announce the change; and if he had, he kept a clear view of loyalty. "You don't resign if the man who has to make decisions makes one."[41]

Johnson, faced with a number of pressing decisions, was confounded by the cacophony from Congress, the Lippmann element of the press, increasing numbers of dissident students and faculty members on campuses across the nation, the Joint Chiefs of Staff, Westy, and his own advisors.

The Joint Chiefs weighed in on the side of Westy's three divisions, and recommended one of them come from the Republic of Korea (ROK). Mac

Bundy, joining those favoring escalation, suggested that more U.S. forces in South Vietnam would be an important bargaining chip in any future peace negotiations. Bundy, Rusk, and McNamara offered the opinion that a massive infusion of allied troops into the southern highlands below the DMZ would serve "as a show of force and deterrent."[42]

Then Maxwell Taylor dropped into the Washington whirligig. Back for "consultations," he came to warn the president not to send more soldiers to South Vietnam. Johnson, out of respect for Taylor, always gave him a careful hearing—even when Taylor said things that ran against LBJ's grain. And Taylor, this time, marshalled considerable force of logic to hurl at his fellow military men and the commander in chief.

He had already lost the fight to keep combat troops out; his new strategy focused on delay, on slicing numbers thinly and minimizing American commitment—something that naturally disturbed a general's psyche. He picked up a point already made to LBJ: "We will soon have to decide whether to try and get by with indigenous forces or to supplement them with Third Country troops, largely if not exclusively U.S." That decision involved reconsidering the army chief of staff's recommendation to send a division to Vietnam, and Taylor said that "considerable additional study is required before we are prepared to make a recommendation either for the introduction of a division or for the assignment of its mission."[43]

Mission bothered him because it would doubtless involve combat, and he doubted that Caucasians were suited to guerrilla war in Asian jungles. Then, too, the more Americans took over fighting roles, the more Saigon would let them. Finally there would come a crossover point at which the South Vietnamese would abdicate to their giant ally and Vietnam would become America's war. Then the United States would, as George Ball kept saying, indeed become "a puppet of our puppet."[44] Taylor pretty well persuaded LBJ to back away from heavy troop assignments, but he had trouble with the Joint Chiefs.

Meeting them on March 29, the ambassador must have felt the undercurrent of resentment. A general he was, but one who thought like a civilian, a number chopper who seemed to have forgotten the old military fear of fighting a war with too little and too few.

Taylor remembered rightly enough: He did not want the U.S. Army lost in the far reaches of Asia on the tag end of a hopeless logistical line, struggling against racial prejudice, enemies, hostile friends, a vile climate, and on a dismal battleground. As louder peace words were spoken everywhere, as Rolling Thunder hit the north but failed to bring a peace with victory,

Taylor had been thinking about ways to slow the rush to war and at the same time provide an acceptable way out of Vietnam, a way that would save American face by *looking* like victory.

In effect he borrowed Gen. Henri Navarre's idea of enclaves. Navarre had wanted to hold certain strong points along the Vietnamese coastline as major French bases. Fortified, they could throw back attacks, and their persistence would sustain France's dominion. Taylor modified the idea and put it in American terms: enclaves could be testing grounds for U.S. forces. American troops patrolling enclave perimeters would find out whether white soldiers could fight in Asia. And, as long as the enclaves persisted, America, like France, would hold Vietnam. The enclaves had other merits: They would be important logistical bases and they would provide shelter for the ARVN as it expanded and finally took over holding the coastline. Then the United States could declare victory and leave.[45]

Taylor's timidity ran counter to a message brought from Westmoreland. Enclaves wouldn't do; they would pin American troops in "an inglorious, static" situation that would rob them of mobility and bring fighting to population centers.[46] Westy's view showed something of a plan working in his mind. "Search and destroy" missions became his hallmark—operations reminiscent of the U.S. "search and find" raids conducted during the Philippines Insurrection. The difference was modern technology. Westy would use American airmobility to put firepower and manpower wherever enemy units might be found. It was sound idea as long as the enemy showed up in great numbers and stayed around to fight.[47]

Taylor won something of a victory at the National Security Council meeting on April 1. Although the JCS got a full hearing and Westy's worries were completely explored, the president did not see the need for all the troops the generals wanted. He liked Taylor's argument that no real emergency existed in Saigon and, hearing John McCone's worries that increasing numbers of men created the need for greater numbers, LBJ took a middle course. He approved only two more Marine battalions—one for Da Nang, another for Phu Bai—and endorsed wider operational activities for men on the ground, but left the details to McNamara and Rusk. He also agreed to an intensified Rolling Thunder program according to his concept of "slowly ascending tempo." The president accepted only one Westy request, but not fully: An additional eighteen thousand to twenty thousand men were authorized to begin building a broad logistical base in the south as a hedge against future needs. It was an important decision, boosting the authorized U.S. troop level in South Vietnam to 40,000 men. But LBJ did it reluctantly, and with a firm desire for a reassessment of the whole Asian situation.

Go to Honolulu, the president told McNamara, pull together officials from Washington, from CINCPAC, in-country people from Saigon, take a full look at the war and bring back unified recommendations for future action. McNamara convened a small group on April 20: John McNaughton, Bill Bundy from State, Bus Wheeler, Admiral Sharp, Westy, and Taylor. The meeting may have had the underlying purpose of sandbagging Max Taylor.

Of all the attendees, the ambassador arrived the most irked. He had, he thought, been sold down the river after the Washington meetings. No dummy, he guessed that much had happened after he returned to Saigon—much that would reshape the south's future, and all of it without his knowledge. He knew a few details because they came in the form of troop deployment notices. Taylor, assuming the enclave plan still operative, had read through some apparently routine cable traffic from the JCS to CINCPAC on April 14 and discovered a message that jolted him mightily: a report on the plan to dispatch the 173d Airborne Brigade to the Bien Hoa-Vung Tau area as additional security. Stung, he complained loudly in a cable to the State Department: "This comes as a complete surprise in view of the understanding reached in Washington that we would experiment with the Marines in a counterinsurgency role before bringing in other U.S. contingents." He wanted the deployment delayed until "we can sort out all matters relating to it." He added a waspish last paragraph: "Recent actions relating to the introduction of U.S. ground forces have tended to create an impression of eagerness in some quarters to deploy forces into South Vietnam which I find difficult to understand."[48]

He had reasons aplenty for confusion and pique. Consider an April 15 missive, apparently approved by LBJ, that proposed mixing U.S. troops into ARVN units, a brigade for the Bien Hoa-Vung Tao area, and "the introduction of several battalions into coastal enclaves." All of those actions had been preceded by a strong presidential idea that "something new must be added in the south."[49]

Taylor would have been even more furious had he known the behind-the-scenes maneuvering to manage him. A number of his friends were involved. Mac Bundy, fending an increasingly fractious LBJ, suggested that giving direct orders to the famous ambassador—a Kennedy friend—might lead to a public resignation that could be most sticky. He pushed the conference idea. Slow things a bit, Bundy urged: "I am sure we can turn him around if we give him a little time to come aboard." Taylor's protégé Westy had grown increasingly enthusiastic about getting more troops as he noted the softening of McNamara's views on escalation, and even moderate Bus Wheeler accepted the harsher JCS push for more men, munitions, money, and force.[50]

These friends corrupted the political and military systems by conniving to send orders around the ambassador. Even "Oley" Sharp, as the CINCPAC was known, shared some of the blame—but he found himself in the almost untenable spot of being under Taylor while having to carry out direct orders from the JCS.

As the Honolulu meeting evolved, Taylor sat in Sharp's sumptuous headquarters and listened in mounting shock. He realized that an avalanche of escalation now threatened to bury the south. McNamara had more clout than anyone else at the meeting, and he soon made it clear that a renewed sense of unity would come from the discussions.

The ambassador tried to delay the rush toward a new consensus, saying that he needed clear reasoning for further deployments in order to convince the Saigon regime to accept them. "It is not going to be easy," he said, "to get . . . concurrence for the large scale introduction of foreign troops unless the need is clear and explicit."[51] But he sensed the drift of things all too clearly. Momentum overran him.

Clearly the JCS had bypassed him with their appeal for massive commitments. Just as clearly, the president had joined the fervency by being ready to Americanize the war—he apparently wanted U.S. officials filtered into southern provincial administrations for better management. Nothing worse could have been suggested from Taylor's standpoint. Already worried that too many U.S. troops would allow South Vietnam to slacken its war effort, the ambassador thought civil administrators would achieve the total elimination of southern sovereignty—by America, not North Vietnamese. That would go George Ball one better: the United States would become its *own* puppet.

Feeling betrayed—especially by his friend McNamara—Taylor sulked in the growing realization that LBJ's muscle flexed the whole Honolulu gathering. Taylor realized that LBJ "was the fellow with the black snake whip behind them [the JCS] saying, 'Let's get going—now!'. . . He did all this behind my back. . . . Once he made his decision, he couldn't get going fast enough."[52] If he wanted to continue resisting—and he did—Taylor's will wilted in a conversation with McNamara. What the defense secretary said is not recorded, but he plainly pressed for consensus on sending three divisions to South Vietnam—for a total of eighty-two thousand U.S. troops,[53] with more likely to be needed.

When convinced that the president "was going to get all the ground forces in [South Vietnam] the field commander wanted, and get them there as fast as he could," Taylor joined the effort.[54]

Not only did he join, he made a total conversion—to the point of exceeding everyone's else's optimism at the meeting. The majority, as reported by the chairman, thought that victory—in the form of denying victory to North Vietnam and the VC—could come in "a year or two," but Taylor burbled that it might happen in "a matter of months."[55]

Oley Sharp, responsible for Rolling Thunder, caught the main drift of things as he read McNamara's report of the meeting: The air and ground war in the south would intensify, and diminish in the north. His reading of McNamara's report brought a wry observation: "As with most conferences that Secretary McNamara attended, the published results somehow tended to reflect his own views, not necessarily a consensus."[56]

McNamara rushed back to Washington and a series of talks with LBJ and other Vietnam advisors. Things were rapidly becoming more complex. While the JCS moved ahead with plans to carry out the Honolulu proposals, antiwar voices rose at home.

"Teach-ins," a variation of the famed civil rights "sit-ins," began on several U.S. campuses. Faculty members talked to both public and student groups about the morality and sensibleness of the Vietnam "war." These gatherings grew in number and size—some fifteen thousand to twenty thousand protesters rallied in Washington on April 17—and greatly bothered LBJ and many in the White House. The antiwar ralliers represented an alternative view of U.S. foreign policy—to some degree shared by Sen. Bill Fulbright—and as such undercut presidential constitutional authority. Johnson reacted with predictable pungency and ranted about sniping from the sidelines. He took some comfort from J. Edgar Hoover's report that radical groups like the Students for a Democratic Society [SDS] were "largely infiltrated by communists," and from the FBI director's assertion that Reds wanted to spread dissent widely and shake American's confidence in the government.[57] The North Vietnamese clearly took the unrest in America's streets as confirmation that they could outlast the Americans.

Many of the naysayers were people who attracted attention. Some of Johnson's advisors wanted to debate such luminaries as Hans Morganthau, Walter Lippmann, and even Senator Fulbright. Johnson, however, wanted nothing done by his people that might dignify opposition in any way, so the "debates" tended toward a campus upheaval with undertones only longtime academics like Mac Bundy, Walt Rostow, and Daniel Ellsberg could appreciate for the moment.[58]

As far as George Ball could tell, protesters were about his only allies now that Max Taylor was marching to the president's drum. Called, along with Rusk, to the White House on April 20, he heard the results of the Honolulu conference. The enemy seemed to be spreading across South Vietnam like a

Red tide, taking control of the backcountry. McNamara's Honolulu colleagues recommended increasing commitments now and probably later. While an unruffled Rusk sat twirling his spectacles as the president talked, Ball broke in with great emotion: please, he told LBJ, do not take "such a hazardous leap into space" without another survey of settlement chances. At this precise moment, Ball suggested, rushing on beyond his own reason, there might be a good chance for negotiations.

A raised presidential brow and half smile greeted that outburst. "All right, George, I'll give you until tomorrow morning to get me a settlement plan." Then, with force, "If you can pull a rabbit out of the hat, I'm all for it!"[59]

Working feverishly, Ball quickly produced a sixteen-page document headed, "Should We Try to Move Toward a Vietnamese Settlement Now?" He had something of a rationale for his ideas in North Vietnam's answer to a seventeen-nation invitation for peace negotiations. Ball put it this way: "I believe that Hanoi . . . has put out a feeler—in its peculiar Oriental way—that we should not ignore." Knowing he was stalling and seeing diplomatic phantoms, Ball nonetheless sent his top-secret memo to the White House that night because "I could not let us take this tragically definitive step without employing all available tactics to slow the process."[60]

A shrewd assessor of men, Ball glossed his argument to Johnson's taste. Recommending the president delay decision for a few days "to test the diplomatic water," he suggested that "you may still wish to commit the additional forces only provisionally—with the understanding that deployments might be changed at any time prior to actual landings in South Viet-Nam or that they might be stretched out over a longer time span." Pragmatist ever, Ball got down to details—in the McNamara manner. More U.S. troops would mean more U.S. casualties, as the secretary of defense himself had said. Their presence would also change world opinion of the war and induce Hanoi to meet or exceed American numbers.

As for action, America's efforts had been formidable. In ten weeks, U.S. planes had made more than 2,800 sorties. The number rapidly rose from 122 sorties per week during February's first half to 604 per week by mid-April, and more than thirty-two targets had been either destroyed or damaged. Ball admitted that U.S. troop deployments and word of more to come had improved South Vietnamese morale "and increased stability in Saigon," and that "heavy air attacks in the South and air strikes against the North have—at least for the time being—somewhat impaired morale among the Viet Cong and decreased their efficiency." And yet, Ball emphasized, nothing indicated that "our air strikes have . . . halted or slowed down the infiltration efforts of the North Vietnamese."

Still sounding like McNamara, Ball highlighted the importance of the coming rainy season in Vietnam: Rain will hinder U.S. air activity, he reminded the president, and stressed that "the free movement of our forces . . . whether by air or road transport—will be restricted." There were also indications that the VC were concentrating in anticipation of operating in the rain against airfields, cities, and other exposed points. That brought Ball to the crux of his problem: "Should we try to set in train a possible diplomatic solution before the rainy season or should we wait until fall? Looking at the issue through Hanoi's eyes, waiting before serious negotiations might give an indication whether they [the North Vietnamese] can exploit their tactical advantage during the rainy season. . . . If they should succeed in a spectacular way in attacking an isolated point of prominence in the interior . . . their bargaining position would be substantially improved."

On the other hand, if the South Vietnamese and the Americans survived the rainy season relatively intact, and without allowing an important VC success, Hanoi might lose enough heart to accept a diplomatic end "on terms we could accept." What about the risks of staying away from negotiations? They were high, Ball thought, for sound reasons:

1. We cannot continue to bomb the North and use napalm against South Vietnamese villages without a progressive erosion of our world position. . . .
2. I doubt that the American people will be willing to accept substantially increased casualties if the war continues over a substantial period of time and there are no signs of active diplomacy. . . .
3. We cannot expect Peiping and Moscow to sit still over a long period while we bomb North Viet-Nam on a systematic basis.

Ball bravely recommended creating a coalition government in South Vietnam without U.S. intervention, a general amnesty, and dared to suggest that "reunification would be permitted at a specified future date if desired by the people of South Viet-Nam and their Government."[61]

Had Ball pulled the rabbit? Not quite. At an 11 A.M. White House meeting the next day, Ball took some consolation in noting that LBJ had read the memo carefully during his "night reading," but realized that his magic had not been enough "to fight off the hounds of war."

LBJ's interest, though, had been piqued. Bill Moyers called the next day to ask for a copy of the memo. "The President," said Moyers, "is very interested in your idea," and wanted to get some people together "to do nothing for three or four days but ponder the peaceful alternatives in Southeast Asia."[62]

Encouraged, Ball went to an 11:15 A.M. White House meeting on the twenty-first with the president, McNamara, Rusk, Mac Bundy, John McCone, and Admiral Raborn. McNamara, facts abristle, crisply summarized the Honolulu discussions and his interpretation of their results. Ball, emboldened by prior approval, remarked that escalation along the lines mentioned would change America's relationship to the war and would make world reaction "very difficult." Again he suggested a careful examination of Hanoi's four-point proposal of April 8.[63]

Johnson thought carefully and looked hard at Ball; clearly unhappy with most of what he'd heard, the president squirmed for something else. What, he shot at Ball, were the alternatives to current U.S. Vietnam policy? The undersecretary said there were several and he would, with the president's consent, prepare a study of the issue. Go ahead, LBJ told him.

McCone next entered the discussion. Intelligence, he said, indicated that escalation would beget escalation and produce a stalemate.

Pensive, hunched in his big cabinet chair, squinting at McNamara, LBJ probed: Why didn't the Honolulu group suggest heavier air attacks against the north?

McNamara, straight, calm, and combed, said that might provoke Chinese reaction.

"Are we pulling away from our theory that bombing will turn 'em off?" asked LBJ.

No, McNamara shot back, "That wasn't our theory. We wanted to lift morale; we wanted to push them toward negotiations—we've done that."

A turn toward Rusk. What about world reaction to the bombing? LBJ wondered. "Will they let us go on?"

Rusk, careful, certain of the rightness of calling the aggressors' bluffs, seemed unworried. Johnson grumped that the United States seemed to be losing the propaganda war. Waving a big hand, peering from one to another of his advisors, he explained some of his frustrations. "They [the Communists] meet and have a party line. They follow it through. And then you get Walter [Lippmann] and Fulbright and connections."

Ball, seizing on the uneasy pause that followed, tried again. In America, "intellectual opinion is against us." As for foreign countries, some "will stay with us because they need us," he said, but many believed that in time the U.S. world position would erode.

McNamara, irked with meanderings, a man without doubt of his own course, broke in. The United States is not losing the propaganda war, he told the president. "You *have* said you are ready to talk."

Johnson refused the flattery. "I'd give us a C-minus and we ought to have an A. . . . In a very few days, we need an initiative." No one left the meeting greatly enthused.

The same cast reached the White House at about 12:30 P.M. the next day, this time joined by Cyrus Vance, Bill Bundy, John McNaughton, and General Wheeler. Obviously the president wanted action, so discussion centered more on what should be done than on philosophies or speculations. Tacitly acknowledging that Ball still labored alone in his vineyard, the president heard brief remarks on the Honolulu recommendations and finally approved them.

No National Security Action Memorandum was issued from the meeting, nor were there public announcements of what would be done. Johnson complained that some newsmen apparently knew about the Hawaii meeting and that the *New York Times* might even break the news of U.S. troops in offensive operations. Rusk, the president said, had called the *Times* to try to stop the story, but "was too gentle . . . on killing it."[64]

Rumor turned into fact. Hanson Baldwin, the *New York Times* military analyst, presented fairly accurate figures on troop increases and outlined new rules of engagement.[65]

From any point of view, the spring looked to be Ball's "Slough of Despond." Haunted by the specter of the holocaust he saw ahead, desperate to turn the stampede, Ball realized his efforts were foredoomed. Where he saw possibilities in Hanoi's four points, his colleagues bombarded LBJ with suspicions and disdain for "enemy" ideas—although, unknown to Ball, a few quietly agreed.[66] Depressed, not daunted, the undersecretary worked on a major policy proposal for LBJ. Titled "A Plan for a Political Resolution in South Viet-Nam," Ball's proposal enjoyed important outside help—which he knew he needed.

Working alone against heavy odds, he wondered how the president could "be expected to adopt the heresies of an Under Secretary against the contrary views of his whole top command?" So he turned to former Secretary of State Dean Acheson and Washington lawyer Lloyd Cutler, who helped him craft a plan resembling his last one, one that provided amnesty to all VC who quit fighting, installation of a constitutional government in the south with all citizens of whatever persuasion involved, adoption of coherent and doable social and economic programs, and withdrawal of foreign troops with the end of insurgency and consolidation of security. Paying attention to substantive and procedural issues, the plan also addressed implementation.

Ball, however, knew that the only way to sell his program to the South Vietnamese would be through Max Taylor. Trusting nothing to the normal cable procedures, Ball sent an assistant to Saigon. But no support came from that committed enthusiast, to Ball's great sadness: "The episode confirmed an opinion I had not wanted to accept. America had become a prisoner of whatever Saigon military clique was momentarily in power. . . . each clique understood how to exploit its own weakness. If we demanded anything significant of it, it would collapse; so we never made any serious demands."[67]

More than that, all of his efforts confirmed his peculiar isolation as the president's devil's advocate. Even when Bill Bundy sometimes sounded sympathetic, probably because of his CIA backgrounding in France's dismal Vietnam experience, he came down on the forceful side. And when Ball tried to bell him by asking for help on a peace plan, Bundy dodged. If the flabby moral courage of colleagues left Ball rueful, Bob McNamara's outright deceit hurt the most. Ball never ran around his superiors, and when he drafted one of his negative responses to majority views, he always sent Rusk, McNamara, and Mac Bundy a copy, and sometimes others. Often McNamara would call and announce: "I'm coming over to see you because I want to talk about that very interesting memorandum." Once in Ball's office, McNamara—polite, relaxed in an effulgence of knowledge and camaraderie—would say "there was almost no difference between us and he was very much in accord with my views," and that they should both talk to the president. But McNamara usually forgot, somewhere between State and the White House, what he had said. Shocked at first, finally merely cynical about McNamara's charades, Ball remembered what usually happened:

> I would come in before the President and the President would ask me to state my position which I would do at some length; then would turn to Bob, and McNamara would shoot me down in flames, pulling out all kinds of statistics which I had never seen before. McNamara was a genius at that, and then Rusk would pick up the theme, and I would be pretty well decimated by all but the President who would say, "Well, we haven't quite answered George's concern."

Johnson seemed to like the point-counterpoint exercise by this oddly dynamic duo, and used it often to clear his perspective.

Ball never called McNamara's hand about the torpedoings. "I don't think he wanted to try to explain why he had done that."[68] Apparently suffering increasing doubts that victory was attainable, McNamara doffed them before LBJ. In those agonizing Vietnam meetings, the defense secretary held an omniscient line that required iron confidence—and as the news grew worse and the bombs did not win, scuttling George Ball helped sustain his eroding ego.[69]

Everyone's ego needed boosting quickly. The North Vietnamese launched their expected spring offensive in early May, 1965, and this time significant main-force units were involved. A full VC regiment briefly held Song Be, capital of Phouc Long Province, near Cambodia. A heavy American air response, including transporting an ARVN regiment to the battle area, restored the situation. Not long afterward, in a series of heavy actions at Ba Gia, near the coast in Quang Ngai Province, a VC regiment wrecked an ARVN battalion and almost neutralized another coming to its relief.

Throughout May a disastrous series of South Vietnamese defeats forced abandonment of several district headquarters towns. Americans had participated in these battles and gotten a close look at the ARVN's weaknesses. Nor were Americans immune to embarrassment: A Special Forces camp at Duc Co was besieged for two months.[70]

chapter
SEVEN

"No Acceptable Option"

John Kennedy had said how it would be: "The troops will march in; the bands will play; the crowds will cheer; and in four days everyone will have forgotten. Then we will be told we have to send in more troops. It's like taking a drink. The effect wears off, and you have to have another."[1]

Military reverses strengthened demands for sending more help to South Vietnam, and Johnson began listening more seriously. He had been bending slowly toward more commitment for some time; had, in fact, asked Congress in May for a $700,000 supplemental appropriation for Vietnam and the Dominican Republic. A brief flurry of carping in the House and Senate threatened to provoke a major debate on Vietnam, but the Dominican Republic diverted attention. Even though a queasy worry about more men trickling into Southeast Asia tinged some speeches, a general sentiment to avoid showing divided opinions kept opposition muted. Still, some important complaints were aired. Fulbright and one or two other senators had asked hard questions of Rusk and other administration officials concerning the Dominican situation and, by extension, Vietnam. Even favorable senators, more than a few, expressed doubts about "sneaking" into war.[2]

Although irked by doubters, Johnson respected the power of Congress and sought to keep on its good side. He wanted reaffirmation of support and, as Bill Bundy said, he got it by what "can only be described a gimmick"—the supplemental appropriation. If Congress approved the funding request, it would coincidentally approve the policies that made the request necessary. Debate divided along pro and con Vietnam views, with some interesting dashes of chauvinism and cynicism thrown in.

Several members knew they were trapped by the presence of Americans in Vietnam—they had to support them—and some resented the fact. Wayne Morse of Oregon, a chronic carper, ridiculed his Senate colleagues who voted for the appropriation with reservations. "Whom do they think they are kidding. . . . I think the White House must be laughing at their 'reservation.' It is only votes that are binding upon the Pentagon or the White House, not the opinions of Senators of how the Executive should exercise the powers Senators are going to vote him today."

That brought a sharp rebuke from Everett Dirksen: "I want the word to go out to those who represent us in Vietnam that we back home . . . are in their corner if they need us. It would be a sorry spectacle, indeed, if word should be sent out . . . by shortwave: 'You have been let down by the U.S. Senate,' as the Senator from Oregon wants us to do."

Morse returned fire: "We've heard it, now, from within the Senate, as well as from the White House: 'Criticize the warmaking policy of this administration, and you aid and abet the Communists.'"

That division bubbled, LBJ knew, and it bothered him. The president tried to smooth the waters by meeting with congressional leaders between 6:30 and 8 P.M. on Sunday, May 2, before submitting the appropriation bill—but he got rolling and restive about public sniping and, according to a *Washington Post* story appearing the next day, LBJ glared at Fulbright and "implied that Congress ought to show the world it really backs up his policies." On the fourth, the day the bill went up, the president invited senior members of the House and Senate Foreign Policy, Armed Services and Appropriations Committees—32 senators and 108 representatives—to meet him, the vice president, Rusk, McNamara, some staff and, for the first part of the meeting, members of the press. Convening at a little after 10 o'clock in the morning, everyone stood as LBJ entered and took the podium.

For about half an hour he talked about Vietnam and made a series of important points. He reaffirmed U.S. commitment to South Vietnam and said the Communist objective was "not simply the conquest of the south," but also "to show that the American commitment is worthless . . . and once they succeed in doing that, the gates are down and the road is open to endless expansion and to endless conquest." Next he accurately summed up his own dilemma: "We can't go north and we shouldn't go south, and we can't negotiate. So what should we do?" The answer, he said, was to continue helping the South Vietnamese until peace could intervene. Then he threw a bone to antiwarriors as he hit on a lingering truth about Vietnam, a truth that re-erupted now and then to chastise all U.S. policy makers: there could be "no military solution to the problem of Vietnam and we all realize that. We know that we must find . . . a path to peaceful settlement."[3] He might have noted that military strength could help the peace process, as it had in the Dominican Republic.

Amorphous disconsolation in Congress did not kill supplemental appropriations—all concerns notwithstanding. An overwhelming House approval of 408-7 outdid the Senate ratio of 88-3, and LBJ signed the bill on May 7, 1965. At the ceremony, a subdued but resolute chief executive pledged to the people of South Vietnam that "America keeps her promises. And we will back up those promises with all the resources that we need." Lest there be doubts, he promised, too, that "we will use our power with restraint and we will use it with all the wisdom that we can command. But we will use it."[4]

If the president took some satisfaction in feeling that the appropriation bill amounted to a blessing of his Vietnam policies, he did not show it—he remained determined.[5] But he paid attention to fringes of opposition, fringes that were increasingly irksome and loud.

Bill Fulbright's switch from help to hindrance angered the president. He knew his old friend doubted the wisdom of the whole Vietnam business, and as long as he carped privately, LBJ joshed him: "Well, Bill, what have you been doing today to damage the Republic?"[6] But public dissent provoked a stronger reaction. Bobby Kennedy, newly elected senator from New York, sat with LBJ in the little room off the Oval Office and asked for a short bombing halt. While Kennedy's faintness could be understood, old friend Mike Mansfield's growing and obvious objections stung with the deeper point of good intentions.

To blunt this kind of attack, also possibly to calm some of "those little shits on the campuses" and their "egghead" professors, and accommodate some urges within the administration, the president finally called a halt to bombing in North Vietnam on May 12, 1965. Code-named Mayflower, the secret pause had a purpose beyond mere propaganda. A diplomatic note, delivered to North Vietnamese representatives in Moscow, sought to open ways to negotiation. The note said the United States was "very hopeful that . . . this first pause in the air attacks may meet with a response which will permit further and more extended suspension of this form of military action in the expectation of equally constructive actions by the other side in the future."[7]

And some contact occurred. A senior North Vietnamese diplomat in Paris talked with French foreign office officials and said that the four points his country had outlined earlier were not prior conditions to talks but rather "working principles for negotiation." American diplomats thanked the French and asked to be kept informed.[8]

There is some doubt about the sincerity of American interest. Bill Bundy recorded highly skeptical State Department reaction. The North Vietnamese talked "in riddles" and used "carefully chosen and nuanced words and phrases." A careful study—"deconstruction"—of the northern message showed no modification of the north's long-stated position. Some effort at follow-up suggested to LBJ that another bombing pause might be useful— if and when Hanoi's rhetoric cleared. In June, Blair Seaborn re-explored his North Vietnamese contacts with fairly negative results, although French diplomats still had vague talks going in Paris. Over all of these rumors hung a miasma of unreality—as if both sides sidled by each other in pirouetting displacement maneuvers. Suspicion inhibited rapprochement. If Americans puzzled over Hanoi's meanings, Hanoi viewed the Yankee venture as a "worn out trick."[9]

How much Johnson knew of the diplomatic posturing is uncertain. He did know the bombing halt had good and bad sides. It might clarify a lot of thinking—he told some of his White House staff that it could "clear a path either toward the restoration of peace or toward increased military action."[10] At a White House meeting of the NSC on May 18, he mused, "My judgment is the public has never wanted us to stop the bombing. . . . If we hold off this bombing longer, people are going to say, 'What in the world is happening?'. . . I would say to Mansfield, Kennedy, [and] Fulbright that we notified the other people—and for six days we have held off bombing. Nothing happened. We had no illusions that anything would happen. But we were willing to be surprised. We are anxious to pursue every diplomatic adventure to get peace. But we can't throw our gun away." The NSC agreed, and the bombing halt ended that day.[11]

MOMENTUM

By June the portents ran heavily toward massive American commitment in Southeast Asia. General Westmoreland, growing stronger in his righteousness because of enemy action, called for more men, and Admiral Sharp— along with the JCS and Bus Wheeler—agreed that massive intervention seemed the only way to save the south.

George Ball, clinging to shreds of humor midst catastrophe, saw the American willingness to administer artificial respiration to a corpselike South Vietnam as a perfect example of George Santayana's wry definition of fanaticism: "Redoubling your effort when you have forgotten your aim."[12]

Ball had a limited perspective, prescient though it would prove, and could not know the full malignity of LBJ's crisis. And make no mistake, Lyndon Johnson did, indeed, face a crisis of engulfing agony as June, 1965, advanced.

He had pushed Vietnam ahead of him since the terrible day of JFK's death, had wished it away, tended it one-handedly, left it to those he trusted—and all the while he knew it lurked in wait for him. Too many promises, too much ringing rhetoric, too many people already in South Vietnam demanded fulfillment, achievement, and support. He knew all this, yet nothing in that knowledge made his task any easier. As usual, he gave ear to a close group of advisors while at the same time musing about Vietnam with White House visitors, Lady Bird—sometimes even with the White House domestic staff.[13]

He consulted close friends constantly—especially such trusted advisors as Clark Clifford, Abe Fortas, and General Eisenhower. As misfortunes piled on disasters in Vietnam, Fortas quietly but firmly upheld the president's morale. A good friend with the wisdom of familiarity, Fortas knew how and when to suggest changes in course. For him, the spring of 1965 was not a time for shifting aims. General Eisenhower remained a firm believer in sticking it out in Vietnam and encouraged LBJ at every opportunity. Clark Clifford, though, had different ideas—and they would have the impact of the unexpected.

Clifford knew much about Vietnam, indeed about all U.S. foreign policy, as a result of service on the President's Foreign Intelligence Advisory Board—a committee that offered external evaluation of intelligence issues. In early April, LBJ asked his old friend to start looking closely at the situation in Vietnam and to think about what ought to be done. Those ponderings raised Clifford's consciousness and he grew concerned about the depth of American commitment to Saigon. Vague worries concentrated in early May, after Johnson sought his comments on a highly confidential letter from John McCone. The outgoing head of the CIA put South Vietnam's condition starkly and said that if defeat were to be averted, massive numbers of U.S. troops were needed. As more Americans poured into the war zone, he thought more and harder air strikes against the north essential—crippling damage must be done to the north's war-making machinery. Without full pressure, the conflict would grind on and American patience evaporate. This logic had merit, but it had more merit when reversed. As Clifford realized that, he reached "a personal conclusion about Vietnam: we should start looking for a settlement, even if it did not meet our original objectives."

Judiciously, as befitted a distinguished attorney, Clifford reacted to McCone's views: "I believe our ground forces in South Vietnam should be kept to a minimum. . . . This could be a quagmire. It could turn into an open ended commitment. . . . I continue to believe that the constant probing of every avenue leading to a possible settlement will ultimately be fruitful. It won't be what we want, but we can learn to live with it."[14]

Johnson read Clifford's observations with care and probably noted that at last George Ball had an impressive ally. But Clifford's dissenting voice merely added to the babble. Knowing his thinking time was gone, the president began an infinitely careful process of resolution.

BOILING POINT

The president knew he and his country faced a crack in time itself, a moment that might force the fates and cast the future. Nothing proved so baffling to him, so frustrating, so damnably uncertain, as trying to see Vietnam clearly through the angry Asian mists. And he found he could never quite get ahead of the monster growing ten thousand miles away. Just as he felt some sense of control, in came another top-priority message, another summons from the battlefield—more men must come or South Vietnam is doomed. It happened again during the first week of June.

Worries still wafted across the country over the Honolulu decision to send more men when Westy submitted an urgent request for forty-four battalions—an immediate increase of 41,000 men, for a total of 123,000. But even this heavy support might not be enough, and COMUSMACV hinted that perhaps another 52,000 might be needed. One thing about Westy's staff work, it was good and efficient. His needs were couched in definite, professional-sounding terms, not vague, civilian sorts of rounded figures and unknown organizations: twenty-two army and twelve Marine maneuver battalions (infantry, mechanized infantry, or armor),[15] with supporting artillery, engineer, air defense, and helicopter battalions, plus navy and air force combat units and support troops.

He had good reasons for what he sought. Considering recent ARVN defeats and the obvious VC and North Vietnamese buildup,

> I see no course of action open to us except to reinforce our efforts in South
> Vietnam with additional U.S. or Third Country forces as rapidly as is
> practical during the critical weeks ahead. Additionally, studies must continue
> and plans [be] develope[d] to deploy even greater forces . . . to attain our

objectives or counter enemy initiatives. Ground forces deployed to selected areas along the coast and inland will be used both offensively and defensively. . . .

Although they have not yet engaged the enemy in strength, I am convinced that U.S. troops with their energy, mobility, and firepower can successfully take the fight to the VC.[16]

Westy also urged emphasis on airmobile forces, feeling that U.S. mobility had confused the enemy and offered the best chance of keeping the offensive. Like most Western professional soldiers, he thought in offensive terms. He put forth his views firmly in a message sent a few days after his blockbuster request for men: the south's survival depended on "a substantial and hard-hitting offensive capability on the ground to convince the VC they cannot win." Why? Because Hanoi and its VC allies were shifting to "big-unit" war. Westy believed this and it shaped much of his planning that hectic spring.[17] The impending challenges also demanded some clarification of his field command authority. Could he order U.S. forces to battle in aid of threatened ARVN units? Oley Sharp, his immediate superior, said yes, he could, but cautioned him to be careful not to allow a large U.S. unit to lose its first action!

When Westy's wish list reached Washington, the Pentagon and the White House erupted in disbelief. America's field commander put it with glacial clarity: It was time to get in or get out. And, if America got in, it would take lots of men and treasure and time beyond guessing. What brought COMUSMACV to this moment of truth? Had the Da Nang and later landings gone to his head? Or had he, in the much more rational reaction, simply realized that South Vietnam's forces could not handle the growing strength of the VC?

Westy had already made his feelings clear and stood ready to fight as best his forces allowed. Political decisions were beyond his writ, but he worried. And Washington worried—piercingly—about Westy. The Pentagon, along with the White House, glimpsed a frightening point with awful clarity: Westy intended "to take the war to the enemy," which would likely be costly in men and money.[18]

Reason tended to get swept away in the emergency atmosphere of early June. Few doubted—Ball did, as well as some U.S. ambassadors in the Far East—that South Vietnam tilted toward collapse and that U.S. troops alone could save the day. How would they do it? Westy, coached by his operations chief, Brig. Gen. William E. DePuy, adopted a new iteration of Paul Harkins's attrition plan. DePuy's concept aimed at unleashing an unstoppable American mincing machine against the enemy with which "we are going to stomp them to death."[19]

ACTION FROM AGONY

A good many people close to the decision makers guessed the trending of things. Veteran LBJ watchers, those who survived his daily shifts in mood and demeanor, felt a kind of hardening, although he kept probing and questioning and second-guessing his own prejudices. Some few wanted to claim, later, a special feeling about the president's commitment. And yet nobody really knew. He played everything into his feelings, as usual, and dropped hints for divergent purposes. All those who knew him noted his caution in momentous moments; even these, though, missed the almost formal processes that let him examine facts with an especially patriotic conscience.

A few who were close to the president wondered if he listened enough to himself, to them, to the public, to the Joint Chiefs of Staff, to dissidents, to anyone. So closed a personality comes to decisions in ways that are maddening to the curious, but always by personal choice.

Still reaching for information, the president summoned the special advisory council he had created back in September, 1964—a group of old government hands, with experience, probity, and intelligence. The "Wise Men," as they were known, had an impressive official title—President's Consultants on Foreign Affairs—but everyone used the shorter, dressier designation. The members preferred it and endeavored to live up to it. They were each distinguished, and together formidable: Dean Acheson, Eugene R. Black, Gen. of the Army Omar N. Bradley, John Cowles, Arthur Dean, Allen Dulles, Roswell Gilpatric, Paul G. Hoffman, George Kistiakowsky, Arthur Larson, Morris I. Leibman, Robert Lovett, John McCloy, Teodoro Moscoso, James Perkins, and James J. Wadsworth. They blended the talents of former cabinet and subcabinet appointees, former CIA directors, men of high military renown, economic wizardry, and matchless international scope.

They came to a two-day White House meeting, July 8–9, 1965, broke into various panels, read background papers, and listened to briefings. General Bradley, Gilpatric, Kistiakowsky, Larson, and McCloy comprised the Vietnam panel. They met on the eighth with Rusk, McNamara, Ambassador Llewellyn Thompson, and Bill Bundy. In general, the panel accepted the seriousness of Saigon's plight and also the dismal portents of its fall. Thailand, they thought, could not be held, and bad reactions would follow in Japan and India. Most of all, the effects on Europe bothered them—"le Grand Charles" had worked hard to divide America from the continent, and failure in Indochina would help confirm his argument that the U.S. probably could not defend Europe. The panel thought a major defeat would be awfully awkward; equally so, simply pulling out. A suggestion of taking the whole mess to the UN received short shrift because, as Bradley thought, it would confess too much eagerness to quit.

Consequently, the general view supported sending whatever forces would sustain the south. A few felt that U.S. efforts so far had been "too restrained" and may have given Hanoi false expectations. Whatever decisions were made, the panel urged full public disclosure—a point made fervently by Roswell Gilpatric in a note to Mac Bundy on July 9.

After the meeting on the eighth, LBJ gathered a small group in the Cabinet Room for drinks and conversation. He came in at a little after 6:30 P.M. and went around the table, shaking hands. Everyone waited to hear him and then "to impart their wisdom." Acheson sat at the table, along with Bradley, Cowles, Dean, Lovett, and McCloy. Others present included Rusk, George Ball, McNamara, Treasury Secretary Henry Fowler, and Mac Bundy. A satisfying group, indeed, LBJ could note. Looking at them, cherishing the power at his command, he took his seat and began putting the group into his picture. There were problems that plagued decision, he said, and began to outline various impediments to getting on with some kind of policy in Vietnam. Outsiders could not really know the pressures coming from a generally negative press, from carping congressmen who needed to worry only about their districts or states and not the fate of the nation, from a fuzzy group of so-called intellectuals who enjoyed the luxury of uninformed complaint.

Johnson did not notice, as he warmed to his recollection of wrongs, the reaction of some listeners. Old hands like Rusk, McNamara, Ball, Bundy, and other staffers waited patiently for news. But Acheson, his coldly efficient mind biased against frippery, seethed. And yet, the president's "tirade" had a curious effect on the former secretary of state. He had come to the table with some doubts about further involvement in Vietnam; the more he listened to presidential self-pity the more impatient he got. Finally he "blew his top," broke in, and scolded LBJ. The president, he said, was completely right about Vietnam: He had no choice but to get on with it. Acheson offered the bristling assessment that "explanations were not as important as successful action." That opened the door—every one of the Wise Men urged strong pressure in Vietnam.[20]

Johnson listened carefully, probing for nuances. Bob Lovett and John McCloy expressed some worries, but both men reluctantly agreed that LBJ had "to go in." The collective view of the Wise Men carried a good deal of weight, especially fitting, as it did, with Bob McNamara's rising bellicosity.

Apparently he had been influenced by Westy's "force ratios" argument of recent weeks.

Cocksure always in the labyrinths of numbers, McNamara found solace in formulae—Westy had one: counterinsurgency doctrine postulated that friendly forces had to outnumber guerrilla opponents by 10 to 1 for victory. The army chief of staff's recent gloomy forecast of the possible need for five hundred thousand men reflected that estimate. McNamara knew the president would not commit a half-million men, so he found ways to justify fewer. The arithmetic lacked elegance, even logic, but it had an arcane kind of confusion that teased the brain. Westy's staff tried a novel way of slicing numbers. If only NVA regulars in the south were counted, a hundred thousand VC would be eliminated, leaving the enemy 72 battalions, or fifty thousand men. South Vietnam boasted 133 battalions. Now, add the American factor, maximizing it by the tricky idea of "force multipliers": one U.S. Army battalion—with its modern mobility and firepower—equaled two of the enemy's, and each Marine battalion equaled three of the enemy's. So calculated, U.S. and South Vietnamese strength could be put at 172 battalions against 72 for the NVA. The total came out to a ratio of only 2.4 to 1—hardly the required 10 to 1—but a nimble shift of strategic definition took care of the discrepancy. Westy remained fixed on the idea that Giap's men were moving toward waging large-unit war, so 2.5 to 1 looked like more than enough to "stomp them to death."

Johnson bothered little with the coils of numbers—but he knew McNamara understood these things, so there must be something to the idea. Still, the secretary of defense seemed almost panicked by South Vietnam's approaching coma—he even sent B-52 heavy bombers into action. Huge, they could dump thirty-seven thousand pounds of bombs per plane over a considerable spread of terrain. They came unannounced, their bombs falling silently and exploding in awful flashing rows of dirt and death. Because the enemy liked to avoid battle by hiding under the thick jungle canopy, B-52s should have been just the weapon to blast them out of the war.[21]

That seemed an unusual touch of terror, coming from the usually unruffled defense secretary. Maybe, agitated as he seemed, McNamara should go out again and check the ground close up. Dutifully he went to Saigon in mid-July, taking with him Bus Wheeler and Cabot Lodge, who had been selected to return as ambassador at the end of the month.

Those who watched McNamara during his typically whirlwind survey of everything in Vietnam saw only the calm, congealed manager whose command of facts and people reached awesome dimensions. As it happened, his trip came at an important political moment in Saigon—the early weeks of the Ky-Thieu government. Almost inured to South Vietnamese instability, McNamara staged his interaction with the new regime in strictly official ways.

One thing about McNamara, he had an eye for his place in the news. Carefully casual, ever efficiently looking at things, a man on top of every situation, he projected the kind of Yankee drive greatly needed in the south. As he looked around, he could notice things were different in Saigon. Greed reached new heights of invention but the city clogged under smoke and crowds and a kind of raucous blending of old charms and new churls. An anticipation of waiting for the American deluge charged the air, but McNamara came with special things to see. Met by members of the country team, escorted to MACV headquarters, he and his group were treated to an interesting argument between the military and diplomatic people. Westy's arguments were made and recorded; Max Taylor and Alex Johnson demurred at the speedy buildup. They conceded the need for U.S. troops, but hoped to slow the flood of Americanization.

Westy caught the drift early. McNamara listened to him with only half an ear—he already agreed with the forty-four battalion request! In fact, he had asked for estimates on how many more men might be needed to deny victory to the North Vietnamese. Unperturbed by the estimate of a 275,000-man total, McNamara listened favorably to a three-phased MACV plan: first to stop losing, next to go on the attack in vital areas and reinstate pacification, and finally to mop up. It all sounded good, but no one ventured a guess as to how long it would take.[22]

At last the secretary met with the new government's leading figures, Nguyen Cao Ky and Nguyen Van Thieu. Adopting a formal, bustling kind of dynamism, McNamara paid scant attention to the people and bore down on a list of twenty-five questions he had sent in advance. A shrewd interpreter sat in on the meetings, not to McNamara's credit in history, and watched as the Vietnamese played their cards exactly as planned:

Q. How many allied troops would South Vietnam need by the end of the year?

A. Forty-four battalions, plus one for Saigon security.

Q. How would the South Vietnamese people accept so large a foreig force?

A. Americans were not regarded, in general, as colonialists—they woul slip the old French brand. Any possible entanglement would be avoided if U.S. forces operated mainly in the hinterlands, as Westy's pla prescribed.

Interpreter Bui Diem, later Saigon's ambassador to Washington, saw McNamara as "precise but affable, scribbling on a yellow pad," firing endless questions about troops, organization, logistics, and management, "as though he was bent on finding all the factors and components for the solution of some grand mathematical equation."[23] If McNamara had any impression of the new government he was working to support, it failed to appear in person or in documents. He had apparently formed a bad impression of Ky earlier, but he remained impassively correct, as did the Vietnamese.

Cyrus Vance, McNamara's deputy, interrupted the meeting with a cable saying that LBJ's "current intention" was to approve the forty-four battalion program, along with various deficit funding possibilities, and he was even contemplating calling up reserves. McNamara did not get all the answers he wanted from Westy or his staff about U.S. strategy in Vietnam (and thinks, to this day, he should have pressed for them). Finally he returned to Washington to file a report he had written before reaching Saigon.[24]

When he got back, he discovered that LBJ planned a complete review of the Vietnam situation as he prepared to make the decision so long hanging fire.

It all started at 10:40 A.M. on July 21, 1965, with the usual suspects dragooned for what all knew to be decisive times. On the agenda lay Westmoreland's request for massive intervention, buttressed by his clear belief that South Vietnam had no future without it. A colloquy began without the president, and some ideas surfaced about how the South Vietnamese wanted to use U.S. troops and how they finally agreed with the enclaves, then the "ink spots," and finally independent operations. Battle seemed the only option; Lodge acknowledged that channels were not open for negotiations. "If I thought a diplomatic move would be successful, I would be for it," he said. "Now it would harden the enemy."

Fears about enemy propaganda claims that Americans and South Vietnamese plotted a northern invasion triggered assertions by McNamara and others that measured responses—layered reserve call-ups and moderate budget increases—should be evidence enough "that we are not taking over North Vietnam, nor do we want to." McNamara emphasized that the United States needed to distance itself from Ky's brash boasts about "going north."

A phantom backdrop to all the talk lurked unspoken: If LBJ decreed acceptance of Westy's crisis program, how should it be implemented, and how should it be told to the public? Within a week, most thought, a public announcement should detail what would be done and why.

At 11:30, the president walked into the Cabinet Room. If he noticed that the green drapes were drawn and the room dimmed in artificial light, he gave no sign. Nothing dimmed his presence—larger than most men, bulkier in build and aura, LBJ filled the place. In a gray suit set off by a pale blue, high-collared shirt and blue-flecked tie, his face grave, a bit worn and studious, he looked the part of president. Striding quickly to his high-backed chair, he nodded to those seated at the table and sat down.

Softly he said, nodding to McNamara, "Would you please begin, Bob." So began a week of meetings, one after the other. All views were tested. McNamara stuck to Westy's guns and presented the case forcefully, with total command of facts and figures, and without the slightest hesitation. Subscribing to COMUSMACV's views on the crisis, the defense secretary went straight into the problems of providing the troops needed and keeping them operational in Vietnam. To sustain 200,000 men there, a number likely to be increased, he recommended calling up reserves at a rate of about 235,000 a year. By mid-1966, McNamara said, another 600,000 men would be available. He talked of support troops, of logistical areas, of all the mysterious needs of a modern and warring field army. As usual, most in the audience thought McNamara's was an impressive, highly professional performance—assuming basic premises were accepted.

Johnson listened with care when McNamara finished, the president leaned back in his chair, and pointed a long, yellow pencil at the defense secretary. Voice lowered almost to a whisper—so that everyone strained to hear—LBJ said, "What I would like to know is what has happened in recent months that requires this kind of decision on my part. What are the alternatives? I want this discussed in full detail, from everyone around this table."

Jack Valenti, sitting a little to the right and behind the president, watched him closely—there was no shaking of the pencil hand, no sign of nervousness, just the kind of intensity he brought to decisive moments. "He had summoned his disciplines," Valenti noted. "I knew he was beginning to circle the problem, approaching it from all sides, determined to find its soft spots, analyzing the chessboard, figuring with that rigorous intensity he brought to bear on any difficult problem what turns in the road would be permissible and how deep into uncharted territory he was prepared to go."[25]

LBJ had a knack for fixing on hard points and digging. He heard McNamara and Wheeler explain the need for more men. Seventy-five thousand could protect bases; more men would turn the tide to allied favor. Another hundred thousand for the present would not cause the Chinese or Russians to intervene. Clearly, something bothered Johnson. Fiddling with his tie clasp, he finally said that more men might produce greater casualties.

Wheeler disputed that: "The more men we have there the greater the likelihood of small losses."

Dissatisfied, tapping the pad in front of him, crouched in his chair, LBJ said, "Tell me this. What will happen if we put in 100,000 more and then two, three years later you tell me you need 500,000 more? How would you expect me to respond to that? And what makes you think if we put in 100,000 men, Ho Chi Minh won't put in another 100,000, and match us every bit of the way?"

Wheeler leaped to the challenge. "This means greater bodies of men from North Vietnam, which will allow us to cream them."

His response hardly calmed the president, who grumped about lack of good intelligence from the north and sagged wearily in his chair when Admiral Raborn told him that the CIA had a task force working on that very problem.

Nothing he heard that morning pleased the president. He told George Ball that he wanted to hear his assessment of other alternatives in the afternoon. And, as the president walked out of the Cabinet Room, he decided to invite Clark Clifford to the afternoon session.

Clifford came in a bit late to join "the most remarkable series of meetings that I had attended" in nearly thirty years. When he walked in he heard Ball intoning a familiar litany: "We can't win. The war will be long and protracted, with heavy casualties. The most we can hope for is a messy conclusion. We must measure this long-term price against the short-term loss that will result from a withdrawal." Ball obviously had trekked this course often, but he still attacked with zest. Almost every Great Captain, he told the president, at some time had to retreat—and this looked like one of those moments. "We can't even find the enemy in Vietnam," Ball observed. "We can't see him and we can't find him. He's indigenous to the country, and he always has access to much better intelligence. . . . I have grave doubts that any Western army can successfully fight Orientals in an Asian jungle." That old Taylor worry struck home with LBJ—Ball would come back to Western capability time and again. "What we are doing," said Ball "is giving cobalt treatment to a terminal cancer case. A long, protracted war will disclose our weakness, not our strength."[26]

Johnson looked hard at Ball and, almost with anguish, asked if withdrawal would not destroy America's credibility in the Far East and Europe. "If we were helping a country with a stable, viable government, it would be a vastly different story," Ball replied.

Clifford listened sadly as everyone else weighed in against Ball. His proposal was too late, represented a radical policy shift, and offered no indication of benefits, they said. Rusk and Lodge nailed Ball's coffin shut with calmly reasoned statements about the threat to world peace if America flunked the Vietnam test.

The next day the JCS had the podium, and LBJ opened with his estimate of the options: an "elegant bug-out;" maintain current U.S. strength and lose slowly; or add 100,000 men with the realization that more might be needed to prevent defeat. As the president listened to the military professionals, he realized they could not promise success with *any* numbers committed. They had come to accept denying a northern victory as their definition of success—and what it would take to convince the North Vietnamese they could not win, nobody knew. Finally, LBJ pushed Adm. David McDonald, the Chief of Naval Operations, to say that the United States could not win an all-out war, but was at the point of "get out now or pour in more men."

McNamara stridently supported what was called Plan I: sending 100,000 men, making a public announcement of bigger commitment, announcing a reserve call-up, and budgeting $2 billion to cover the cost. But LBJ's mind had shifted and McNamara missed the signals. The president wound up humiliating his defense secretary by publicly rejecting Plan I and accepting Plan III, which called for 100,000 men without a reserve call-up and only a $1 billion budget. It was a cruel moment for the hard-driving technocrat—to be told in public that his plan, agreed to with the military, would not fly. As McNamara's biographer said, "Johnson would make them fight not as past wars had been fought, with the public fully aware of the commitment and behind the fighting men; they would tiptoe into war."

It was one of Johnson's mean moments—those moments when he made subordinates feel like subordinates, brought them down to mortal status, and rode over them. And he knew what he'd done. After the meeting he slipped out a side door and said to Horace Busby, nodding toward McNamara, "Think we'll get a resignation out of him?" He knew there would be no resignation of that kind—just resignation to the realities of the administration.[27] And McNamara must have realized why Johnson picked Plan III—he did not want to fight for all the money or all the men.

Clifford grew increasingly depressed through the meetings of the twenty-first and twenty-second, and found himself feeling for George Ball more than ever. As he left the White House on the twenty-second, a guard told him the president wanted him. He went back to the little study off the Oval Office and found LBJ waiting there with Mac Bundy. What did Clifford think? Nothing if not honest, Clifford said, "The way the military acted today reminded me of the way they dealt with President Truman during the Korean War. Some of what General Wheeler said today was ridiculous." Looking at his meeting notes, Clifford quoted, "'the more men we have, the greater the likelihood of small losses. And if they infiltrate more men into the South, it will allow us to cream them.' These are disturbing statements. I don't believe they are being straight with us." Clifford boldly added that the president did not need to commit the country to heavy investments in Vietnam. "If you overplay the decision now under consideration, the nation will be committed to win a ground war in Asia. I asked myself two questions today as I listened to McNamara and the Chiefs. First, can a military victory be won? And second, what do we have if we do win? Based on what we have heard, I do not know the answer to either question."[28]

CLOSING ARGUMENTS

On Friday, July 23, 1965, Clark Clifford found himself in a kind of alliance with George Ball. He had read most of Ball's memoranda to the president, thought them persuasive, agreed with them, had said so, but feared that, in Ball's apt quoting of Emerson, "Things are in the saddle and ride mankind."[29]

There came one last chance to convince the president. Just before seven that night he got a call from LBJ. Come, he said, you and Marny, to Camp David tomorrow. Bob and Margie McNamara were coming, a few others, and "we would relax, and we would have a chance to talk privately about Vietnam." Accepting instantly, Clifford knew that "the stage was now set for the final argument." And that argument would be difficult. Bill Moyers, briefly doffing his impartial role as press secretary, had told Clifford that "it would take a miraculous effort to change the President's course—requiring not only a change in Johnson's mind, but also in Rusk's, McNamara's, and [Mac] Bundy's."

If George Ball had long felt like the "Lone Ranger," Clifford shared the feeling now. He had prepared often for tough courtroom moments, for hard-nosed judges and mean situations, but the Camp David meeting looked to be the hardest challenge of his life. George Ball, in passing the torch, put his faith in Clifford—the only one, he thought, "who had even the slightest chance to stem the rush toward disaster." Dubious of his persuasive powers, Clifford promised "a very hard and long talk" with Johnson. Impressive energies worked for war in the president's councils: Could LBJ, Clifford wondered, "reject the advice of his three top national security advisers—all inherited from Kennedy—as well as the unanimous advice of the Joint Chiefs of Staff and the Ambassador in Vietnam, himself a former Chairman of the Joint Chiefs of Staff? Could he change a policy that had the support of a substantial majority of the American public?"[30]

Clifford assessed his opponent in the time before leaving for Camp David. McNamara held the key, he knew, "in the process driving the President toward approval of Westmoreland's request"—a request that, six months earlier, Clifford knew McNamara would have rejected. What had happened? "Bob's mastery of facts and his analytical skills had led him, I felt, into a logical fallacy, but his reputation for personal integrity and the force of his personality were carrying the case against those few voices calling for a different course." Clifford had high respect and personal regard for McNamara, and probably did not fully grasp the psychological blow LBJ had just delivered him. The defense secretary, nevertheless, would be a tough opponent, and Clifford intended to fight him on utterly impersonal grounds.[31]

CAMP DAVID, JULY 25–26, 1965

Saturday proved a fine day for a helicopter ride to Camp David. The Cliffords joined the McNamaras, their son Craig, and Luci and Pat Nugent for the twenty-five minute flight to the mountains. Nothing about Vietnam clouded the holiday atmosphere.

Camp David looked glorious; a big compound, more rustic than luxurious, it boasted relaxingly isolated cabins for visitors. The newcomers found others ahead of them: Sen. and Mrs. Birch Bayh of Indiana, Supreme Court Justice Arthur J. Goldberg, who would be sworn in the next day as U.S. Ambassador to the UN (that was a story in itself), Jack Valenti, and Horace Busby. Everyone joined the Johnsons for dinner. The president struck Clifford as unusually subdued.

Most of Sunday passed in relaxation. Clifford worried about the coming bout and rehearsed his notes carefully. Keep it simple, he thought, stick to basics, things the president had heard before, but put them firmly into an overall U.S.-world context and in such order as to break McNamara's confidence. At 5 P.M. the call came to join the president at Aspen Lodge, a spacious building with a glassed-in living room that looked out over a gorgeous Maryland tableau.

Clifford had seen it often, and bits of it—Ike's golf course, furniture installed by different users—reminded him of other presidents he'd advised. This time Clifford saw things with a special clarity as he groped for arguments to fend off war.

They were in a hunting lodge with a big fireplace on one side. A large rectangular dining table served as the centerpiece. At the head of the table, his back to the fireplace, Johnson occupied his usual chair. Next on his right sat Clifford, curly hair coiffed carefully, thin face lined and serious, his papers arranged neatly in front of him. Straight across from him sat McNamara, hair slicked down, glasses aligned, fussing over a neat stack of notes. To McNamara's left sat Goldberg, round and energetic, his angular face set off by heavy-rimmed glasses, calm but curious in an unaccustomed role. Valenti, the note taker, sat poised on Clifford's right and, next to him, Busby.

Deferring to Goldberg, LBJ opened by talking about taking the Vietnam imbroglio to the UN and asked Clifford's opinion. It was too risky, Clifford said, for too little gain. Then he plunged into his own brief. He echoed many of George Ball's views, blending in his own as he argued against creating an impression that the United States was replacing the South Vietnamese to win a big Asian war. Why? Because the president needed to keep his options open and not be pinned to any particular course just yet. Knowing LBJ's penchant for personalizing most everything, Clifford said that the Vietnam situation was no one's fault. "The bombing might have worked, but it hasn't. A commitment like the one that we have made in Vietnam can change as conditions change. A failure to engage in an all-out war will not lower our international prestige. This is not the last inning in the struggle against communism. We must pick those spots where the stakes are highest for us and we have the greatest ability to prevail."

McNamara listened woodenly as Clifford went on with mounting emotion. He hated the war. If America sent more troops, so would the North Vietnamese. And if they ran short, China and Russia would help them. If America won, the prize would be long occupation of a war-torn, feckless land; if it lost after a massive effort, the result would be a disaster—the possible loss of more than fifty thousand men in five years. "It will ruin us," he said flatly. Then, turning directly to the president, he urged LBJ to hold on for the time being; send in a few more men, not a lot. After the coming monsoons, make another probe for negotiations, search for "an honorable way out." Lower America's expectations in Asia. "Let the best minds in your Administration look for a way out, not ways to win this unwinnable war. I can't see anything but catastrophe for my country."

Johnson thought briefly, then turned to the secretary of defense. Crisply, in his firm staccato voice, McNamara disagreed with Clifford's assessment of the Vietnam situation. Adding nothing new, he rehashed his earlier arguments. South Vietnam would fall without more U.S. troops, which would damage America's world prestige. Only quick action could prevent quick defeat. He was again the essential McNamara in action—unfazed, cool, certain in his convictions.

When McNamara finished, LBJ turned off debate—much to Clifford's disappointment. "Perhaps he sensed the futility of further debate," Clifford mused, "the lines were drawn clearly; he had heard the arguments on both sides, and there was little else to say." The meeting broke up, guests going to their cottages. While they waited to hear if they were going home or to dinner, Clifford noticed that LBJ walked out of the lodge, got into a car alone, and began driving around the camp area. He drove for an hour, came back to the lodge, got out, and began walking by himself.[32]

At last Johnson walked slowly back to Aspen Lodge. Looking a little less troubled, he opened the door to the big living-dining room and went in. He had accepted the best of no acceptable options.[33]

ENVOI

At a midday Washington press conference on July 28—deliberately not scheduled for prime time to subdue its impact—Lyndon Johnson made a major Vietnam speech, one that historians have oddly branded minor. He announced that more troops would go to Vietnam. He made no great fuss, made no special pronouncement, but he did speak of purposes. "What are our goals in that war-stained land? . . . We intend to convince the Communists that we cannot be defeated by force of arms or by superior power. They are not easily convinced. In recent months they have greatly increased their fighting forces, their attacks, and the number of incidents. I have asked the commanding general, General Westmoreland, what more he needs to meet this mounting aggression. He has told me. We will meet his needs."

The president dissembled deliberately by downplaying the number of men that were going—citing the earlier figure of 125,000 instead of the 175,000 actually agreed to—but he gave some specifics.[34]

"I have today ordered to Vietnam the Air Mobile Division and certain other forces," he announced, adding that "additional forces will be needed later, and they will be sent as requested." All of these actions would require a hike in the monthly draft calls—from seventeen thousand to thirty-five thousand—and an invigorated enlistment campaign.

An end to the fighting had been rigorously sought. The president commented on fifteen fruitless efforts to start talks with the North Vietnamese. So, he said, "we are going to continue to persist, if persist we must, until death and desolation have led to the same conference table where others could now join us at a much smaller cost."

Solemnly and earnestly Johnson added that

> I do not find it easy to send the flower of our youth, our finest young fighting men, into battle. I have spoken . . . of the divisions and the forces and the battalions and the units. But I know them all, every one. I have seen them in a thousand streets, of a hundred towns, in every State in this Union—working and laughing, building, and filled with hope and life. I think that I know, too, how their mothers weep and how their families sorrow.
>
> This is the most agonizing and the most painful duty of your President.[35]

Men still marched but no bands played.

chapter
EIGHT

Asian War, Western Style

lmost no one involved in the decision to enlarge America's part in the war felt good about what had happened. The president regarded the whole business as "painful," the result of South Vietnam's imminent demise, and was irked that "we have very little alternative to what we are doing."[1] A widening war brought all kinds of unforseen costs in its wake. With the Great Society bills rising, too, Johnson wrestled with the puzzle of financing two wars. As usual, in matters of figures, he sought McNamara's help.

Bob McNamara—himself depressed by a wrong-going war and smarting over LBJ's failure to call up reserves—met the challenge. He wrestled with cost factors, working to hold estimates down so that the expected $8 billion overrun coming in 1966 did not hit the headlines. He knew that the president feared a major congressional debate on war financing— that kind of open argument might well put the hawks in charge and produce a wider, fiercer war, and sink Johnson's domestic crusade. So McNamara, number-cruncher extraordinary, devised a cunning dodge. He ordered the Pentagon's money people to develop budgets based on the idea that fighting in Vietnam would stop at the end of the fiscal year— by June 30, 1967.

The president guessed that Congress would "give him the war, but not the Great Society," so he pushed boundaries of truth in constructing the coming budget. Both he and McNamara encouraged ignorance in various branches of government. The JCS, Admiral Sharp, and General Westmoreland urged large sums for a large war and chafed under the Defense Department's parsimony; LBJ's domestic troops pushed Great Society programs in virtual ignorance of military needs; the Council of Economic Advisors and Treasury Secretary Henry Fowler worked in a miasma of numbers, puzzled and unconvinced by low war estimates, but unable to penetrate Johnson's optimism and McNamara's smoke screen.[2]

What led McNamara to an artificial war estimate? One of his biographers caught the secretary's point about the June 30, 1967, cutoff date:

> This was arbitrary but made sense when the government faced a crisis . . . and . . . many agencies had to plan and allot funds on some common basis. The purpose of the cutoff was to let the military pay for its immediate needs but to disallow long-lead-time items justified on possible levels of conflict that were not certain. A very important dimension of budgeting for Vietnam . . . was that federal law made misestimation a crime. Thus a simple, uniform assumption, so long as McNamara said it was arbitrary, kept him and hundreds of government workers within the law.[3]

For the moment, however neither McNamara nor the president nor important congressional leaders wanted a tax increase. Johnson had a firm fix on congressional practice and knew he could get a war tax only by "wrapping himself in the flag" and accepting the fact of a big conflict. One of his economic advisors pointed out that "Johnson at that time was a dove. . . . As Toynbee says, it's easy as hell to get a democracy to hate somebody. He literally was afraid he'd lose control."[4]

If Johnson really doubted his control it was because he feared that if the radical right grew because of the war, he might have a hard fight for moderation. He might have won that fight but preferred no contest—and McNamara may well have given Johnson the out he most wanted. Arthur Krock, powerful head of the *New York Times*'s Washington bureau, speculated that the secretary of defense predicted an exit from Vietnam by the middle of 1967 and that Johnson jumped at the unlikely bait.[5]

But as McNamara planned and got caught up in force numbers and logistical details, he felt almost pulled apart by the excitement of a bigger war and the growing suspicion that even a bigger war was unwinnable. He began to filter some concern to LBJ[6] and to some of his own friends but still he exuded public optimism. Finally the war business overcame him and he began to turn his public views into a personal delusion. In a few months, when talking about the upcoming budget, he would boast: "Never before has this country been able to field and support in combat so large a force in so short a time over so great a distance, without calling up the reserves, and without applying price, wage and material controls to our civilian economy."[7]

And, as the enormous efficiency of the Vietnam buildup became clear, he would add with proprietary excitement that "we moved 100,000 men 10,000 miles in 100 days."[8] On television in August, 1965, the secretary of defense talked about North Vietnamese withdrawals and cited a positive body count: Between May and July, the enemy lost seven thousand men, while U.S. and allied losses were only three thousand.[9]

At the same time, McNamara's doubts ran deeper through late 1965 and early 1966—so deep they almost broke his psyche. Increasingly nervous, fearful of losing outward control, the super manager became a haunted war minister.

His growing doubts reflected an important shift in the outlook of several high-ranking defense officials—especially that of Assistant Secretary of Defense John McNaughton. McNaughton remains hard to see—he skirted the edges of the power he used like a youthful éminence grise. A year before, McNaughton's gyrations under McNamara's protection branded him a nearly hysterical hawk full of imaginative but baffling notions. Now, with various fats in the Vietnam cauldron, McNaughton returned to his contrariwise musings—musings with significance because Robert McNamara listened, and because, despite his arrogance and systems analyst jargon, he had a good reputation in the arms-control business.

What influence McNaughton actually held over McNamara remains mysterious; whether he led or followed is uncertain—but he had impact. Mechanistic, statistically minded, nearly a logician, McNaughton became a close confidant of McNamara's. He kept a hard face toward the war à la LBJ, but showed a softer profile in an exchange of private, highly secret memos with his boss that reveal mutually advancing unease.

Almost a bellwether of mounting confusion in the Defense Department, he leaked his doubts in conspiratorial talks with White House staffer Michael Forrestal, who, he found, shared some of his worries but clung to the notion that the U.S. government still controlled any foreign events it wanted. McNaughton knew how to play the Washington game and wanted to stay in it. So, like McNamara, he managed a duplicitous muffling of himself.

While he doubted the course the government pursued, he defended it "almost rudely." McNaughton continued his nimble role of proing and conning, following a chartless course of whims and warnings that saved his job. But his shifting mind resulted in a nervousness like McNamara's, so that boss and worker came to seem surprisingly alike as both planned war with faith fading.[10] In time, McNaughton's caution would look like realism.[11]

George Ball, faith long gone, found his fears escalating along with the fighting. He took little comfort from Rusk's worries about whether or not the United States should escalate,[12] since those worries did not translate into direct opposition. Having himself rejected the domino theory as an unsupported assertion,[13] Ball watched in mounting frustration as that theory shifted from geography to psychology. The old theory posited that neighboring states might fall to Communism in the wake of one country going under, which meant that if South Vietnam were absorbed by the north, Cambodia and Laos might also be lost. Geography, though, offered a possible alternative buffer: another anti-Communist bulwark might be built in Thailand without much loss of Western prestige. But the psychological theory left no options. Failure of U.S. strength anywhere would undermine world confidence in America's strengths and purposes, to let Vietnam go would amount to loosening America's grip everywhere.[14]

As that idea took hold, Ball fumed as he listened to colleagues wistfully wondering how North Vietnam could be brought to negotiation. Ball pointed out that everything was going the north's way, and that by sticking to their guns the North Vietnamese had every chance of winning. Then, too, the United States offered nothing but southern victory as a basis for peace. Hanoi would be foolish to alter its policies. "The battle-hardened leaders in Hanoi," Ball observed, "had no interest in mechanisms that would facilitate their crying 'Uncle'. . . their interest was in forcing us to go home."[15] While Johnson looked vainly for peace signals from the north, Ball hoped for a shift in American aims.

Those who waged the growing American war were frustrated in the wake of Johnson's escalation. True, he shared COMUSMACV's alarms about the south's pending ruin; true, he accepted Westy's call for forty-four battalions and more; true, he agreed to more and wider bombing—and yet, withal, he withheld things like the call-up of reserves, an unlimited budget, and a declaration of war. He seemed, to the Joint Chiefs and Westy and the men deep in Vietnam, not to know he had accepted war. Instead of waging it openly, he shied from the word and spoke of no change in the policy of helping South Vietnam stay free. What the military minds missed was fundamental: Johnson knew America had slipped into war, but he wanted it to remain limited, kept within bounds politics would permit. And he would test those bounds carefully.

But the president missed something equally fundamental: Waging limited war often depends more on the enemy than on domestic realities. And he, along with most of his advisors, missed the fanatical devotion of the North Vietnamese to the reunification of Vietnam. No one should have missed this point—thousands of casualties, years of effort, Hanoi's persistence and amazing resilience, was evidence aplenty.

WESTERN UNCLE

Most of the war fighters missed that point, too, for a time. As northern reinforcements poured south, Westy's optimism faded into predictions of a long war. He scrapped his earlier guess that only 300,000 men would be needed by the end of 1966—now 400,000 at least must come, and as many as 600,000 might be needed by the end of 1967. McNamara accepted those alarming numbers without public qualm, kept them secret, and stuck to the June 30, 1967, budget cutoff date and to his public promise to fight the most economical war in American history.

For their part, the South Vietnamese had mixed reactions to the heavy American commitment. The new government—with General Thieu as chief of state and Air Vice Marshal Ky as prime minister—which had toppled the civilian regime of Prime Minister Phan Huy Quat in mid-June, had some stability but looked squarely at its problems of consolidation and rejuvenation of the war. A large infusion of U.S. troops, needed as they certainly were, might play into the propaganda hands of the VC and North Vietnamese. South Vietnam more than ever, would look like a Yankee puppet. Bill Bundy echoed that idea when he suggested that "our . . . intervention would appear to be turning the conflict into a white man's war."[16] More than that, the ARVN's weaknesses had not been corrected. Defeats of the spring and summer had erased the best South Vietnamese mobile battalions; officer training lagged, as did recruiting, and a malaise of stagnation pervaded the armed services.

Historian Dave R. Palmer aptly observed that "American soldiers have never been characterized as light travelers, and those who fought in Vietnam were no exceptions." More Americans meant more of all things American—dispensed from the massive PXs blooming around the large bases. And, of course, the PXs leaked their wares to Saigon's—and other—streets. That leakage negated the main purpose behind such lavish support for the GIs: to keep, in Westy's words, "American soldiers and their dollars on their bases and out of towns and cities."[17] All the men and all their luxuries nearly ruined South Vietnam's tottering economy; despite the best efforts of both governments to minimize inflation, it soared to almost ruinous levels by 1966.

Inflation and increased hordes of U.S. servicemen looking for girls, booze, and diversion fanned the already rampant corruption, which further weakened the Thieu-Ky government.[18]

Most Americans already in country were encouraged by the U.S. commitment of more men to the Vietnam conflict. But not all of them. Some American advisors—men like John Paul Vann and others who wondered why the United States kept on—fixed jaundiced eyes on certain ARVN units and commanders and saw them as ineffectual. To some extent the charges were true, but the blame needed spreading. American advisors, many of them energetic, competent, and loyal to their mission of helping the ARVN, sometimes lacked perspective on their allies. They came, some of them, to share the MACV view that the ARVN could not be trusted and so should be shunted clear of the real war that U.S. troops waged. In their minds, the more Americans, the better the chances for victory.

Vann had, not long after he returned to Vietnam in March, 1965, come to the conclusion that "we are going to lose this war." To friends back in Denver he explained that southern "moral degeneration," coupled with the amazing discipline of the North Vietnamese, shifted the odds north of the DMZ. "This country [South Vietnam]," he said, "has pissed away its opportunities so long it is now force of habit—and apparently nothing is going to change them." Increased bombing, Vann thought, would not accomplish much, and he raged against the foolish optimism of southern leaders who pranced behind American firepower.[19] So, even though publicly accepting more Americans in the fray, Vann and others privately doubted success.

American servicemen grew into a great, pervasive presence in South Vietnam as the legions Lyndon Johnson had authorized poured across the Pacific and swelled MACV's troop strength by the end of 1965 to nearly 185,000 men.[20] By then, some of the advance elements had already been hammered in battles that did much to unhinge McNamara's positive certainties. Those battles were part of General Giap's strategy for escalating the war in 1965.

THE DONG XUAN CAMPAIGN

The Montagnard word for river was *Ia*, which is important because the first major confrontation of the new, American war came in the valley of the River Drang.

The location is important, far more than the derivation of the name, for the people who fought there, the things they did, and the fearsomeness of everything in that place will always be associated in history with the Battle of the Ia Drang Valley. The action in the valley had all kinds of interesting antecedents—all of them caused by the VC and North Vietnamese and by fears they generated.

An important background element was Gen. Vo Nguyen Giap's plan to cut South Vietnam in two in a *Dong Xuan* (winter–spring) offensive late in 1965—an objective much talked about at MACV and in Washington, and one of the reasons LBJ decided to escalate the war. Rumors had Giap's big attack hitting in various places, but splitting South Vietnam across its middle seemed a certain aim.

Actually, Giap hoped to win the war by capturing the central highlands and driving to the sea along the Route 19, Pleiku–Qui Nhon, axis. That drive would dishearten the ARVN and topple the already shaky Saigon regime. An ancient proverb partly dictated North Vietnamese strategy: "He who controls the Central Highlands controls South Vietnam," which had a modern corollary: "He who controls Route 19 controls the Central Highlands."[21]

Giap's plan had plausibility and his tactics were deft. He chose a line of attack that would further his objective and terrain suited to an attacking force of three NVA infantry divisions. Vietnam's central highlands are steep, craggy, nearly roadless jungled hills that offered cover for his nimble infantry and might confuse American reaction. When he launched his divisions from Cambodian bases he expected help from local VC units, and guessed that holding attacks around Saigon and other urban areas would limit South Vietnamese and U.S. reinforcements for the main battle zone. He had a problem, though, one he probably did not anticipate.

Allied commanders knew where Giap planned to attack because intelligence officers had done an accurate job of estimating the time and place. This concentrated Westy's attention on where and how to call Giap's hand. In a sense, Westy had made preliminary moves already. For one thing, he agreed with Giap's own theory that mobility would make the difference in the inhospitable areas where the enemy clustered. Mobility and vaunted American firepower—if they could be brought to bear in dense jungle conditions—ought to answer the nagging question of whether GIs could be effective in a hostile, Asian land.[22] That conviction made Westy's selection of troops easy: He would use the 1st Cavalry Division. Not only was it the first full U.S. division on the ground—it arrived in Vietnam from Fort Benning, Georgia, on September 11, 1965—but it was also an airmobile force, the most maneuverable unit in the MACV arsenal. Dave R. Palmer best describes it in *Summons of the Trumpet:*

> The 1st Cavalry travelled on wings and rotors rather than legs and wheels. It had nearly 450 helicopters, five times as many as were found in a normal infantry division. It was an infantry-artillery-cavalry-aviation organization which went to war on the wind. Everything hinged on the helicopter: firepower, maneuver, command and control, reconnaissance, logistics, even administration. Jungles and mountains were not serious obstacles to it, nor were wide rivers or great expanses or a dearth of roads.[23]

If MACV headquarters nursed some doubts about how Americans would do against enemy regulars, the air cavalry people had no doubts at all—they would bring a new dimension to the Vietnam War, a dimension that would put the North Vietnamese permanently on the defensive. Destruction would come to the enemy at the hands of one of the army's most fa-mous—or infamous—units, the 7th Cavalry, known for its regimental song "Garry Owen" and for Custer's Last Stand. The men of the modern 7th Cavalry unfortunately had some old problems—like Custer's men, they did not know all they needed to know about their commander's strategy or tactical intentions, about the coming operations, or about the coming battle-fields. Nor did they know much about the enemy—except that NVA regulars were somewhere in large numbers. The air cavalry would do the usual infantry thing: find the enemy, fix him, fight him, and finish him.

Not "blooded" in Vietnam fighting, the men of the 1st Cavalry Division still had some veteran canniness and knew that much hung on their performance—if they flushed a big enemy force, the first battle would set a vital tone. They spoiled for a fight.

As it happened, the North Vietnamese high command agreed completely about the importance of drawing first blood. North Vietnam had been infil-trating regular units into the south for some time, but by late 1965 the plan to split South Vietnam apart for a quick win had been postponed indefi-nitely. President Johnson's July decision to send large numbers of troops to the south altered northern plans. The North Vietnamese knew they would have to engage the Americans. What they did not know was if they could overcome vaunted Yankee firepower and mobility. So they, too, spoiled for a fight.

Everything but the stage was set. And the stage depended on a series of complex variables. One exit from Uncle Ho's trail snaked into South Vietnam from Cambodia near an imposing mountain known as the Chu Pong[24] Massif, which offered an almost perfect assembly point for infiltrators aiming at the Civilian Irregular Defense Group [CIDG]/U.S. Special Forces base near Plei Me, about thirty miles southwest of Pleiku. That base figured heavily in the plans of Brig. Gen. Chu Huy Man, the NVA commander, and one of Giap's old friends.[25] He directed two full regiments to rendezvous at Chu Pong.

Since basic northern strategy had shifted from controlling the highlands to engaging the Americans, the choice of ground became more important than ever. If General Man could control the battlefield, he might well negate allied mobility, or at least limit its effectiveness. Employing standard NVA tactics, he plotted to suck ARVN troops into an ambush from which he guessed the Americans would try to rescue them by swarming in with their helicopters. He would destroy the rescuers and take over the area. The base at Plei Me took center stage.[26]

"NUMBERS . . . ARE A LANGUAGE TO ME"

It was all going wrong. Everybody's predictions had shifted. Even what it was the United States wanted to accomplish in Vietnam had changed. Robert McNamara had helped sell the notion that U.S. policy remained fixed on denying victory to the North Vietnamese. Now, in late November, Barry Zorthian, the public relations man in the Saigon embassy, could be heard telling reporters something different. "The name of the game has changed," he briefed a small group of favorites. "Now we're going to win." There would be no more of the namby-pambiness about denying victory to the enemy. Westy had tested things in Vietnam and in Washington and come up with a winning plan. It would be costly, it might require as many as 750,000 Americans, but victory would crown U.S. efforts.[27]

The defense secretary knew better. John McNaughton had been warning him and, in an early November memo to LBJ, McNamara had voiced a few more hesitant doubts as whiffs of hard fighting reached the department. The president read depressing estimates of more men needed. The Phase I deployments, McNamara said, had saved South Vietnam, but sticking with present arrangements likely would produce nothing more than a "compromise outcome," which the secretary labeled probably "unstable, difficult to sell domestically, and damaging to 'U.S. political effectiveness on the world scene.'"

Uncertain about policy, even more uncertain about success, McNamara lamented the failure of the Saigon government to make economic progress and its creeping loss of interior control and national authority. He confessed amazement at Hanoi's resilience. New enemy numbers negated earlier U.S. projections. Not an optimist about the ability of U.S. technological wizardry to sweep the fields, McNamara saw the bleak possibility of cutting U.S. losses and abandoning South Vietnam—a possibility he rejected because too much had been invested to quit, or even to lower public expectations about the war. Despite his own pessimism, the defense secretary told LBJ that in order to avoid stagnation, even "disintegration," more men must go to Vietnam in accordance with the planned program. However, the additions should be tied to a bombing halt of some duration to give Ho Chi Minh a chance—if he wanted it—to negotiate, and also to convince America and the world that everything had been done for peace. Most importantly, he added that "it would probably tend to reduce the dangers of escalation after we resumed the bombing."

Few other documents pack the import of this fifteen-page November 3, 1965, memo. It reveals a beleaguered soul riding two horses on divergent tracks. And it is, in some ways, a sad confession of mental and moral bankruptcy. Numbers spoke to him, he said, and their message was alarming: In the summer of 1965 Hanoi had more than 71,000 regulars in the south (up from 6,000), cadres were up to 40,000 (more than a third higher), and guerrillas counted 110,000 (a fifth more than at year's beginning). These numbers told another story, one that McNamara knew but hated to admit: the bombing had not crippled the north's capacity to overmatch U.S. reinforcements.

Bravely McNamara told the president that "none of these actions assures success . . . the odds are even that despite our effort, we will be faced in early 1967 with stagnation at a higher level and with a need to decide whether to deploy Phase III forces, probably in Laos as well as in South Vietnam."[28] More than that, he suspected that by early 1967 American losses might run between 500 to 800 men a month. The tone of the memo, its miasmatic details between hard points, shows that McNamara realized he had made horrendously bad guesses about numbers and duration—points LBJ would not miss. The secretary's credibility was at stake and slipping.

In late November, McNamara departed for a NATO gathering in Paris—without plans to visit Saigon. An urgent request from Westy changed his plans; the general wanted forty battalions instead of twenty-eight for his second phase increments! All previous calculations were out the window. McNamara went from Paris to Saigon to argue on the ground.

Visits by VIPs always churned juices at MACV headquarters. Westy's staff had a well-orchestrated scenario to impress high-level snoopers from Washington, CINCPAC, or from the allies. Handsome, crisply uniformed field-grade officers (majors or colonels), reinforced by legible maps, slides, pointers, and a good loudspeaker system, followed the general to the podium, echoed his welcome, and delivered the word for the moment. Skilled speakers, these briefers dazzled listeners with a barrage of military jargon buttressed with tales of fine units, well-run operations, enemy body counts, the high morale of U.S. forces, and devastating air strikes—all done with an air of dauntless optimism.

McNamara understood that kind of treatment. An old hand himself at dazzling brass, he usually tried to get out of Saigon and see something of the field. This time, though, he wanted to huddle closely with Westy. The people who came with the secretary of defense—General Wheeler, General Johnson, and Admiral Sharp—awed even the most jaded headquarters hands. Rumors ran the gamut about the coming powwow. Was Westy in trouble? He seemed unflustered as the briefings continued.

Not unaware of the McNamara numbers fetish, staffers concentrated on them. They reported that "The VC/PAVN [People's Army of Vietnam] buildup rate is predicated to be double that of U.S. projected forces." McNamara listened intently to the effect of these enemy increments. "This development has already reduced the November battalion equivalent ratio from an anticipated 3.2 to 1, to 2.8 to 1, and it will be further reduced to 2.5 to 1 by the end of the year." Predictions were bad. "If the trend continues, the December 1966 battalion equivalent ratio, even with the additions planned, will be 2.1 to 1."[29] Obviously more Americans were the answer.

Questions told the briefers something: The visitors were concerned about the recent battles between U.S. units, the VC, and the NVA. There had been several encounters, but actions in one operation called Silver Bayonet, caught the visitors' attention. This campaign involved the airmobile 1st Cavalry Division, which Westy had sent to find General Man's troops in the Ia Drang Valley. Aimed at finding the enemy in large numbers somewhere in Pleiku Province, Silver Bayonet began on October 23, 1965, and ran through November 20.[30] Although it had begun quietly enough, things quickly heated up for the 1st Cav, and its casualties were what caught the attention of all the flag officers descending on Saigon. What had happened?

Westy said he thought U.S. operations since the July commitments had been successful, the Ia Drang operations especially so. He had long believed that high mobility would allow massive U.S. firepower superiority to dominate Vietnamese battlefields. If that were true, his search-and-destroy strategy—a strategy of attrition—would finally save South Vietnam, even win the war. If any of his colleagues doubted it, he offered a nearly on-the-scene briefing by the man who had commanded the main fight in the Ia Drang Valley, the first real test of airmobile doctrine.

The brass boarded helicopters and rode northeastward over the recent Ia Drang battle site toward An Khe. A sleepy hill town on Route 19, An Khe had been enlarged by chopping back the jungle. It had the kind of busy barrenness to mark it an important military base. It had, too, that November 29, a number of resting troopers who watched the glittering entourage arrive with some bemusement. What were *they* doing in a war zone? How did *they* like the stifling heat and the choking dust spraying all over them on touchdown?

Unfazed and clearly expected, the visitors went quickly to a briefing tent with the 1st Cavalry Division's commander, Maj. Gen. Harry W. O. Kinnard, who had arranged presentations by his own staff and by Lt. Col. Harold G. Moore, the man in charge at Landing Zone (LZ) X-Ray.

LANDING ZONE X-RAY

Kinnard discussed the overall activities of his division in recent months, confessed there were more than 230 U.S. soldiers in body bags, and another 240 or so wounded, but boasted of nearly 3,500 NVA casualties.[31] He also lauded the nearly fifty thousand helo sorties during the Ia Drang campaign with only four shot down. Then he turned the meeting over to the tall, blue-eyed, wiry Hal Moore. A West Pointer, twenty-year soldier, and veteran of some of the toughest combat yet in Vietnam, Moore had qualms about briefing McNamara: "I had heard the secretary of defense had a fearsome reputation as a human computer, insensitive to people."[32] And there he sat in the front, glasses squared, without expression.

Moore knew he had only a short time in which to talk about what the 1st Battalion, 7th Cavalry—his men—had done at X-Ray. He had maybe twenty minutes. He would use no notes, notes would have interfered with the implosion of feeling that battle memories bring, with the pallid faces of the living, the wounded, and the dead. Moore did have a map and a pointer. He glanced at the tent full of high-ranking officers and civilians, then turned to the map and back in his thoughts. How can emotion be translated into sere fact?

Men were facts of varying kinds. The ground they walked and bled over was fact, too. The heat, the dust, the dryness, the Ia Drang Valley, Chu Pong, the LZ—all these were facts. But they were more—they were talismans in blood that froze a slice of wonder forever in his mind. Moore began with his orders to find the enemy, went to a quick description of the Plei Me fight that had frustrated North Vietnamese plans and sent them back toward the Chu Pong Massif. He talked then of selecting the LZ because it could handle from eight to ten helicopters; of anxious moments on November 14, 1965, when his first companies were landing right in front of the mountain; of wondering if Charlie looked down on everything his understrength battalion did; of the long, fiery hours until extraction on November 16. Moore managed somehow to keep his briefing professional as he let memories of the battle come. The roar of rotors and support planes, the dust, the heat, the man-high anthills, the smell of dry elephant grass, the green tracer patterns, the sharp popping of small-arms fire, the shouting, cries, growls, the thunderous shelling engulfed him once again.

It all flooded back in an angry, terrible tempo, but Moore rigidly edited memory as the fire touched his mind.

His listeners would know about the B-52s' first commitment to ground support as they pounded Chu Pong Mountain with 5,000 bombs;[33] they would know, too, of the awesome fire support the battalion received from big guns arrayed at LZ Falcon, of the 33,108 rounds of 105mm shells sheeting in from about five miles east of X-Ray; of the reinforcements helicoptered in under fire. So Moore talked about the enemy, their cool unconcern for casualties, their discipline. And he talked about his men. That was the hardest part, because he cherished them so, had seen them grow in battle. He groped for words to tell their valor.

Could his audience know about the noncommissioned officers, those corporals and sergeants and specialists who knit the companies together? About the lieutenants and the captains who held their lines against attacks of sometimes more than 10 to 1? Of the wounded officers and men who refused to quit, the men on the M-60 machine guns who held their positions until overrun, and the "grunts" who died alone in the grass, often surrounded by enemy dead? Could he tell them anything sensible about the platoon that got lost several hundred meters from his main perimeter and, with its lieutenant dead, held on under a sergeant who called in covering artillery fire to within twenty-five yards of his squad-sized line of effectives? Could he squeeze into coherence the forty-eight hours without sleep he and his eight hundred men endured under constant attack or imminent threat by more than two thousand North Vietnamese who were constantly reinforced?

He could not talk about the tragedy at LZ Albany, the disaster that befell Lt. Col. Robert McDade's 2d Battalion, 7th Cavalry, but he knew it had overtones of the Little Big Horn.

What of his emotional refusal to depart the battlefield when relief came because he would not leave anyone behind, living or dead, and he feared three sergeants from C Company were lost? He had been awake for forty-eight hours, he had won the battle, but the flush was still on, and he could not bear the thought of men missing. Weeping, wildly waving his rifle, he shouted, "I won't leave without my NCOs. I won't leave without them." He kept men searching until everyone was found.[34]

He could talk numbers, not happy ones, but numbers that the sober defense secretary could grasp: His battalion had suffered 79 killed and 121 wounded, none missing; enemy killed and wounded totaled nearly 2,000; captured enemy arms included "fifty-seven AK-47s, fifty-four SKS carbines, seventeen Degtyarev automatic rifles, four Maxim heavy machine guns, five RPG-2 rocket launchers, two 82mm mortar tubes, two 9mm ChiCom pistols, and six enemy medic kits. Engineers collected and destroyed another hundred rifles and machine guns, three hundred to four hundred hand grenades, seven thousand rounds of ammunition, three cases of RPG rockets, and 150 entrenching tools."[35]

Moore added that "brave American soldiers and the M-16 rifle won a victory" at X-Ray. The men made the difference, of course. As JFK once remarked, "any danger spot is tenable if men—brave men—will make it so."[36]

Winning always sounds good, and Hal Moore described victory coming from the cooperation of all arms and from courage. Finally he stepped away from his map, faced the secretary of defense, and said, "Sir, that completes my presentation." In the silence that followed, Westy, sitting near the secretary, basked in an "impressive" performance and determined to recommend a Presidential Unit Citation for Moore's battalion. McNamara got up, walked to Moore, looked him straight in the eye, and shook his hand firmly, without words.

There were no questions, and McNamara would tell Westy those were the best briefings he had heard "during his 5 years in office."[37] Numbers made things clear to him, and the numbers he had heard changed the equations in McNamara's mind. Lots of Americans were dying. Things were going wrong.

They were going wrong in ways beyond numbers. Lessons always follow battles, and Ia Drang had many for both sides. In some ways it had echoes of First Bull Run in the American Civil War, which bathed the South in hubris and depressed the North. But both sides counted LZ X-Ray a victory. Clearly the air cavalry concept had proved itself by the massive casualties inflicted against comparatively few losses. The enemy had withdrawn, left the field—another measure of success. For their part, the North Vietnamese would have taken even more casualties if necessary to learn how to fight the helicopters and the massive American use of air support and artillery fire. They learned, so they thought, to "hold on to the buckles" of the Americans, to pull in and fight them closely. That negated the U.S. firepower advantage and forced a decision on the ground.

Moore knew his battle had importance and assessed it shrewdly as marking a sea change in the Vietnam War. Decisions would have to be made in Washington and in Hanoi, and they would have to be made soon.[38]

Probably the best quick appreciation of what had happened came from *New York Times* reporter Neil Sheehan, who arrived at X-Ray during the cleanup. Standing near Hal Moore's anthill command post, he mused that "this could be the most significant battle of the Vietnam War since Ap Bac."[39] True.

Still trying to find the new boundaries of Vietnamese reality, McNamara went up to Da Nang for a look at the Marines. He liked them, although he guessed their unbridled optimism came more from habit than perception. Still, he enjoyed hearing that pacification seemed to be going well in I Corps territory—though he probably flinched at the total honesty of a briefing colonel who admitted that "once the Marines seemed to have pacified an area, they moved on, and there was a tendency of the Vietcong to come back, and do just as well as before."

The National Broadcasting Corporation's Sander Vanocur hitched a ride back to Saigon with McNamara, and the secretary asked his view of the visit. When Vanocur confessed depression, McNamara wondered why. Vanocur replied that "we were going to be spread too thin, that it seemed to him a bottomless pit. 'Every pit has its bottom, Mr. Vanocur,'" said the icy man of numbers.[40]

But the numbers were melting in the shifting fog of war. Westmoreland—the man most everybody trusted to save South Vietnam and burnish American honor—seemed proud of his attrition scheme, which looked suspiciously like Paul Harkins's old "kill the enemy" program. But now Westy was fudging his optimism by saying that "the war had been characterized by an overestimation of the Vietnamese," and that more men were needed to press the attack. Losses, he conceded, would mount on both sides.[41] Vietnam had a way of dulling martial minds, it seemed—and of quenching vision, too.

There was another surprise for Secretary McNamara. A visit with Prime Minister Ky melted more numbers. After two years of Westy's attrition, Ky said, the Saigon government expected to control only 50 percent of the country—15 percent less than he had guessed back in July.[42]

A lot of people pointed to the survival of South Vietnam as proof that LBJ's July commitment had saved the situation. Probably. But how much was enough?

CHANGED ILLUSIONS

Always before, the trip back from Saigon had seemed long; this time it seemed hardly long enough. McNamara worked on planes, generally editing facts written before finding. He had a notion of conditions before his visit to MACV, but this time he seemed to have gone through the looking glass. His frightful glimmering of error now shone in certainty. People in the Pentagon saw it immediately. Some of the bounce had gone, a deeper seriousness touched his eyes. People in the White House saw it, too, when McNamara arrived on November 30 for a quick meeting with the president. Chester Cooper, Mac Bundy's Vietnam deputy, noticed that McNamara looked "concerned . . . grave, either about what he saw in Saigon or about the upcoming meeting giving the news to LBJ, or both."[43]

Both, of course, because he had seen things that cracked his confidence and he had to confess mistakes. McNamara handed a grim-faced president a three-page supplement to his November 3 memo. The addition noted alarming changes in the Vietnam situation and warned of "the increased infiltration from the North and the increased willingness of the Communist forces to stand and fight." Still clinging to numbers, even contradictory ones, McNamara pointed out that North Vietnam could have more than 150 battalions in the south by the end of the next year, when, he hoped, enemy "losses can be made to equal his input." If McNamara looked worried, so did LBJ. Somber and beleaguered, he listened to an anguished man. McNamara's news briefings had shifted, too, from predicting relatively quick success to voicing the probability of a long war.

Johnson surveyed his war minister with a shrewd eye to body language. It was evident the man's firmament had gone soft. He'd guessed wrong about the bombing, obviously; hordes were coming south on the Ho Chi Minh Trail. And he'd guessed wrong about how the enemy would fight and how many GIs it would take to prevail. Concern etched the defense secretary's usually placid visage. Too much waffling in the government over the last few months had left him as confused as the president. Back in July, the certainty that Giap planned a swift victory spurred Johnson to escalate; then reports of an enemy policy shift back toward the guerrilla stage of war cast doubt on whether many more Americans were necessary; now, although Giap did not aim at quick victory, he seemed willing to commit big units to big battles.

All of this confusion made Westy's bludgeoning seem reasonable, after all. What did McNamara want him to do? LBJ wondered.

Send what Westy wanted, came the reply. That seemed the only course that would prevent failure and preserve an option or two for success. Beef up American troop strength to four hundred thousand by December, 1966, but recognize that more—perhaps as many as two hundred thousand more men—might have to go in 1967.

If we do all this, LBJ asked, will things get better? Awash in mea culpas, the secretary made another confession: "deployments of the kind I have recommended will not guarantee success." Even worse, "U.S. killed-in-action can be expected to reach 1,000 a month." Warmed to the fullness of truth, he said that "the odds are even that we will be faced in early 1967 with a 'no-decision' at an even higher level" of loss.[44]

McNamara already had bundles of information from MACV: proposed deployment schedules, logistical support requirements, the million details of spreading from a small conflict to a major war. He would have been depressed to know that Westy had not finished planning the 1966 campaign and that while McNamara spoke bleakly with LBJ of higher war costs, their field commander was gathering more data for a conference with Oley Sharp in Honolulu—data that would push the numbers higher than ever.[45]

Aware of LBJ's discomfort with these new uncertainties, aware of rising public protest against the war, at the end of November, 1965, McNamara offered the president a dissembler's gambit: Going back to his suggestions of bombing pauses, McNamara pointed out that it would likely defuse much domestic unrest to make a splashy effort to get Hanoi into negotiations. "It is my belief that there should be a three or four week pause in . . . bombing the North before we either greatly increase our troop deployments to Vietnam or intensify our strikes against the North. . . . we must lay a foundation in the minds of the American public and in world opinion for such an enlarged phase of the war, and . . . we should give North Vietnam a face-saving chance to stop the aggression."[46]

WOBBLING TOWARD DECISION

McNamara's dithering bothered LBJ, and his restless harping on a bombing pause brought his judgment into question. Johnson could hardly have missed the inconsistency.[47] Since the secretary kept urging more men and more force, what sort of terms could be offered Hanoi? Surrender? Good question.

Few others in the White House inner circle wanted the bombing stopped. Dean Rusk took a hard line. A pause should come "only when and if the chances were significantly greater than they appear that Hanoi would respond by reciprocal actions." As for foreign opinion, Rusk suggested that a pause would become imperative "only if we are about to reach the advance stages of an extrapolated Rolling Thunder program, involving extensive air operations in the Hanoi/Haiphong area" sometime in the future.[48]

The soft-spoken secretary of state had nerves of steel, and his World War II experience taught him the virtues of toughing war out. Then, too, he understood his boss probably better than anyone else in the cabinet. Shared backgrounds and prejudices gave them an almost telepathic empathy, and Rusk knew Johnson would not "cut and run." Rusk agreed fully.[49]

To pause or not to pause stirred a great debate in the administration that might have produced a general review of national Vietnam policy. That did not happen because almost every one of the policy makers was locked into small niches of the larger situation. Mac Bundy wanted to look at broader things, but pressures from the Oval Office kept him mired in details and manning barricades against dissension. Rusk saw no real need to disinter bones merely to rebury them. The president fretted that everything he and his advisors did seemed to darken the "black cloud" of Vietnam. Jack Valenti, valiantly trying to relieve pressures on the president, saw Vietnam as "a fungus on the face of the Johnson Administration. The more you itched, the more fungus grew, the more you had to itch." That fungus spread everywhere, Valenti noted. "No matter what we turned our hands and minds to, there was Vietnam, its contagion infecting everything that it touched, and it seemed to touch everything."[50]

Besieged himself, McNamara shared LBJ's frustrations with no new ideas, with the old strategy, the same old escalation, the same old North Vietnamese countermeasures. He looked desperately for fresh notions—and hence latched gleefully onto a proposal from some Harvard and Massachusetts Institute of Technology faculty members to build an electronic barrier along the seventeenth parallel from the coast westward to Laos. This high-tech barrier would consist of a line of small, sensitive sensors that could detect footfalls, air-droppable mines, and hostile fire. Supported by Marine strong points along the line, the sensors would slow enemy infiltration southward. If they worked, maybe the bombing would become redundant and the North Vietnamese would agree to talk.[51] Anything that might halt bombing attracted McNamara, so he supported the idea strongly.

He kept pushing for a bombing halt. Deep in his mind lurked the notion that a pause would slow the inexorable escalation that skewed all rational figures.

Old Washington hand that he was, McNamara cast a net for helpers. He found that Rusk, the hard-line opponent of a bombing pause, had softened a bit and might be willing to support a limited stoppage. Mac Bundy thought nothing would be lost by a halt and joined the group. The three of them sought an audience with Johnson in early December. When they met at the LBJ Ranch on the seventh, they knew they had a hard sell ahead. The president remembered that the six-day bombing halt in May had fizzled, opening the way for a flood of supplies along the Ho Chi Minh Trail. Skeptical, to say the least, Johnson listened to a recital of recent rumors of diplomatic activity from various quarters.

Peace rumors always were rife, but recent ones came from a speech made at the UN by Janos Peter, the Hungarian foreign minister, who flatly stated that Hanoi would agree to talks if the United States stopped bombing. He repeated the statement in a meeting with Dean Rusk and said the talks could be in Budapest. Aware that this overture had more substance than most, Rusk gave the Hungarian chargé d'affaires a fourteen-point U.S. peace plan for Vietnam that softened preconditions, welcomed "unconditional negotiations," accepted Hanoi's four points as discussable, allowed VC participation in peace talks, left reunification to the Vietnamese, and dangled a unilateral bombing halt.[52]

Always more relaxed at the ranch, LBJ still took a tough line as he listened to his three guests. They were united in thinking that something might be gained from a pause. Finally, pushing as he always did to get all the facts out, Johnson revealed his deep worry. "If we should stop for a while," he mused, "and Hanoi did nothing in return . . . would we not have trouble resuming the bombing?" No, came the return speculation; the United States would gain enough sympathy by trying for peace to cover any future necessities. Unconvinced, Johnson pressed the point. "Are you sure it will be that easy?" None of them saw resumption of bombing or troop reinforcements "as a serious problem."[53]

The president could not have missed the touch of cynicism in Mac Bundy's position. He advocated the halt, but thought it ought to be "hard-nosed, and we should expect that it will not lead to negotiations, but it will strengthen your hand both at home and abroad as a determined man of peace facing a very tough course in 1966."[54] Cynicism did not bother the president—he probed for varying views for any reasons.

No conclusion came from the Texas talks, which hardly surprised, though it must surely have frustrated, the visitors. Johnson often stalled over big decisions—to the point of sorely testing the patience of his advisors.

Still worried about a pause, the advantage it might give the enemy, and about how to renew things later, he kept pondering. The coming of the Christmas season brought some diversions, not all of them happy, but one of them potentially useful: Prime Minister Harold Wilson was en route to Washington and might work to end Vietnam's agonies.

Every year, the President of the United States lighted the huge Christmas tree on the Ellipse, across Executive Avenue from the White House. Set for December 17, 1965, that moment loomed as a special opportunity to indicate some initiative distinctly different intended for Southeast Asia, especially since Wilson would sit on the rostrum with LBJ for the effulgent moment. Johnson knew an announced bombing pause would please Wilson, perhaps help him in Britain's political lists, and help calm world opinion. With that in mind, he asked faithful, woefully overworked Jack Valenti to get with George Ball, Bill Moyers, and Mac Bundy to see if something important might be worked out.

When Valenti got the uncommonly small group together, he noted interesting results. Although Mac Bundy had touted a pause in Texas, his mind had shifted some and, when talking with Ball and Valenti, he leaned against it. Ball wanted it, as did Valenti. The president wanted a report on the meeting and Jack knew he had to buttress his own views carefully so that reason would triumph over mere dovishness.

ANOTHER GLIMPSE OF THE BLACK CLOUD

"We are in quicksand," Valenti wrote LBJ as Tuesday evening, December 14, ended. "The war is going to be hard and bitter and bloody days are ahead." Nothing good loomed on the Vietnam horizon. "The longer the war goes the deeper goes the bitterness and higher go the walls of hate." There must be a better way, Valenti urged. "Thus, we need to do all we can NOW to end the fighting before we are in so deep we can never get out."

No direction looked weatherable to this most loyal aide. Bombing the north only hardens enemy resolve, he said, despite contrary U.S. military views. He had talked with Ambassador Llewellyn Thompson, who had been the U.S. Moscow man, and asked what he thought about a bombing pause. Thompson urged it, said he thought it would be "received with relief and hope in Moscow" because the Russians would be able to get out of "the painted corner they've been in and possibly may move toward helping in a settlement." Shoring up the strong side, Valenti said that fighting should proceed apace in the south; that would cool suggestions that American boys would be sacrificed by a bombing lull. He took something of Rusk's, McNamara's, and Bundy's Texas line when he said that bombing could resume without trouble if Hanoi gave no hint of interest.

Assessing shrewdly his boss's concern about China, Valenti argued that "a pause would take some of the heat off the Chinese—and possibly deter them from moving in greater weight to Hanoi. Moreover, it would give Hanoi less dependency on the Chinese, and thereby allow the North more freedom of negotiating movement."

Valenti saw important domestic political advantages in that leftist arguments would, for a moment, be blunted. Looking out over the White House ramparts, Valenti thought a bombing pause "would allow third [world] countries, both friends and neutrals, more breathing room, and possibly edge the thrust of world opinion in a direction more congenial to us."

Closeness to the president lent Valenti a kind of charming candor. "But, above everything and all else," he confessed, "the largest logic for a pause is simply that it is the best alternative we have now to an endless, bloody war where there is no light in the tunnel." Trouble, he thought, would most likely come from the Republicans, "who are urging the blockade and quarantine of Haiphong. There is logic here, as Bundy pointed out, and we'll have to find some sound reason for not doing it—though if the pause is ineffective after a time, it is always there for us to do." Buttressing the prohalt argument, Valenti addressed LBJ's main worry. "Simply stated, sir, the pause doesn't disallow us any alternatives for a harder push. But it would give us opportunities for possible talks. And the hope is worth the try."[55]

Knowing that Valenti understood his deep desire to get peace talks going, LBJ grilled him for more than an hour to test how "firm my . . . recommendation was."

A sober president greeted Valenti, Mac Bundy, Rusk, McNamara, and George Ball in the Cabinet Room just after 9 A.M. on December 17. Johnson talked of preliminary words with Prime Minister Wilson and his ideas about Vietnam, then rambled on for a bit about the UN and the media. Nothing bad done by the VC got publicized Johnson observed, while every little thing the United States did in Vietnam was portrayed as some kind of atrocity. "Everything that is being written is done to make the world hate us," LBJ lamented.

George Ball, picking up on an important point, observed, "There is something of a racial element in what we do to the North, but it is not there when the North hits the South."

Sitting in his big chair, Johnson nodded. "They do such a better propaganda job than we do. On NBC today it was all about what we are doing wrong. . . . Harold Wilson told me his line has been steady since my Baltimore speech. Wilson is telling his opposition to bring the VC to the conference table and he will produce the president."

Leaning forward, clasping and unclasping his big hands, Johnson made a fervent assertion: "I am willing to take any gamble on stopping the bombing if I think I have some hope of something happening that is good." He had talked to Fulbright, to Walter Lippmann, and to other opponents of the war and had not turned them—"but we must listen to what they are saying."

As though he had not listened and had forgotten his original position, McNamara blurted, "Mr. President, we will increase bombing. It is inevitable. We must step up our attacks."

Ball then took up his old and lonesome cudgel. "I am holding a heretical view," he confessed, "but I think the bombings in the North are having a negative effect. If we look hard at the bombing in North Vietnam it is not producing a salutary effect." Looking hard at the president, Ball did a quick survey of the bombing situation. "We started bombing, one," he reminded his listeners, "to raise morale; two, to interdict supplies; and three, to get Hanoi to change its mind.

"The first is not needed anymore. Bombing hasn't served the other two reasons. We can restrict supplies only to a critical level, no lower. Obviously we are not breaking the will of the North. They are digging in, taking a hardening line." Drawing on experience, Ball added, "I was in charge of bombing surveys in World War II and bombing never wins a war. . . . The one hope we have is to stop the bombing and seize every opportunity not to resume. Meanwhile conduct the war in the South with redoubled effort."[56]

Ball's last point caught Johnson's attention. "That has great appeal to me," he enthused. Problems came with the Joint Chiefs, he guessed; they would oppose any pause.

"I can take on the chiefs," McNamara, his jaw set, said tartly.

But the president had another worry: Could the American people be sold on a bombing stoppage? McNamara finessed the question. "The Navy and the Air Force are conducting 3,000 sorties in the North. There is no way to stop the bombing in the North except as part of a political move."

A look at Rusk. "I don't think the bombing has caused the North to escalate," the secretary added disagreeing with Ball. "They are determined to do so, regardless of bombing. We tell the Russians, you ask us to pause, and we pause, now what will you do for us?"

McNamara returned to the attack. "You really need several of these moves. We have one pause, we need more."

Gazing around the table, LBJ relaxed his stand a bit. "I have no objection to stopping the bombing. What are the objections?" There were none, just affirmations.

Leaning on the table, his eyes set in a distant stare, LBJ asked, "Should we not have someone moving throughout the world, trying for peace with other countries?" No one answered. Slowly, coming back to the moment, Johnson asked McNamara if he wanted to talk to the chiefs about the pause.

No, the secretary wanted only to know the president's desires. "We will decide what we want and impose it on them," McNamara replied. "Before you decide, I cannot deliver. After you decide, I can deliver."

Obviously swaying, LBJ cautioned against openly announcing a halt. Weather and the Christmas season could be used as reasons while trying to sell Hanoi on peace. No peace efforts—which he thought must be made—could succeed while the bombing continued.

He looked sharply at McNamara. "Bob can say to the chiefs that we have a heavy budget, and the possibility of a tax bill, controls on the economy, the danger of inflation, the killing of the Great Society. Therefore," the president added with emphasis, "we need to make sure diplomats talk before the roof falls in on us in Congress and the diplomats tell us they can't talk with bombs dropping."

Another moment's brooding, then, looking at them all, he continued: "The weakest chink in our armor is American public opinion. Our people won't stand firm in the face of heavy losses, and they can bring down the government." Looking into the future, he added, "we are going to suffer big political losses, every president does in off-years, but ours will be bigger."

Still not quite settled on a decision, he put it off. "Let us meet again tomorrow and inspect what we have said today." He got up, followed by the others.

Later while reviewing the meeting with Valenti, LBJ asked his views. The presidential aide carefully assessed what he'd seen and heard. The course seemed right, he said, "so long as we bomb we will never get the North to a conference table."

Sitting tiredly in his Oval Office chair, the president agreed. "You are right," he said. "Every night I try to put myself in the shoes of Ho Chi Minh. I try to think what he is thinking. I try to feel what he is feeling. It's not easy, because I don't know him."

Leaning back, eyes fixed on the ceiling, the president murmured, "God, we have got to find a way to end this war, we've got to find a way. We must keep trying."

Sitting up, LBJ looked squarely at Valenti and told him to schedule a noon meeting the next day and to include Abe Fortas, Clark Clifford, and Alex Johnson with the others. Since there had been an agreement with Saigon to permit a Christmas pause of a few days, the argument would be about whether to extend the time.[57]

Johnson met with the group at 12:35 P.M. on December 18. Each participant looked at a summary of the previous day's discussion. The president jumped right to the point: A talk with the chairman of the Joint Chiefs had revealed the professional view clearly enough. "The military says a month's pause would undo all we have done."

"That's baloney," McNamara snapped, reacting quickly, angry that his own brass would undermine his idea.

"I don't think so," Johnson quickly disagreed. "I think it contains serious military risks. It is inaccurate to say suspension of bombing carries no military risk."

Rusk doubted a pause would be long if nothing came from the north. Johnson agreed. Some haggling went on about the starting date, with most thinking a short time line important. A discussion of loose points continued, with LBJ fussing about public reaction. McNamara, joined by Mac Bundy, temporized. "We can resume bombing at any time," he reminded the president. Which may not have been precisely so—a pause might well encourage the rest of the world to think the war was cooling down and a resumption would brand the United States as an insincere peace seeker. The argument continued, with Rusk willing to risk a pause to convince the American people their government sought a diplomatic solution.

"It is our deepest national purpose to achieve our goals by peace, not war," Rusk said, twirling his glasses in his serious pose. He coolly stated a rational case. "If there is one chance in ten, or twenty, that a step of this sort could lead to a settlement on [the basis of] the Geneva agreements and the 17th parallel, I would take it." A pause, Rusk mused, might put responsibility for prolonging the war squarely on Hanoi.

Abe Fortas and Clark Clifford sat in on the discussion and both weighed in against a pause. Fortas thought it would show American vacillation, and failure would bring hard-rightist demands for enemy extermination. "There is danger," Fortas pointed out, "that Hanoi would greet the pause as visible evidence that the protests in this country have had an effect on the government."

Clifford, flawlessly suited, his hands typically in front of him, fingers making a portentous tent for his words, guessed a pause would be fruitless, since the North Vietnamese would "reject any proposed settlement until they realized that they could not win and they were far from that stage." He added, with his carefully crafted subdued emphasis, that "I don't like the president to take a posture that is clearly unproductive. It might end up being viewed as a gimmick. Timing during the Christmas holidays is inopportune."[58]

McNamara jumped in with a courageous clincher: "The military solution to the problem is not certain. . . . Ultimately we must find . . . a diplomatic solution."

Hunched in his big chair, frowning, intent, LBJ looked at the defense secretary. "What you are saying," Johnson made it a sharp statement, not a question, "is that no matter what we do militarily, there is no sure victory."

"That's right," McNamara confessed uncomfortably, "we have been too optimistic." Then, firmly, unflustered, serious, he made an astounding admission: "Our military action approach is an unacceptable way to a successful conclusion." There might be a slim chance to influence northern actions by shifting bombing targets and intensity, but he could promise nothing.

Irked, not just a little confused, LBJ showed less anger than puzzlement. He fell back on his old penchant for personalizing things and voiced the wish that he could get into Ho's mind. Leaning back, pencil waving, the president speculated on the need for dedication. "What troubles me more is their doubt as to our will to see this thing through."

After slogging through the tortured logic of the last several hours, LBJ pitched a rhetorical question: "What problems do we get into if we don't bomb during Christmas, and tell the Russians we are willing to go farther? You say the Russians won't and can't do any more unless we stop bombing, and yet, they probably won't do anything."

No one spoke.

Tired, Johnson stood up, stretched, glanced around the table, sighed, looked at McNamara, and said, "we'll take the pause." With that, he left the room.[59]

chapter
NINE

Different Ways
to Peace

S keptics seem always to cluster around rumors of peace; they see peace as a time of weakness, and peacemakers not as God's children but as the Devil's playmates. Those skeptics, however, who saw LBJ's peace gestures as false or soft were wrong. He fervently wanted a way out of the war that stained the nation and soured the people. "There can be no losers in peace," he told Congress in November, 1963, "and no victors in war."[1]

But the president rejected a peace without equity—both sides must want it enough to yield victory for the future. Would the bombing halt bring fair negotiations? Recent and positive indications—such as Dean Rusk's report of the Hungarian foreign minister's UN pronouncement that Hanoi would talk if the United States stopped bombing the north, and Mac Bundy's private conversation with Soviet ambassador Anatoly Dobrynin, who mentioned that a bombing halt would give Moscow a chance to push Hanoi toward a cease-fire[2]—Johnson doubted. Peace usually comes after one side is beaten or war grinds toward stalemate, and neither of those conditions prevailed in South Vietnam. So, more from hope than certainty, the President of the United States launched a worldwide "Christmas peace offensive"[3] during the complete bombing halt that began December 24, 1965.

Johnson threw himself into his massive peace venture with all his fulminating energy—despite the specter of strong right-wing reaction if the bombing halt produced nothing but more war.[4] If it was going to be done, it would be done well and with much media panoply. Johnson started on December 27 by receiving McNamara at the ranch. The two of them talked in the living room until nearly 11 P.M. No notes were taken, so the subject can only be conjectured, but their subsequent actions tell something of the topic. Johnson began a prodigious phone campaign, despite the hour. He asked Dean Rusk to tell the Saigon embassy that he planned on extending the bombing halt "for several days, possibly into the middle of next week," and followed that with "dozens of phone calls,"[5] to a variety of people, including two reliable aides, George Ball and W. Averell Harriman.

That late-night call on December 28 remained etched in Ball's memory. At his family house in Florida for the Christmas holidays, the undersecretary of state hoped for a well-earned respite from war, rumors of war and peace, and from the rigors of the Johnson administration. No such luck. The president's unmistakable voice filled the room: "George, you wanted a pause, and I'm giving you one. Now I need you to get it going. I'm sending a plane for you in the morning."[6]

Harriman remembered getting similar orders: "Averell, have you got your bags packed?"

"Well, it's always packed, Mr. President."

Johnson boomed on. "Bob McNamara is here with me. He's got an airplane waiting for you to take you to Europe."

"Where do you want me to go?"

"That's for you to decide," LBJ replied. He then explained that he planned an extension of the Christmas bombing pause and he wanted international support for peace negotiations with North Vietnam.

Harriman caught McNamara's plane at eight that night. "I had no instructions, of course, except the general instructions which he gave me."[7]

As it happened, Harriman went to Poland—where he knew many officials—and won some support for mediation. The foreign minister agreed to go to Hanoi, and the Polish government offered other efforts. "They took the President's position seriously," Harriman reported, "possibly because I knew the Poles over the years, and gave them my assurance that the President was serious in this move." Harriman later learned that the foreign minister's hasty trip to Hanoi was encouraged by Moscow and opposed by Peking. He also learned that the Polish visit coincided with Alexander Shelepin's Hanoi jaunt—but he never discovered if the two men talked. The

Polish emissary found Hanoi unready to negotiate but perhaps not hopelessly so. Harriman, however, doubted there was even a crack of light in the northern position.[8]

When Ball reached Washington on the twenty-ninth, he found the president churning with excitement for what struck Ball as a gigantic "diplomatic extravaganza." Word had gone to America's Pacific allies of an extended bombing stoppage, to the Russians because Ambassador Dobrynin had talked of a halt, to UN secretary general U Thant, and to others so as to make sure Hanoi got the word. The president further proposed sending a barrage of spokesmen for the American endeavor over a wide span of the planet.

Ball, doubting the virtues of so showy an effort, nonetheless had to admire LBJ's "bully pulpit" diplomacy. Ever anxious to make things personal, the president's new plan at least had his own brand of originality. Johnson's message to the world was that the United States had halted the bombing of North Vietnam, and reciprocal restraint from Hanoi would influence America toward negotiations.

Johnson, realist though he remained, had hopes and would remember wistfully the heady days of probing. He talked nightly about it to Lady Bird and she, too, scanned the headlines for any hint of hope coming from the "Paul Reveres . . . riding all over the world."[9]

The president worked hard at this campaign and later said that

> This was one of the most widespread diplomatic campaigns of my
> Presidency, and it was criticized for that very reason—because it was so
> extensive and so well publicized. But we wanted to overlook no
> opportunity for peace, and we wanted the world to be informed. The
> Communists were using every possible channel of communication—
> propaganda, diplomacy, gossip, interviews, and conversations—as well
> as every forum from the United Nations to the world's teahouses to
> spread their line. But it seemed that in the eyes of American and foreign
> critics the United States could only do either too much or too little.[10]

Ball, while thinking the whole "spectacle futile and unbecoming,"[11] nonetheless helped orchestrate Johnson's touristic drama. Since the president relied as much on old friends as on diplomats, Ball cooperated with Harriman's missions to Poland, to Tito's Yugoslavia, and to other places he thought possibly helpful; Mac Bundy's to Canada; Ambassador Foy D. Kohler's across Moscow to the Kremlin; and Arthur Goldberg's to General de Gaulle and on to London for talks with Prime Minster Harold Wilson, then to Rome for a visit with the Holy Father (Johnson boasted the propaganda coup of sending a Jew to the Vatican) and also discussions with the Italian government. Hubert Humphrey, carrying the imprimatur of second in the American command, went to Manila for the inauguration of a new Philippine president and on to meet with Prime Minister Lal Bahadur Shastri of India. At each of these august occasions, Humphrey talked with other high officials in attendance, including Chairman Kosygin of the USSR. Ball journeyed to Puerto Rico, where he buttonholed Sen. Bill Fulbright, just coming off the eighteenth green, and then went on to Florida to brief the Senate's minority and majority leaders, Everett Dirksen and Mike Mansfield. Assistant Secretary of State for African Affairs G. Mennen Williams talked with various African leaders, while Tom Mann explained the U.S. position to South American officials.

Unconvinced about formal diplomacy, despite Rusk's strong support, LBJ kept other channels working. Coincidentally with contacting Ball, Johnson asked Henry Byroade, U.S. ambassador to Burma, to contact his North Vietnamese counterpart in Rangoon with news of the bombing halt and a request for reciprocal action.[12] Hanoi's consul general promised prompt transmission.

Johnson had the same message delivered to the North Vietnamese embassy in Moscow in January, 1966—this time with an invitation to direct and confidential talks. Their reply was that the United States had no right to bomb in the first place, and the only acceptable agenda for peace remained Hanoi's four-point plan. That same discouragement came back from Rangoon with an added specific: Settlement could come "only when the United States government has accepted the four-point stand of the government of the Democratic Republic of Vietnam," demonstrated "by actual deeds." Johnson got the picture clearly enough: "Hanoi was not interested in negotiating; it was demanding a settlement on its own terms."[13]

Frustrated, hardly surprised, the president made the "peace offensive" an important point in his State of the Union message on January 12, 1966. That message received careful massaging by the president and all of his writing staff because it would be his best chance to wrap his vision of peace and hopes for general betterment into a challenge for Congress to tackle a Great Society agenda as ambitious as he had thrust upon the previous session, an agenda to push them and, with any kind of luck, excite them. Much of the Great Society's program had been achieved but much remained to be done. Critics muttered that he wanted too much, that the economy could not stand all his social reforms coincidentally with war in Vietnam.

But LBJ knew better. What mattered was the country's heart. The country could do anything its heart willed. He knew that heart, had felt it as he toured the nation and watched the faces of children and teachers and parents who hoped for so much from his education programs. He saw it in the shining faces and eyes of black Americans when he talked about voting rights as the breaker of all lingering chains. He responded himself to the pulsing in those long, late White House hours laboring through the "night reading" in the growing certainty that time would be short to finish an American miracle. So he worked his staff beyond endurance to construct a 1966 State of the Union message to match challenge, opportunity and vision. To Joe Califano and Jack Valenti, embroiled in the churning excitements of their president's hopes, that message grew into a kind of Promethean world promise. The burden he would hand his congressional colleagues, his unfolding humanitarian dream, he kept closely guarded.

President Johnson walked in briskly on Wednesday, January 12, smiled around the House, greeted Vice President Humphrey and Speaker McCormack, took a measured stance, stuck to his teleprompter, and spoke of his hopes, of the War on Poverty, of the legislative load coming to Congress— over and through it all, he said, stalked war in Vietnam. America could wage both wars, he said.

> We will continue to meet the needs of our people by continuing to develop the Great Society. . . . I have come here to recommend that you, the representatives of the richest Nation on earth . . . bring the urgent decencies of life to all of your fellow Americans.

He surveyed the House, caught a glimpse of Lady Bird and Luci and her fiance, Pat Nugent, in the Gallery, along with some of the White House staff wives,[14] then went on.

> There are men who cry out: We must sacrifice. Well, let us rather ask them: Who will they sacrifice? Are they going to sacrifice the children who seek the learning, or the sick who need medical care, or the families who will dwell in squalor now brightened by the hope of home? Will they sacrifice opportunity for the distressed, the beauty of our land, the hope of our poor?

Next he came to one of the crunches:

> I believe that we can continue the Great Society while we fight in Vietnam. But if there are some who do not believe this, then, in the name of justice, let them call for the contribution of those who live in

the fullness of our blessing, rather than try to strip it from the hands of those that are most in need.

He promised again to stick by America's commitment to the war-worn South Vietnamese, then acknowledged the odd nature of the conflict.

> The war in Vietnam is not [World War II and Korea]. . . . Yet, finally, war is always the same. It is young men dying in the fullness of their promise. It is trying to kill a man that you do not even know well enough to hate. . . . Therefore, to know war is to know that there is still madness in this world.

Finally, he talked of the difficulties in making peace.

> For twenty days now we and our Vietnamese allies have dropped no bombs in North Vietnam.
> Able and experienced spokesmen have visited . . . more than forty countries. We have talked to more than a hundred governments. . . .[15] We have talked to the United Nations. . . .
> We have also made it clear . . . that there are no arbitrary limits to our search for peace. We stand by the Geneva agreements of 1954 and 1962. We will meet at any conference table, we will discuss any proposals—four points or fourteen or forty—and we will consider the views of any group. We will work for a ceasefire now or once discussions have begun. We will respond if others reduce their use of force, and we will withdraw our soldiers once South Vietnam is securely guaranteed the right to shape its own future.
> We have said all this, and we have asked—and hoped—and we have waited for a response.
> So far, we have received no response to prove either success or failure.[16]

Thirty-five days into the bombing halt—and three days before it ended— Ho Chi Minh wrote to various heads of governments "interested in the Vietnam situation." He denounced U.S. peace efforts as "deceitful" and "hypocritical," and demanded a U.S. troop withdrawal, at the same time insisting that the National Liberation Front be accepted as "the sole genuine representative of the people of South Vietnam." For Ho, the solution was his terms or nothing.[17]

Johnson, a cynic in the making, learned with wry disgust that North Vietnam capitalized on the halt by pouring men and supplies through the DMZ and along Ho's trail. Others were surprised, even appalled, at Hanoi's brash enterprise. The president, though, realized that Hanoi had never agreed to anything—the waves of men and material rolling southward were the fruits of American generosity. All the "frenetic to-ing and fro-ing" (the phrase is George Ball's) of the great peace offensive came to nothing.

Johnson, never a blinkered optimist about the peace mongering he tried, had talked with various groups about what to do if bombing had to resume. In a series of sessions with congressional leaders and other respected advisors, LBJ garnered enough divergent views to permit any kind of action. On January 25, sitting in the Cabinet Room with a bipartisan congressional group, he heard Rusk lament the fruitlessness of peace efforts, then listened as Speaker McCormack urged hard action to protect U.S. soldiers. Representative Gerald Ford, like most of those present, wondered what the options were, and the president recited his triple choices: pull out, bomb more, or do nothing. For him, the question was when to resume bombing.

What, Ford wondered, did LBJ's advisors suggest? State, Defense, the JCS, all recommend early resumption, said Johnson. That clinched it for Ford. "If your advisers say bombing is necessary—I'm for it," he said.

Mike Mansfield, the Senate majority leader and calm, studious, fair-minded old friend who did not like anything about the Vietnam situation, urged caution. Continue the lull. Resumption of the attacks would, he guessed, increase U.S. casualties, kill more North Vietnamese civilians, and increase international opposition. He suggested that the more the United States destroyed of the north, the more "we treat with China instead of North Viet Nam."

Earnest and rumpled, Everett Dirksen expressed his own view in that rumbling, cavernous, cathedral voice of his: "I am [as] sensitive to young blood as any man. You could withdraw. This would be a disaster. You could let this be a war of attrition. Keep what we have. Be patient. But this is expensive and wearing. It doesn't reduce casualties. [The] country wouldn't support you. . . . Or you can fight. . . . Let's do what is necessary to win. I don't believe you have any other choice."[18]

LBJ, hunched in his big chair, nodded at Dirksen's sympathetic words, then turned to hear what his longtime mentor and confidant, Georgia's Richard Russell, had to say. "I didn't want to get in there, but we are there," sighed Russell. "We are prepared to fight a war. We are *not* fighting. I think we have gone too far in this lull—although I recognize the reason. This pause has cost you militarily." Then, hitting LBJ's most sensitive nerve, he added, "We are going to lose a lot of boys as a result—casualties of our care for peace. For God's sake, don't start the bombing half way. Let them know they are in a war. We killed civilians in World War II and nobody opposed. I'd rather kill them than have American boys die. Please, Mr. President, don't get one foot back in it. Go all the way."

Bill Fulbright, the increasingly unhappy liberal who began to suspect LBJ had tricked him and the whole Senate into backing the Tonkin Gulf Resolution, twisted, shifted, frowned in irked body language, and announced he opposed renewed bombing. "If we win, what do we do?" he wondered. "Do we stay there forever?" Then, switching to public reaction, he said, "There has never been American discontent like this. . . . I think we should play for time." Then he touched another raw Johnson nerve: "Nobody believed the Chinese would come in Korea—but they did."

The leadership, in general, wanted the president to do more than he proposed; certainly the overwhelming opinion favored resumed and heavier bombing. Still, Johnson listened to others over the next several days. George Ball cautioned about China, and LBJ asked McNamara, Rusk, Mac Bundy, Admiral Raborn, and Ball about that point in a January 26 meeting, again in the Cabinet Room. The secretary of defense's answer: "I believe we can tell China we do not intend to destroy the political institutions in North Vietnam."

Next day, the twenty-seventh, the president expanded his advisory group a bit to include Bill Moyers and Bus Wheeler. Valenti, taking notes, reported Wheeler urged expanded interdiction and Johnson questioned whether that would increase the chances of China intervening. Wheeler doubted it, nor did he think the Russians would enter. McNamara added that he did not know how much expansion would be required to "stop the flow of supplies. We could actually quadruple intensity on certain targets. We need more facts."

LBJ brought in still more people over the next few days. Clark Clifford thought, like Russell, that the North Vietnamese had to feel harder war and added that "if we don't bomb, China will be . . . bolder than us." Then suggested that the bombing halt might prove to be a deterrent to real peace if it sparked a "phony peace bid"—a point accepted by Wheeler and rejected by Bundy and McNamara. Ambassador Goldberg thought the bombing halt had helped America's international position.

Johnson listened to every shade of opinion and finally confessed his nagging worry about more delay: "I've played out my pause—not from 115 countries have I gotten anything. I want . . . to evolve . . . political and peace moves—initiatives of my own." Why? "Because . . . the Fulbrights and the Morses will be under the table and the hard liners will take over unless we take initiatives. . . . So let us keep [the] peace emphasis on."[19] As pressure mounted to get tougher, the president held tighter reins on operations against the north: The reckless scattering of bombs in populated areas would not only annoy world opinion but also kill civilians.

Most of LBJ's advisors grasped his concern, some more than others—all saw the strain of worry in his face.

Lady Bird Johnson had a special worry about it all as she listened to her husband worry about what to do if "nothing, nothing, nothing comes of the peace offensive. . . ."[20]

And when nothing happened, Johnson sank deeper into cynicism. Bombing halts obviously were snares and delusions, but this one seemed to have salved some stray diplomatic consciences. Rusk, stoic that he was, accepted the results philosophically. He had begun with honest hopes, but when they were dashed he recommended the bombing resume. Ball maintained his gallant consistency: "We at least broke the momentum of escalation."[21] And he kept trying, although his convictions began to shimmy a little.

Dauntless peacemaker that he was, Ball did not wear blinders. The rising furies of war wore on his optimism, as they did on everyone's. He remained committed to disengagement, but he could not ignore some of its dangers. In June, 1965, he had sent the president a secret memorandum titled "United States Commitments Regarding the Defense of South Viet-Nam," in which he tried to show American legal guarantees eroded by the instability of the South Vietnamese government. At the end of this shrewd legalistic opinion, Ball looked behind his hopes to assess the costs of simply dumping Vietnam. Legally it could be done without dishonor, he thought, but responsibility came to haunt him. "In the longer term," he admitted, "we must judge a decision to withdraw assistance from South Viet-Nam primarily in terms of its effect on the ability of the United States to maintain its role of world leadership."[22]

Clinging to the idea that a U.S. withdrawal could somehow be achieved without sloughing Western obligations, Ball made a valiant try in early January to prevent more bombing. One Ball memo suggested various ways of involving the UN in the peace process, although he had small confidence in that venture. Grasping at whatever Asian reeds waved, Ball pointed to a possible peace signal through Prince Souvanna Phouma of Laos and, in a reinforcing memo, Ball chided against the resumption of bombing. Never on the ropes, he kept urging further U.S. peace efforts as long as the bombing halt prevailed, including strong reendorsement of a six-power conference, a cease-fire effort, and renewed urging that the cochairmen of the Geneva conference (USSR and UK) reconvene that body.

As hope of even a partial peace fueled his desperation, Ball randomly urged a Geneva conference on Cambodia, revived International Commission meetings on the Geneva proposals, a new appeal from nonaligned nations, and, although he had some contempt for the UN, Ball thought the secretary general, along with the pope, might be asked to continue trying for peace. Finally, Ball played on Johnson's worry about China's response to urge a light-handed approach to war.[23]

Johnson noted with sardonic expectation that as nothing happened on the peace front, pressure from the great "beast" of the far right mounted to hit the north harder. Ball, feeling the urge toward escalation, made a frantic try to support Johnson's reluctance to up the ante. On January 20 LBJ read a memo titled "Should We Resume Bombing," which concluded that air strikes had failed to achieve any of the desired effects. Furthermore, Ball made the case that fiercer attacks had every chance of pulling North Vietnam's Communist friends into open support.[24]

Ball failed to convince LBJ that bombing halts did anything more than serve Hanoi's purposes. Believing that the North Vietnamese needed to feel the heat, Johnson told the congressional leadership and the National Security Council that peace's pathway lay through the woes of war.

On January 31, 1966, bombing resumed, albeit at a lower level than before.

HONOLULU—NEW PERSPECTIVES

Of all the White House coterie engaged in president watching, Jack Valenti most felt the poignancy of LBJ's pessimism about the chances for peace. Close enough to feel nuances coming from that restless engine of a man, Valenti, on January 21, 1966, sent him a memo suggesting possible ways to end the war. Chief among his suggestions was one that would take LBJ to Honolulu for a personal effort at shoring up the South Vietnamese government. "The President could appear with Prime Minister Ky and stress the political, economic, and social future . . . once the fighting has stopped."

All kinds of good things might flow from such a gathering. Valenti suggested that "it would be very helpful for the world to see the cordial relations between Ky and the President and their combined faith in the kind of world that can be built without fighting in South Vietnam."[25]

Johnson mulled the idea of a meeting with the new Vietnamese leadership and liked it. Until recent weeks he had had grave doubts about the survival of the new regime in Saigon. However, Prime Minister Ky had presented a kind of "state of the nation" summary to the Armed Forces Congress on January 15 that cheered Johnson. In it, Ky voiced three objectives for his nation: defeat the enemy and rebuild the countryside; "stabilize the economy; and . . . build a democracy."

The president told Valenti, Mac Bundy, and Dean Rusk to plan the Honolulu meeting, then threw himself into preparations with his usual verve.[26] He expected everyone to be ready to accept invitations. Word went to Premier Ky and President Thieu on February 4 that President Johnson expected to meet them at CINCPAC headquarters in Honolulu two days later.

Honolulu in 1966 had more ambience than in later, tourist-ridden years. The U.S. presidential party arrived late on February 5 and was greeted by Admiral Sharp and General Westmoreland. Johnson had last seen Westy at West Point, several years before, and greeted him and his wife, Kitsy, gleefully. "I have a present for you," the president said, pointing to "Stevie"— Katherine Stevens Westmoreland, the general's sixteen-year-old daughter, who LBJ had brought along as a birthday surprise for Kitsy.[27]

In that spirit of hope and kindness, LBJ swarmed on Honolulu and prepared for the first session of meetings he had determined would be significant.

Some of the veteran media folk following the LBJ trail might have shared cynical suspicions that Johnson had engineered the hasty trip to take the limelight from Bill Fulbright's touted senatorial hearings on Vietnam.[28] If so, they were right and wrong. Certainly the president chafed at the Arkansas senator's public exposure of the Vietnam tragedy before an American and world public unschooled in the realities of that arcane place; chafed, too, at public argument over presidential authority to keep sending men to Asia. However, actor par excellence that he was, Johnson missed few chances for upstaging. Still, he came to Honolulu more to change a war than to divert its impact. He came, too, to size up the new allied leaders—with some apprehensions.

Those allies likewise came with apprehensions. Various reputations preceded Johnson and his cohorts. South Vietnamese experience and prejudice cast a kind of dark mythos around Yankee leaders charging to Saigon's defense. Saigon's leaders came to Honolulu determined to be enlightened but not absorbed.

They came on the afternoon of the sixth without much fanfare or Yankee panoply. Prime Minister Ky arrived more subdued and better prepared than expected; so did President Thieu and the third South Vietnamese representative, defense minister Gen. Nguyen Huu Co. They were met at the airport by LBJ, and had to work at not being overwhelmed by the careful arrangements for the meeting.[29]

Official sessions began the next morning. The Vietnamese noted the "high-powered team" from Washington, which included McNamara, John McNaughton, generals Wheeler, Westmoreland, and Maxwell Taylor, Admiral Sharp, Dean Rusk, Secretary of Agriculture Orville Freeman, Secretary of Health, Education, and Welfare John Gardner, AID director David Bell, and ambassadors Lodge, Harriman, and Leonard Unger.

Johnson, sitting in the middle of the U.S. group, began by announcing a new and different theme: "We are here to talk especially of the works of peace. We will leave here determined not only to achieve victory over aggression, but to win victory over hunger, disease, and despair. We are making a reality out of the hopes of the common people."

It happened that Ky had some indication of LBJ's agenda—beyond remarks about "the other war" the president had made in his State of the Union address—and had prepared ahead. With Johnson's opening exhortation fading in the background, Ky began to talk of his country's problems and his intentions for its future. Confidently, forcefully, the prime minister said, "we were deluding ourselves with the idea that our weakness could not be remedied while we were fighting a war . . . . It has taken a long time to realize that we will not completely drive out the aggressor until we make a start at eliminating . . . political and social defects. We must be indestructible, not vulnerable."

Ky pledged a social revolution—an attack on such Johnsonian bugaboos as disease, ignorance, and totalitarian authority.

Johnson listened in growing admiration as Ky's crisp presentation continued.

> I do not mean that we have to cure every one of our ills before we go to
> the peace table, but we must have a record of considerably more
> progress than we have been able to accomplish so far. We must create a
> society that will be able to withstand the false appeals of Commu-
> nism. . . . where each individual can feel that he has a future, that he
> has respect and dignity, and that he has some chance for himself and for
> his children to live in an atmosphere where all is not disappointment,
> despair, and dejection.[30]

He concluded with a Johnsonian peroration:

> A program for a better society can be established and launched by
> any type of government, Communist or non-Communist, dictatorial or
> democratic. But such a program cannot be carried forward for long if it
> is not administered by a really democratic government, one which is put

into office by the people themselves and which has the confidence of the people.[31]

Arranging his papers, Ky looked at Johnson, whose eyes had been fastened on him during the speech. Smiling broadly, leaning across the big table, Johnson said, "Boy, you speak just like an American."[32]

From that moment on, the two leaders were friends. Ky liked Johnson's "get it done" style, and fancied himself in the same image. As they walked together toward one of the conference sessions, Ky urged modernization of TV communications in Vietnam "as a medium of information and propaganda." There were just two airborne stations in the whole country, Ky said.

Johnson turned around and raised his voice: "Where's the USIS man?" When the man appeared, Johnson told him about the problem and said, "Do something right now, please."

With in a month television flickered across the South. Ky noted that "if my request had gone through normal channels it would have taken a couple of years."[33]

Ky was fascinated by Johnson's fierce dedication to social reform,[34] and thought the whole gathering had been a great success.

As they prepared the text of a joint announcement of the conference's results, LBJ made it clear he wanted more than a mere recitation of the obvious. As everyone sat again around Oley Sharp's huge conference table for the last session, Johnson crammed on his glasses, held the total text of the communiqué in his big hand and read it aloud, stabbing a finger at each action paragraph. Fixing every official present with those heavy-browed eyes, he pushed the paper and said he wanted action. He held a blueprint, he said, a bible that both sides would follow and, at each subsequent meeting (there would be several he thought), check for progress. Glancing around the table, Johnson growled, "You men who are responsible for these departments, . . . bear in mind we are going to give you an examination and the finals will be on just what you have done." Old Johnson hands admired his style; newcomers were dazzled, a few intimidated, as Johnson scowled on.

For instance, he would expect specific data about building democracy in rural areas. Like McNamara, he wanted numbers on how much had been built, when, and where. Waving the suddenly precious document, he quoted, "larger outputs, more efficient production to improve credit, handicraft, light industry, rural electrification [that brought memories!]. Are those just phrases, high-sounding words, or have you coonskins on the wall?"

Westy, listening and watching, chuckled to himself at the puzzlement the

Vietnamese must be experiencing over Johnson's last words. What were coonskins?[35]

Again, stabbing the paper, LBJ quoted: "The President pledges he will dispatch teams of experts." Loudly, "Well, we better do something besides dispatching. They should get out there." Musingly, he read on, "we are going to train health personnel." Looking up, he asked, "How many health personnel?"

He then used a story to make his point: "You don't want to be like the fellow who was playing poker. When he made a big bet they called him and said: 'What have you got?' He said: 'Aces,' and they asked: 'How many?' He said: 'One aces.'" Smiling but serious, Johnson said, "we have talked about training personnel—for health, for education, for other things. When we come back and check and I ask how many we have trained, I don't want you to say: 'One personnel.'" That lightened the session.[36]

The result was the Declaration of Honolulu, which pledged the Saigon government to end social injustice, to establish a stable economy, and to provide a better lifestyle under true democracy for the entire country. Significantly, the South Vietnamese government promised something most Americans there found doubtful indeed: to draft a new constitution in the next few months, present it for national debate, and then to a general vote on ratification. A permanent government would be elected under that constitution.

In addition, Ky and his associates opened the door to Vietnamese fighting for the other side. The communiqué announced an "open arms" program that invited VC and NVA soldiers to "come and join in this national revolutionary adventure. . . . come and work through constitutional democracy to build together that life of dignity, freedom and peace those in the North would deny the people of Vietnam."[37]

Ky, Thieu, and Co noted that things military had been ignored at the meeting. Johnson, near the end, explained why. "We want to be able honestly and truthfully to say that this has not been a military build-up conference here in Honolulu." Then, looking at Ky, he added, "We have been talking about building a society, following the outlines of the prime minister's speech yesterday."[38]

Pretty well pleased with the conference results, Johnson invited Ky, Thieu, Westmoreland, and one or two others to his hotel suite for drinks and an informal assessment of things. Flattered at the attention, Ky basked further when LBJ leaned close and whispered, "come into my bedroom for a moment." Ky followed, wondering what special secrets the president wanted to share with him. Johnson closed the door, leaned earnestly toward him, and said, "I wondered if you would like to have an autographed picture of me." A bit nonplussed at the anticlimax, Ky pleasantly accepted. Then Johnson broached the real subject of the tête-à-tête: Would Ky object if Vice President Humphrey went back with him to Vietnam the next day? "I would like Humphrey to come with you and start the policy ball rolling, to get some action on the things we have talked about."

Ky agreed quickly, but said, "I didn't even know Mr. Humphrey was here."

Johnson grinned conspiratorially. "He isn't, but he will be here by the time your plane takes off."[39]

One of the things LBJ had been considering before going to Honolulu had been a fresh pitch to U.S. allies about Vietnam—and he'd thought about sending Hubert Humphrey on a tour, accompanied by Jack Valenti and Averell Harriman.

Thereby hung a different tale, one that showed LBJ working on various levels in personal matters. The "Happy Warrior" could carry brimming optimism in an empty bucket and would make a positive spokesman for America's Asian crusade—now. "Now" is the operative word because for nearly a year Humphrey had stood like a wayward child outside the pale of prominence. His obvious opposition to bombing and urging of caution in Vietnam alienated Johnson, and the president shoved his deputy into the same chill he, himself, had sometimes felt under the Kennedys. That isolation shattered Humphrey. Always on the fringes, he had shuffled in an almost piteous quest for information and useful things to do. Typically, the vice president strove desperately to please and thus inch his way once more into LBJ's confidence and councils.

Ingratiating goodness, relentless optimism fanned by humor, and a nearly unshakable smile made Humphrey into a kind of caricature of himself—at least to many newsmen and to later historians. He is often portrayed as a tragicomic shadow wafting in LBJ's wings, hardly a man, more a substance. No fool, though, the vice president could hide his strong mind and will behind that feckless image. Often well-informed and wiser than guessed, Hubert Humphrey pursued his own pathways of persuasion.

Some observers found Humphrey's position sad, but, at the same time, felt that he brought trouble on himself. Too weak and pleasant to stand against LBJ's raucous image, Humphrey seemed a wistful toady on the trails of power.[40]

People close to him—family, staff, and old friends—knew a man different from the jester at Johnson's table. Humphrey's smile sometimes faded into a stony-faced scowl, and his cheerful voice settled into anger—not often, for more than most he forgave things—but sometimes. Deep within him,

Humphrey kept an iron grace that made him seem, somehow, more than mortal.

Johnson began pulling him back to the center of things a few days before leaving for Honolulu. The president had thought of inviting Humphrey to the meeting, but worried about both himself and the vice president being out of the country simultaneously. Keep a loose schedule, LBJ had said; after the conference he might ask Humphrey to do some traveling.

Fortunately the vice president's calendar was clean, because the call came with barely a day's notice. Humphrey was somewhat taken aback because, "after a year, more of isolation than participation, I was about to embark on a major trip in a delicate area, with no time for specific preparation, no briefing papers reviewed ahead of time, no time for study in depth."[41]

Some advance study would have helped, but in Los Angeles, on the way back from Honolulu, a nearly ebullient president greeted Humphrey. Confident, refreshed in the feeling that things were getting better in Vietnam, Johnson said he thought victory might just happen. Westmoreland increasingly impressed him, and he told Humphrey that Ky and Thieu were surprisingly strong. The time had come to collect information on the good things America was doing in Vietnam and what new efforts would be made toward pacification. The president said he wanted his deputy to tour Asia with news about Honolulu, about the declaration, and the emphasis on "the other war." Johnson, hearing Humphrey's steady urging of pacification, had begun to call the nonmilitary efforts in South Vietnam "Hubert's War." Humphrey's selection as deputy on mission made sense, then, on both political and logical grounds. His role as LBJ's missionary offered him a stage beyond puppetry—and he used it. Despite short notice, a grinding schedule, and unforeseen crises, Humphrey's mission did good things and garnered some sobering impressions.

There were rumors that Johnson carried conspiracies in his psyche. He did, of course, in the deepest political sense; he did not in the normal run of affairs. The suspicion came from his absolute largeness, from his simply bulking over everyone else and filling so much more than his own space; suspicion came, too, from his huge complexities. The real LBJ remained elusive. So it happened that the conferees who sat with him in the big sessions and small at Honolulu saw only a piece of him and, hence, only a piece of what happened.

Johnson's compelling energy made it difficult, nearly impossible, for him to function on only one level. In Honolulu he had several conferences going simultaneously, each separated from the other but somehow oddly linked.

A separate conference on military matters ran as a backdrop to the Honolulu headlines. Westy had been there when the U.S. entourage arrived in haste; he had gone early to press Oley Sharp for more men than the seventy-one battalions approved back in July. Although sympathetic, Admiral Sharp still needed persuading. It was, after all, his responsibility to oversee military activities in Vietnam, and he took the job seriously. Why did Westy need more troops? How many more? When would they be needed?

General Westmoreland rarely made a move without staff work to back him, so he had answers. He wanted seventy-nine more U.S. battalions and twenty-three from the allies—which would raise America's ground commitment to 429,000 men. Once more he pitched for additional communications, engineer, air maintenance, and port units; without those logistical elements it would be difficult "to utilize the combat troops fully in sustained operations."[42]

During some of the political sessions in Honolulu, McNamara and General Wheeler discussed Westy's needs in depth. They agreed with the new number but cautioned COMUSMACV that the reserves likely would not be called up, which would make it impossible to provide all the support units needed. Do your best, Westy was told, with help from the navy, air force, civilian contract agencies, and simply by making do.

President Johnson took the need for increased numbers without visible shock, but struck his field general as "intense, perturbed, uncertain how to proceed with the Vietnam problem, torn by the apparent magnitude of it." His worries spilled over into anticipation: Westmoreland was to have a televised press conference. "I hope you don't pull a MacArthur on me," Johnson said, adding, "General, I have a lot riding on you."[43]

Westy had no intention of criticizing the war and ignored the admonition, but he resisted Johnson's efforts to lure him into predicting how long the war would last. To the press, Westy gave an impressively honest and professional assessment of the Vietnam situation. "The nature of the enemy is such," he said firmly, "that we cannot expect him to be defeated by a single battle or series of battles. He will have to be ferreted out over a period of time, which will involve many campaigns, many operations."[44]

Back in Washington, Johnson took an increasingly hard look at everything about Vietnam. At a White House meeting on February 24, a tired Hubert Humphrey reported that his short-term view of Vietnam encouraged him; he accepted the idea that "the tide of battle has turned. . . . We need to understand that this battle can be won." Johnson's new emphasis on "the other war" pleased Humphrey. The reorganization of the U.S. embassy in

Saigon to give Deputy Ambassador William J. Porter control over nonmilitary programs, for example, showed serious Yankee purpose. Beyond Vietnam, the vice president found agreement among the allies with the idea that the war ranked as only a part of a larger struggle, but not much promise of direct support. Australia, among the most loyal of the group, would try to triple its 1,500-man Vietnam contingent; South Korea planned to send another army division and a marine regiment, for a total of 45,000 troops; and the Philippines would send about 2,000 men. But most of the Association of Southeast Asian Nations [ASEAN] seemed "ready to fight in Vietnam to the last American."[45]

Humphrey reported that rising American dissent clouded many of his foreign discussions. Johnson bristled and fumed. Why can't Americans dissent privately? he wondered. Not since the Civil War had such public opposition appeared. Outsiders simply could not understand why prominent Americans lambasted the president, the government, and government policies. Humphrey jumped in soothingly. At least, he observed, the Honolulu conference had focused domestic and foreign attention on "the other war," and that had some calming effect.[46]

Military discussions in Washington were long and thorny. Westy's need for more men upset McNamara and Wheeler, but they recognized the cause: the North Vietnamese had simply overmatched the U.S. buildup. While all prudent planning indicated that seventy-one battalions should be enough, enemy recruiting changed all that. During the military planning meetings in Honolulu, McNamara, Rusk, McNaughton, and Bill Bundy drafted a memorandum that served as a blueprint for Westy's operations in 1966. In it, priorities were set for opening roads and rail lines and for securing densely populated areas and food producing areas. The guidance to Westy was that allied "military units were to destroy enemy forces at a rate at least as high as the enemy's capability to put more men in the field."

Satisfied, COMUSMACV returned to Saigon secure in knowing that "in setting the goals for 1966, senior civilian authorities acting for the President formally directed that I proceed as I had planned."[47]

Johnson, however, could not escape a sense of déjà vu. In many depressing ways, the American situation remained roughly what it had been a year before. What would it be a year hence? McNamara gave no really encouraging news and Johnson faced an old question: How much is enough?

No matter where he looked, LBJ faced some facet of the war in Vietnam.[48] The First Lady, watching the lines deepen in her husband's face, knew that his "cloud of troubles" grew heavier. She noted, sadly, that "Vietnam . . . is about two thirds of what we talk about these days," and heard him talk often of his personal concern for Americans wounded and dying so far from home. "There's not a mother in the world," he said often, "who cares more about it than I do, because I have two hundred thousand of them over there—and they think I am in charge, and if I am not, God help them—who the Hell is!"[49]

During his sobering reassessment after Honolulu, LBJ felt poignantly something he had said in the State of the Union speech: "The cup of peril is full in Vietnam." He knew now that peril washed beyond Asia, that it eddied in Washington and stained the White House hallways.[50]

"THE END MEN LOOKED FOR COMETH NOT"

Through all this miasma of despond, Johnson kept a certainty about objective. He recognized that in Vietnam, people were the purpose of the war. Various others tacitly agreed, although tempering their agreement with serious worries about the fighting. Still, the president pushed.

McGeorge Bundy, national security advisor par excellence, finally decided to quit. This came as no surprise—time and issues and passions passed under various bridges while the president and Bundy skirmished around problems. Relationships like theirs are hard to describe: different ages, different levels of power, different backgrounds, prejudices, and different ways of seeing things separated them, but an enduring affection bound them together. Bundy, the quintessential Kennedian, watched and listened and came to admire the bulking, brash, and bombastic Texan whose pragmatic political prowess gave Camelot a chance. Openness stood as the real crunch between these two strong personalities. Bundy believed that the president should admit he'd changed the scope of American commitment in Vietnam, that he should step before the cameras and say that things were different—that the enemy had escalated and that America had to meet the challenge.

But the president hesitated. He feared such an admission could trigger a debate that might yet derail the Great Society bills working through Congress. Bundy sympathized with Johnson's dilemma, but felt forthright confession would be better than evasion. He believed the American people were tough enough to accept a changed situation and would respect an administration honest enough to say so. Bundy said he "really didn't think that the Gulf of Tonkin resolution meant to the Senate 150,000 troops." Commanders in chief are supposed to lead people, Bundy kept believing, but understood that Johnson hung hoist on a petard of demand and necessity. Necessity forced him to press the Great Society, while public support demanded candor about Vietnam.

Bundy came to know that "there was a temperamental difference in the two of us that made me not very useful to him." Bundy thought that resigning would best serve the president and the country. Still, he had a decent respect for the rightness of things and "didn't want to go in a way that criticized the decision, because I agreed with the basic decision."[51]

Good fortune smiled on both LBJ and his friend: The Ford Foundation was looking for a president, and no one better fitted the needs of that international and cultural organization which did so much for mankind than Mac Bundy.

Knowing his departure was fast approaching, Bundy tried hard to sell LBJ on one of his deputies, Robert Komer, as successor. Komer, in turn, thought Bill Moyers was the man for the job. Moyers wanted it, and everyone guessed he had the surest track to the post. Still, LBJ dawdled. Bundy feared that if his office were vacant the president's contacts with Vietnam and the world would shrink to words from Rusk and McNamara, and then only "when decisions had to be taken, the great thing LBJ did not like to do."

Bundy pressed Johnson hard before he left office on February 28, 1966, and, not long after he departed, Komer responded to a presidential summons.

"I want you," said the president, "to go over there and sit in Bundy's chair and I want you to do Bundy's job for me, just temporary. And I don't want anybody in town to know that you're there."

Puzzled, Komer asked, "Not even McNamara and [Walt] Rostow?"

"I guess you'll have to do business with them," Johnson growled, "but goddamn it, if I read a word in the press, you're blown and you are out on your fat ass."

"Mr. President," Komer said, in his booming tones, "I'll try." Johnson cut him off. "Remember, I don't want to hear a goddamn thing."[52]

Johnson's covert appointment made it difficult for Komer to function forcefully. There seemed to be something tentative in the ways LBJ used him. Nevertheless, Komer found his short-lived job immensely enlightening.[53] Close association showed Komer that LBJ's interest still focused on the Great Society, but he resolutely refused to cut himself off from outside views on Vietnam. Still, as Mrs. Johnson noted, Vietnam filled a lot of conversation, much presidential musing, and increasing amounts of television time and media space.

Komer could see clearly that Johnson's real interest in winning hearts and minds in South Vietnam had not percolated much beyond Deputy Ambassador Porter's office in the Saigon embassy (Porter would be underestimated as a shrewd assessor of pacification's possibilities).[54] Speeches and admonitions around Admiral Sharp's conference table produced agreements about agricultural aid, about health and education, and other key civilian areas—but actual efforts were fragmented and uncoordinated, with various agencies clinging to their own agendas without concern for total effect.[55]

None of these facts went unnoticed by the president. One day, near the end of March, he called the chunky, confident Komer into the Oval Office and looked at him hard. Pulling him into the little office to the side, where he could press people more closely, Johnson sat Komer down. Puzzled, but convinced something he would not like threatened, Komer listened in amazement as LBJ said, "Bob, I've decided to put you in charge of the other war in Vietnam."

"What other war, Mr. President?"

"That's what we need to figure out."[56]

Komer had just caught one of Johnson's "fastball" ideas. "If you didn't get out of the way," Komer noted, "you caught it in your gut." He tried to slow things down.

Pulling his thinning hair back nervously, Komer said, "Mr. President . . . I think there are a couple of things I ought to tell you, if you'll listen. First of all, Mr. President, I don't know anything about the Far East. This is the one area of the world I never had any dealings with. I've dealt with everything else, as you know, but not the Far East. I have never been to Vietnam. I don't even know where the damn place is."

"Bob," LBJ said, sweeping Komer into his confidence, "let me tell you. I've got a lot of people who say they're experts and they tell me all sorts of different things. Maybe we need somebody who's not an expert."

Komer continued his wriggling. "Mr. President, I've never been west of San Francisco. I don't know anything about Asia."

"You'll learn," LBJ said firmly.

Komer kept trying to explain that Asia had never been his bailiwick; he wasn't literate about things there, it just seemed not a good idea. The president stuck to his scheme, but, finally noticing that Komer looked really depressed, he said, "I'll tell you what, we're going to pay you top dollar, too." Then he added, "You better go right over and see McNamara."

That triggered Komer's common sense: The fact the president had said "nothing about Rusk, no mention of Rusk at all," made it clear that McNamara had pacification under his wing.

Then Johnson ushered Komer out. He had him, and he knew it. As Komer left the Oval Office, he spotted Marvin Watson sitting at his desk.

"Marvin, the President just told me he's going to give me a new job and pay me top dollar. What the hell does that mean?"

"Oh," Watson quipped, "you're going to get paid as much as I am."

"Jeez," thought Komer as he groped toward a different world.[57]

Because Washington resonates to titles, Jack Valenti suggested Komer be given one to convey power: "White House Special Assistant for Peaceful Reconstruction in Vietnam."[58] The new Special Assistant for odd jobs, as Komer put it, made a quick trip to the Pentagon and told McNamara about his assignment.

"Well," asked the secretary of defense, "what's the first thing you're going to do?"

Komer, who admired that direct kind of question, said "The first thing I'm going to do is get on a plane and hightail my butt out to Vietnam. I want to see the place I'm supposed to be dealing with."

Nodding behind his squared away glasses, McNamara said, "That's the smartest thing you can do. I'm very impressed with your answer."

In Saigon Komer started his course in the strange process called pacification.[59]

Over time, Johnson and Komer may have wondered what they had done, but the appointment proved remarkably right.

Johnson and Komer were not working on a new idea in stressing "the other war." Even Gen. Paul Harkins, neolithic thinker that he seemed, understood something of the need for winning the "hearts and minds" of South Vietnamese civilians. How to do that bothered him, though, and he did not push it effectively. But America had waged war against guerrillas before—against Emilio Aguinaldo's patriots, against the fierce Moros of the southern Philippines, with Edward Lansdale against the Huks—and had done fairly well. Legacies from early days in Vietnam remained and Komer found that he had something to build on.

Fortunately, that blustery, tough-minded man picked up information like a sponge. Soon he knew some of the early history of pacification, and realized that more than casual thought had been given to the advisory program in the years up to 1965. Before America moved to "take over the war," a good many gifted, dedicated, hopeful advisors fanned into Vietnam's hinterlands with multiple missions to prop up local village chiefs, support the militias, harass the VC, offer administrative and military advice on local control problems, and offer direct medical and crop assistance with help from such U.S. agencies as AID and special agricultural missions.[60]

Various types of advising were tried. In the early 1960s, as JFK expanded America's assistance program, army officers and men were sent to aid different ARVN units—armies, corps, divisions, regiments, even battalions. The army also sent men to help in the provinces. Help in the backcountry received high priority because the VC killed provincial and village chiefs who were loyal to Saigon.

After Diem's fall, rural protection efforts decayed as Vietnamese officials became embroiled in personal political wars.

By the time General Westmoreland became COMUSMACV in June, 1964, pacification had fallen far behind America's big war. Westy was not unsympathetic to "the other war." As deputy to Harkins, he watched as the MAAG, sent subsector advisory teams into thirteen districts around Saigon in April and May, 1964.[61] Westy also heard reports of the remarkable dedication and achievements of the advisory corps—reports that influenced his decision to implement an important civilian assistance program of his own which he called Hop Tac—("cooperation" in Vietnamese). "It was designed," he said, "to gradually expand security and government control and services—pacification—outward from Saigon into six provinces that form a kind of horse collar about the city."[62]

In a way, this idea negates a little the notion that Westy lacked inspiration and was the quintessential "book soldier." Brigadier Gen. James Lawton Collins of the MACV staff saw Hop Tac as "a laboratory experiment in pacification," and he had a sound point. Westy ignored his own strategic philosophy of search and destroy as he thought about his new plan. "For several years," he said, "priority for ARVN actions against the VC had been based on wherever the insurgents were strongest. I considered it better to accept temporary setbacks in some regions while using the government's limited resources to secure the more critical areas, such as Saigon and its environs, then gradually to expand outward as those areas were secured."

As Westy saw it, Hop Tac would be a politico-military effort, with troops working outward from Saigon according to an expanding circle plan. When enemy forces were shoved from each zone, "saturation patrolling and ambushes" would stifle any return attempts and security could be handed over to the militia and a heavier police force. Civilian agencies then would provide schools, medical care, water, and agricultural help. The aim of all this: winning the people away from VC promises of better things later. "It was," Westy reported, "'a spreading oil spot'" concept; if it worked around Saigon, he would try it around other large cities.[63]

Although Westy pushed the program in mid-1964 as new, it had long roots. An "oil spot" (tache d'huile) plan dated back to pre–Dien Bien Phu days, there were overtones in Maxwell Taylor's enclave scheme, and the CIA experimented with a similar idea in Vietnam's highlands in 1961.[64]

Success depended on the quality of the new subsector advisors fanning out around Saigon. Most were outstanding. Consider, for special example, the story of Capt. James Floyd Ray.[65]

Born into a military family on August 17, 1937, Ray had the busy, traveling kind of youth army children know. He enjoyed it, especially the years at West Point, New York, where his father did a stint on the Military Academy's faculty. Devoted to things military, Ray entered the U.S. Military Academy in 1955. With customary verve, he became adept in intramural sports and a star in the chapel choir and glee club. His academic record impressed everyone. He stood second in his class academically upon graduation in 1959, was a cadet battalion commander, and a national debating champion.

West Point graduates have a remarkable record in winning Rhodes scholarships to Oxford University in England. James Ray's selection to a Rhodes scarcely surprised anyone who knew him. With an interest in international problems sparked by his travels, Ray focused on politics at Oxford. Again, it would scarcely have surprised his friends to hear that he took a first degree in philosophy, politics, and economics.

During his third Oxford year, Ray married Charlotte Walters of Tyler, Texas. They seemed a model pair: He, handsome and witty; she beautiful and with a sense of humor to match his—and they both loved the last Oxford year.

Back in the United States, Ray was sent to the Infantry School at Fort Benning, Georgia, where he finished at the head of his class and "the most promising junior officer [his commanding officer] had met in 23 years of service." From Benning, the Rays went across the country to Fort Lewis, Washington, where Jim took charge of the worst company on the base and turned it into the best.

A brief preparation course at Fort Bragg, North Carolina, barely acquainted him with the complexities of Vietnam. Arriving in Saigon on August 23, 1964, Ray plunged into the arcanities of "in processing" at MACV offices. There seemed to be a kind of grim humor to the horror stories told to the newcomers, but Ray saw little evidence of trouble in Saigon, and he pictured that city for Charlotte in a letter dated August 24:

> One's first impression is that Saigon is surprisingly French, particularly in its architecture, and in its appearance is far less oriental than I expected. Second, one is struck by a sense of decay, of an apex passed.

The city reminds one of nothing so much as a woman who only recently was glamorous in a fairly good imitation of fashion, but who suddenly and with merciless swiftness has lost her youth.

Ray's arrival coincided with the launching of General Westmoreland's Hop Tac program, so a heavy part of his initial briefings focused on "the spreading oil stain concept: 1) clearing 2) securing, 3) developing." He understood that Westy's policy drew much from Diem's old strategic hamlet program: district populations would be screened, Popular Forces would be activated and trained, communities would be fortified, communications would be improved, the people would be organized for security and development, and hamlet committees would be elected in an effort to bring a touch of spreading democracy to the backcountry.

Like most new arrivals in Vietnam, Ray wondered about his assignment. That he would be a "Civil Affairs, Psy Operations and Strategic Hamlet advisor," he knew; where seemed various. At last he got word: He would go to Nha Be District, Gia Dinh Province, Capital Military District, some five miles out of Saigon. He understood that chain of command—a sensitive topic to the South Vietnamese—and knew his role was purely "advisory." It worked out that his U.S. superior in Saigon would be an artilleryman, Colonel Sapp, of III Corps, "a rather elderly looking gentleman," who seemed "pleasant." Commander of the Vietnamese Capital Military District was Brig. Gen. Duong Ngoc Lam, and the province chief, was Colonel Trang. Ray would be advisor to the Nha Be District Chief, Captain Truong.

Ray first grasped some of his particular realities on August 27 when he went around Saigon doing initial paperwork for his coming assignment. He had already gotten a specific task from Colonel Sapp: Prepare an analysis of the degree of pacification of the strategic hamlets in Nha Be District "set against a similar ARVN analysis." Ray understood that his job was "to discover what we need to do in the district, and how it can be done." Word was that local Vietnamese failed to take advantage of much of the assistance already available to them from AID's Official Mission offices. Ray would work on that. "Second, I am to learn what I can of their & VC political organization." Apparently the VC did a lot in the district, since the district chief, Captain Truong "claims the VC plan to levy . . . taxes in the district and he claims also to know the 6 collectors."

By the time Ray reached his district on Friday, the twenty-eighth, he had considerable knowledge of it: The population was 39,821, plus 10,500 children under twelve in an area of "90 square miles, with 9 villages and 34 Strategic Hamlets." His initial impression:

First we stopped off to meet Capt Truong, who seemed to be genuinely glad to see me and eager to please. He showed me the office he had prepared for me—a token, I am sure. He also mentioned lunch at his house next week. After such pleasantries in Amvietoise [American, Vietnamese, French], we drove to the oil storage compound, where I viewed my new house. It was really appalling, I must admit, as regards sanitation.

Oil gave Ray's assignment special importance—or rather the oil storage tanks belonging to Shell, Esso, and Caltex near Nha Be. His concern extended to the security of "this rather lucrative target," so his house was located inside the wire fence surrounding the tank farm. "House" loosely described the odd shelter he was provided. With no latrine, no real kitchen, no refrigerator, and barely a pallet for sleeping, it ranked fairly high on the local comfort scale.

Ray slowly made it livable. Saigon provided a refrigerator almost too large to get into the house, and various visits to the PX and Saigon's bountiful black markets provided such luxuries as music and books.

Food proved a lingering mystery. Some of Saigon's restaurants were excellent—the My Chanh especially—and delighted his near-gourmet taste. Others were terrible; food in the field often seemed one of the horrors of war. Sometimes dining at Captain Truong's house provided tasty diversion from field rations. A poor cook, Ray frequented the Saigon officers' club—although he worried about being in the city, for "madness lies here. Surely if Dante had known the place he would have placed here all those who spend much time doing nothing."[66]

Ray plunged in to help on as many fronts as energy and allied bureaucracies allowed. He set up and taught English classes that became so popular they nearly did him in. He also sought to organize schools, turned his advisory group medic loose on the local population, and struggled manfully to create a sense of urgency in Captain Truong. There were VC units roaming the area around Nha Be, often in it, and Ray tried to stiffen Truong's determination to invigorate the local militia. Interminable delays, ironclad excuses, and general unconcern frustrated him; vexing, obnoxious, stupefying problems dogged every day—but especially the nights, when VC infiltrators worked at worming through the district. As Ray patiently dealt with these problems, he slowly, inexorably, began to make a difference.

Truong seemed to have the right idea, but he wallowed in a kind of wistful ennui. Captain Trac, commander of the two-company garrison, showed more concern for the district, especially the tank farm. Although Ray liked them both, he warmed a bit more to Trac, whose concern for "le poverte de mon peuple," was touching. Trac resented Troung, "who lives like a lord of the manor—for instance, he has an extensive Imperial Household Guard, but they sleep on bare earth." Trac's worries sparked Ray's, and he groped for quick ways to improve local living conditions.

His whole district needed virtually everything—enough to stagger the capacities of even the agricultural aid people—but Ray, in his diary, fixed on one thing first: "A major project . . . must be to introduce some standards of public hygiene." During a visit with the head man of Nha Be township on September 5, Ray looked at the village market (a self-help project), and then toured the school. "Suggested," Ray wrote that night, "they include a latrine in the future classroom building plans, and build in a little training in SANTÉ PUBLIQUE." An afternoon survey of another self-help project, billed as part of the agricultural mission's "pig/corn program: a pigsty," revealed unsuspected layers of corruption and bureaucracy. Corn had to be bought, although the sacks were clearly labeled "Donated by the people. . . ." Obviously several hands were sifting corn. A late visit to a new strategic hamlet, built to replace burned Saigon housing, gave Ray a comprehensive look at civil affairs problems.

The people's needs were staggering. Ray and Captain Troung wrestled with ways to start turkey farming. Most of all, though, they worried about water. "Water," Ray noted, "is an unexpected problem—there is none during the dry season, which means only one rice crop per year—and 6 months of unemployment." He and Truong looked "for alternate means of employment, such as the pig program and a brick factory." Practical always, Ray wanted to find another source of water—"but the river is salty, and it takes a 200 meter well."

So much needed doing, so many people asked for so much help, that Ray—like most early comers faced with the awful inadequacies everywhere—flailed around in search of swift fixes. Maybe, he mused to Charlotte, a scholarship program could be funded that would send a Nha Be student to the United States.

His energy never flagged, though, despite bureaucratic snarls locally and in Saigon. He pushed the engineers for building equipment, the ordnance people for better weapons, and he remained determined to improve the command problems surrounding him. Ray had no real command authority. He could urge, persuade, exemplify, fulminate, and suggest, but he could not order his Vietnamese counterparts. Worse, the command arrangements between Truong and Trac seemed incoherent; who did what, where, when, and why baffled a man trained in U.S. Army organization. Although he persisted, Ray came slowly to the conclusion that the problem lay somewhere in the psyche of the mysterious East.

Persistence did have its rewards, at least now and then. In October 1964, Ray went with Troung to observe "the dispersal of USOM [U.S. Official Mission] funds to 400 families who had moved—voluntarily—into new hamlets, 500 piasters each. They seemed quite happy with the sum." Ray's quiet suggestion that, while the people were gathered, the team medic might talk to them pleased Truong immensely. But progress seemed stymied by the spread of the status quo.

That afternoon, for instance, still pleased about a tiny success, Ray toured the district medical facilities with some visiting USOM officials. "They were properly appalled at the District Health Center, and at one of the hamlet aid stations a pig wandered in. Everyone . . . thought we were doctors and a huge crowd gathered to seek help. Schultz [the medic] and I set and splinted a broken finger (using a palm frond splint I whittled). What a pity we could not do more for them; they really wanted help. USOM team departed promising efforts to help. We'll see."[67]

Overwhelmed with "opportunities," the young West Pointer tried to get his Vietnamese advisees to send honest reports to Saigon. Pointing out that one of Hop Tac's main points aimed at finding out pacification's progress by stressing both population screening and elimination of the VC infrastructure, Ray questioned the statistics going forward. Nha Be's reports generally showed a well-screened population and no real VC threats. Since the VC infrastructure had hardly been disturbed in the district, Ray urged an open admission that, by the government's own criteria, none of the hamlets had completed pacification! Truong listened respectfully.

As for Westy's Hop Tac plan, Ray liked the idea but deplored its execution. Too many inspections of little things, usually done without sufficient notice and in adversarial modes, irked everyone. One of the problems seemed to be that military inspectors were fuddled by the civilian activities they surveyed. Changes in that program seemed essential to preserve its sound purposes.

As he roamed his codomain, Ray noted the heavy overgrowth of grass that choked a lot of the farming area and also provided interesting hiding places for any lurking VC. He and Troung tried to launch a grass cutting program in early September, which involved them in oleaginous encounters with Saigon officialdom. Two weeks later, three majors descended from MACV to inspect the grass cutting—which had not begun!

Sweeping the district always with critical eyes, Ray turned more and more attention to martial matters. At first glance, Captain Trac's tank farm defense plan looked good—at least, considering his resources. But, and Ray would find this a perennial condition, too much reliance rested on static positions, probably easily bypassed. And the positions were too dispersed to help each other. Perhaps, Ray hoped, helicopters would provide quick reinforcements in an emergency.

Trying to improve things, Ray discovered that the static outposts represented more than a place, they represented a mind-set nearly impossible to break. Ray suggested to Troung and Trac that flare ships would brighten their prospects of holding positions. Most of all, the American urged sending frequent patrols out into the countryside to find, engage, and beat the VC. Trac appeared to listen, reluctantly, to this uncommon enthusiasm. Ray could promise, and deliver within about fifteen minutes, two Hueys for support of any mobile operations; with the aid of one or two flare ships, the VC might be glimpsed flitting in the brush. That sounded useful to Trac, and Truong had no objection.

Early efforts must have amused the Vietnamese. On Monday, September 14, an early-morning report of 150 VC three miles from Nha Be triggered a major sweep. Ray's armed helicopters arrived, swooshed over a wide area, and found nothing. The Vietnamese had no more luck on the ground. Ray figured the "VC presumably dispersed to the west, spooked by the first sound of the Hueys." But, in good Fort Benning style, he critiqued the ground operations: "far too slow in getting moving—and our first action was to throw half a dozen 60mm mortar rounds for reasons as yet unclear."

Truong and Trac were impressed, however, and Ray found less resistance in the future to the use of gunships and flare ships. Problems centered around the readiness of militia troops who remained woefully unprepared. Let Ray describe an especially frustrating action on September 8–9, 1964:

> The operation was, at least from my point of view, even more disappointing than expected. We got off to a late start, and soon found that one boat (which was quite large) could not go under a bridge until the tide ran out. So we waited for a boat from the other side to arrive, and transferred by sampan. Arrived at the central hamlet, which is very long and narrow, around 1015. Met the hamlet chief, who was at work on a community center . . . and then set up shop at a villager's house where we drank coconut milk and tea for an hour or so. The house was interesting—a Buddhist family altar, with photograph of the dead father. Furniture consisted mainly of plain mahogany platforms: beds.

Went then to look at a 30-man Ngia-Quon post, on the border of Binh Chan district. It has quite a lot of wire within the last 30 meters, but seems not to be oriented toward the major threat. They patrol at night by sampan only: there is no defense in depth. But at night they must provide guards for the hamlet from their forces.

Ate lunch with Truong on the boat ride home—a box lunch that was surely the most dangerous part of the day.

That expedition fitted a general picture of inertia that seemed to permeate the Regional and Popular Forces. They bothered Ray with their VC-like black pajama garb (he conceded there was some poetic justice because the VC often wore ARVN uniforms). He also knew they needed guidance and training (for which nobody seemed to claim responsibility) and that their arms were outdated and their ammunition unreliable—that they shied from meeting the well-armed and drilled VC seemed the better part of valor.

In time, special training for the local defense forces improved their condition and brought recruits to their ranks. Ray took constant interest in improving these forces and attended all ceremonies for graduating training classes or deployments of new units. He had a lot to do with initiating the local defense training program, which finally earned a visit from Westmoreland in January, 1965. Westy's entourage nearly flooded Nha Be; it certainly unnerved Ray's superior, Colonel Sapp, who rushed from Saigon to be seen. Once, during those ceremonial rounds, there was a glitch and Colonel Sapp fussed about what Ray planned to do about it. A veteran by then, Ray just smiled and said, "stand here and worry about it, sir."[68]

Keeping the pressure on, Ray stressed coordination of RF/PF efforts with the police and kept banging away at command and control issues until some coordination happened. That led him to vent a rare boast: "I don't really think they would have resolved those matters without my urging"!

Most of all, though, Jim Ray worked—and that brought him an unexpected problem. Once, not long after arriving in Nha Be, he invited Captain Trac to a modest dinner. As they sat chatting afterward, Trac suddenly asked in Amvietoise, "Why are you working so hard here?" First flustered, then amused, Ray talked of why he liked his job: it was the best in South Vietnam[69] because it demanded the skills of a diplomat, foreign aid administrator, and military advisor. Still, the Yankee work ethic disturbed his cohorts. His badgering forced action where inconvenient and turned Nha Be District from passivity into aggressive pursuit of the VC. One of Ray's most pleasant surprises came in November, 1964, when the district police chief "staggered me by soliciting my comments on how to inspect check-point operations."

He did a lot more than coordinate command. His English classes won many friends, and his concern for self-help programs insured the success of the brick factory, the free distribution of corn, a general policing of the entire district, and much greater RF/PF efficiency. In short, he had better prepared the district for a war that he saw on January 7, 1965, as "coming closer to home lately." Two days after penning that observation, he and Captain Trac plotted an ambush for some aggressive VC. Jim Ray was killed that night while trying to aid one of Trac's men.[70]

James Floyd Ray represents America's greatest triumph in South Vietnam. He and so many advisors like him brought energy, wisdom, sympathy, and deep personal concern to the Vietnamese around them. They were truly "the best and the brightest," and they left behind not victory in military terms, but hope, humanity, and the greater love of man. They were not wasted, for they sowed mercy and reaped the future for a remote and ravaged land.[71]

THE MARINE WAY

Marines are different—not ornerier or more conceited, just different. And they like it. Best of coordinators when necessary, willing sustainers of the army under the worst conditions, veterans of all kinds of hard time—including, especially, Guadalcanal—Marines cling to an uncommon pride of hardness. And although they do coordinate with the army, coordination usually poses problems—so much so that army commanders grumble about leatherneck assistance and look upon working with them as a kind of family interoperability problem.

Of course, the army posed particular problems of its own in Vietnam. Pacification is an unusually interesting example of how the two services diverged in program concepts, methods, applications, and varying truths. Interestingly enough, they had the same ideas—and that caused the main problem: Who had bragging rights?

Assigned to the northern provinces, up in the I Corps zone, the Marines were close to the DMZ—close to the route the enemy would take in a mass invasion of the south. It was just where they wanted to be for several reasons. Not only did they sit in a potential hot seat, they were ensconced in something of a cul-de-sac; from Da Nang to the DMZ, the Annamite Range swings close to the coast, with Highway 1 sometimes winding its way edgily close to the ocean. In that mountain-girt region, the Marines were a good distance from Saigon and MACV, so they did things in their area much as they wanted them done.

They were there, too, because General Westmoreland had a special appreciation of them. He, unlike most army brass, had once served with a Marine division, and thus understood the logistical background of the Marine beachhead philosophy. They were accustomed to sustaining themselves from the sea and could move inland without worrying unduly about bases and protected lines of communication. He liked it, too, that Marine battalions were heavy in infantry—their four companies each had two hundred men, which gave them considerable staying power. But he did not like the early tactics he saw Lt. Gen. Lewis W. Walt employing throughout his zone.[72]

Walt, sticking to tested counterinsurgency tactics, established beachheads, then combed the country between them, tying them together in a security network. Gradually the cleared areas would expand. This scheme had the hearty support of the Fleet Marine Force, Pacific, commander, Lt. Gen. Victor H. "Brute" Krulak, who watched happily the successes earned by Walt's program through 1965.[73]

Obviously the Marine plan resembled the "ink spot" idea—indeed, General Krulak called it the "'spreading ink blot' formula"—and a good many people in Saigon and Washington liked it. But the Marines' successes were not the army's, and Westy dismissed them quickly: "The idea seemed to be effective," he told Krulak, but there simply wasn't time to do it that way. Krulak—never a shrinking violet—erupted that there wasn't time to "do it any other way; if we left the people to the enemy, glorious victories in the hinterland would be little more than blows in the air—and we would end up losing the war." But Bob McNamara backed Westy's view. "A good idea," he opined late in 1965, "but too slow."[74]

Neither Krulak nor General Walt could get higher brass to listen to the stories of places like Le My, where Marines were doing much the same things that Jim Ray had done. One comment from the district chief hit home with Krulak, who was looking approvingly at civil progress in the community. "All of this has meaning only if you are going to stay."[75] Thereby hung the whole problem of U.S. policy in Vietnam. All of America's efforts were transitory. When the Americans cleaned up a village and moved on, back came the VC to wreak vengeance as the price of sticking with Saigon.

Marines have a near fetish for making things tidy. They devised special ways not only to control their area, but also to negate VC influence. Long experience in guerrilla operations—Haiti and Nicaragua, knowledge of British doings in Malaya during the 1950s—gave them a head start. And they had a tough-minded, innovative commander in Lew Walt.

Walt encouraged a special scheme that did much good. Called the Combined Action Program (CAP), it mixed a squad of Marine volunteers coached in Vietnamese culture into a platoon of RF or PF troops. The Marines would move into a village, live with the people, get to know them, and work on civic projects. In tactical operations, the Marine squad leader, by written agreement with the South Vietnamese corps commanders, commanded the force, with the militia platoon leader as his assistant. Not only did this increase security in the villages, it greatly improved RF/PF morale in the combined units and turned them into aggressive pursuers of the VC. Walt kept expanding the program until I Corps had "114 CAP units comprised of about two thousand American marines and naval corpsmen and three thousand Popular Forces soldiers" guarding some 350 villages.[76]

Westy grudgingly agreed that the idea worked and approved the use of some army troops with territorials, but he worried that it was too troop-intensive, would duplicate advisory efforts, and would involve Americans in actions best handled by Saigon's forces. Westy came increasingly to the notion that the big war was his and that pacification was Saigon's problem.

Marine efforts did replicate some of the U.S. Army's advisory efforts, and that turned out well. The I Corps record of making and protecting friends, harassing foes, and holding the area tightly secure showed the fine things that could be done by men intent on doing them. Good is hard to see in war, but in Vietnam's "other wars" came some flashes of good amidst the carnage.

Just how much did Johnson know about the good things going on in Vietnam? General Walt paid him a White House visit in February, 1966. Johnson enjoyed talking with military men when they were fresh from the field. The straight-backed Walt impressed LBJ as being a "Marine's Marine," and the president liked what he said.

Johnson always listened intently to news of what U.S. troops were doing to help the Vietnamese people—building schools, dispensaries, offering medical care. Walt's account of the CAP story excited LBJ, and he thrilled to the news of "young Americans in the midst of war's horrors . . . keeping their humanity, their loyalty to each other and to their country, and most important, their compassion for the men, women, and children around them."[77]

War's paradoxes baffled always: Good coming out of chaos; brotherhood from conflict; humanity from sacrifice. Was there, somehow some silver lining in the black cloud lowering on the White House? It all seemed so puzzling to the embattled commander in chief. Scattered reports indicated pacification was making progress; others suggested that results were patchy, diffused, and uncoordinated. That was why LBJ ordered Bob Komer to Vietnam. A lot depended on him because the big war continued and other challenges were coming.

Other Wars

pparently endless lines of protesters marched in front of the White House, chanting antiwar slogans and carrying Viet Cong banners; they were sometimes whipped to various frenzies by speakers or by occasional hecklers who jeered and waved America's star-spangled banner. All kinds of obscenities made up the jargon of a new generation turned against old things, old ideas, even old people often embodied in parents and the odd prejudices parents seemed to carry from the 1940s and '50s, years of conflict and of minds closed by the Communist bugaboo. Most of those young protesters had no shame in calling for Uncle Ho's triumph, no pride in America's wrongful crusade against the Vietnamese; they floundered in search of a focus for their frustrations, a focus they could hate—and they found that focus in LBJ.

What they shouted, yelled, and sang before the White House many thought went unheard inside—but their noises were more for themselves than for the Satan they thought resided inside the house whose color painted over a decadent darkness of evil. They would have been tickled to know their new Beelzebub heard them—as did his whole family. Luci Johnson remembers with grim clarity the last words she heard at night during the hectic years, the words that woke her in the morning: "Hey, Hey, LBJ, How

Many Kids Did You Kill Today?" She explained that "People think the President is isolated but on the north side of the White House those residents literally hear every ounce of complaint. Forget the media [telling] us, we can hear it."[1]

The marchers had been coming in growing numbers through 1965, encouraged by politicized professorial "teach-ins" as well as an individual kind of canted idealism—and there is nothing more dangerous than activist idealism just waiting to be aimed. Slowly, protesters slipped into the rowdy discipline of a "movement." They spawned leaders of high energy—the names of Timothy Leary, Tom Hayden, Abbie Hoffman, and Jerry Rubin resonate from those years—who pushed radical ideas beyond original notions. They were occasionally duped by Communists circulating among them, and their very numbers gave them, sometimes, a moblike kind of revolutionary anger. Many of them believed in the rhetoric of rejection, perhaps boasting of American decline in an effort to hide uncertainty if not a real fear of the draft, which probably fueled antiwar sentiment as much as did ideology.

Rigged so that college students won easy exemptions—in an attempt to correct some errors of the World War II draft—Selective Service boards tended to select the underprivileged who had little chance for college. And the heaviest burden seemed to fall on blacks—as any fair counting of troops in the field would verify. Harlem's Rep. Adam Clayton Powell, Jr., ranted loudly against the May, 1966, Selective Service plan to use qualification test scores for high school seniors and undergraduate and graduate college students to determine deferments if monthly draft calls went above thirty thousand. It was a racist ploy, thundered Powell, to dragoon blacks to the Vietnam slaughterhouse.

National test day, May 14, saw over 750,000 male college students take the exam. Well over half of them received a Students for a Democratic Society (SDS) counter-draft exam with such stimulating questions as "how many South Vietnamese deserted in 1965?" The testing program came to an abrupt end; not so, opposition to the draft.[2]

Enlisting to fight against immoral, colonialist repression gave rational cover to many who simply shirked. "Hell no, I won't go," became the chorus of draft-card burners encouraged by high-sounding words of opposition coming from America's campuses, from distinguished intellectuals, even from members of Congress (Sen. Wayne Morse endorsed legal marches and protests). That opposition would fuse in time with other areas of protest into a stronger, tougher movement, but one laced with fatal disagreements about doctrine and objective. A hoped-for close alliance with Stokely Carmichael's Student Nonviolent Coordinating Committee (SNCC) and other dissident black elements did not happen; nor did alignment with American labor. But the movement, nonetheless, rose to a kind of prominence—a success that led to gluttony and overreaching which finally broke its power.[3]

Rallies, marches, and great crowds milling around the Pentagon, the White House, in big cities and small, were avidly presented on network TV and in newspapers, as were comments by some of the most radical antiwarriors who asked for volunteers to fight against Americans in Vietnam. These visible antagonisms gave more than comfort to the enemy, they convinced Hanoi that the American people—like the French after Dien Bien Phu—would not sustain the war. North Vietnam would win by simply hanging on. A North Vietnamese newspaper gloated that the American "debates on the Vietnamese problem, will become increasingly fiercer [sic]. The United States Imperialistic rear will be the scene of great confusion, which in turn will exert great influence upon the morale of the United States servicemen on the front line. That is why the Johnson clique is very perplexed and afraid, faced with the ever stronger anti-war movement which, like a sharp knife, is stabbing them in the back."[4]

As a kind of religious zeal worked through the movement, churches took sides. Many church groups denounced the protesters; others offered support. For a time the press caricatured the rebels as "bearded bums" in an "acne alliance." President Eisenhower had no time for them, but the most profound preachment against them came from one of America's greatest orators, Everett Dirksen. "The spectacle of young men willing to perjure themselves to avoid the draft," he thundered, "and willing to let the world know that they do not support other young Americans arrayed in battle in Vietnam in the cause of freedom is enough to make any person loyal to his country weep."

Doris Kearns, herself of the protest era, speculated that "the peace movement developed essentially outside the established political system. This was both the source of its strength and its undoing."[5] She goes on to suggest that ignorance of history proved to be the movement's worst enemy. Untouched by the experiences of their elders, the protesters saw Vietnam as a civil war in a small land beyond America's writ. As for the domino theory, it seemed a feeble construct of deluded thinking, and no one's thinking seemed more deluded than Lyndon Johnson's.

Johnson had some sympathy for the young rebels. It was the kids who were deluded—he did not blame them because he knew they lacked perspective. "Why should I listen to all those student peaceniks marching up and down the streets?" he asked. "They were barely in their cradles in the dark days of World War II; they never experienced the ravages of Adolf Hitler; they were only in nursery school during the Korean War; they wouldn't know a Communist if they tripped over one." Their teachers deserved the most blame, Johnson thought, because they prated about peace coming to the good people, the "soft and . . . nice."[6]

Johnson's own experience of history taught that force sometimes has to be met with force. Weakness in the pre–World War I and II and Korean War eras forced Britain, France, and America into war. Failure to stop Communism in Vietnam would bring on greater conflict in the future. That, the youngsters could not know—but Johnson surely did.

If what the criers on Pennsylvania Avenue wanted was to irk the president, they failed; they bothered him, yes, but mainly they pained him. He was, by all measurements, on their side—the most ardent rebel of them all. They marched, sang, and cried for a more decent country, one to stand against even its own oppressions—but Lyndon Johnson made it happen. Dimly at first, then more clearly, he grasped the dream of the Great Society, shaped it, pushed it, willed it into being. Johnson's triumph made no difference to those who saw only the nightmare of Vietnam. America's streets became baffling extensions of a maddening war.

Some critics—Kearns among them—say that Johnson could not stand all the public outcry, that he adopted a siege mentality, turned inward and against his real and fancied enemies. He doubtless did shun the ones who made the easy judgment of paranoia, of "projection and conspiracy;" he did seek solace in discrediting detractors. The White House has, sometimes, too public a face, bulks too large in the world's fears; those who work there are sometimes hostage to the images they see on TV, read in the papers, and hear through the walls. They can come to a different reality that projects friends as enemies and enemies larger than life. That view comes sometimes to high executives and reflects the distortions of eminence more than the specters of dementia.

President Johnson lost no touch with reality; it crowded him from all sides. The protesters were symptoms of a national malaise fueled by war and by deep divisions in the union. That malaise limited presidential influence and showed cracks in the country's consensus. Always a realist about public moods, Johnson measured his sagging repute against the things he wanted to do. George Ball constantly brandished failing national will as a rising threat and Johnson knew it was coming. Which would distrust wreck first, the domestic war or the one in Asia? He would have to ride a rising crest of anger as he sought to win them both.

Street conflict amounted to an odd kind of civil war—a mixture of peaceful demonstrations and direct combat between protestors, police, and sometimes the National Guard. Those defense forces were often overtaxed during the course of 1965, a year in which more than a hundred thousand protesters marched or milled in antiwar rallies.

The temperature of the movement rose and fell in almost direct relation to fiery campus teach-ins. For instance, in March, after an all-night denunciation of U.S. "aggression" in Vietnam by fourteen Michigan University professors, a nationwide telephone campaign launched a countrywide campus crusade that culminated in a May 15–16 national teach-in in Washington. Covered on network television, by foreign corespondents, by all the media, this event triggered a frisson of loathing in J. Edgar Hoover. His FBI dutifully announced that at least twenty-six of the teach-in's sponsors were Communists.

But the war escalated through the year. The number of picketers grew proportionally in front of the White House, their messages angrier and more pro–Viet Cong. Twenty thousand massed around the Washington Monument and sought money to help the oppressed VC. Militancy grew as new, smaller, carefully directed groups like the SDS aimed at widespread campus disruption. Trainloads of troops were harassed as "butchers." A fairly hot summer seemed a cool prelude to the winter campaign. October nearly brought another revolution—this one in the United States. Over one hundred thousand people thronged Fifth Avenue in New York. Again, Hoover's henchmen reported heavy Communist sponsorship. There were immolations, and guidelines were circulated on how to avoid the draft. Even revered child authority Dr. Benjamin Spock took the road in protest against the Vietnam War as he gave speeches on "Raising Our Children in a Cold War Age."

Police sometimes overreacted during demonstrations and mass gatherings. They were tired, scared, and irritated, and they often swung hasty truncheons, striking out in anger and hurting people. That sort of storm-troop reaction touched America's undercurrent of sympathy for underdogs; it also touched a latent national reverence for freedom of speech. Listen to former professor Gale McGee, senator from Wyoming, speaking to the country:

> As one who has vigorously defended America's tough stand in Vietnam. . . . [I caution that] we must not destroy our fundamental freedoms in the name of preserving them. This we do if we ban pickets or smear them as communists. I am sure there must be some communists in the ranks. But I deplore labeling every protest movement as commu-

nist-inspired. . . . This smears the overwhelming majority of the protestors in a way detrimental to their free right to object, or to oppose.[7]

McGee was right. The Communist label created a great underswell of fright across America, especially on the campuses; so much so that many professors and students who shared McGee's concern about First Amendment rights were muffled in fear of jobs or reputations. And it became, for many old-line liberals, almost as difficult to speak out against war protesters as it was for protesters to protest. Those who dared were branded as warmongers as hysteria swept the land in a morbid reprise of McCarthyism.

For the administration, the civil conflict's main challenge loomed clear enough: preserving freedom and order simultaneously.[8]

THE FULBRIGHT OFFENSIVE

Senator J. William Fulbright, idealistic Democrat from Arkansas, ranked a longtime friend of LBJ's. They had helped each other in the Senate and generated, over the years, considerable mutual respect. They had their differences—Fulbright, for example, resented Johnson's lukewarm support of Adlai Stevenson in the 1952 presidential campaign—but both were southern liberals and that pulled them together more often than not.[9] In Johnson's early presidency Fulbright had supported him with strength and eloquence; the senator defended the Tonkin Gulf Resolution before his Foreign Relations Committee and the whole Senate. And Fulbright campaigned hard for LBJ in 1964. But over the next two years, Fulbright grew increasingly concerned about Vietnam. He frequently trekked to 1600 Pennsylvania Avenue and shared his worries with the president, who listened carefully during those private sessions in the first half of 1965. Fulbright understood LBJ's political dilemma if the United States pulled out of Vietnam without some kind of settlement. It seemed to Fulbright that creation of a kind of Titoist state looked like the best arrangement for South Vietnam. That would deny the south to both sides and give LBJ something to cover an American withdrawal. Although he heard his Arkansas friend, Johnson remained unpersuaded and Fulbright finally spoke out against U.S. policy in Southeast Asia—although he avoided personalizing his criticism.

Be it said for the senator, he tried to keep his closeness with Johnson. But Johnson, finding it almost impossible to separate public and personal positions, broke their friendship. A year later, when their relationship had cooled, LBJ wrote Fulbright a semiconciliatory letter: "I listen to everyone . . . but I . . . take the responsibility for deciding the policy. . . . I have a fondness for you and Betty that is real."[10] Much later, in his final evening at the White House, he reminisced with Joe Califano and talked of Bill Fulbright nostalgically. Vietnam and civil rights had estranged them he knew, the Dominican matter also, but the Tonkin attacks had created the first gulf. Johnson could recall Fulbright's lamenting, as he reviewed Vietnam in early 1966, that he had not really understood the Tonkin Gulf Resolution. That sparked one of Johnson's quips: "For a Rhodes scholar to say that he didn't know what was in that resolution is more than this hillbilly will ever believe."

But on that last night, quips and quarrels were muted. The president looked back in sorrow at some of the things he had allowed himself to say about Fulbright over the past hectic years. "Perhaps it would have been different with Fulbright," he thought, "if we had only talked to him more, had him over here more, found some things to agree with him on." And then a final summation: "We never should have let the fight become so personal."[11]

But personal it became. And it was a sense of personal betrayal that led to Fulbright's most direct attack on the president's Vietnam policy. Feeling that he had been misled when Johnson sought passage of the Tonkin Gulf Resolution—lied to, in fact, about Johnson's future intentions, and lied to later by administration officials—Fulbright, as chairman of the Senate Committee on Foreign Relations, decided to hold open hearings on America's actions in Vietnam.[12] Scheduled for early 1966, these hearings had every potential for launching a national debate on Vietnam—a debate that might fracture the country, paralyze the commander in chief's power to continue the war, and hand victory to Hanoi on a television screen.

Senators love televised hearings. They get their makeup just right, sit lazily behind their microphones and, when they get the floor, ask portentous questions, either as hits off their colleagues or to make points at home. Fulbright, as chairman, understood his committee's thespian needs, gave them exposure, and ran the Committee on Foreign Relations with professional charm. His disarming earnestness, his querying eyes, and his intelligent words muffled in a soft, southern drawl all lent a sense of honest fact-finding to his own special star chamber.[13]

Administration people were sure that all congressional committee chairmen took nasty delight in summoning executive branch officials to the Hill, sitting them in front of microphones and cameras, and treating them often with snide contempt. That had some validity, of course, but Fulbright seemed above cheap posturing. Still, he could be tough, his questions exacting, his debating skills fearsome—and his colleagues were not all above a pose or two. And, as he prepared for his hearings, some qualms ran through State and Defense—qualms that somehow did not ruffle the secretaries of those departments, nor some of the other witnesses called to defend the U.S. position in Vietnam.

Johnson fussed always about the time various congressional hearings took, about the number of hours members of the administration spent away from their jobs just to mollify a political whim. These hearings had such dismal possibilities that Johnson's anger seemed oddly muted in frustration. Fulbright's television circus would not only help the enemy, it would lend a good deal of legitimacy to the antiwar movement. More and more people could chuck patriotism as anti-American. He had, in a way, upstaged Fulbright with the Honolulu conference and had taken most of the potential witnesses with him. Fulbright persisted.

But Johnson's worries waned as the senator botched the hearings. His hard grilling of such American stalwarts as Maxwell Taylor and Dean Rusk worked against him. They were formidable as they sat looking up at their accusers and responded firmly, patiently, witheringly. Taylor stuck to his guns about Vietnam, holding to the belief that American policy would prevail and that South Vietnam could be denied to the Communists.

Dean Rusk's formidable integrity, his solid support of the U.S. position, and his calm refusal to be ruffled scored heavily, as did his prepared statement, "The U.S. Commitment in Viet-Nam: Fundamental Issues." His solemn final comment pretty well finished the inquisition: "Gentlemen, I think a simple answer to the question, what are we doing in South Viet-Nam, is to say that for more than a decade we have been taking sides in a cause in which we have a vital stake."[14]

Rusk's earnest testimony put the best possible face on America's efforts in Southeast Asia—and it made considerable impact across the country. Two days later, Sunday, February 20, Lady Bird Johnson noted in her diary that "the week had been a terrific strain . . . and then on Thursday and Friday, I had the feeling that it was our inning—that we won with General Maxwell Taylor and Secretary Rusk."[15]

Fulbright's offensive faded without much added fanfare—but, as antiwar feelings grew in Congress, the senator kept on the scent.

THE JOHNSON REVOLUTION—SECOND PHASE

Mounting anger in Congress and the country not only irked the president, it alarmed him because of his Great Society programs. They were likely victims of mounting national frustration. Right-wingers, the ones LBJ most feared, called for more aggressive policies in Vietnam. John Cornelius Stennis, a Mississippi Democrat and chairman of LBJ's old Preparedness Subcommittee of the Senate Armed Services Committee, finally did lead a campaign to relegate the Great Society "to the rear" in order to free resources to crush the enemy in Vietnam. Johnson worried that Stennis's attitude might spread throughout the senate's conservative southern bloc and derail the whole domestic program. Richard Russell's staunch control of his colleagues could hardly be expected to stand against a fervid burst of patriotism.[16]

By mid-1966, Johnson's Great Society had made astounding legislative progress. The campaign began in December, 1965, at the LBJ Ranch. Joe Califano, an increasingly needed henchman on the domestic front, arrived with a loose-leaf book labeled "The Great Society—A Second Year Legislative Program." Between those covers were proposed bills to be enacted by the second session of the 89th Congress—bills to complete the Great Society, bills to make another American Revolution.

Califano found the president seated behind his desk in the ranch office; the book was placed on end in front of LBJ so he could look closely as his assistant turned the pages. The White House staff waging the domestic war had heard LBJ's September 16 statement that "we mean to show that this Nation's dream of a Great Society does not stop at the water's edge: and that it is not just an American dream. All are welcome to share in it. All are invited to contribute to it." Those words guided the staff in proposing a huge program of social improvements, a program to serve as a model for the world.

Clearly excited at what he brought to the ranch, Califano went through the pages, noting that "we were serving up plenty of butter to go with the guns, a grand design. . . . As he went through my proposals, Johnson approved a vast international health initiative (which among other things, set the goal, eventually achieved in 1980, to eradicate smallpox from the face of the earth by 1975), and international population, education, and food programs." All these were dear to LBJ's heart, and his enthusiasm soon matched Califano's.

Johnson's memory amazed people—William Bundy stood in awe of it—but it had a shrewd selectivity to it that could befuddle political friends and foes. It was at its best when Johnson wanted to recall a thing he'd done or promised to do. And he remembered that day, leaning back in his chair, things he had promised. He greeted proposals to reshape the Executive Branch with pleasure. A new Department of Housing and Urban Development won his approval, as did a reorganization of the Department of Health, Education, and Welfare, renovation of the Civil Service System, a four-year term for House members, and some changes in the electoral college. In the civil rights area—a field already boasting such victories as the Civil Rights Act of 1964 and the Voting Rights Act of 1965—Johnson agreed to proposals for fair jury selection, protection of civil rights workers, and an important fair-housing plan.

The president greeted with pleasure the idea of a new Department of Transportation, but his face squibbed up with a malodorous reaction to a proposal to spend public money on a supersonic jet transport. He went along with the idea, Califano noted, "because it was the hot button for the powerful Washington senators, Warren Magnuson, who chaired the Commerce Committee (on which we were dependent for our auto-safety program and most consumer legislation), and Henry (Scoop) Jackson, a key supporter on Vietnam and environmental programs."

It came as no surprise to Califano that Johnson beamed at a demonstration cities proposal, under which a five- to ten-year effort would aim at turning some hard-core slums into "a modern area with a total approach—new homes, schools, parks, community centers and open spaces," along with health and police facilities. New parks won his warm endorsement, as did historic building preservation plans, a trail and scenic road system, a clean rivers plan, and "tough new clean-air legislation."

A massive scheme for local health planning, modernization of hospitals, the education of doctors and paramedics, plus a Committee on Mental Retardation earned quick support.

Johnson wanted to do much for education: stimulate school construction and modernization for the poor, pass a GI Bill for cold warriors, provide school breakfasts and lunches, and press for enlargement of kindergarten and summer programs for underprivileged children.

The president accepted a plan for campaign-reform legislation and fussed about the way American political campaigns were funded—he felt that all federal elections should be publicly underwritten.

After some digression about political funding, Johnson went on to approve for inclusion in the legislative package U.S. participation in the Asian Development Bank (an important cog in his Vietnam machinery), a bicentennial commission to plan celebrations of American's two-hundredth birthday, rent supplements, extended unemployment benefits, increased minimum wages, truth-in-lending and packaging bills, repeal of the law permitting state right-to-work laws, and improved anticrime measures.

When the session ended, Califano reflected on "an extraordinary experience. In less than two hours, this President had blessed a massive second-year program that would astound the Congress and the country when he unveiled it in his State of the Union message on January 12, 1966."[17]

Johnson taxed his entire domestic staff in putting the message together.

Bits and pieces were farmed out to different people and, at length, the president even allowed Dick Goodwin, he of the splendid speech-writing talents, back to the White House. As the message was massaged into shape, Califano grasped its real scope better than most. "The budget and legislative program, that Johnson would present," he wrote later, "would amount to a public declaration that he was going to get his Great Society while he fought the war."

And, memorably, on the evening of January 12, President Johnson challenged Congress to stay the course of guns and butter.[18] Reaction had run well to the massive workload Johnson piled on Congress. His message had smoothed some ruffled liberal feathers, gave enough to the hawks for the nonce, and scotched any notion that he would allow anything to stint his revolution for the little man. And Congress went to work right enough. When the session ended, an avalanche of bills had passed. Together with the work of the first session, the 89th Congress had pretty well given LBJ the revolution he coveted. Let Joe Califano sum up the achievements: "When the 89th Congress adjourned on October 22, 1966, Johnson's legislative accomplishments were already monumental. Indeed, with the President asking for 113 major measures and getting 97 passed, the second session of the 89th Congress had exceeded the output of the first, in which 87 measures were requested and 84 passed."

This whirlwind lifted Joseph Califano to the high, clear air of a better, caring world, took him to new heights, and spread Canaan before him. He never forgot it. "Did we legislate too much?" he mused much later. "Perhaps. Did we stub our toes? Of course." But all these came from a belief in the rights of man, an ennobling belief that touched things done with the fiery zest of change.[19]

Overall, LBJ had proposed two hundred bills to a sympathetic Congress that enacted 187 for a .935 average. Johnson knew he had done more than any other American president to advance the people's cause in America, but he lamented the lack of appreciation. He lamented, too, clear evidence that the honeymoon was over. Vietnam's "black cloud" wafted doubt across the country and the Congress. Although the president counted victories for the Great Society, he needed victories in Vietnam to shore up rents in the Union. Unfortunately, there were none. Nothing but troubles spilled from America's embattled ally, and casting darker shadows through the White House.

NGUYEN CAO KY'S CIVIL WAR

Premier Ky returned home after his meeting with LBJ in Honolulu full of enthusiasm. If Johnson had not called him "the Churchill of the East," he had certainly shown much friendship and confidence. Ky felt that he had a kind of American mandate to get his government consolidated for heavier war against the Viet Cong. To carry out that mandate—which comported well with his own estimate of his destiny—Ky knew he would either have to come to some kind of understanding with southern dissident Buddhists or force their acceptance of the new government. Understanding seemed highly unlikely since the dissidents were led by a highly political priest (bonze), Thich Tri Quang.

Tri Quang had a firm grasp of the impact of the news media and knew how to mix religious mysticism with political policies in a fine brew of trouble. For years he had fought for civilian rule in Vietnam, and had suffered for it. When Diem had permitted Nhu to launch an attack on Buddhist pagodas, Tri Quang took refuge in the American embassy and emerged later as a kind of hero. Seating himself in Hue, Tri Quang began a campaign of Buddhist unification into a religious and secular power by shrewdly creating two organizations that became political and spiritual forces that helped topple Diem's, Khanh's, and Huong's governments.

Nguyen Cao Ky came from a Buddhist family, and Tri Quang may have thought he had a ringer at court—after all, Ky's youth and political naivete made him ripe for manipulation. Ky, shrewder than most thought, refused the role of puppet. First he tried reason. Inviting various Buddhist groups to his house, he told them that he recognized they represented a large segment of the Vietnamese population, were entitled to be heard, and that he did not really oppose their aims. "I'm willing to discuss any problems you put forward," he repeated time and again, "but if you believe in the destiny of South Vietnam, if you want us to survive against Communism, which is an enemy of your religion, surely it's time we united against the common foe."

Ky realized that Tri Quang wanted to be the power behind South Vietnamese affairs.[20] Tri Quang pretty well proved the point by loosing a series of Buddhist demonstrations in various Vietnamese cities, especially in Hue and Da Nang.

Just what happened in the ensuing confusion, in what sequence, comes variously from the sources. Ky's recollections make him the flamboyant hero of the story; Westy's memory relegated the entire mess to the status of "foolishness,"[21] although he kept a closer eye than guessed on everything happening in the I Corps area.

Ky's first action against the Buddhists focused on one of their closest ARVN friends, Gen. Nguyen Chanh Thi, commander of the South Vietnamese I Corps. Thi's constant cooperation with the Buddhists and apparent conniving to advance their goals made him suspicious to Ky and Thieu and others in the government. Truth be told, he and Ky were destined to clash because of their similarities. "General Thi was in many ways like Ky," Westy noted. "They looked somewhat alike: suave, wiry, mustached, flamboyant, swaggering. Both had infinite courage."[22]

When word reached Saigon that Thi had encouraged the Buddhists to think that his I Corps would not fight them if they staged national demonstrations, Ky had enough. To him, Thi "was nursing ambitions to become an old-fashioned warlord," as he encouraged something of a Buddhist secession movement. On March 10, 1966, Ky, backed by Thieu (who thought Buddhist power was exaggerated)[23] and the military directorate, sacked the I Corps commander and precipitated a major political crisis.[24]

Tri Quang, delighted at Ky's blunder in removing the widely popular General Thi, gleefully loosed his minions in all directions. A day later, the United Buddhist Church called for elections to pick a civilian government. Ambassador Lodge told LBJ that elections held before a constitution was drafted, without election laws, "is to court a wildly irresponsible mess."[25]

Following their election demand, Buddhists and students flooded the streets in Da Nang, Hue, Hoi An, and many other large towns, calling for an end to military rule. Some strikes followed these demonstrations. In Saigon, gangs of toughs seized the opportunity to trash autos and store windows. Most policemen—bewildered, outnumbered, some sympathizing with the crowds—stood idle. Rumors lay a hazy dread across most of the south as demonstrations expanded. When the Da Nang port closed and troops began to take sides, Ky's government teetered on the brink.

As civil war threatened to engulf the country, it looked as though the Buddhists might succeed in paralyzing Saigon's war effort, cut Vietnam in two, and perhaps force secession of the central part of the country and hand victory to Hanoi. They would have denied such a purpose and meant it; but their political naivete exceeded their ambitions. On the other hand, their determination went unguessed for a time and their numbers were undercounted.

Presiding over this chaos, Tri Quang held court at his headquarters in Hue's Dieude temple. From there he issued myriad media appeals—his followers held the radio station, and TV crews always seemed at hand for one of his appearances. He had some thoughts of winning by nonviolence what the VC could not win by killing. His Gandhi-like smile seemed more a smirk to Ky as declarations, pronouncements, and pleas wafted through world capitals. Meantime, some of his followers were brandishing antigovernment and anti-American banners in a thinly veiled attempt to provoke Americans as they watched the news at home and to pressure Cabot Lodge to urge the government to abdicate.[26]

The whole thing seemed, to some Westerners, a kind of Eastern tragicomedy. While the south's fabric frazzled, U.S. troops were dying. One irked embassy official stormed at Stanley Karnow, "What are we doing here? We're fighting to save these people, and they're fighting each other!"[27]

Westy urged Lodge to emphasize American irritation as disturbances escalated over a three-week period. The ambassador reminded Ky that 228 Americans had died "fighting for South Vietnam," in the I Corps area during that period. Westy also had a special briefing about the rising enemy threat in the I Corps region given to Thieu, Ky, and other government officials.

As the unrest increased, General Walt put both Hue and Da Nang off limits to his Marines.

Ky, worried that the situation seemed to be running past Tri Quang's or anyone else's control, announced the formation of a special committee to draft a constitution. When that received approval by referendum, elections would be held as soon as possible, perhaps by year's end. This apparent concession to democracy by Ky sparked even fiercer dissident attacks. In the rising fervor, about three thousand troops from the crack ARVN 1st Division paraded in Hue and shouted for the government to go.

Thieu and Ky at last decided to move—they could wait no longer and preserve any kind of credibility for their administration. Scuffing up charges that Da Nang had become a Communist held city, they informed Lodge (who heartily agreed) and MACV that three South Vietnamese marine battalions would go to Da Nang in the hope that a show of force would crumple opposition and frighten the Communists out. Westy, trying to play a correct game of noninterference, advised General Walt to hew to a neutral course. But the U.S. Marines were furious—they, not the Communists, held Da Nang!

From this point the players elude a program as the story eludes a script.

Ky, taking with him Defense Minister Nguyen Huu Co, two South Vietnamese Marine battalions, some field police and military security elements, a psychological operations team or two, and a command group, swooped down on the Da Nang air base on April 4. They arrived, according to the *New York Times* of April 5, in six U.S. troop transports with American pilots, or, according to Westy's faulty memory, by sea and one "old C-47 aircraft previously given the South Vietnamese" because he refused involvement in a purely Vietnamese problem.[28]

Arrival brought a rude shock to the invaders. General Walt had closed the base because some two thousand ARVN dissidents were marching toward the field. A Marine truck managed to get stuck and block a bridge south of Da Nang, which cut the approaching force in half. In the confusion, General Walt secured an agreement from the dissidents not to attack Ky's men if they did not advance on Da Nang.

But the agreement fizzled—the dissident's commander wanted to make a show and trained four guns on the base. Angry, Walt sent an officer to stop this move, which threatened U.S. planes. Landing his helicopter directly under the offending guns, Walt's emissary noted that two of the guns were U.S.-made 155mm howitzers. While he talked with the opposing commander, U.S. Marine fighter-bombers circled overhead, Marine artillery moved into position, and a Marine infantry battalion deployed for action. An ultimatum: Rather than see American planes and men killed by guns loaned to the dissidents by the United States, the Marines would open fire.

An uneasy truce lingered. The terrible noonday heat came and faded. Ky's men were clumped near their planes and endured hours of vicious taunts and curses from local citizens ringing the base fence. Ky finally went back to Saigon with his bravado wilted and much face lost. Some of his junta colleagues began to shun meetings with him in a feeling that his recklessness had weakened the government.

There can be danger in a proud man humbled. Ky took council of his ego, surveyed the damage to his future, and plotted his own redemption.

As it happened, he had some time. Thieu, consciously or not, worked to extend that grace period. On April 11, the day after the last of Ky's useless force returned from Da Nang, Thieu called together a national political congress, with all shades of Vietnamese political opinion included. According to Thieu, the congress would arrange for an orderly shift of power to civilians, and he gave some assurance that he and Ky would retire after the election. A couple of days later, Thieu decreed a constitutional assembly election within six months.[29]

Depending on who read Thieu's decree, it seemed sufficiently vague or nothing less than total surrender to Tri Quang's demands. That arch dissident, reading it his way, toured the northern provinces calming agitators and urging defected soldiers to return to the ARVN and the war.

Ky also received inadvertent help from the U.S. embassy, which found itself in the awkward position of not knowing whose side it ought to be on. If Thieu really marched toward democracy, fine; but a growing suspicion of Communist infiltration of the Buddhists raised questions about how fair any elections might be. That left the United States in the pretzeled posture of not really wanting what it had all along said it wanted.[30]

Lodge left the country for a time, in line with a hands-off policy apparently declaimed in Washington. Ky, plotting quietly, learned that no less than five White House crisis meetings were held between April 9 and 20, and that various plans for Vietnam were discussed. Ky wryly noted that "the decision, insofar as there was any decision, was to make no change in the policy."[31]

In this period of stupefied stasis, General Westmoreland also left the country. He assessed the situation as relatively calm; a new ARVN I Corps commander seemed to be making some progress in calming unrest and, with Tri Quang almost subdued, stability appeared to be at hand. So COMUSMACV went to Honolulu on May 12 for conferences with CINCPAC and a bit of rest and relaxation.

Two days later, Westy, on the beach with his family, received an urgent summons to the phone. Secretary Rusk told him that things were not so calm, after all. Ky, staying in his office, had sent perhaps two thousand Vietnamese airborne troops to "liberate" Da Nang from new crops of Communists. The ARVN forces took the radio station, the mayor's office, and I Corps headquarters. Surprised though he was, Westy said he would have approved the action had he been consulted. "Despite the Buddhists' proclamations that all they were after was a civilian government they were actually trying to get a government they could dominate," the general said. "Had Thieu and Ky given in to that, turmoil by Catholics, the religious sects, labor, whatever, would have been the result."[32] And COMUSMACV saw no reason to cut short his vacation since the government seemed to have everything in hand. He did not yet know that Thieu and the rest of the junta had not known a thing about Ky's commando raid.

Westy rationalized that a quick return would signal undue American worry so he determined he should stay in Honolulu.

Bob McNamara disagreed, however, and the general returned to Saigon on May 20, where he found the I Corps area situation had deteriorated into idiocy. General Thi had gone back to Hue to help calm things; his replacement, Gen. Ton That Dinh, also relieved, refused to accept reality and tried to carry on by giving Thi de facto command of the 1st ARVN Division. The new commander, Gen. Huynh Van Cao, for whom Westy felt sorry, lacked any desire to command anything; he simply wanted out and he tried not to get in.

Reluctant though Cao was, he did go to Hue in an effort to talk 1st Division officers into a return of loyalty. This mission a failure, he returned to Da Nang, where he found himself confronted by an aggressive National Police chief, Col. Nguyen Ngoc Loan. Loan wanted permission to attack the Buddhist pagodas, which were, he said, minifortresses. Cao, a Catholic, timidly ducked the issue—he thought it would only make things worse.

Lew Walt was probably the man most confused by Ky's venture. The Marine general became irked when a South Vietnamese plane began circling some Buddhist artillery emplacements. He did not know that Ky had ordered a plane to circle the guns and drop a message that a single round fired would bring destruction to the guns and gunners. General Walt, still puzzled by the circus around him, threatened to shoot the plane down. Ky called Lodge and pronounced his own threat: "I must ask you if this is the policy of your government. If it is true, then I am going to fly up to Da Nang in ten minutes and lead the planes in action, just to see if the Americans have the courage to shoot down the prime minister of Vietnam." Lodge promised a quick talk with Walt, but Ky flew to Da Nang anyway. On the ground, he ordered heavy guns trained on the U.S. Marine base. "If Americans start to shoot down our planes," he ordered, "destroy the marine base."[33]

Walt asked Ky to visit him. Ky replied that he had no time. In a few minutes came another, stronger, request. Again Ky refused. Finally, Walt asked if he could come to Ky. Sorry, still busy.

Then Walt announced he had instructions from an agitated Washington to talk to Ky before he left Da Nang. Furious, Ky finally relented. Walt wanted to know why he hadn't been informed of the mission. Ky suggested it was none of his business. Walt said he commanded the U.S. Marines in Da Nang and also served as advisor to the South Vietnamese command; he thought he deserved to be in the information loop.

"In normal military operations, perhaps, General," Ky replied in some dudgeon. "This is an internal problem—the people versus the government. . . . I'm trying to . . . restore the authority of the central government. Suppose a unit under your command rebelled against your authority? Would you tolerate it?"

No, of course not, Walt replied, his own attitude beginning to soften. He wondered aloud if Ky intended to attack Hue, and showed relief when the prime minister said he intended to interdict the roads north and south of Da Nang and so starve out militants in Hue and the two provinces below. That should work.

Wait. Farce is still to come.

Pacification progressed in Da Nang, but pockets of dissidents persisted. When Ky ordered his air force to smash them, Walt grew alarmed: Such attacks might hit innocent civilians, as well as some of the Americans remaining in the city. He tried to persuade the local air force commander not to attack. The man said he had direct orders; he would attack. When Walt heard that South Vietnamese piston-engined planes were taking off from the air base, he alerted four U.S. jets. Hearing of rocket attacks that wounded three Marines in the American compound, Walt sent two jets to orbit above the South Vietnamese planes. If they fired one more round, the Marine general told the local air commander, U.S. jets would shoot them down. Equally tough, the local commander sent four planes to orbit above Walt's craft. Playing the old game of hand pyramids, Walt sent up two more jets in a fourth threatening tier.

Some unrest sputtered in the wake of Da Nang's flying circus. Tri Quang, in Hue, called for more demonstrations, although he seemed increasingly isolated. He knew he would have trouble holding the movement together after Da Nang and the coming government thrust toward Hue. Whether at his instigation or not, the Buddhists resorted to sporadic acts of protest as their collective power drained away. Parades, hunger strikes, immolations— all were fading gestures of a losing cause. A nun who burned herself at the Dieude temple on May 29 sent a message to President Johnson condemning America's support for the Saigon government. Her death, said Tri Quang, had been caused by Johnson.

Although LBJ had watched the chaos in middle Vietnam with dismay, he refused to panic. Replying to various statements like the nun's, he said that suicides were "tragic and unnecessary," and asked the Vietnamese people to rally behind the government.

Ky's soldiers reached Hue early in June and tried peaceful suasion rather than mass murder. The most recalcitrant protesters were imprisoned; Tri Quang, whom Ky increasingly detested, was detained in a Saigon hospital.

Ky's civil war ended. His government triumphed, at some cost, but firmly and in a way more lasting than anyone guessed. He had been lucky in the fact that the VC and their northern brethren, caught in the general confusion, failed to take advantage of the southern madness. "We lost an opportunity," Ho Chi Minh's deputy confessed.[34]

As for LBJ, his view of the whole charade reflected what he heard from Lodge and others in Saigon, USA. His summary: "I always believed that if Tri Quang and some of his principal followers were not actually pro-Communist, at least their movement had been deeply penetrated by Hanoi's agents."[35]

Even more than the in-country Americans, Johnson wanted hard evidence of progress toward democracy in South Vietnam. Elections were the best evidence, and Ky and Thieu stuck to their Honolulu—and more recent— promise. In June, an election law drafting committee presented the government with rules under which a constituent assembly would be chosen to draft a national constitution. In September about two-thirds of the eligible voters registered and, despite serious VC threats and interference, nearly 80 percent of the registered population voted. President Johnson had worked with the Vietnamese to assure fair elections by outside observers. Overall reports were highly favorable, although one ghastly blooper came from a Texas clergyman earnestly watching the polls in a place he persisted in calling "South Vietcong."[36]

Some observers, jaded by the south's arcane political processes, found the elections rotely predictable. Others, though, found them surprising, a brave assertion of Vietnamese determination for stability. Westy, now with some sophisticated understanding of the Vietnamese people, regarded the Buddhist crisis in much calmer light than either the embassy or the White House and said he felt the election was "a most noteworthy achievement."[37]

Austere Brahmin Henry Cabot Lodge offered LBJ a sober view of what had happened: "For the Vietnamese to have voted in such large numbers in the face of terrorism shows their willingness to defy the Viet Cong in order to take a step which they believe is a step forward for their country."[38]

There was, in the American reaction, a good deal of sophistry, comforting delusion, and large amounts of hubris.

Nerve-wracking as the Buddhist crisis had been, LBJ took great comfort in Thieu and Ky carrying out their promise. They showed the kind of reliability the president had long wanted to see in Vietnam. Maybe, for a time, the United States and its faltering protégé could get on with the real war—a war that showed no sign of waning.

chapter

ELEVEN

How Much Is Enough?

L yndon Johnson packed more raw energy into himself than several
average people, energy churned to action by an abiding passion for
making things better. He had always been that way, but opportunities of the presidency charged him to a zealot's pitch. Lady Bird
worried about him, about his endangered heart, his weight, his drink-
ing, the woeful weariness she often saw slumping him down, and she fought
to keep life calm in the White House. She read him pretty well. "His mood,"
she knew "was a barometer of how things were going."[1]

Few things triggered an LBJ down mood faster than losing friends in his
official family. It was hard enough losing Mac Bundy, although the job he
took seemed ideal. But to lose Jack Valenti. . . . What would the offices be
without that dynamic, quick-witted aide with the right word and easy pen?
Jack had been through it all since that awful day in Dallas, through the Great
Society origins and victories, through the hard decisions about Vietnam in
1965, always on the lookout to smooth the president's path. Johnson knew
he had not always given back the good he got from Valenti—he knew he
had a strange tendency to vent harshness on his close colleagues and he had
been pretty hard on Jack at times, sometimes in front of others. There existed between the two men, though, an understanding beyond surface bruises.

Valenti shrugged off horrendous outbursts with an occasional tightened lip, but always with patience. "Because I felt so secure in my relationship with the president," Valenti wrote, "while these moments embarrassed me, and sometimes pushed me into a kind of blue despair, it never unhinged my enduring respect for him, or caused me to believe I was flung out into the cold. . . . I knew he cared about me and trusted me and needed me."[2]

Valenti realized, as did some others close to the Oval Office, that sudden rages often were the president's way of venting; he could rant and rail at the staff when necessity forced him to feign cordiality with others.[3] And he had a personal way of making amends—no direct apology came, but dinner invitations did, personal favors, a casual hug and a smile.

It would be harder with Valenti gone though. The president hated the prospect, but, as with Mac Bundy, the opportunity stifled argument. Valenti had been offered the presidency of the Motion Picture Association of America [MPAA].

For Valenti the prospects were both good and sad. He needed to find a better paying job, "had debts to pay, and . . . needed to earn more money for my family." But Jack hesitated. He could rationalize that "White House assignments are transient duties. . . . Even presidents must leave after eight years;" but against that came LBJ's own assertion that "he needed me."

By April, 1966, negotiations had progressed to the stage of acceptance, and Jack and Mary Margaret went to dinner with the Johnsons. While explaining his reason for taking the post—money—Jack revealed a contract provision that would release him for any presidential needs.

Valenti lamented the timing—he had tried to institute a complete change of White House staffers in Bundy's wake. Walt Whitman Rostow was pretty clearly the president's choice to serve as Bundy's replacement, and that erudite, affable, able student of international affairs got the job on April 1, 1966. California called, and Valenti worried that he "never was able to finalize my suggestions about a new team in the White House." Valenti had urged a clearly LBJ team on the president because "if we have fallen down anywhere it is [in] our inability to dramatize and communicate the fantastic strikes and breakthroughs of the Johnson administration—that contribute to a higher quality of life everywhere in the world."[4]

In a way, Valenti's hesitancy to leave came from caring too much about LBJ. He knew he would miss the White House, but not the zest of power that came with working there: LBJ would need him often, and, as president of the MPAA, he would exert power of his own.

Johnson had a personal flair with people he cherished. Jack received one of the most moving letters of his life on April 25, 1966, in which his boss acknowledged his resignation:

> You know how much I will miss your companionship, your good cheer, your brilliant mind, and your storehouse of information. You have been some very special something to me for a long time—first because of Mary Margaret, and then Courtenay, but really all the time—it was you yourself.
>
> I guess I just didn't want to admit that a man should need another man quite so much. . . .
>
> You have served your country with devotion and distinction, and you can always be as proud, or prouder, of that, as you are of your fifty-one missions. You served me, though, even more—and I thank you, and love you, and am very proud of you.[5]

The contractual provision permitting Valenti to depart the movie world anytime the president called made the move palatable for both of them. The first summons came in October—the president wanted Jack to help with a conference in Manila—just three months after Valenti's resignation took effect in June, 1966.

By that time the loyal opponent in Johnson's official family had also departed: George Ball resigned in September.

Where now would come an inner circle voice for hesitation?

ASIAN ROUNDUP

Bad news clustered in from Vietnam. Just when it seemed things were improving after the directorate quelled the Buddhist problems, the military situation began to deteriorate. Puzzled by mixed signals from the battlefront, LBJ asked McNamara to go once more to Saigon. What was happening out there?

For two days in October, the defense secretary, who had not visited Saigon in a year, listened to MACV briefers give their usual numerical recitation of troops, logistics, body counts, engagements, sorties by allied ground and air forces, estimates of enemy strength and intentions, topped by various favorable prognoses. He sat, unflappable, mentally toting numbers, face masked, reactions hidden. Briefings finished, the secretary sped away on a quick circuit of field units.

Nothing substituted for a close, personal look. McNamara saw evidence everywhere of the amazing American buildup. Westy's long-desired strong logistical base had become a reality. Construction at places like the Cam Ranh Bay complex in the II Corps area had created a massive center that included a deepwater port, a jet airfield, and almost unlimited depots of food, ammunition, and other military needs.[6] Westy's seizure of the initiative could be seen in a radically changed operational tempo—U.S. attacks were taking the war to the enemy in almost every tactical zone. On the ground McNamara found far more optimism than came through the information channels.

There were problems, though, and McNamara, after arriving back in Washington, gave a careful assessment to the president.

He found himself less pessimistic than a year earlier, yet he hardly felt enthused. "My concern continues . . . because *I see no reasonable way to bring the war to an end soon.*" The enemy had adapted to the situation by waging a war of attrition and, although this had cost more than sixty thousand North Vietnamese casualties a year, a depressing fact remained: "*It appears that he can more than replace his losses by infiltration from North Vietnam and recruitment in South Vietnam.*"

His earlier fears about pacification deepened. Compared to two or four years ago, VC guerrilla forces were larger, attacks and harassment had increased, more roads and railroads were closed, agricultural production was down, "we control little, if any, more of the population; the VC political infrastructure thrives in most of the country . . . full security exists nowhere (not even behind the U.S. Marines' lines and in Saigon); in the countryside, the enemy almost completely controls the night."

As Johnson knew, McNamara had long worried about the bombing program. "*The ROLLING THUNDER program of bombing the North [has not] either significantly affected infiltration or cracked the morale of Hanoi.*"

What should be done? McNamara rang changes on old notions—keep up military pressure, redouble pacification efforts, but he came to a new idea, one germinating for some time in his almost desperate psyche. "Specifically, we must *improve our position by getting ourselves into a military posture that we credibly would maintain indefinitely—a posture that makes trying to 'wait us out' less attractive.*"

McNamara recommended a five-part course of action:

1. Stabilize U.S. forces in Vietnam at somewhere around 470,000 men. This would signal the world that the United States intended to stick by the south as long as necessary.

2. "Install a barrier" near the seventeenth parallel, a line to run from the sea "across the neck of South Vietnam . . . and across the trails

in Laos," a mix of fences, wire, sensors, guns, aircraft and mobile units, and air-droppable mines. Cost: about $1 billion.

3. Stabilize Rolling Thunder sorties at some reasonable rate.
4. Push pacification vigorously, with RF/PF forces assigned to stay in their operational areas and become friends with the locals.
5. Work toward negotiations, while also working to divide Hanoi from the VC.

In summary, McNamara said that final triumph *"lies in girding, openly, for a longer war and in taking actions immediately which will in 12 to 18 months give clear evidence that the continuing costs and risks to the American people are acceptably limited, that the formula for success has been found, and that the end of the war is merely a matter of time."*

Under that broad umbrella, McNamara made tactical suggestions for fine-tuning the American efforts. He also urged that "the bulk of the ARVN should be shifted to pacification"—a radically different conclusion from his earlier Vietnam assessment.[7]

McNamara's whole tone had changed. Certainty of success had faded; victory had become negotiable. A close look at his report shows the strain of bifurcated logic; it also shows the secretary trying a shrewd game of pandering to LBJ's prejudices. Although the president certainly wanted to "win," he had come recently to believe that winning depended on pacification. So McNamara sugarcoated the bitter medicine of an indefinite conflict with emphasis on the "other war." That fuddled the issue sufficiently to cover the secretary's growing despair and keep the president's confidence.

If Johnson held McNamara in undiminished regard, he had some misgivings about the shifting perspectives coming from the secretary of defense. Military news, which LBJ consumed with an amateur's passion, seemed good. Others felt good about Vietnam; Lodge had encouraging words. As always when confronted with puzzles, Johnson wanted more information.

What he needed more than information, though, was new perspectives and different ideas, maybe even outsiders' views. How best to get them?

Johnson remembered that several months before President Chung Hee Park of South Korea had suggested a meeting of the heads of all nations helping South Vietnam, and that in August, 1966, Thailand's leaders had also suggested an Asian conference on Vietnam. Johnson discussed the matter with President Ferdinand Marcos of the Philippines when he came to Washington in September. The United States would be glad to participate in such a conference, but Asian leaders should organize it. Marcos got the point. He consulted other nations and soon invited leaders of South Vietnam,

Australia, New Zealand, the United States, South Korea, and Thailand to meet in Manila on October 24–25, 1966, for a close look at the Vietnam War in the context of Asia's future.[8]

The president accepted and told Lady Bird he wanted her to go. The trip was no spur of the moment junket, but the State Department and White House staff, especially advance man Bill Moyers, carefully arranged it to be spontaneous.

They went in October with a fairly large official party that included Dean Rusk and a number of eager reporters. *Air Force One* and four other big jets carried them all in considerable ease. Once over the Pacific, LBJ, wrapped in a "gaudy lounging robe," collected the press people around him and talked about his new vision. The West, he boomed, had been too long in appreciating the East. Sitting, walking, and gesturing seven miles above the water, the president warmed to his subject. "Asians are sensitive people. . . . [President] Marcos said, 'You're all the time talking about the unity of Europe, why never about the unity of Asia?'" That hit home with Johnson. "When they see this big blue plane flying in," he said, "they're going to realize we're interested in the unity of Asia." There were problems that LBJ grasped painfully. Racial prejudice had something to do with Western aloofness. Back when Americans fought in the Philippines during the Spanish-American War, and afterward, against Emilio Aguinaldo's "insurgents," the Filipinos had been "little brown brothers."

Prejudice bothered Johnson. Some among the accompanying writers saw the troubled soul wrapped in that gown, watched him sip apple juice, breathe into a moisturizer to save his voice, and suffer for the Asians.

"He could . . . envision power lines down the Mekong Valley," one reporter noted, "lush and ordered fields of rice and new agricultural crops, sanitized villages secure and happy." Johnson needed that kind of vision, enlarged on of course, because "he could not function without such a vision up there ahead somewhere."[9]

The first stop was Honolulu, where the president's people were wrapped in leis and LBJ talked about Hawaiian statehood and America's growing appreciation of Asia.

Next it was on to Samoa, then New Zealand, where the Johnsons were ensconced in the governor-general's house. A motorcade to Parliament turned into a triumphal procession through some sixty thousand happy New Zealanders, but it did have bitter reminders of home. Outside the imposing Parliament building a group of protesters carried familiar signs—"Hey, Hey, LBJ, How Many Kids Have You Killed Today?" and "Withdraw from Vietnam." But the protesters were raucously outnumbered.[10]

At the airport after lunch the Johnsons bid a large farewell and boarded *Air Force One* with Prime Minister and Lady Keith Holyoake for the next stage of the tour—Australia. There, enthusiasm matched New Zealand's.

In Melbourne, despite some paint spattering his limousine, Johnson sank into the luxury of an old-time political rally. Thousands thronged the streets and he reacted typically—standing up in the car, hat waving, cheering back to the people, "Hurray for Australia, Hurray!" Throwing himself into the mood of his admirers, Johnson's energy awed Prime Minister Harold Holt, who huffed and puffed to keep up with a guest who swarmed among the multitudes.

Sydney produced more protesters, but most of the city reacted to Johnson's own enthusiasm. Somebody gave him two kangaroos, which he accepted, quipping that he would put them on the ranch and might "ride one of them down to the Post Office at Hye."

At Canberra, something of the frontier spirit charmed both Johnsons. Mrs. Holt enjoyed watching LBJ's joy with the crowds. "Your husband," she said, turning to Lady Bird, "is a romantic man." Which brought an emphatic "He *is*."[11]

Filipinos greeting *Air Force One* on October 23 showed their own enthusiasm. They had the familiarity of shared dangers, a pride of history, and the grace of old friends. En route to Manila, LBJ saw policemen trying to hold the people back. Stop, he said, "I am traveling 26,000 miles to see these people, and I can't do it if the police push them away."[12]

Shortly after his arrival in Manila, Johnson began a round of talks with various heads of state. Marcos came to see him, and they voiced high hopes for the coming session. Johnson then called at President Park's suite. Later Thailand's prime minister, Thanom Kittikachorn, a friendly, ever-smiling man of deep capacities, came to Johnson's suite.

To those watching the evening's visits, Johnson's careful reticence and his self-effacement were obvious; he kept himself tightly reined and in the background throughout the conference. Bill Moyers noted LBJ's plan to be "a twenty-percent man. . . . He's going to listen eighty percent, talk twenty percent." Most of all, the president worked to avoid any impression of influencing the proceedings or dominating his colleagues. Avoiding shoulder-to-shoulder pictures, standing a step below the others in groups, the tall Texan kept a reasonably level head with all the Asians.[13]

The Johnsons joined in the lavish barrio fiesta held on the grounds of Malacañang palace Tuesday evening, October 25. In the shifting lantern light the lovely old residence of Spanish governors, American governors-general, and now of Philippine presidents, glowed behind huge banyan trees; its arches shadowy, mysterious, fetching. Inside, music beckoned people to the floor and LBJ, wearing a splendid barong tagalog, impressed Imelda Marcos with his dancing prowess. Lady Bird, in a dress presented by Mrs. Marcos, danced with a member of the Bayanihan dance troupe.[14]

The president survived the conference handily, despite working two agendas simultaneously. Official results were good. He carefully pushed the idea that Asia should come into world perspective at last, that the Vietnam War ranked as only one of many things happening in the most populated part of the globe. Slowly a sense of regional pride and mutual concern emerged. At the end of two long working days, the conferees each spoke. Johnson's remarks were short but heartfelt. He celebrated the emergence of important principles—resistance to aggression, commitment to reconstruction, pacification, regional development. "I have seen the banners that say 'We want peace' and I say 'So do I.' I have seen their banners that say 'We hate war' and I say 'So do I.'" The way he said it made the difference; people listened and believed.

The summit produced a "Declaration of the Goals of Freedom" from the seven nations assembled. Their goals included freedom from aggression, hunger, illiteracy, and disease, and freedom to build "a region of security, order, and progress, and to work for peace throughout Asia and [the] Pacific."

A communiqué accompanying the declaration contained a real surprise: The allies engaged in Vietnam pledged to withdraw all their forces within six months after North Vietnamese aggression definitively stopped. This came straight from Johnson, inspired by a visit he'd had with Soviet foreign minister Andrey Gromyko two weeks before. There had been doubts and resistance from some of the allies, especially from South Vietnam and Korea, and from the U.S. State Department. Such a statement, some thought, might read as an excuse to quit the war. But Johnson bulled ahead and got the language he wanted. "Nobody can accuse us of a soft attitude," he argued. "If anyone doubts the basis of our commitment, they will find that we have more troops in Vietnam than there are words in the new Webster's Dictionary."[15]

Johnson worked after hours on his second agenda. He had asked General Westmoreland to join him in Manila—Westy and Kitsy had just visited the ranch in August, so the general seemed surprised at another summons. Surely the president knew his thinking. When he arrived, Westy raised a questioning eye upon noting that neither Bus Wheeler nor Oley Sharp were present to join in military briefings. Johnson confessed he had made the decision himself; he wanted Westy "to occupy the center of the stage as the senior military officer at the conference." That left the general flattered, wondering if the ranch summons had been for sizing purposes, and fueled a thought that he might be taking over "broader responsibilities for management of mission affairs."[16]

Westy joined his South Vietnamese counterpart, Gen. Cao Van Vien, chief of the Joint General Staff, in assessing the war for the conferees. In the evening, U.S. policy talks continued with Johnson, Rusk, Harriman, Bill Bundy, Leonard Unger and Chester Cooper of State, consultants Clark Clifford, Rostow and Robert Komer, John McNaughton of Defense, and the USIA's director, Leonard Marks. Westy, Lodge, and Philip Habib represented the Saigon contingent.

Long experience listening to briefings lent Westy a special ear, and he had an acute antenna for nuances. Clearly Johnson had new information on troop assignments from McNamara and Wheeler; just as clearly he had some new move in mind about management of pacification and obviously Bob Komer would be a key figure. Listening and learning, COMUSMACV nursed a little anger—nobody had consulted him about the six-month withdrawal idea.

There were other bothers for the general. At a luncheon with Harriman and William Blair, U.S. ambassador to the Philippines, Westy came close to disillusionment. Harriman, he of the famed hard line in Moscow, talked of Russian intentions as Westy listened, incredulous. "I can tell you, General Westmoreland, categorically, the Russians are doing everything they can to bring peace in Vietnam." The general almost blurted a reminder of the supply torrents coming to the north from Russia, but he bit his tongue. Harriman seemed happy in his fancies.

Fancies were bad enough, but the president's personal discussion of Secretary McNamara's report chilled the general. Not only did the secretary's possible troop numbers sound alarming, but the president's concern about bombing had bad overtones. When LBJ asked him to present his ideas about Rolling Thunder, Westy was ready. He had ordered a special group to prepare him a study on that subject so he could dictate a cogent response while shaving on the morning of October 24—and he put his feelings bluntly. The air campaign against the north, Westy wrote, has been nothing more than "creeping escalation," and has not affected the enemy war effort. American airpower had been misused and produced results far less than possible. Now that Hanoi had a formidable air defense system and more MIGs for high-altitude combat, American casualties would escalate, "perhaps more than we will be willing . . . to sustain, given the present limitation on targets." His recommendation was to bomb "lucrative targets" near Hanoi and Haiphong harbor, to hit North Vietnam hard enough to prove that America had far more power than it had used.[17] Westy doubted his views would be heeded.

At the moment he had a more immediate crisis on his hands. Johnson had called Westy to his suite—Rostow, Lodge, and Bill Moyers were already there. How about a presidential visit to Vietnam at two o'clock the next afternoon? Floored, the general said it could not be handled—security made it impossible. Johnson hunched up, huffed, and got mad. "Dammit," he snapped, "if that's the way you feel about it, I won't go." Westy scrambled to make amends.

Two o'clock, he said, simply left no time to make anyplace secure. A later time, say five o'clock, would be fine. Johnson accepted and Westy rushed to prepare for the presidential visit. Frantic calls to various staff officers alerted them to something, but Westy kept the full details shrouded in a cover scheme. Bring in some twenty-five hundred troops for an awards ceremony at Cam Ranh Bay, he said. He would also brief commanders on the Manila conference. He ordered his staff to pull in some hospital patients—ostensibly to make room for expected casualties at the Nha Trang air force hospital—build and decorate a reviewing stand, and do all the other myriad things a sudden martial convocation demanded. Westy then took off for Cam Ranh Bay himself. Arriving in midmorning, he found most of his bogus plan going well. Flying down to Saigon, Westy told his chief of staff, Bill Rosson, the true story, then went back to Cam Ranh Bay with a clutch of higher-ranking MACV staff officers in tow. Miraculously, the cover plan worked; newsmen did not know what was happening until after they were airborne from Manila. In fact, LBJ arrived a half-hour early—another security dodge —but everything went smoothly.

Johnson, in subdued ranch attire, got in Westy's jeep to review the troops. Obviously moved, LBJ's excitement touched Westy and he boasted that "no Commander in Chief in our history has ever had finer troops than these." Johnson walked the lines of men, saw that some were obviously just in from the field, and proudly pinned on medals. Everything slowed down because the men wanted to shake Johnson's hand, to get his autograph, and he tried to accommodate them.[18] Finally on the reviewing stand, he surprised Westy by pinning the Distinguished Service Medal on him. Sweat soaked Johnson's shirt but rising inspiration made him impervious to the heat. He spoke emotionally to those young Americans: "We believe in you. We know you are going to get the job done. And soon, when peace can come to the world, we will receive you back in your homeland with open arms, with great pride and with great thanks."

Later, in the hospital, the president looked men in the eye, shook hands, and murmured his personal admiration and gratitude.

He next spoke briefly at the officer's mess, then visited the enlisted men's mess, where he went through the chow line and ate with men who came in with their rifles slung on their backs. Soaked to the skin, Johnson accompanied Westy back to the officer's mess for a talk with the major unit commanders.

It was dark when LBJ's jeep rolled toward the airfield and, when it drew close to the presidential plane, he could see and hear that the runways were lined with cheering troops. Moved more deeply than any watcher could remember, he waved, boarded *Air Force One*, and flew back to Manila.

Wrapped in the comforts of the aircraft, Johnson thought back on the dramatic hours he had spent visiting troops in Vietnam. He felt then, and would repeat his memories often, that "I have never been more moved by any group I have talked to, never in my life." Westy's boast about his men seemed an understatement.[19]

From Manila, the Johnsons flew to Bangkok, Thailand, then Malaysia, and finally to Seoul, Korea, where they climbed the steps of the city hall and turned to face an enormous mass of humanity that "swayed like wheat" and teetered on the edge of frenzy.

Johnson asked President Park how many people he thought were in the crowd. Park asked someone with them, then turned back to LBJ and said about two million. Stunned, Johnson looked again at the human avalanche. Park misunderstood his expression apparently, because he apologized. "I'm sorry, that's all the people we have." Johnson loved that moment and told the story often.[20]

As he had in Vietnam, the president mingled with GIs in Korea. Visiting the men guarding the thirty-eighth parallel, he waxed eloquent about America's heroic past, recalling an entirely fictional great-great grandfather who died in the Alamo—an exaggeration that stuck with him and fueled something of the poisonous "credibility gap" to come.

On Wednesday, November 2, 1966, Johnson spoke to the Korean national assembly about a better Asian future. He boasted of Korea's "modern miracle," and about a new Asia looming on the horizon. Korea's success and Asia's bright future stemmed, he said, from stopping aggression in Korea in the 1950s. Similar aggression, he said, would be stopped in Vietnam, a place where Korea's fine soldiers were fighting side by side with Vietnamese, Australians, New Zealanders, and Americans, for freedom. He had seen millions of faces on his tour, he said, "And I have been deeply encouraged. So I leave today with a deep sense of confidence in the future of Asia and the Pacific." Weary but enthused, the touring party started home from Kimpo Airport on that same day.

The president could take pride in knowing that he had accomplished a good deal on his trip. He recognized in time that the Goals of Freedom declaration really spelled out the core of his own foreign policy, or Johnson Doctrine: combating aggression, poverty, illiteracy, and disease; cooperation in social, economic, and cultural areas "on a regional basis"; and a constant search for peace. Simply by showing up in Manila, by sharing leadership and by waxing warm to people who wanted warmth, he did much to advance America's image.[21] And his constant emphasis on the importance of Asia in the world turned Asian heads toward the west in a kind of common recognition. Add to that the salient fact that Johnson changed the whole thrust of American foreign policy, refocusing it eastward and giving the United States a truly world perspective. If some criticized him for a perspective only as broad as Blanco County and as deep as the Pedernales, others realized that keeping faith with his roots freed Johnson's vision for the world. And if some belittled the trip as typical Johnson grandstanding, others saw it as Homeric theater.

Hugh Sidey put it this way:

> If eloquence was not always in abundance, or even if good taste sometimes faltered, it was nevertheless pure Johnson and it was drama of raw energy and a remarkable amount of sincerity. Because of that it succeeded. It was a remarkable adventure also because . . . the Manila summit, around which the whole thing was constructed, was planned with care. The event flowed from restrained start to reasonable end, giving a sense of purpose.[22]

WINTER OF DISCONTENT

Just about an hour out from touchdown at Dulles, *Air Force One* hit a patch of terrible weather. Big as it was, the plane twisted, rolled, bucked, and did gyrations to pale an aeronautical engineer. Lady Bird sat terrified, clutching the arm of a State Department officer. She glanced at Ashton Gonella, who "looked ready to faint." Liz Carpenter, who hated to fly anyway, kept sending questions to the pilot.

What omens in so turbulent an ending to an odyssey for peace?

A safe landing at about 8 P.M. disgorged a weary, relieved group into the welcome of friends and dignitaries. Under a big banner that proclaimed, "Well Done, Mr. President," Johnson accepted a twenty-one-gun salute and heard the national anthem before greeting Hubert Humphrey, the chief justice and members of the Supreme Court, cabinet members, diplomats, senators and congressmen, and many friends. Standing in a light rain, the president then recounted what he had seen and hoped, and recited a prayer he had heard offered in an Australian church: "O God, Who has bound us together in the bundle of life, give us grace to understand how our lives depend upon the courage, the industry, the honesty, and the integrity of our fellow men, that we may be mindful of their needs and grateful for their faithfulness, and faithful in our responsibilities to them."[23]

Fatigue took the Johnsons to the ranch for rest. But the president kept mulling what he'd learned. He knew that the troop number question would not go away. Talking with McNamara and Wheeler, thinking over Westy's ideas, Johnson wanted more military data. Wheeler reinforced the JCS position, which dovetailed, somewhat, with Westy's ideas. But Westy wanted something like seven hundred thousand men by 1968, and even with those, could not offer a certain time for withdrawal. Various bombing programs were meshed with the troop issue. And everything impinged on the budget, which had to be presented soon. It would contain a hefty $9.1 billion supplement for the war before the new fiscal year, 1968, began.

Tired but restless, LBJ asked a steady stream of people to the ranch for consultations on money, Great Society programs, and martial matters. To all of these conferences LBJ brought a new perspective. He felt, for the first time in many arduous months, untrammeled by carpers. Before the Asian trek, black depression had stalked him; he confessed to Jack Valenti during a White House dinner in September that he would not run again. If he could find an honorable way to chuck the job, pass it to Hubert Humphrey, he would—but he would be accused of political conniving. "We have too many difficult problems and we need leadership that won't be attacked at every turn. We probably need a fresh face."[24]

But the raucously approving crowds that had greeted Lady Bird and him in so many foreign cities buoyed optimism, almost banishing the doubts that clawed at him always.

Johnson wanted to be the greatest American president—a drive stemming from two desires: to be needed and loved. But the war in Vietnam diminished all that he did and befogged his future. Deep within him, though, near that keep of wounds and insecurities, he had a reservoir of will to rise to his own image. How? By creating the Great Society *and* saving South Vietnam.

Basking in the Asian kudos, replenished in his need to be needed, the president's freshened mind churned with several possible moves in Vietnam. He weighed them carefully during his working break at the ranch in early November, 1966. But before he acted he wanted to hear McNamara and Wheeler again.

The defense secretary and JCS chairman came to the ranch twice that month, and both times they talked about troop needs. Johnson had discussed numbers with Westy in Manila, and also with Thieu and Ky and their military people. Westy wanted the allies to contribute "their proportional share" of troops. Johnson liked the idea and linked it to population percentages. With that in mind, he listened as McNamara and Wheeler told him about a recent CINCPAC planning conference at which they again had been urged to authorize changes in rules of engagement and an end to restraints on the air campaign in North Vietnam, on cross-border incursions, and on special operations—even in the southern half of the DMZ. The Pacific command brass wanted their plan adopted in toto; piecemeal actions had done virtually nothing to gain advantage in the war. They urged mining ports, a naval quarantine, and raids into Cambodia and Laos. Knowing all too clearly the current drift of presidential biases, the planners boasted that their whole package "will support intensified and accelerated revolutionary development and nation building programs."[25] The buzzwords were right but the timing was wrong. Neither the secretary of defense nor General Wheeler any longer agreed with open-ended troop commitments.

All through Friday, November 4, and into Saturday, Johnson, Wheeler, and McNamara worked on a compromise plan. By late Saturday the president had accepted a new level of deployments. McNamara told newsmen assembled in the yard outside the ranch house that more men would go to Vietnam, but at a "substantially slower rate." That meant good news about the draft, he added. For four months, calls would drop sharply.

To veterans of the White House press corps, McNamara's performance showed his usual sharp command of numbers, details, but also a different kind of diffidence. Citing a new study based on prisoner interrogations, he said that allied air and ground attacks had hurt North Vietnamese morale, denied them sanctuaries, and cut their food supplies. Enemy body count, he boasted, now topped a thousand a week. Those veteran snoopers waited for his estimate of how all this related to the course of the war, but they waited in vain. McNamara closed the conference without venturing any further prognosis.

The president, with a clear eye toward the elections, had worked with McNamara and Wheeler on an entirely new approach to Vietnam. Always in favor of giving Westy what he needed, fearing to deny American soldiers anything essential, Johnson at last accepted that limits would have to be set on troop commitments—that the United States simply could not continue pouring blood and treasure into an ultimate uncertainty.

The ranch talks, and reports of them, had both foreign and domestic significance. The president, more than any other American, appreciated the domestic significance of his Vietnam plans: Congressional elections would occur in 1966 and, because of the clustering crises, they might be a war referendum.

Experience taught LBJ that the party in power always loses congressional seats in midterm elections, but he expected more than the usual losses. And right he was—the Democrats lost forty-seven house seats and eight governorships, which signaled growing unease and a desire for some kind of change. Whether or not the vote amounted to a referendum on the war depended on points of view. Johnson took it as more than usual disaffection with the "ins," yet resisted the thought of total rejection.[26] But the tiger's back he rode grew thinner and sharper as the odds in his race against time grew longer.

The "substantially slower rate" of troop deployments announced the sea change in American strategy. McNamara gets credit for winning this policy shift, but LBJ, tuned to varied political sirens, already leaned toward some kind of hedging. Still, compromise had not come easily because of differing views on future policy in South Vietnam. None of the ranch discussants wanted cross-border operations that might widen the war, so they rejected that JCS desire. Their discussions were influenced, too, by war costs.[27]

There would be troops for Westy. The president would not strand the men already ensnarled in "that bitch of a war." He would not let them wither as some lost tokens of freedom. He had a sense of the rightness of what America had promised, and that made Vietnam an extension of his conscience, a place where his and America's honor merged.

At the ranch, in those hectic days of bargaining, Johnson must have had some questions about McNamara. Fervent still, full of nervous certainty, the secretary of defense seemed almost at war with himself. Yet he seemed correct about the need for capping American troop levels. If it went against LBJ's grain to question Westy's needs, he followed the lead of the best numbers man he ever knew. Agitated though he was, McNamara kept presidential perspective and suggested sending only enough reinforcements to let Westy hold the initiative while enhancing the South Vietnamese armed forces; he recommended a ceiling of 470,000 men for Vietnam.

Clearly something had happened between McNamara's Saigon visit and the Manila conversations, because Westy's expectations had dwindled. After calling for 700,000 men by 1968, he talked in Manila about a need for only 500,000 by the end of that year. McNamara's shrinking enthusiasm had obviously been communicated. Some observers thought that the secretary had already discussed the 470,000-man ceiling with him and that Westy had wriggled for more in Manila. But he came a long way. To John

McNaughton in Defense, whose predilections were becoming dovish as he looked hard at what his computer told him about force increments and enemy capacity to counterescalate, Westy suggested a total of 480,000 men by the end of 1967 and a cap of 500,000 by the end of 1968. Those numbers, he said, were sufficient "even if infiltration went on at a high level," although he might need more for Delta operations.[28] Oley Sharp, an apostle of quick success, urged no less than 570,000 American soldiers in Vietnam by the end of 1967.[29]

Johnson, and hence Westy, had been sandbagged by one of the best of the Whiz Kids, Alain Enthoven, assistant secretary of defense for systems analysis. Numbers coming from MACV were, by Enthoven's analysis, unrealistically high. "We were amazed at how little real planning lay behind the requests," Enthoven said.[30] If he or his cohorts knew anything of how military staffs planned is unclear; what is clear is that they doubted any numbers but their own.

Buttressed by fellow devotees of figures, McNamara enlarged his own growing disenchantment. Instead of men, he turned to technology and encouraged the barrier line so long in his fancy. If it worked, it would not only reduce infiltration across the DMZ and the Laotian corridor, but also the need for heavy bombing in the "extended battle area" above the DMZ. Westy shuddered at the thought of the line, but, eventually accepted it as a means of channeling infiltrators into prepared fire zones. In a kind of high-tech fiasco, the whole idea fizzled—to the cynical delight of newsmen who dubbed it McNamara's line, to go along with such other design duds as the Edsel and the TFX experimental fighter.[31]

McNamara, who had a solid grasp of protecting his rear, developed a nimble defense for the shifting face of the war. First, he argued that Westy's troop requests had been met "at or near the time requested." Second, strategy dictated changes. After all, the main purpose of U.S. forces in South Vietnam remained the frustration of enemy offensive capabilities and pacification of cleared areas. McNamara saw two ways to achieve these results: one, continue to increase allied forces "as rapidly as possible, and without limit, and employ them primarily in large-scale 'seek out and destroy' operations" against main-force enemy units; two, stick to the same strategy, "but build friendly forces only to that level required to neutralize the large enemy units and prevent them from interfering with the pacification program."

McNamara favored the second choice for three reasons. First, enemy forces had not been attrited quickly enough either to break morale or reach the critical cross-over point where the allies were killing more men than the enemy could replace; second, deployment of more than 470,000 Americans in 1967 would probably smother South Vietnam under ruinous inflation; third, "endless escalation of U.S. deployments" would likely not be acceptable to Americans at home nor show determination to stay for the duration.

Out of the Texas talks came definite numbers: 470,000 U.S. troops, 52,000 allied troops, and "less than half of the ARVN. The remainder of the ARVN, plus a portion of the U.S. force, would give priority to improving the pacification effort."[32]

Those numbers should have cooled the unrest seeping across the United States, but other events obscured the good news.

All through the past year, Defense Department officials and LBJ had boasted of the almost "surgical" bombing campaign against North Vietnam, a campaign in which the president became personally involved by selecting targets to minimize civilian casualties. That some civilians would die everyone understood, but heroic measures were promised to minimize death in the streets of North Vietnam.

That image vanished with a Christmas Day, 1966, front-page *New York Times* story by the assistant managing editor, Harrison Salisbury, who had been allowed to visit North Vietnam. There he was given tours of Hanoi and surrounding areas, where he saw extensive bomb damage. His Christmas present to America was a devastating indictment of U.S. bombing policy.

For three weeks his stories painted a grim picture of indiscriminate killing of civilians, of a fearsome air campaign aimed almost specifically at populated areas, of children dead or maimed. And Salisbury did much damage with lurid accounts of bombed-out churches, rows of gutted homes, and repeated attacks on nonmilitary targets. Barry Goldwater and others denounced his stories as Communist propaganda; and they did run pretty close to some Hanoi accounts of Yankee atrocities.[33]

Exaggeration caused most of the problem. Bombs were not, then, the "smart" weapons of more recent times; even so-called precision bombing caused a good deal of collateral damage, which the North Vietnamese magnified into deliberate savagery. As Philip Goulding, assistant secretary of defense for information, recognized, "we had been gradually convincing the people of the United States that all our bombs always fell upon the targets at which they were directed, that we killed no civilians. . . . We should have known better."[34]

McNamara, especially, fumed at Salisbury's dispatches. Not only did he and Bus Wheeler do a weekly stint of target selection, but they paid exacting attention to protecting a buffer zone along the Chinese border that avoided MIG airfields and ports. The president joined them in these target sessions and worried constantly about hitting civilians—"take this SAM [surface-to-air missile] site out and that SAM site out, but that is too close to Hanoi."[35]

Johnson saw Salisbury's articles in sour perspective and knew that with each installment, the so-called credibility gap widened. He later noted that "in spite of reports that give the opposite impression, the vast majority of our airmen made strenuous efforts to avoid civilian casualties. They were not totally successful . . . and that was a constant source of sorrow to me. But they tried, and their orders were clear."[36] As for Salisbury's *New York Times* articles, they were sharp reminders that truth is in the venom of the teller.

Johnson had agreed to a complete halt to bombing North Vietnam for two days during the Christmas holidays. Salisbury's fearsomely graphic articles may have encouraged the president to repeat the halt from December 31, 1966 to January 2, 1967, as a segment of a partial cessation that lasted seventy-eight days, from December 23, 1966 to March 1, 1967. These stoppages coincided with some abortive peace feelers through British, Polish, papal, UN, and South Vietnamese sources.[37] Although deeply opposed to these halts, Johnson usually yielded to advisors who saw glimmers of hope or breaks in the war. He sympathized with military authorities like Oley Sharp, who saw bombing halts as signs of American weakness and as cornucopias of supplies to enemy. Halts also cost U.S. pilots' lives because North Vietnam used each respite to increase its air defenses.

Admiral Sharp, the agitated CINCPAC who was convinced that massive air attacks could ruin North Vietnam, had been able to escalate Rolling Thunder to 13,200 sorties a month, and had been cleared to hit a strategic bridge, "a railroad classification yard, . . . a vehicle depot, a cement plant, two power plants, and elements of the Thai Nguyen steel plant." Since some of these objectives were inside the Hanoi Prohibited Area, they had required special approval from Washington—an approval abruptly withdrawn before most of them were attacked. Infuriated, Sharp scolded Bus Wheeler: "The American people can become aroused either for or against this war. At the moment, with no end in sight, they are more apt to become aroused against it. It's up to us to convince our people and Hanoi that there is an end in sight and that it is clearly defeat for Hanoi."[38]

To bomb or not to bomb—that long argument made a frustrating end to a winter of discontent.

PUZZLES FOR THE PRESIDENT

Troop numbers became Lyndon Johnson's greatest ambiguity. Bob McNamara, the master calculator, schemed to cap commitments in Vietnam, but the cap became a floating constant. Actually, the enemy proved to be the complex variable. Estimates of North Vietnamese infiltration kept escalating—there seemed no end to how many men that small country could muster for the war. As numbers rose, so did Johnson's puzzlement.

Johnson could look back on 1966 as "an upbeat year" for Vietnam, although things had deteriorated a bit toward the end and hopes for peace had been as illusory as ever. Would 1967 bring more good military news, better chances for peace? Or was LBJ's race with time nearing a crucial moment in the angst of civil chaos? While news had been good from Southeast Asia, news from America's streets had been hectic, strife-torn, and messy. Johnson saw several horrid possibilities in domestic troubles—they might rend the body social, they might slow or halt the administration's civil rights crusade, and they might curtail U.S. efforts in Vietnam.

Myriad as were his troubles, Johnson did not scatter his worries. His many years in the Senate taught him the need for compartmentalization, and Johnson's mind generally worked in packages—never better than in the early years of his presidency, when he focused piercingly on getting JFK's legislation through Congress and on designing and building his own Great Society.

But the war, at last, had eroded the walls of his mind. It snaked into his psyche in subtleties of conversation, sudden questions to visitors about their views on Vietnam. Jack Valenti had seen the war as a "fungus on the face of the . . . Administration," but Jack was no longer handy to share the uncertainties. Mac Bundy was gone, too—he of the crisp assurances, the pithy memo, that odd amalgam of arrogance and courtesy. And Bill Moyers was preparing to go into newspaper publishing at the end of the year. Who would ride herd on the reporters? Who would replace his quickened mind, his sober advice, his energetic self? Yet even Bill, the nearly surrogate son, showed signs of irritation, and rumor had it that he had begun to oppose the war.

Was the war winnable? Johnson had known for two years, even in the darkest days of South Vietnamese fecklessness, that U.S. power could deny victory to Uncle Ho. Military people, mostly funneling their statistics through McNamara's mind, fed the White House continuous casualty ratios. "At the beginning of 1965," LBJ heard, "the ratio of enemy-to-allied casualties was estimated at 2.2 to 1. The next year this ratio was 3.3 to 1, and in 1967" it would rise to 3.9 to 1. Desertions were included in the victory-in-sight equation: VC desertions to the south in 1965 totaled 11,000, the number rose to 20,000 in 1966, and 1967 estimates called for 27,000. Captured enemy documents gave a rosier glow to MACV's message by confessing the

Communists had lost control of over a million South Vietnamese during the last half of 1966.[39]

Organized and invigorated, pacification seemed to offer the best hope to South Vietnam, whose people would have to save themselves, go to full mobilization, retrain the ARVN for anti-Viet Cong activities, and leave the "big war" to Westy's command.

The president recognized the need for change and a closer look at his colleagues. What about the administration's Vietnam team? Were its arteries hardening?

Johnson, wanting an intense review of Vietnam activities, especially a close look at pacification, called for another meeting, this time on Guam, in March, 1967. He picked Guam for the gathering site, he said, because that small island offered good security and was close enough to Vietnam so that participants would not be far from their war assignments.[40]

REORGANIZATION

The president had come to an important decision and knew, before he left for Guam, how he would quicken America's efforts in the war. McNamara had been pushing for reorganization of the U.S. command in Saigon. Combining all military and civil activities under Westmoreland, perhaps making him a theater commander in the Douglas MacArthur mode, seemed a good idea. He had broached it to LBJ, with a hint that Westy remembered in Manila. The president pondered; he had already made a move toward consolidating pacification activities in the White House, but how could things be pulled together on the ground? Was it a good idea to put everything under the military commander? Johnson talked it over with Bob Komer, undoubtedly with Rusk, probably with John Roche, a liberal former Brandeis University professor who had become an increasingly trusted speechwriter-cum-Vietnam-aide,[41] and with Walt Rostow.

Air Force One touched down at Guam on March 20 and was greeted by the airmen of Anderson Air Force Base, who had been waiting in a drenching rain. Johnson stood before his bedraggled audience under an umbrella held by Maj. Gen. William Crumm, host and commander of the B-52 force on the island. Westy, among the listeners, hid his amusement: "One of the first things a young officer learned in the old Army was that an officer in uniform never pushes a baby carriage, never carries a large bundle under an arm, and never holds an umbrella. Nobody apparently had ever contemplated the situation in which Bill Crumm found himself."[42]

Guam, heavy with history from World War II and loud with sounds of B-52s leaving for South Vietnam, had a more warlike look than Honolulu or Manila. The conferees found comforts few and quarters cramped. With the official guest house too small for the conferees, many were housed in private houses given up by their owners. No great headquarters conference room was available, so meetings were held in the officers' club.

As far as security was concerned, a Russian trawler rode at anchor out beyond the long runway.

Never one to lose control of the agenda, Johnson quickly introduced a new Saigon team. Ambassador Lodge would be replaced by veteran diplomat Ellsworth Bunker. Johnson praised the job Lodge had done: In two tough tours he had borne America's banner well, made hard decisions, and had done much to sustain Prime Minister Ky and President Thieu. The president introduced Deputy Ambassador Eugene M. Locke, a Texas friend of LBJ's and an astute lawyer-politico. To no one's particular surprise, Johnson presented Bob Komer as the head of South Vietnamese pacification. David Lilienthal, former head of both the Tennessee Valley Authority and the Atomic Energy Commission, came as a special advisor to South Vietnam on postwar economic development. He had not especially wanted the job, but the LBJ "treatment" dazzled him into acceptance.[43]

Johnson's control of the agenda nearly slipped during the first session when Thieu and Ky took stage center and presented the new South Vietnamese constitution, literally hot off the press and offered proudly. They had a right to be proud. Their country embattled, their culture unaccustomed to democracy (although not unaccustomed to fictive elections), they had triumphantly piloted a new constitution through the Constituent Assembly—albeit with a night-long session just before presentation. Still, here it was; done, as promised. The president's happiness could be heard by everyone at the conference. He looked at the constitution, he said, "just as proudly as I looked at Lynda, my first baby."[44]

Behind the basking, most must have felt the president's unease. Some rumors had it that North Vietnam teetered on the brink of a peace feeler; others that Hanoi's morale had never been more bellicose. Westmoreland kept expecting to reach the grail-like crossover line [the point when enemy losses would exceed the ability to replace them], but the general remained vague about timing. As for policies decided in Honolulu and Manila, the president had some doubts about follow-up. Obviously pacification lagged; obviously, too, Rolling Thunder lagged in results and consumed men and ordnance in discouraging amounts. All of this had direct impact in the United States and put terrific pressure on what Johnson called "the absolutely vital political base in the country."

But the president concealed his worries, returned happy thanks for

Vietnam's constitutional progress, and declared the main purposes of the meeting to be cementing good relations between the new American team and the new Saigon authorities, to emphasize the importance of Lilienthal's postwar economic planning, to examine southern land reform plans, and to emphasize the growing importance of pacification efforts.

Johnson disappointed Westmoreland a bit by turning away from the idea of making him the U.S. ambassador and putting everything in his hands. Still, Westy would have more responsibility under the new arrangement. He would run the war and have pacification under his wing. Not only that, he would also have a military deputy, Gen. Creighton W. Abrams, who would work on improving the Republic of Vietnam's armed forces. That put Bob Komer in a fascinating position, one that showed the height of administrative and political originality: he would be deputy to Westy for pacification. In his charge would be all civilian and military agencies involved in various levels of winning the hearts and minds of southern civilians. This unique arrangement, for which Komer deserves much credit, made almost everybody happy—after they all got to know each other. It would be announced when Bunker took over in Saigon in late May.

Although billed as a nonmilitary gathering, the conferees heard much about the war. Westy came with the feeling that "there is an amazing lack of initiative in planning for the future by the higher echelons of government. There seems to be a tendency to recognize a problem and assume that it will be solved . . . by . . . fading away . . . [because] we are so sensitive about world opinion."[45] He did not, of course, spill this thought before his colleagues around the table—an august group that included General Wheeler, Admiral Sharp, various AID officials, roving ambassadors, and all kinds of South Vietnamese representatives[46]—but he talked candidly about prospects. Unless U.S. pressure cracked the VC, or Hanoi withdrew, he told the president and others, "this war could go on indefinitely. . . . But we are making progress . . . we have found that we can fight the guerrilla. We can fight in the swamps . . . [and] in the mountains. We can fight the Main Force. We can fight in the jungle."

Silence greeted his report. Westmoreland—did he gloat?—saw shock around the table. David Lilienthal, who heard Westy say the war might linger for ten years without increased military pressure, looked at LBJ. "The look on the President's face. . . . Ten years, my God! . . . Imagined I could read the President's mind: 'think of the mothers of eight year old kids: could they possibly face up to that?'"[47]

Without fanfare, but with a determination old LBJ hands knew was unswervable, the president cut off much military optimism about numbers or spheres of action. Clearly he intended to reduce the U.S. commitment and put more of the war's burden on South Vietnamese shoulders. If he seemed to mimic the secretary of defense, he did—although not for dovish reasons but rather political ones. Without some evidence of reinvigorated South Vietnamese efforts that would allow reduced U.S. aid, American public opinion might stop the war.

The president's plans were thus made clear: He wanted a coordinated and effective pacification program, and he would follow the old military maxim of giving the generals half of what they asked for while doubling their mission!

Nonetheless, the conferees departed Guam in some optimism. America's effort would continue under new management, and Ho Chi Minh's recent release of an exchange of letters between himself and LBJ only reinforced the American contention that North Vietnam had no interest in negotiations.[48]

Westy and Komer worked on their new alignment during the return trip to Saigon and for two days after their arrival—and they hammered out an amazingly functional arrangement. They had interesting views of each other in time. "The Lord knows the President handed me a volatile character in Bob Komer," Westy recalled. "The nickname 'Blowtorch' was all too apt. . . . Yet Komer was the man for the job. He pushed himself and his people hard. He had imaginative ideas, usually sound. Striped pants might work later, but at the start, abrasion was in order and Bob Komer worked overtime at that."[49]

Komer, in turn, liked the general and got along with him:

Westy thought I was hell on wheels. The way I did it was to say, "Westy, we both went to the Harvard Business School." He was there for thirteen weeks or something like that, he adored the place. . . . I threw out "Yes, Sirs" all over the place. But Westy understood what LBJ told him, which was, "I want performance in Komer's field." . . . And I sold him on the idea that . . . you make me head of pacification and I report to you and if anything goes wrong they're all going to blame me and nobody's going to blame you. And if everything goes right. . . . And Westy understood that. . . . I'd say Westy was pretty good.[50]

So skillfully did the blending occur that military men thought LBJ had resolved the old civil-military controversy about pacification in their favor, and Komer knew it had been solved jointly.

When Ambassador Bunker arrived in Saigon on April 25, 1967, he announced the absorption of the old embassy Office of Civil Operations (which had tried to coordinate all civilian agencies working in the field) by Komer's Civil Operations and Revolutionary Development Support (CORDS) operation.[51]

Bunker, a veteran of the Dominican Republic crisis, quickly won the admiration of both Americans and South Vietnamese. Tall, thin, ramrod straight, a properly taciturn Vermonter with thin white hair and cool blue eyes, Bunker came to his task with a towering reputation for courage, honesty, coolness under fire, and personal reserve. South Vietnamese who did not know him well quickly dubbed him "Mr. Refrigerator," but in time the nickname changed to "blue-eyed sorcerer." One high-placed South Vietnamese official said they needed a "Vietnamese Bunker to lead us against Ho Chi Minh."[52]

Johnson hoped the new team would succeed. Always a realist, he looked ahead to the limits of his credibility. Lilienthal, novice that he was, found Johnson's Guam performance magnificent, but Johnson assessed his performance against hopes for the Great Society, against a less than enthusiastic reception to his State of the Union message with its request for a 6 percent income surcharge, its promise to stick in Vietnam, and its "time of testing" theme.[53] If Westy's long look proved true, if his requested 80,500 man minimum reinforcement (which might result in a protracted, though successful, frustration of North Vietnamese success) were sent, Johnson likely would lose his race with time, lose the Great Society, and be the first American president to lose a war.

He had often counseled others that the American public was the best ally and the worst enemy a president could have—depending on the depth of the crises faced. He knew that he, more than Westy, was approaching the crossover line—indeed, the Gallup Polls indicated he had already sunk below general approval[54] and that he must move swiftly to save his domestic program and the war.

RETURN OF A GLADIATOR

Come back to the States, the president told his field commander, and issue public reports from the front. Though uncomfortable on public view and uncertain of the propriety of his visit, good soldier Westmoreland complied.[55]

No fool, Westy knew LBJ needed him back home for public relations reasons. He also knew that in Washington he would have a chance to work on McNamara and others about things essential in Vietnam. He would have an opportunity to address a joint session of congress—a spectacular first for an active field commander—and to make other important speeches.

Johnson expected fine performances from Westy, who had an all-American-boy face and attitude, a voice to match his earnest gaze and granite jaw, and somehow always a razor-creased and crisp look, as though he dared any uniform to wrinkle. In short, he was a model TV subject. Wisely, Johnson made no attempt to coach his general—he would say whatever he wanted to say.

At New York's Waldorf-Astoria Hotel on April 24, 1967, Westmoreland made his first report. The president scanned the remarks carefully and enjoyed the strong message from his general. He spared no criticism of North Vietnamese infiltration, terrorism, and murder; he explained the enemy's coordinated war effort aimed at both military and diplomatic operations; he stressed American efforts to avoid civilian casualties, the courage of the South Vietnamese, and the special qualities of America's men at arms. Westy avoided an open boast of early success. "Although the military picture is favorable . . . , the end is not in sight." North Vietnam cherished active hopes of winning the war in the streets of Washington, Westy felt and, indeed, America's stick-to-itiveness would play a crucial part in the outcome. Deftly fending some tough questions, the general explained that the strategic and tactical situation was interwoven. "It is going to be a question of putting maximum pressure on the enemy anywhere and everywhere we can. We will have to grind him down." The United States indeed waged a war of attrition, he said, "and the only alternative is a war of annihilation."

The Johnsons invited Kitsy and Westy to the White House on April 26, where the general had a chance to do some lobbying at dinner. Seated between the president and Sen. Richard Russell, he explained his ideas on Vietnam's future. On the twenty-seventh, Westy met twice with LBJ, McNamara, Rusk, Cyrus Vance, Undersecretary of State Nicholas Katzenbach, Bus Wheeler and Rostow in the Cabinet Room. The issue, not surprisingly, was more troops for Vietnam.

Westy had the persistence of his beliefs, clearly, and said that the successes achieved with a relatively small U.S. force encouraged him to think more rapid progress could be made if he had more men. He suggested a limited reserve call-up to provide enough force to bring America's involvement to a close. He also sought permission to drive into Laos and Cambodia. Referring to the two plans he had submitted recently, he said the "minimum essential force" of 80,500 men would bring the U.S. complement in South Vietnam to 550,000 and the optimum force of 200,000 would bring the total to 670,000. Although the smaller number would not open the gates to U.S. defeat, "it will be nip and tuck to oppose the reinforcements the enemy is capable of providing."[56] He urged the larger number, which would let him destroy North Vietnamese sanctuaries in Laos and Cambodia.

A student of body language, Westy felt that LBJ leaned toward calling up reserves but that McNamara hesitated. By far the most hawkish comments came from Rostow, who suggested that U.S. forces "invade the southern part of North Vietnam . . . to block infiltration routes." Only Westy picked up that idea and it died in a whelm of silence.[57]

Wriggle as he might, COMUSMACV could not elude Secretary McNamara's constant questioning about how long America's crusade would continue under each of the troop plans. Reluctantly, with caveats about continued bombing of North Vietnam and the Laotian panhandle, Westy answered, "With the optimum force, about three years; with the minimum force, at least five."[58]

The president had two pertinent queries: "When we add divisions can't the enemy add divisions?" and "If so, where does it all end?"

Westy said he guessed the crossover point had been reached in all but the two northern provinces of South Vietnam.

"At what point," asked an anxious commander in chief, "does the enemy ask for volunteers" from potential allies?

"That is a good question," Westy replied.[59]

Disturbed, Johnson closed the discussion. Westy got the clear impression that no decision had been made.

On Friday, April 28, 1967, General Westmoreland walked into an enthusiastic House and Senate, and was introduced. After taking in the scene, he confidently placed his manuscript on the podium and began to speak. America would succeed in Vietnam—he avoided the word "victory." But success, he emphasized, depended on the national will. The enemy, he said, believed "our Achilles heel to be our resolve." Then to the subject dearest to him and to everyone listening: "Our soldiers, sailors, airmen, marines, and coast guardsmen in Vietnam are the finest ever fielded by our nation. . . . These men understand the conflict. . . . They believe in what they are doing. . . . Backed at home by resolve, confidence, patience, determination, and continued support, we will prevail in Vietnam over Communist aggression."

Overwhelmed by the cheers and applause, Westy sought a decent end to his performance. He turned and saluted the President of the Senate, the Speaker of the House, and the members—an inspiration that touched the country.[60]

But Johnson's hopes for a propaganda coup were dashed before Westy arrived in Washington. As Westy spoke in New York and remarked that dissent encouraged the enemy, he earned a barrage of antiadministration venom. Johnson's motives for having the general on tour were impugned, and Westy must have been glad to get back to a war he had some chance of understanding.

The antiwar movement burgeoned. On April 4, Martin Luther King, Jr., spoke in New York City to a crowd of more than one hundred thousand. In a ringing "Declaration of Independence from the War in Vietnam,"[61] he flayed the United States for killing twenty civilians for every VC warrior. "So far we may have killed a million of them—mostly children." These numbers were first circulated in some Communist propaganda pieces and had no other basis of support. But they gained wide circulation because King quoted them.[62]

For Lyndon Johnson, 1967 opened with Vietnam optimism that drained to despair with spring.

chapter

TWELVE

"Lyndon Lives in a Cloud of Troubles"

U nlike most houses, the White House is never utterly still—total repose eludes it, along with the people it shelters. A staff is always alert in the Situation Room, history stalks the hallways, and sometimes, surely, ghosts of troubles met hover in the wings. At about 4:30 in the morning on June 5, 1967, Lady Bird heard "that most dread and frightening sound that can happen in this house—the sudden ringing of the telephone in the middle of the night. It can never be good news."[1] Jarred awake, she answered it. The Situation Room wanted to speak to the president immediately.[2]

"Yes," she heard her husband answer. Silence, some questions. Caught in "an almost unbearable wave of sympathy," she asked what had happened. "We have a war on our hands—in the Middle East," he said and settled back. Walt Rostow had called to say that the war LBJ had feared might come had begun. Lady Bird could not go back to sleep, but shook when the phone jangled nerves again in about an hour. More talk, more silences, then a kiss from Lady Bird. She knew, as he got up and began watching the news, that the house they shared had powers of its own, that "in this place there are thermometers of trouble somewhere in the world."[3]

A little before eight o'clock, the phone rang again. The president was still in his bedroom, surrounded by television and newspaper accounts of what had happened between Israel and Egypt. McNamara, dispassionately as possible, spoke a sobering and unprecedented warning: "Mr. President, the hot line is up." That teletype link between Moscow and Washington had been installed to make possible the cooling of world tensions—it had never been used for that purpose before. Johnson hardly seemed surprised. For weeks he had feared Middle East escalations and felt, deep inside, that trouble between the Arab nations and Israel loomed "far more dangerous than the war in Southeast Asia."[4] And now the hot line was up.

SIX DAYS TO AVERNUS

Burdens sometimes hang long in history. Especially old faults among peoples linger, buried maybe for an age, but lurking fallow in memories, waiting to erupt. Burdens of conscience, blood, and race can make actual changes in the bounds of reason. Troubles spread thickly woven between the Jews and Arabs, worse far in the times since the British quit the Middle East and left unfulfilled a homeland to mend the Diaspora. If the Jews were God's chosen, the twentieth century seemed still some kind of testing time for them, a century of horror, of dying, of myrrh-stained blood running in Canaan's rivers toward a place carved in iron from an earth bleached of tears—left only with the Wall. They had come after Hitler's holocaust to their hard scrabble Zion to nurse a promise from a dream.

Fielding a chaos of claims, injustices, and loose ends of war, the UN, in 1947, sought a simple division of Palestine into two states—one Jewish, one Arab—with Jerusalem internationalized. Accepted by the Jews, the plan infuriated the Arabs and fighting began. Israel declared its independence on May 14, 1948, only to be invaded the next day by neighboring Arab states. UN-arranged cease-fires jockeyed a nervous peace between outbreaks in 1948 and 1949. Full-scale war erupted in 1956. Israel won and agreed to UN settlement in the full flush of victory. In June, 1967, Israel again watched an ominous gathering of Arab hosts—and decided that a preemptive attack seemed the better part of valor. Israel's airmen and tankers would sweep the skies and the desert, and the war would end in a cease-fire with Israeli troops overrunning the Sinai Peninsula, clearing the Gulf of Aqaba to Sharm al-Sheikh and nudging Egypt's borders.

There were unexpected wages of success. Egyptian passions, frustrated, turned to fury and long recrimination. Gamal Abdel Nasser, head of the United Arab Republic [UAR], blamed the United States and other Israeli allies for the early massive air strikes that wiped out the Egyptian Air Force, and orchestrated a round-robin of broken diplomatic relations. During the war itself, a series of errors on both sides nearly caused a world conflict. And an Israeli attack on an American communications ship, the USS *Liberty*, nearly caused a breach between Washington and Tel Aviv.

Far more than they knew, the Israelis owed their final extrication from a badly overextended condition to the coolness of Lyndon Johnson. Concerned that a Mid-East war had potential for mass havoc, Johnson had initiated contact with Soviet foreign minister Andrei Gromyko a few minutes after hearing of the Israeli attack on June 5. "We feel," he said, "it is very important that the United Nations Security Council succeed in bringing the fighting to an end as quickly as possible and are ready to cooperate with all members of the Council to that end."

McNamara's message about the hot line might mean there was a Russian response—or something else. Johnson went to the Situation Room at about 8:15 that Monday morning. Small, unadorned, the room had an almost cell-like quality, relieved only by maps, desks, and some active staff members. The president later would learn that the hot line terminated in the Pentagon but had been extended into the White House that morning on the explosive orders of the secretary of defense.

Tinged with strangeness and no little mystery, "Molink," as technicians called the special teletype system, was installed in August, 1963, in the wake of JFK's Russian troubles, and had seen only test use and an annual New Year's message exchange.

Johnson was joined in the Situation Room by McNamara, Rusk, Walt Rostow, George Christian, and Bill Macomber, assistant secretary of state for congressional relations. Translators began intoning a message from Chairman Aleksei Kosygin.

As Johnson settled into his chair, he looked around the room and felt the tension. Two things came through clearly: First, this crisis had world overtones and could lead to nuclear war; second, like the crisis in the Dominican Republic, it was happening on his watch. He would work it as he had that one—up close and personal.

Kosygin, it turned out, had angry questions. Outraged by the Israeli attack, the chairman thought the United States had known about it and possibly condoned it; he demanded answers. As Johnson pondered his response, he realized the unusual impact of the hot line. Quick communication, of course, had virtues, but the hot line brought together people who could act. That was good and bad. Wrong words would produce wrong actions. Slowly, carefully, determined to set a tone of calmness and deliberation, LBJ told Kosygin that the United States shared Russia's surprise at the attack, disavowed any fore-knowledge or complicity, and pledged to urge Israel toward a cease-fire. Kosygin cooled down.

America heated up. At a news briefing early that morning, Robert McCloskey, a State Department spokesman, fielded questions about U.S. policy toward the conflict and finally said, "Our position is neutral in thought, word, and deed."[5] Johnson read the meaning correctly as a remark to reassure everyone the United States did not intend to go to war, but as the words carried across the country, telegrams and phone calls piled up at the White House. The American Jewish community had erupted.

Already concerned that American reaction lagged as the Mid-East crisis smoldered, Abe Fortas called to urge that LBJ "refrain from getting into the 'neutrality issue,'" which he thought might mean invoking the Neutrality Act. Many other Jews shared that worry; strict neutrality would nullify all previous promises of aid and comfort for Israel. The error of intention required quick correction, and Dean Rusk went before a national television audience to recount American commitments to Israel and present UN moves toward peace.[6]

As the first days dragged, Johnson became irritated with the strident cries for action. Not only did a vocal portion of American Jewry demand nearly total extinction of Egypt and no quarter for the Arabs, some reflected a puzzling paradox of views on Vietnam. "Dammit," Johnson fumed to Harry McPherson, "they want me to protect Israel, but they don't want me to do anything about Vietnam." As questions continued to pour into the White House, Johnson told Joe Califano to call Arthur Krim, Lew Wasserman, and Ed Weisl, assure them that the United States stood with Israel and to "get that word out and the Jewish community off his back."[7]

A memo from two of his White House staffers urging a presidential message to calm a June 8 Jewish rally in Lafayette Square, right across Pennsylvania Avenue from the White House, drew a flash response.[8] When he saw one of the memo's authors in the hall outside the Oval Office, Johnson waved a big right fist. "You Zionist dupe," he yelled. "Why can't you see I'm doing all I can for Israel. That's what you should be telling people when they ask for a message from the President for their rally."[9]

Johnson remained icily calm and impartial in diplomacy. Following usual practice, he formed a special committee of the National Security Council to coordinate U.S. actions. Going beyond the normal membership, he brought in trusted advisors from outside. Knowing well George Ball's coolness in a crisis, LBJ sent word for him. Rostow tracked him down in Chicago early on June 5, and asked, "Don't you know there's a war on?" The president, said Rostow, wanted Ball and Mac Bundy in Washington, pronto.

Ball demurred. He had two speaking engagements that day, and it was simply too late to cancel them. "This one by luck I was able to avoid," Ball later crowed. Mac Bundy, however, "less fortunate than I, was trapped in Washington for several weeks as executive secretary of the Special Committee of the National Security Council for the Middle East Crisis."[10]

That assignment must have seemed doubly familiar to Bundy—not just because of his Johnson years, but also because of the famed "ExCom" group during the Cuban missile crisis. Johnson also asked Dean Acheson to join the special advisors, and he participated in a couple of meetings.[11]

No one advised anything other than leaving the crisis up to the UN—despite its wide repute for languor. Fortunately the Russians agreed, and LBJ pushed Ambassador Goldberg (whose Jewishness caused some small dubiety) to call for a UN cease-fire. Johnson made it clear, through Goldberg, that the United States would support a Moscow demand that the Israelis fall back to the 1956 armistice borders—with one addition: "a commitment of all parties to refrain from 'acts of force regardless of their nature.'" America's plan aimed at opening the Gulf of Aqaba and the withdrawal of all forces from the Sinai.

The Arabs and their Russian allies would agree to a cease-fire if Israeli troops quit the Sinai; more, they wanted to achieve a total solution to the Middle Eastern problem.[12]

Israel disagreed, so UN activities stalled on the night of the first day of the war, military operations continued, and Johnson was left to fend the concerns of his frequent houseguest, Mathilde Krim, and his old friend, Justice Fortas.

Johnson endured, too, a visit from Gov. John Love of Colorado—just returned from Bangkok, Tokyo, and eight days in Vietnam—who could not "see how a military victory can be won," and suggested that "'political types' would be more effective in the management of the nonmilitary phases."[13]

Tuesday, June 6, 1967, dawned sunny and pleasant, with a prediction of no more than eighty-five degrees. In the Situation Room, temperature measured anxiety. Present at 6:40 A.M. were the conscience keepers and decision makers of the United States of America. Johnson took his place at the head, Hubert Humphrey joined him, along with Rusk, McNamara, Nick Katzenbach, Mac Bundy, Rostow, Clark Clifford (just over from his handy office), and Ambassador Llewellyn Thompson, in from Moscow for the crisis.

Lady Bird, ever worried about her husband and his friends who labored all hours, usually without food, followed Johnson over from the mansion, went to the White House staff mess, and helped the steward bring breakfast to "the crisis center of America." She found her husband and his cohorts talking with hushed concern about a message off the hot line. Kosygin wanted quicker UN action on a cease-fire.

Johnson, rigidly controlled, agreed with the chairman, but noted that there were problems. All kinds of rumors floated as fact in the air of war. Egypt, beleaguered, nearly humiliated along with its Russian suppliers, lashed at phantoms. Knowing the Mediterranean-based U.S. Sixth Fleet had carriers and strong air capability, Cairo claimed U.S. planes had joined in Israeli attacks on Egypt. Absurd though it might sound to Washington and to América, the charge seemed reasonable in the areas of tumult.

From the Situation Room, LBJ went to a congressional leadership breakfast at nine o'clock. There he assayed the Middle Eastern situation in detail, won praise for moderation, and used the moment to press for prevention of a national rail strike, "which all agreed would be disastrous."[14]

At 7:45 P.M. on the sixth, Johnson activated the hot line, to tell Chairman Kosygin that the UN had adopted a cease-fire resolution. A few minutes later, the president faced television cameras and announced: "The cease-fire vote of the Security Council opens a hopeful path away from danger in the Middle East. . . . The United States has warmly supported this resolution. . . . We believe a cease-fire is the necessary 'first step', in the words of the resolution itself . . . toward what we all must hope will be a new time of settled peace and progress for all the peoples of the Middle East. It is toward this end that we shall *now* strive."[15]

On the third day of the war, Israeli acceptance of a cease-fire failed of Arab agreement. An understandable disbelief suffused Arab reality. Never had defeat engulfed so quickly. Old Jerusalem had fallen and Israeli soldiers offered prayers at the Wailing Wall.

Johnson agreed with a National Security Council assessment issued at noon that Egypt had suffered a "stunning loss," that Nasser reeled under both military and psychological defeat, and that Russia, too, shared these humiliations—which prompted caution for the moment. "One thing we should do now," said Johnson, "is to develop as few heroes and as few heels as we can." The full council, encouraged and subdued, agreed.[16] Good news came by evening that a cease-fire held between Jordan and Israel.

Confusing word came in early the next day about an attack on an American ship off the Sinai coast. A glitch in Pentagon intelligence reporting left Johnson at the mercy of television accounts for some agonizing time. Finally, shards of news confirmed that a state-of-the-art U.S. Navy electronic surveillance ship, the USS *Liberty,* had been attacked with considerable loss of life. The question in everyone's mind was, Who did it?

Johnson, who had been on the hot line with Kosygin early in the day addressing cease-fire problems, contacted the chairman again at 11:00 A.M. to report that U.S. carrier planes were investigating a serious incident near the Sinai. A few minutes later, the president met with the Special Security Committee in the Situation Room. Rumors had been fleshed with a few facts: the *Liberty* had been hit by planes and motor-torpedo boats; at least thirty-one crewmen were dead, and possibly 171 wounded. Heavy in the Situation Room hung the questions: Had the Russians or the Egyptians attacked? How to react?

While debate sputtered, word came from the Israelis: It was *they* who had attacked the *Liberty*. As Dean Rusk noted, "that didn't please us, although an Israeli attack . . . was far easier to deal with."[17] No one around that big wooden table really believed the Israeli explanation that the whole thing had been a mistake based on ignorance of *Liberty*'s position or mission. Clark Clifford exploded. He urged Johnson to handle the attack as harshly "as if the Arabs or Russians had done it." Insist on punishment of those responsible, he ranted, adding that he found it "inconceivable that [the attack] was an accident."[18] Dean Rusk broke his stoicism to urge reparations, punishment, and apologies. He found the whole Israeli story "incomprehensible" because the attack had lasted too long to be an accident. "I didn't believe them then," he recalled later, "and I don't believe them to this day."[19]

Johnson calmly accepted Israel's apology and reparations. In the secrecy of the Situation Room, though, he agreed with Clifford and asked him to chair a special investigation of what had happened. Clifford would later recommend that the Israeli government "be held completely responsible." In his memoirs he worried the problem: "Having been for so long a staunch supporter of Israel, I was particularly troubled by this incident. . . . I never felt the Israelis made adequate restitution or explanation for their action . . . though I did not believe this tragic incident justified a break between the U.S. and Israel."[20]

Johnson downplayed the episode as simply the fortunes of war. He used the hot line again to inform Kosygin that U.S. carrier aircraft would continue to make investigation flights and not engage in aggressive action, and asked the chairman to so inform the Arabs. Kosygin did; the hot line had performed as intended.[21]

By the afternoon of June 8, Nasser's United Arab Republic had accepted the UN cease-fire arrangements, but Russia introduced a resolution accusing Israel of violating the cease-fire resolutions of June 6 and 7. Syria seemed to be the problem; Russia had a special relationship with that small nation and held out for its territory. In fierce fighting on June 9, Israel occupied Syria's Golan Heights.

Johnson kept pressing, as did Goldberg, for an end to the fighting. On June 10, Israel agreed to accept the full cease-fire resolution. By late morning LBJ thought "we could see the end of the road." He had spent a nervous night—complaining to the White House physician of left shoulder pains, which triggered heart worries—but finally went to sleep around six in the morning. Several urgent calls from Walt Rostow were deflected, as was one from Dean Rusk. Johnson awoke at about 8 A.M., just in time to hear that "Mr. Kosygin wants the President to come to the equipment as soon as possible." In the Situation Room at 8:57 A.M., Johnson munched on melon balls, sipped his tea, and at 9:05 read a Molink message that chilled everyone present. Israel, Kosygin said, had ignored all Security Council dicta about a cease-fire. A "very crucial moment" approached, one that might force "independent decision" on Moscow. A catastrophe loomed, Kosygin warned, unless Israel halted military operations unconditionally. If not, the chairman said, "the Soviet Union would take 'necessary actions, including military.'" Rusk, disbelieving, asked Ambassador Thompson to verify the word "military." He did.

A cold stillness settled over the room.

In the agonizing tenseness Johnson swung calmly toward McNamara. "Where is the Sixth Fleet now?" he asked, quietly. McNamara spoke on the phone, then turned back to the president and said, "It is approximately three hundred miles west of the Syrian coast."

The president, again very quietly, asked, "How fast do these carriers normally travel?"

McNamara almost whispered, "About twenty-five knots. Traveling normally, they are some ten to twelve hours away from the Syrian coast."

Johnson considered a problem in geometric timing. Since Russian intelligence ships tracked the U.S. fleet, word would swiftly reach Moscow of any sudden change in sailing patterns. Order the fleet to change course, he told McNamara softly. Instead of cruising a normal one hundred miles off the Syrian cost, have it cruise along at fifty miles. One challenge deserved another. If Kosygin was bluffing, Johnson was not.[22]

Several more hot-line exchanges occurred during the morning. Slowly, Kosygin's irritation subsided, and with it the threat of a nuclear exchange. Later on that dramatic day a final cease-fire went into effect between all Arab and Israeli forces.

America's commander in chief performed superbly throughout the Six-Day War. He gathered the right advisors and listened to them; his calm firmness held the UN effort together; his determined forbearance avoided a lasting breach with Israel, with American Jewry, even with the UAR; and his adroit threat of force kept a balance of wisdom in Moscow. He played the war close to his chest, the power tools in his hands, the decisions always his—and the result was what Lyndon Johnson yearned for in Vietnam: peace with hope for the future.

LOWERING CLOUDS ON A COLD TRAIL

Few moments of satisfaction came anymore. If Johnson and his advisors worked wonders for peace in the Middle East they had no chance to bask in the glory—back on their desks were the eddying issues of the war they could not stop. Timing remained the crucial issue. Jack Valenti, looking ahead, once quoted a line from Alexis de Tocqueville's *Democracy in America* that struck home with Johnson: "The people grow tired of a confusion whose end is not in sight."[23] Valenti might have offered some good precedents— for instance, Britain's long, finally victorious struggle against Napoleon. But precedents seemed, somehow, small comfort against the unknown. How long? How long? Johnson's probes for predictions always resulted in hedged uncertainties.

How long tangled with *if,* in a maze of collateral questions. *If* more men went to Westy, *if* more targets opened above the DMZ, *if* raids were allowed in Laos and Cambodia, *if* the ARVN improved, *if* pacification spread, then, maybe, the north would lose heart and give up in three or four years. With less men, fewer targets, and no cross-border operations, the whole thing would take longer. But, no one knew *how much* longer.

So, for the commander in chief, the question remained: How many men for Westy? Not so subtle changes in cabinet attitudes affected this perennial question. McNamara had grown gloomy trying to reconcile feelings with ambition. In mid-May, following up on Westmoreland's plans for maximum and minimum forces, the secretary of defense worked closely with John McNaughton's systems people on a response. On May 19, the secretary delivered a tough, twenty-two page memo to the president that was largely McNaughton's work. Struck by McNaughton's blast that "a feeling is widely and strongly held that 'the Establishment' is out of its mind," and has no war rationale,[24] McNamara let his own doubts show:

> This memorandum is written at a time when there appears to be no attractive course of action. The probabilities are that Hanoi has decided not to negotiate until the American electorate has been heard in November, 1968. Continuation of our present moderate policy, while avoiding a larger war, will not change Hanoi's mind, so is not enough to satisfy the American people; increased force levels and actions against

the North are likely to get us in even deeper in Southeast Asia and into a serious confrontation, if not war, with China and Russia. . . . So we must choose between imperfect alternatives.

Having played on Johnson's China worries, McNamara went on with a kind of personal recapitulation about how the United States got into what had become an unpopular war. Americans, he said, "want the war ended and expect their President to end it. Successfully, or else." Realistically, McNamara admitted that America's softening commitment affected policies in Hanoi.

Even though Westmoreland claimed success in the war against main enemy forces, pacification lagged. The South Vietnamese government reeked with corruption and internal dry rot and was, in fact, "moribund" as it presided over a people interested only in being left alone. McNamara reserved his hardest hits for the ARVN, calling it "tired, passive, and accommodation-prone." He guessed that Hanoi had a clear notion that the United States might win the large war, but lose the whole thing in the villages and American streets. More than that, there seemed little hope for negotiations. "They seem . . . determined to match U.S. military expansion of the conflict."[25]

As Deborah Shapley says, "it was quite an evolution from this former proponent of signaling-and-bargaining war."[26]

Surveying possible options, McNamara rejected giving Westy two hundred thousand men. That option would force a reserve call-up, create a huge bulge in the defense budget, lead to almost indiscriminate destruction of North Vietnam, and would not win the war. And, picking a Westmoreland scab, McNamara wondered if the crossover point really had been reached, why were more troops necessary? Whatever numbers went to Vietnam, he argued, "the enemy . . . will maintain the military 'stalemate' by matching our . . . deployments." The secretary's reference to "stalemate" was important.

He urged the president to follow what was called Course B, an option that would send another thirty thousand men to Vietnam, deny attacks in Laos and Cambodia, and limit bombing to twenty degrees north latitude. With words about a "cool drive to settle the war" by making crystal clear the main objective—not guaranteeing a free South Vietnam, only one rid of outside interference in self-determination—he came down in favor of less help for Westy. In essence, he simply wanted to stabilize the war. There were pros and cons, of course. Stabilization might deflate South Vietnam, encourage antiwar sentiment at home, and convince North Vietnam of victory. But, in McNamara's cautious assessment, although Course B "will not win the

Vietnam war in a military sense in a short time," it would contain the conflict and fit into an integrated strategy involving military, pacification, and diplomatic action "that gets things moving toward a successful outcome in a few years. More than that cannot be expected."[27]

One thing he did not say, despite the implications, was that the war seemed to him unwinnable. Ironically, at the same time Ellsworth Bunker's optimism grew with each day of service in Saigon.[28]

Everybody seemed to have a different opinion about the troop problem. Johnson, with his ferretlike skill, winkled opinions from casual visitors and stored those ideas in his mind as he cast and recast the odds.

Looking at his White House advisors, the president assessed a changing mood. Dean Rusk remained a cool, committed hawk, though always willing to negotiate or to trim the bombing. Security advisor Walt Rostow had no doubt that victory would come, although in May, 1967, even he advised concentrating bombing in southern North Vietnam and Laos.[29] McNamara and his steady, reliable deputy, Cy Vance, produced a report in mid-May that advised concentrating all Rolling Thunder missions on the "funnel" through which North Vietnamese supplies flowed southward—an area between seventeen and twenty degrees latitude—"reserving the option to strike [farther north] as necessary to keep the enemy's investment in defense and in repair crews high."[30] Abe Fortas remained strong as ever, as did Clark Clifford, who could see no good coming from any relaxation in the war, especially from any bombing halts.[31] Along the corridors of the West Wing and in the Executive Office Building, ideas shaded into a kind of gloomy gray.

Johnson, despite his reputed boundless capacity for flattered delusion, had an uncanny grasp of nuances. He heard the clamor in Lafayette Park, read the columns, looked at his three television sets, and had no need for tea leaves. He stared squarely at his crossover point. Hawks there were aplenty still, powerful ones who demanded more and nastier war—men like Sen. John Stennis—and LBJ worried that somehow they might shove him out on a nuclear limb,[32] so he nodded to them as he could. There were also many doves who lampooned his bloodthirsty streak, had no knowledge of his agonizing care about civilian casualties,[33] and saw the war in dangerously moralistic tones. He had a steersman's nightmare on his hands.

He had steering problems, too, with the whole business of approaching Hanoi. To some extent, hawks and doves flocked together over peacemaking. Some wanted to stop bombing outright, do anything necessary to induce Hanoi to the peace table, even to the point of abandoning South Vietnam: the unilateral crowd. Others wanted no overtures without a clear military edge: the negotiate-from-strength people. Johnson increasingly found himself somewhere in the middle. Experience made him wary of unrequited bombing halts that opened a clear channel for North Vietnamese reinforcements. At the same time, the realist in him lent some understanding of Hanoi's position. He regretted failed efforts at direct contact with Ho Chi Minh, regretted, too, a poorly managed attempt in early 1967 to get Great Britain and the Soviet Union (cochairmen of the Geneva conference) to mediate. Even so, Johnson thought, in mid-1967, that reason might yet prevail on both sides and permit a quid pro quo rapprochement.

Facing an acute dilemma, he again resorted to his favorite tactic: face-to-face contacts. Go back to Vietnam, he ordered McNamara and Bus Wheeler, sound out Bunker and Westy, talk with anyone needed, and bring back a realistic troop plan and general observations on U.S. Vietnam policies.

More immediately, Johnson, at the ranch for a short break, learned that Chairman Kosygin planned a UN visit in mid-June and wanted a meeting. There were lingering issues from the Six-Day War to discuss, Moscow might have a line to Hanoi, and Johnson hoped to pick up a point already raised with Kosygin about an important arms control issue—avoiding emplacement of antiballistic missile (ABM) systems. McNamara put heavy emphasis on limiting these weapons as part of the whole effort toward de-escalating nuclear capabilities.

Nothing seemed more difficult than getting the two heads of state together. It would have been easy, indeed, had Johnson been willing to go the UN; he was not. Easy, too, had Kosygin been willing to go to Washington; he was not. Someone suggested an air force base not far from the UN. The chairman rejected that. Reaching out, Johnson called Richard Hughes, governor of New Jersey, and asked him to pick a place between Washington and New York.

The governor suggested the president's house at Glassboro State College, and Kosygin agreed. Small Glassboro suddenly found itself spotlighted the way Fulton, Missouri, had been when Churchill came to the United States and made his famous "Iron Curtain" speech.[34]

Lady Bird thought "Hollybush" and Glassboro were perfect settings for the talks. "If they expected us to be in big, rich, overpowering country, they certainly wouldn't have found it *there* in that little college town, and that red brick Victorian house with the furniture that looked like what your grandmother probably had."[35]

On June 23, 1967, the Johnsons, including Lynda, arrived at Hollybush just in time to greet the huge black limousine with the hammer-and-sickle pennon. Kosygin and his daughter joined the party and heard the great roaring cheers from a large, friendly crowd, some people carrying signs for

"PEACE." Lady Bird felt the excitement of "a moving moment." Everyone went in the house to see the conference room and greet the conferees—"the stern Gromyko . . . the Russian interpreter . . . our interpreter, Secretary Rusk, Walt Rostow, the affable Dobrynin, and patient and philosophical Llewellyn Thompson" and others.[36]

Too many hopes ride on most summits, and whatever emerges is somehow something of a disappointment. Kosygin and Johnson were closeted with their interpreters in Dr. Robinson's study for the better part of two days. Talks ranged over all kinds of world problems, from hopes that mutual grandchildren could live in peace to Kosygin's recollections of the merciless siege of Leningrad, which left him with a lasting horror of war. Johnson shared those horrors and spoke of things done to lessen Cold War tensions and said the time had come to go farther, to do something serious about ABMs and intercontinental ballistic missiles (ICBMs). Kosygin, employing a tactic he used throughout the talks, switched away from strategic arms issues to angry words about Israel not evacuating conquered territories.

Early tensions, including threats of war, subsided and both men recalled their success with hot-line peacekeeping. Apparently Kosygin had come unprepared for serious arms control talks; he evaded a Johnson suggestion to send McNamara immediately to Moscow and, although impressed with McNamara's hasty summary of the horrors of nuclear war, managed to brush off suggestions of limiting defensive weapons. "When I have trouble sleeping at night," Kosygin told McNamara, "it's because of your offensive missiles, not your defensive missiles."[37] McNamara did not abandon his crusade; his persistence, along with LBJ's, pushed the USSR toward the first Strategic Arms Limitation Talks [SALT] agreements in 1972. But immediate results were small: both sides merely agreed to continue disarmament discussions in Geneva.

Vietnam was by far the most important topic at Glassboro, although soft-pedaled in a minor key. Closeted with Johnson and their interpreters, Kosygin said that a hot-off-the-wire message from Hanoi promised that "if the bombing of the North were stopped, Hanoi's representatives would talk" to the US.[38] The chairman spoke of an emergency and emphasized "that time was short." Johnson voiced worries about what might happen if bombing stopped and the North Vietnamese drove southward. Kosygin thought that swift talks would minimize the risk. Both agreed to cooperate on a message to Hanoi. That message, ready the next day, showed a change in U.S. terms—a hint at willingness to talk as long as neither side took advantage of a truce. Kosygin and Johnson signed it and the message was sent. Nothing came of it—save a closer feeling between the two conferees.[39]

In the helicopter en route to the White House, LBJ said, "Well, I don't think we moved a peg today." Lady Bird understood but, she mused, the Russian guests must have felt the real goodwill of the American public.[40]

Johnson had no time for disappointments. If peace stalled on one front, he would look for some positive signs from Saigon. In mid-June, 1967, news of McNamara's pending descent on that hectic city eddied across the Pacific. In Honolulu, Oley Sharp decided on stellar preparation.

The CINCPAC alerted his subordinate commanders, Pacific Fleet commander Adm. Roy L. Johnson, Pacific Air Force commander Gen. John D. Ryan, General Westmoreland, Seventh Air Force commander Gen. William W. Momyer, and Seventh Fleet commander Vice Adm. John L. Hyland, that the defense secretary was coming prepared to restrict everything more than ever, especially the air war. Sharp said he would not hold back on his own convictions that air strikes against North Vietnam must be increased; the commanders' views in support "would be most helpful."[41] He wanted Westy involved and on track with the overall plans for bombing and ground operations. More than that, Sharp made a special trip to Saigon on June 28 for rehearsals with his principal commanders.

The COMUSMACV did not intend to be outshone. He had his major commanders alerted for comprehensive briefings. Each MACV element would have a segment. "Of course, you'll want to talk about pacification," he said to Bob Komer. "You need a good briefing officer," and Westy promised to provide one.

"No, Westy," Komer replied, "this is a whole new game, this thing we're calling pacification and I am about the only one who knows all the ins and outs. . . . I think I better brief him myself."

Surprised, the general thought about it. "Let's hear what you're going to say," he finally ordered.

Komer's reply shocked him to the core: "Westy, I don't prepare a briefing three weeks ahead. . . . I'll dream it up the night before."

That did it. Westmoreland advised his headquarters that briefings would be done by the officers in charge.

When McNamara, accompanied by Nick Katzenbach and various staffers from Defense and State, arrived at Ton Son Nhut Air Base on July 7, those who watched him bound down the stairs from the big tanker that delivered the team were surprised. He was a changed man. No longer haggard looking, but swaggering again, full of himself and his certainties, he raced into the briefings with the old gusto and arrogance. He had come to set a troop limit and make Westy conform. Katzenbach, a rookie when it came to Vietnam, was there to observe embassy operations and absorb feelings of the war.

Ready for the usual dog and pony show, McNamara rushed to the briefing room, took his accustomed stiff posture, set his glasses, stared straight ahead—and blinked. Westmoreland got up, and opened the session. Komer cheered him silently: "Westy was the most articulate military man in the headquarters anyway. He gave a good performance."

Komer had a humorous brush with disaster during his portion of the briefing when the secretary stopped him cold with a question about numbers. "Those last figures, Bob, you gave on pacification I think are wrong. They contradict the figures on my desk which are . . ." and out they came in serried totes assembled.

Nonplussed, Komer asked, "Where did you get those?"

"From you," snapped McNamara.

Standing in uncomfortable fuddlement, Komer heard the briefing colonel—whose assignment he had resisted earlier—say "Sir, the ambassador's figures are correct. They are the latest. The figures you are quoting are last month's."

To Komer's delight, McNamara's jaw dropped. He stared at the colonel, fussed with papers in his lap, then said, evenly, "That may be so. Thank you very much." Never had that happened at MACV. Komer noted that Westy seethed, that he wanted to kill the offending—and accurate—colonel.[42] But McNamara took the whole thing in stride; he was, indeed, a different man.

Much encouraging information came from the various presentations. Bunker, whom McNamara deeply respected, made an important point: "The situation is not a stalemate." Intelligence thought the nebulous crossover point might have been reached. Oley Sharp harped, as usual, on widening the air war and did it with impressive reasons (enemy antiaircraft fire had declined in efficiency, perhaps from an ammunition shortage; U.S. smart bombs and cluster bombs did devastating damage; and U.S. planes were equipped with electronic countermeasures that reduced casualties),[43] buttressed by well-rehearsed testimony from his air people. But Sharp's hawkishness irked McNamara, who later snubbed the admiral.

Westmoreland had to leave hurriedly—his mother was dying—bringing the meetings to an abrupt close. McNamara's public comments as he departed for Washington were more enthused than ever: Big-unit actions were succeeding, "dramatic" political progress had been made in South Vietnam, and pacification was progressing slowly. But some newshounds saw past the pose to an inner doubt. Doubts McNamara certainly had, but they mixed with a kind of exhilarated optimism. Back in Washington he twice talked of winning—once when he publicly denied a stalemate, and again in a White House meeting on July 11, when he told Clark Clifford "that if we follow the same program we will win the war and end the fighting."[44]

Bus Wheeler agreed with McNamara about there being no stalemate and confirmed a long series of battle successes. Then he confessed disagreement with the secretary about bombing and expressed hope the president would adopt a bold approach to the war.

McNamara downplayed disagreements when he, Wheeler, and Westmoreland saw the president on July 13. They had, he boasted, come to "complete accord" about troop additions. Westy would get about 45,000 men, and agreed on a ceiling of 525,000 by the end of June, 1968. Westmoreland, after heated arguments with McNamara, hewed to the party line and told the president of his "delight" with the final decision.[45] Johnson, whose sources were nearly infallible, knew about arguments between the civilian and military sides in the Pentagon. Nor did he did miss a public argument between Westy and the secretary of defense about the efficiency of operations in Vietnam. When McNamara observed that there were 1.3 million uniformed men in the area, with only 50,000 to 60,000 in a ground combat role, Westy reacted angrily in the press.[46]

Johnson tucked in his mind the fact that McNamara sounded trumpets of success about the land war but showed little enthusiasm for bombing. Throughout this whole troubling period, Johnson kept his own counsel. He revealed little at a press conference held after his July 13 meeting with Westy, Wheeler, and McNamara. Seriously, with the casual confidence of long consideration, he said more troops would be needed and would be sent—that old bent to meet the field commander's needs never really left him—but that final numbers were not ready yet.[47] There would, at any rate, be no need to call up the reserves. Nothing drastic loomed on the horizon. A month later, the numbers were ready: 47,296 more troops were going to Vietnam; the 525,000-man cap would hold.[48] Bombing patterns also would hold.

McNamara could claim partial victory—he had again contained the war, but he had not engaged the issue of ideology. Furthermore, it was becoming increasingly evident that his war-pinching irritated LBJ. Although the president remained cordial, he did not call as often—a significant blow to the secretary, who cherished closeness to the Oval Office.[49]

Johnson began, in a way, acting as his own minister of war. Worried about August hearings on bombing policy announced by hawkish Sen. John Stennis, dissatisfied with the troop-number decision, uncertain that full field needs were being met, he turned toward allies for more help. If more Americans were going over, Johnson thought the allies should ante up also; the American people should expect no less. And he did it with a typically personal pitch by asking Clark Clifford and presidential advisor Maxwell Taylor to make a swing around allied capitals to see how many more troops might be gleaned. Outlining the trip at a White House meeting on July 14, the president said the mission would review Vietnam policy with the allies and let them "know that we are thinking about them, make them feel informed."[50] Clifford had high hopes for success.

Despite LBJ's admonition to avoid publicity about the trip, rumors wafted through Washington news circles. As various articles appeared about Johnson's aides pressing reluctant allies, Clifford and Taylor were embarrassed. All of the countries they would visit, save Korea, had measurable antiwar problems of their own; most U.S. embassies on the proposed route sent urgent messages not to announce they were making a recruiting circuit. President Marcos of the Philippines flatly refused to receive the mission—he had, he rationalized, just visited Vietnam and needed no additional information. Clifford and Taylor briefed the press carefully on a journey designed merely to "reassure our Asian allies, get a firsthand assessment of the situation, and discuss another summit."[51] Already a bit battered, the emissaries left Andrews Air Force Base on July 22, 1967, full panoplied with staffers from Defense and State.

Saigon, their first stop, showed well. Fewer U.S. troops were in evidence—a deliberate Westy design—and the city fairly oozed optimism. Westy and Ellsworth Bunker "gave us the most optimistic progress report I would receive in the course of the war," Clifford noted. He and Taylor met with both Ky and Thieu, talked about the coming presidential election in September, and Clifford harped on the absolute necessity of honest elections. Some tension could be felt between the two Vietnamese leaders—they were to run on the same ticket, with Ky subordinating himself into the vice presidency—but both visitors felt a growing political stability. As for troops, Vietnam expected to add sixty-five thousand men by the end of the year, including fifty thousand RF/PF recruits. Troops would be retained in the ranks longer, and the draft age would drop to eighteen in a semimobilization—exactly what LBJ had hoped for from them.[52]

Numbers did not go up as the trip went on. Clifford became increasingly depressed as capitals came and went.

When he and Taylor returned and briefed Johnson on August 5, 1967, Clifford glumly reported that Australia's Prime Minister Holt had evaded troop questions with boasts about Australia's steady contribution, mentioned his own political problems, and offered little beyond goodwill. New Zealand, where antiwar demonstrations greeted the visitors, could offer no help. Korea was the only bright spot: more support troops would be sent; another division might be possible. Thailand cited guerrilla problems, lack of military leadership, but lots of volunteers. Clifford thought "they are going to come through." Taylor, more veteran at such junkets, felt there would be long-term accretions to troop numbers and praised the improved condition of the ARVN. He worried about America's usual impatience for results because it would take time for allied efforts to coalesce. He suggested to the president that current policies continue, along with efforts to prop up domestic morale.[53]

Clifford became the casualty of the trip. "Privately . . . I told President Johnson I was shocked at the failure of the countries whose security we believed we were defending to do more for themselves." Clifford hardly blinked when Prime Minister Lee Kuan Yew of Singapore—an avid supporter of Johnsonian Asian policies—refused to send a small contingent in support. Clifford had come to recognize the willingness of the Asian countries to take advantage of American concern about the region.[54]

All the differing views served up a hectic mass of confusion. Good news from Vietnam mixed into a doleful melange of domestic woe. The lowering clouds of the antiwar movement grew into a dark backdrop to Johnson's personal crossover point: in mid-July, 47 percent of Americans polled approved of Johnson's performance; in August the ratio fell to 39 percent. Fifty-four percent disapproved of his Vietnam activities—the lowest rating yet.[55] How long could he have guns, butter, and control?

"IT TAKES TWO SIDES TO END A WAR"

In June, a glimmering ray of hope seeped through the diplomatic gloom. Vietnam earned much attention at an international scientific meeting in Paris that month. Casual discussion led two French delegates (one of whom knew Ho Chi Minh of old) to visit Hanoi on a personal peace-seeking mission. They were welcomed by Ho, talked twice with Prime Minister Pham Van Dong, and returned to Paris at the end of July full of enthusiasm. Immediately they contacted an American conference member, Dr. Henry Kissinger. The Frenchmen told Kissinger of their belief that North Vietnam would come to the table as soon as the bombing stopped. Implications were that even a de facto halt would be acceptable without fanfare.

Fuzzy though the contact seemed to LBJ, he authorized Kissinger to state clearly the American negotiating position: bombing of the north would stop if that would lead to prompt discussions. "We were prepared to assume," the president said, "that while discussions were going on, either in secret or in public, North Vietnam would not 'take advantage' of the bombing cessation." This seemed an unambiguous version of the Glassboro terms. No North Vietnamese stand-down before a bombing halt was mentioned, nor were there demands to end all infiltration and support actions. Kissinger told his French colleagues they could inform Hanoi of a major change in the bombing pattern beginning August 24, 1967—there would be no attacks within ten miles of Hanoi's center, and that restriction would continue for sixty days.

Sadly, the channel evaporated, despite the apparently honest interest of one North Vietnamese diplomat. The French negotiators were not allowed back to Hanoi, and within two weeks the North Vietnamese government denounced the whole effort.[56] But Johnson agreed to try to keep the channel open.[57]

Subtle currents eddied behind this change in America's program for peace. McNamara, undaunted in seeking detente, aided by Assistant Secretary of Defense for International Affairs Paul Warnke and Deputy Defense Secretary Paul Nitze, had conceived the modified proposal and persuaded LBJ to accept it. The authors were happy, indeed, when Johnson reiterated their plan during a speech before the National Legislative Conference in San Antonio, where it earned the *nom de paix* "San Antonio Formula."[58]

For the moment, though, the peace trail still ran cold.

"AS COLD WATERS TO A THIRSTY SOUL"

As he scanned the media and listened both to visitors just in from Vietnam and his emissaries around the world, Johnson grew increasingly sure that some radical change must be made in American propaganda. The real story of Vietnam just was not getting across in Saigon or Washington, and certainly not in Hanoi.

At an August 8 meeting with Democratic congressmen, LBJ measured the information gap. Lester Wolff from New York moaned that "nobody sees the light at the end of the tunnel in Vietnam. We are the victims of a poor public relations program," and cited remarks by Gerald Ford about ineffective strategic bombing. Johnson shifted in his big chair, obviously ruffled.

"We are taking out half of the infiltration with our bombing, some reports show," he said, using Rostow's guesses,[59] "but haven't stopped it." Then, warmed to his cudgels, he cautioned, "I am not going to do what Ford says, because we would be in a war with China tonight if we did. . . . We do not want to get the Soviet Union and China into this war." He wanted it clear that stories about a stalemate were untrue; "we are moving along. The kill ratio is 10 to 1. . . . Hanoi is in bad shape. . . . The military situation and pacification are improving." Then, soberly, "much as we want it, there is no easy way out."[60]

If he needed more evidence of the malign effects of bad information, he got it by listening to Senator Stennis's hearings on Vietnam bombing. Long worried about the hearings, Johnson feared that administration policies might be attacked and that careless witnesses might confound the problem. He did not try to coach his cabinet members, but thought some tutelage might be given to military officers—especially known hawks like Admiral Sharp.[61] Military witnesses, dear to Stennis's predilections, were called first so they could air their worries about civilian mismanagement behind committee doors.

Then there was McNamara, himself, whose testimony hardly thrilled the commander in chief. Stennis called the secretary of defense at a little after ten on the morning of August 25. The senator and his colleagues represented a hard-war cabal nearly intolerable to McNamara; he, to them, personified all the errors of a tragic venture retrievable only with force.

McNamara was clearly nervous, eager to declaim and be gone—he had already tried to preempt the agenda by issuing an eight-page statement to the press. Speaking in his usual staccato bursts, armed with data, McNamara made a controlled case for the bombing program. He stuck to the old, original administration line that bombing North Vietnam had always been designed to supplement a vigorous land campaign. He reminded his listeners that it had been instituted at a moment of crisis in South Vietnam to prop up that ally's sagging morale, and had been continued to interdict North Vietnamese infiltration and supplies.

Almost as many bombs had been dropped on North Vietnam as had been dropped on Europe in World War II, yet they had failed to cripple the enemy's war effort. He pointed out that fifteen tons of supplies per day would sustain enemy forces in the south and the North Vietnamese were capable of moving two hundred tons a day. McNamara believed that only a bombing program aimed at large cities would force Ho Chi Minh to quit the war. He refuted military testimony about the terrible effect of civilian control of the targeting process by reviewing the target list. He pointed out that the unstruck targets were mainly minor ones, and that eliminating them would be costly in men and aircraft and results negligible.

In lengthy questioning, some of it pointedly insulting (Strom Thurmond of South Carolina accused him of placating Communists), McNamara defended administration policy—pointing out that both Westmoreland and Wheeler thought they were ahead and would win. Then he offered a plea for continued bombing restraints. Ports, he thought, should remain off limits because of the risk of hitting Soviet ships; so, too, large cities, especially Hanoi. He argued that: "The tragic and long drawn out character of that conflict in the south makes very tempting the prospect of replacing it with some new kind of air campaign against the north. But . . . to pursue this objective would not only be futile but would involve risks to our personnel and our Nation that I am unable to recommend."

Logically sound, even humane, McNamara sounded, but he spoke with arrogance, using haughty words that seemed to make the senators look small and simple—and they resented it.

Johnson resented some of those words, too, especially those that tended to soften a campaign the president had just expanded. The president noted a yawning ditch of disagreement when McNamara talked to reporters during a lunch break in the hearings. One of them picked up on Sen. Stuart Symington's point that McNamara's policy "differed from the military commanders'. He says if you are right we should get out of Vietnam."

Hurriedly, almost fervently, the secretary replied, "Symington . . . is completely wrong. My policies don't differ with those of the Joint Chiefs and I think they would be the first to say it. Their strategy for winning in South Vietnam is exactly the same. . . . I think there is some misunderstanding as to the basis of the argument over the bombing campaign in the North."[62]

Bad as that untruth may have sounded, McNamara's eight-page statement hit Johnson harder. In it, the secretary had effectively demolished any reason for continued bombing of North Vietnam and indicated that escalating it, as Johnson was doing, was fraught with danger. He had, perhaps unthinkingly, trapped himself, though. He used his antibombing stance to push his own peace hopes, which hinged on bombing pauses. Ironically, McNamara had initially urged LBJ to launch the bombing campaign and had supported it resolutely. Obviously, the secretary now spoke with a forked tongue.

Furious at so public a split in the administration—something he had proudly avoided—Johnson took the unprecedented step of disavowing McNamara's comments at a special news conference called on September 1, 1967.[63]

McNamara felt hurt, and probably apprehensive, as the breach with his boss widened dangerously. Then a much wider gap opened, this time between the secretary and the Joint Chiefs of Staff. At a secret meeting in the chairman's office, after hearing McNamara's testimony, the chiefs allegedly vowed to submit a joint resignation. Harold Johnson, army chief of staff, is said to have agreed fully since the military was taking the rap for poor civilian leadership. Varying degrees of acceptance ranged around the table, but in the end they all reportedly decided to resign at a press conference the next morning. Later that day, General Wheeler, stressed to the point of severe chest pains, changed his mind. The resignations did not happen and no one heard about the discussions until after America pulled out of South Vietnam.[64]

Much as he denied it, the hearings had nudged LBJ farther down a hawkish path. In meetings during Stennis's hearings, the president urged more and more targets and talked often about not appearing to do enough to win—so much so that normally aggressive Dean Rusk began to speak against risking border incidents with China.[65]

Shrewdly, Johnson realized that he had, in a sense, fallen victim to news reports of a Vietnamese stalemate and of the hype surrounding military testimony on the Hill. "No longer . . . worried about the stop-the-bombing pitch," he admitted to the Tuesday lunch group that "propaganda about a stalemate has us wobbling now."[66] He stopped the wobbling as he addressed the problems of image, information, and credibility.

Bombing had been pretty thoroughly aired before Stennis's committee and, whatever their opinion—which finally condemned civilian interference with the military—the public had heard both sides of the argument. If the administration's policy seemed soft, because it avoided heavy civilian casualties, it at least showed mercy. Hopefully the path of decency would win a few points on the next presidential poll.

The government's lack of credibility—something Mac Bundy and others had often mentioned—was something Johnson found hard to understand. One issue that had been raised by several in the Tuesday lunches, as well as in the daily press, centered on enemy numbers: How many men did North Vietnam and the VC have in South Vietnam? For months arguments had raged across the Pacific about how to count hostile effectives. In military terms: What was the enemy order of battle? That neither the allied military services nor the CIA could agree on how many enemy troops lurked in the green jungles south of the DMZ baffled the president. Such information went to the heart of what the United States was doing over there, and affected, directly, the whole concept of the body count which had become, somehow, the only real measurement of allied success on the ground.

Trouble emerged with the creation of a new Special National Intelligence Estimate on September 1. In this document, the CIA insisted that 120,000 self-defense forces and secret self-defense forces be included, which would inflate the enemy total to 435,350. Westy's staff thought these forces should be excluded on the grounds of basic inefficiency; besides, if included, these numbers contradicted MACV's official estimates.

Richard Helms proved a tough nut. The National Security Council told Walt Rostow that Helms should "bite the bullet," and join the team. Bob Komer joined the chorus for exclusion, as did Westy's deputy, Gen. Creighton Abrams. "The press reaction to these inflated figures is of . . . concern,"

Abrams cabled on August 20. "We have been projecting an image of success . . . and properly so. Now, when we release the figure of 426–531,000, the newsmen will immediately seize on the point that the enemy force has increased about 120–130,000." From experience, he added, "all available caveats and explanations will not prevent the press from drawing an erroneous and gloomy conclusion as to the meaning of the increase." Ambassador Bunker agreed that the whole thing would turn the credibility gap into a chasm. Johnson used MACV's numbers in press talks.

Helms, realizing there was a growing crisis, sent George Carver to Saigon as a mediator; the JCS joined the propaganda potpourri. Everything went on hold until the disagreements could be melded into a politically acceptable compromise. That the president knew the dimension of this statistical battle is unclear. Political scientist Larry Berman absolves Westmoreland of deliberately deceiving LBJ, and says that "the documents show that LBJ was briefed on the bureaucratic dispute between the CIA-MACV concerning the size of enemy forces," but offers no citation.[67] The Columbia Broadcasting System [CBS] later accused Westy of just such a conspiracy of silence in its special report titled "The Uncounted Enemy: A Vietnam Deception," and the general sued for libel. Thousands of documents were declassified for the trial and the parade of witnesses included McNamara, but no verdict was issued. The trial judge concluded the proceedings with a humanist's epilogue: "Judgments of history are too subtle and too complex to be resolved with the simplicity of a jury's verdict. It may be for the best that the verdict will be left to history."

It seems inconceivable, though, that LBJ with his TVs, his news tickers, and his astounding way of learning everything, had absolutely no knowledge of so large a discrepancy in figures. Whether or not he knew is not as important as what he did with what he knew.

Depression caused by growing public anger and anxiety raised about America's will to stick with the war, all worked some of the same kinds of stress that withered Robert McNamara. Johnson, some would later say, became paranoid and saw old friends who turned "soft" as enemies. While there may have been some who turned, and Johnson may have shown some paranoia, he remained fundamentally true to what seemed to him the best course for the honor of his country. There is no doubt that Johnson did close up somewhat, circle his wagons, and pull in the advisors who remained constant to the moderate course he kept. But he did not close all doors to adverse ideas, he continued to probe for dissonance, to search for alternative ways to get out of "that bitch of a war."[68]

Pressures mounted at home. In October, fifty thousand demonstrators milled around the Pentagon. McNamara watched from his window and saw the untidiness, the disorganization and felt disdain and a moral kind of sympathy. Sloppy emotionalism wasted crowd strength; girls put flowers in the barrels of the guards' rifles, rubbed "their naked breasts in the soldiers' faces. They're spitting on them; they're taunting them. God, it was a mess . . . They did it all wrong. . . . The way to have done it would been Gandhi-like. Had they retained their discipline, they could have achieved their ends. My God, if fifty thousand people had been disciplined and I had been the leader, I absolutely guarantee you I could have shut down the whole goddamn place."[69] He praised the soldiers—who had no ammunition—because they never fired a shot.

McNamara had about expended his own ammunition. He knew it. He hated the exclusion, the messy necessity of dealing with Johnson through Joe Califano, but he remained tied to power by some mystical umbilical cord. He could not go directly to his boss and say I'm tired, I resign. He did it another way, a less straightforward but effective way, that advanced his high-held cause of de-escalation.

His plan perhaps crystallized when Johnson convened the Wise Men on November 1, 1967. Clark Clifford and Walt Rostow suggested the meeting to Johnson; he remembered the usefulness of earlier such gatherings and agreed to call in from beyond government trammels the acutely honest Dean Acheson, Gen. of the Army Omar Bradley, George Ball, Mac Bundy, Arthur Dean, Douglas Dillon, Abe Fortas, and former Undersecretary of State Robert Murphy. Insiders included Averell Harriman, Cabot Lodge, and Maxwell Taylor. Those veteran advisors were to be treated to briefings by the CIA and the JCS in the evening of the first day, after talking with others in the morning and having lunch with the president.

Some of them were shocked listening to McNamara at a Tuesday lunch gathering on October 31.[70] Courteous but nervous, lips quivering, he agonizingly explained that perhaps everything he and Rusk had been trying to do for six years had failed. If that shook some to the core, his assertion over lunch that danger lurked in the continuation of America's policies in Vietnam fueled their consternation. Basic enthusiasm came back to the Wise Men in the evening with positive words from George Carver and Bus Wheeler.

At the next morning's session, despite McNamara's caveat, Johnson heard a unanimous opinion: stand firm in Vietnam. Just how much LBJ needed that affirmation none of the Wise Men knew until later.[71] They knew nothing (nor did McNamara) of a secret assessment in September by CIA director Richard Helms concluding that the United States would not lose too much prestige with factions in Vietnam. Nor did they know about McNamara's blockbuster November 1 memorandum, which would have showed them how far McNamara had drifted.

Some of the Wise Men filed later reports with the president that showed varying shades of agreement on continuing in Vietnam. Taylor and Lodge worried about Westy's tactics, calling his big-battle syndrome too costly. Mac Bundy suggested that LBJ might well question Westy's judgment. For good reasons, Bundy said, civilians had kept out of the "tactical conduct of the war. . . . But now that the principal battleground is in domestic opinion, I believe the Commander-in-Chief has both the right and the duty to go further." He urged Johnson to change his pattern of discussing the war; stop trying to persuade with numbers, most of which had lost either credibility or logic. Instead, take charge, give the people a sense of a presidential policy aimed at gradual success, something to rally around. Without knowing about McNamara's final blast, he said that inconsistencies between the secretary's avowed bombing policies and many new targets confused the public. He thought the president should force McNamara to join with the JCS and draft a rationale for the bombing that was broader than the one he gave the Stennis subcommittee.[72]

Johnson had Rostow compare Bundy's observations with McNamara's November 1 memorandum. McNamara posed what amounted to a huge shift in U.S. policy in Southeast Asia. He argued that the present course would likely cost the United States much heavier casualties, perhaps a total over the next fifteen months of 11,000 to 15,000. That would bring the total number of killed in action to between 24,000 to 30,000, with no light glimmering at the end of a long tunnel. McNamara proposed stabilizing of ground-force strength at 525,000 men, greater reliance on the South Vietnamese, and a unilateral, indefinite halt to the bombing. Since bombing the north did not directly affect the ground war, a halt would cost nothing. In his troubled view, public opinion would force a choice between heavier bombing with expanded ground fighting, or withdrawal from Vietnam. For him there was only one way to avoid polarizing the American mind: stabilize the war and pursue negotiations aggressively.

Johnson circulated this document through his advisors—he wanted a full-scale debate. Returns ran heavily against the secretary. Rostow could not accept McNamara's arguments; Taylor waxed vehement about a "Pull-Out" program that would end, he thought, in a scramble out; nor did he favor a halt to bombing. Rusk opposed an extended bombing halt, saying that "no one has said to me that his view would be changed if we had a prolonged pause in the bombing and there were no response from Hanoi." Clifford could not understand how McNamara derived the idea that a unilateral bombing halt would produce peace talks.

Johnson did an unusual thing: he wrote a "Memorandum for the Record" about McNamara's plan. In it, he stated his own ideas about bombing: Strike remaining targets that had military significance but would not kill too many civilians or risk the involvement of China or the USSR; maintain a routine restrike program for major targets; and try to "remove the drama and public attention given to our North Vietnamese bombing operations." He decided that a unilateral and unrequited halt would be taken by Hanoi and a large segment of America as a sign of "weakening will," but he would play the bombing card if and when the diplomatic climate warmed.

As for an announced policy of stabilization, LBJ rejected it as showing the same weakening will; at the same time, he saw no immediate need for more troops or cross-border raids.[73]

Finally, he went into high gear with a program of good news from Vietnam. He ordered Westy and Bunker back to Washington for consultations. Their reactions to McNamara's plan were predictably negative. Westy thought announced stabilization and a bombing halt "foolish." Bunker opposed a bombing moratorium but liked the idea of a troop ceiling. Johnson, liking what he heard, put both Bunker and Westy on public view.

The ambassador, immaculate as usual, his tall frame straight, his small, round glasses accenting his blue eyes, met the press on November 13. Clearly, carefully, he said that he had just reported to LBJ that "in my view we are making steady progress in Vietnam, not only militarily, but in other ways as well: In the evolution of the constitutional process, in the pacification program, which is, in my view, equally as important as the military situation. There is every prospect, too, that the progress will accelerate."[74]

General Westmoreland knew he had again been called to Washington for public relations purposes. He did well, first at a White House Medal of Honor ceremony for "one of my soldiers," who "despite a serious chest wound . . . had knocked out an enemy machine gun, continued to lead his platoon in a blazing fire fight, braved enemy fire to administer to his wounded, and despite a second wound, crawled beyond the platoon's perimeter to knock out another machine gun." The general praised him "as representative of the stalwart American soldiers in Vietnam."

After conferences with McNamara and Bus Wheeler, Westy went before the armed services committees of both houses, taped a CBS television interview, and dined with the Democratic leadership of the House. His "most important public appearance" occurred on November 21, before the National Press Club. "I permitted myself," he recalled, "the most optimistic appraisal of the way the war was going that I had yet made." No major enemy victories had been scored in more than a year. He did hint that the enemy might be hanging back, waiting to combine a major tactical success with political turmoil in the U.S. for a knockout blow—but the hint was hidden by enthusiasm.

He pushed the optimistic view that not only were U.S. forces pressing the enemy in what he called Phase Three of the war, but also that they worked constantly on improving ARVN capabilities. Phase Four would see the beginning of a drawdown as Americans turned more and more of the war over to the South Vietnamese. Calling it his "withdrawal strategy,"[75] Westy said American efforts were aimed at cutting down enemy strength, and that the war had entered a stage "where the end begins to come into view."[76]

Westy had a personal shock during the visit. Johnson, in a serious private conference, asked what effect his failure to run for reelection would have on morale in Vietnam. His health, he said was not good. Westy said the men would regret his decision but would understand health reasons.

Johnson's propaganda campaign included himself. He struck a positive note at a November 17 press conference while he warned against the American penchant for quick results. Vietnam was not like a football game; there were no quick gains and losses, just a steady kind of oozing down the field. "We are making progress," he boasted. "We are pleased with the results that we are getting. We are inflicting greater losses than we are taking." All official statements for the next two weeks glowed with optimism from Vietnam.

While the good-news push continued—despite Helms and McNamara—Johnson decided that Robert McNamara must be relieved. Gaunt, haggard, he seemed wracked with inner pain and looked barely able to function. Johnson worried about his friend's health, cherished him still with that special kind of respect, and had hoped to keep him aboard.[77] But too many things shoved them apart. First, not necessarily foremost—though certainly nearly so—lurked the close relationship McNamara kept with Bobby Kennedy and the entire Kennedy clan. Johnson knew that his secretary of defense frequented the Kennedy social circle, suspected that he always got an earful about the evils of the war, and guessed that the steady drip of doubt worked into a tortured psyche. Second, perhaps first, were McNamara's own actions swerving away from the course he had done so much to set. Had others drifted so far astray, they would have felt Johnson's anger; although displeasure sometimes seeped into presidential words in meetings with the secretary, Johnson held his temper. Third, there was something else, "some kind of country boy rock-solid quality that wasn't as deep a strain in [McNamara] as it was, say, in Dean Rusk."[78]

LBJ knew, from a late August talk with McNamara, that he coveted the presidency of the World Bank.[79] His loyalty never wavered, and he would stay if necessary, but he would accept the bank job. As it happened, the current bank president had mentioned to McNamara that he planned to depart and that he hoped the secretary might be interested in succeeding him. It also happened that Johnson would nominate a successor since the United States was the largest member of the collegium.[80]

Johnson made the nomination and it met approval from member nations. Reading about the nomination in the papers, McNamara had a long session with LBJ and resigned on November 29, 1967. He later said he did not know whether he resigned or was fired—which either reflected poor memory or dissimulation. He knew of his boss's worries about him, his associations, and his shifting policy firmaments. And his November 1 memo gave notice that he no longer served the team. In effect, he fired himself. A true casualty of the Vietnam War, the former Whiz Kid had been a managerial genius warped into a torn and riddled soul as his plans, numbers, hopes, and promises unraveled.[81]

His leaving gave no joy to a president nearly as weary, nor to a first lady who cared for Bob and Margy McNamara. And she resented the press ruminations while final decision on the nomination lingered. Speculation ran the gamut from outright fired to eased out. Lady Bird noted some of the rumors that "there's a rift between him and Lyndon, that the whole Cabinet is crumbling. . . . A sort of poison is being generated" that might paralyze "constructive action."[82] More than anyone, she knew the toll McNamara's departure took on her husband. On Wednesday, November 29, the day of McNamara's confirmation in his new world role, her husband told her that "except for one, this is the hardest day I have spent in this job." She believed it and ached. "I have seldom felt as sorry for him. The sense of loneliness and separation is deep," even though the secretary would stay until the end of February to wrap up the next defense budget and help his successor find the right buttons to push.[83]

Johnson faced another personal tragedy in McNamara's departure: He had intended to name his loyal and diligent secretary of the treasury, Henry "Joe" Fowler, to the bank job. Fowler, in Johnson's words, "had been waiting for it all the way through. When I told him McNamara was going to get it, tears came to his eyes."[84] The president explained that he had no other choice, and good soldier Fowler understood.

The president gave much thought to McNamara's replacement. He leaned toward Clark Clifford, that urbane, affably cool, Washington lawyer whose counsel soothed a good many chief executives and whose wisdom Johnson noted almost daily. But Johnson moved slowly; his main problem would be to convince Clifford to abandon the freelance freedom of an advisor and accept, once again, the trammels of government office. Timing had to be right for the master orchestrator; a little waiting would have the advantages of fanning interest in a list of possible appointees and of disarming the intended.

Meantime, Johnson pressed the good news offensive, despite McNamara's elevation. The reports of progress from Vietnam won some snickers from the jaded Washington press corps, but the public liked what it heard and, in November, for the first time since July, Johnson's poll ratings went over 50 percent. Bundy's idea that the president ought to take charge had worked.

In the midst of near euphoria about the war, Johnson received some sad personal news from Australia: His friend Harold Holt had disappeared while swimming. The president decided to go to the memorial service. He decided, too, to visit several other places in a heightened quest for peace. He especially wanted to visit Rome. "He felt almost a little boy sort of hope for . . . peace [and] that the Pope just might take some strong role."[85] He called Jack Valenti to temporary duty; with his Catholic connections, he seemed the ideal man to arrange a meeting with His Holiness. Valenti later recorded the seriocomic negotiations and the arcane secrecies involved in bringing the two world leaders together.[86]

For Johnson and his party (Valenti went along) the trip proved tiring and not altogether happy. In Canberra, Johnson talked with Vietnam's newly and duly elected President Thieu. Proud of the budding democracy there, LBJ tried to dissolve an apparent rift between himself and Thieu over the South Vietnamese government negotiating with the NLF—which Johnson encouraged. Thieu's earlier rejection of the idea had confused the American press and a *New York Times* headline proclaimed that "Thieu, Disputing Johnson, Rejects Talks with Foe." Settlement with the VC might split them from Hanoi and secure the south, Johnson thought, and he tried hard to persuade his ally to press that possibility. But Thieu would not budge.

From that inauspicious beginning, the Johnson entourage went to U.S. bases at Korat and Cam Ranh Bay, where the president told U.S. troops, "we're not going to yield. And we're not going to shimmy." He knew the enemy was building up, expected perhaps a kamikaze-type attack soon, and wanted to reassure them of American resolve.[87]

Then to Rome. The pontiff, warm and friendly, listened carefully as Johnson discussed intelligence about conditions in North Vietnam. Direct

U.S.–North Vietnam negotiations, LBJ said, probably would fail because Hanoi could see no advantage in negotiating. He saw some possibilities in pushing talks between the NLF and Saigon, Johnson said, but results would be slow. Would the pope make overtures?

Paul VI said he might do something, but wondered if the Christmas truce might be extended a day or two. Johnson countered with what his military advisors told him about enemy advantages during truces. The pope said he would pray for Johnson's efforts toward peace, adding that "he would like to convey the president's obvious passion for gaining peace to others who might help." Johnson's request for papal intervention in the matter of treatment of war prisoners won instant enthusiasm: "This is a cause close to my heart."[88]

Back home, LBJ encountered a curiously twisted, hostile, utterly wrong *Newsweek* account and some journalistic jaundice about his junketing. Still, the *New York Times* had a flattering thought: "Those who would belittle or even condemn the haste, the extravagance or the corn of some of Mr. Johnson's performances, had best . . . [note] the new signs last week that he remains one of the most formidable political showmen in American history."[89]

The president worked more in the role of juggler during the last months of 1967. On November 15, with Bunker and Westy still in Washington, LBJ met with them and Rusk, McNamara, Richard Helms, Walt Rostow, and George Christian. After a survey of public appearances by the ambassador and the general, Johnson listened to Bunker's report on his visit with the Senate Foreign Affairs Committee. Questions centered mainly on possible negotiations between the VC and Thieu's government. Bunker assured everyone that Thieu wanted to talk, but that the VC were enemies and approaches were tender. Several times during the White House meeting LBJ showed eagerness for quicker action in Vietnam, reminding those present that "the clock is ticking."

Having decided to stick to a moderate course, to keep bombing without obvious increases,[90] and to send a few more men to Westy, LBJ urged everyone at the meeting "to do two things. First, get the number of [unbombed] targets down to the absolute minimum. Second, get the troops out there as rapidly as possible. I want to get these two things behind me."[91]

Other bothers lingered with the year. Questions about how to count bodies filled tedious discussions with statistical arguments and esoteric nit-picking. Johnson's direct notion of straightening out the reporting system brought a storm of reasons why change would enrage an already doubting press. He accepted them, but dubiously. He wrestled with requests from both Westy and Bunker to attack North Vietnamese sanctuaries in Cambodia. He met heavy resistance from Dean Rusk, Bob McNamara, and even Walt Rostow. They feared a dangerously widened war and LBJ held Westy off again.[92]

But reasons for the requests were disturbing, especially to an increasingly nervous commander in chief. The president thought of Westy's recent reports of the intense late September–early October siege of Con Thien, just below the DMZ, and worried anew about North Vietnamese concentrations. Marine tenacity and air strikes broke the siege and killed over two thousand enemy troops. In early November heavy fighting occurred near Dak To, right at the point where South Vietnam, Laos, and Cambodia met. In six days of sporadic but fierce contact, 102 U.S. troops were killed and the enemy lost 636. One hundred two B-52 sorties supported allied efforts, along with 1,116 tactical air attacks.

What caused these heavy contacts? General Wheeler's response reinforced Johnson's own growing suspicions: "The VC are attempting to achieve a dramatic victory and/or draw forces away from pacification."[93]

How soon would the kamikazes come?

Salesman McNamara, July, 1964. Photo by Cecil Stoughton; courtesy LBJ Library Collection

The commander in chief alongside the chairman of the Joint Chiefs of Staff Earle "Bus" Wheeler at the LBJ Ranch, December, 1964. Photo by Yoichi R. Okamoto; courtesy LBJ Library Collection

Bipartisanship, July 1964. Left to right: *Bobby Kennedy, Everett Dirksen, and Hubert Humphrey. Photo by Cecil Stoughton; courtesy LBJ Library Collection*

Jack Valenti in action, January, 1965. Photo by Yoichi R. Okamoto; courtesy LBJ Library Collection

George Ball and the president, February, 1965. Photo by Yoichi R. Okamoto; courtesy LBJ Library Collection

Camp David, March, 1965. Photo by Yoichi R. Okamoto; courtesy LBJ Library Collection

...n conferring with Mac Bundy, September, 1965. Photo by Yoichi R.
...to; courtesy LBJ Library Collection

LBJ and Ike: commanders-in-chief in conference, October 1965. Photo by Yoichi R. Okamoto; courtesy LBJ Library Collection

The shadow of global war: Maxwell Taylor and William Westmoreland, February, 1966. Photo by Yoichi R. Okamoto; courtesy LBJ Library Collection

Private counsel: the president and first lady, April, 1966. Photo by Yoichi R. Okamoto; courtesy LBJ Library Collection

The lingering problem: J. William Fulbright, Mike Mansfield, and the president, June, 1966. Photo by Yoichi R. Okamoto; courtesy LBJ Library Collection

Robert McNamara, June, 1966. Photo by Yoichi R. Okamoto; courtesy LBJ Library Collection

*The president's thanks, July, 1966. Photo by Yoichi R. Okamoto; courtesy LBJ
Library Collection*

Allied review, October, 1966. Left to right: Johnson, William Westmoreland, President Thieu, Premier Ky, Dean Rusk, *and* (far right) Henry Cabot Lodge. *Photo by Yoichi R. Okamoto; courtesy LBJ Library Collection*

The Happy Warrior: Hubert Humphrey at the Cabinet table, February, 1967. Photo by Yoichi R. Okamoto; courtesy LBJ Library Collection

Johnson persuading Nick Katzenbach (left), Dean Rusk, and other members of the State Department, July, 1967. Photo by Yoichi R. Okamoto; courtesy LBJ Library Collection

Ellsworth Bunker and Johnson, November, 1967. Photo by Yoichi R. Okamoto; courtesy LBJ Library Collection

The general with an agenda: Bus Wheeler, February, 1968. Photo by Yoichi R. Okamoto; courtesy LBJ Library Collection

Tuesday Lunch Group, February, 1968. Sitting counterclockwise from LBJ: Dean Rusk, Maxwell Taylor, Tom Johnson, Walt Rostow, George Christian, Clark Clifford, Bus Wheeler, and Robert McNamara. Photo by Yoichi R. Okamoto; courtesy LBJ Library Collection

Man of surprises: Clark Clifford with Walt Rostow (left) *and Maxwell Taylor* (right), *March,* 1968. *Photo by Yoichi R. Okamoto; courtesy LBJ Library Collection*

President Thieu receives Johnson "treatment," July, 1968. *Photo by Yoichi R. Okamoto; courtesy LBJ Library Collection*

The Johnsons at home, January, 1971. Photo by Frank Wolfe; courtesy LBJ Library Collection

chapter
THIRTEEN

"What the Hell Can I Do?"

Lyndon Johnson looked at the coming year with an odd mixture of hope, anxiety, and excitement.[1] An election year, politics would intrude on everything he did—on his domestic program (which already suffered from war erosion), on his Vietnam situation, and on himself as a time of hard personal decision approached. Much of his assessment of the coming months depended on experience. But was Vietnam experience the best of teachers? There, things seemed to fit no patterns in usable American memory.

All of which expanded Johnson's quandary. The war seemed to be going well, corners may have been turned, even Westy had talked in November of a "phase down" in U.S. commitments. Yet something loomed in Vietnam, some pre-Tet or post-Tet action. What?

For North Vietnam the new year dawned in doubt. General Vo Nguyen Giap's strategy of long war had resulted in exactly that; his escalation toward the ultimate phase of a People's War seemed the best way not only to grind down southern and American resolve, but also to win a strong military position before any serious peace negotiations with the enemy.

One bit of knowledge gained from experience had been especially helpful, though at first hard for the North Vietnamese to believe: The Americans were superior at self-destruction. They tended to throw away their best advantages. They stuck close to their artillery bases, overestimated their strengths, and sucked up too much manpower in nonmilitary frills such as PXs and luxuries and mail. Giap knew that although they had five hundred thousand men in South Vietnam, the Americans rarely had a tenth of them actively campaigning. The hero of Dien Bien Phu summed up the U.S. position aptly: "They are greenhorns, not to be compared with the French in their time. They have no idea of jungle fighting." His ultimate insult: "They walk into traps that wouldn't fool a baby."[2]

Harsh as that sounded, America's one-year rotation system did pit mostly "greenhorns" against VC and North Vietnamese troops who had been in the field for years. By refusing to fight a traditional war, a reprise of World War II, the north negated America's advantages. One of Giap's generals put it this way: "We have forced the Americans to eat soup with forks."[3]

That kind of haughtiness sounded good but its wages were in blood. Casualties were the main difference between Giap's war and Westy's. Giap had no fear of body bags to bind his tactics; Westy and the ARVN could ill afford them.

Casualties bothered President Johnson constantly because they piled up for all to see on the six o'clock news. In the dark corridors of his sleepless hours, the president prowled down to the Situation Room and stood, berobed and slippered, reading teletypes about the war, about how many of "his boys" had returned from flying missions that day, about how many of "his boys" had been lost in some nameless green jungle.[4]

That smoldering anguish sensitized LBJ to rumors of heavier conflict. Add to these rumors an interesting subplot: North Vietnamese spokesmen had shifted their international dialogue in December, 1967. Instead of using the usual dodge that talks "might" begin if the United States stopped bombing, they now said talks "would" start. Even UN secretary general U Thant said he had been "reasonably assured" of this possibility.

Add another subplot, one with sufficient undergirding facts to be scary: Various North Vietnamese diplomats and officials had dropped hints to the Viet Cong cadres in the south and other places that the Americans were secretly working toward a coalition government in South Vietnam that would include the VC. A strong hint of confirmation came when a VC agent told South Vietnamese police that he had surfaced to make contact with officials in the U.S. embassy. As this event reached the American press, various antiwar folk in and out of Congress leaped on it as a talisman of breakthroughs. These poisonous rumors reinforced southern worries that their allies might be thinking of selling them out.[5]

These two subplots combined into an interesting diversion as North Vietnam began to inflame its southern allies to a last great surge to victory.

Westy's headquarters intelligence staffers gathered enough rumors and scattered sensor readings from "people sniffers" and movement detectors to keep hordes of analysts sifting information. These analysts were tried and tested in the arcane business of making sense from chaos, professionals at different kinds of cryptics. Much depended on them; the generals could sense things from the pinball flashes on a Vietnam map—but they needed definite dates and troop locations to position reinforcements. The teareaders did pretty well in reporting heavy concentrations in the northern provinces, where enemy eruptions at Con Thien, the preceding "hill fights," confirmed a buildup in the I Corps Tactical Zone—as did heavy infiltration of men and supplies along the Ho Chi Minh Trail and into a Laotian staging area not far from the DMZ. There were other signals: The number of returnees under the south's *Chieu Hoi* program dropped drastically, showing increased intimidation and psy-war actions in the backcountry, and VC propaganda rose to new heights in predicting victory.

These preparations, combined with the peripheral battles in the hills and along the DMZ, dredged up old memories of Giap's actions before smashing the French at Dien Bien Phu.[6] Was he planning something similar? If so, what place in the South bore any resemblance to that ill-fated French outpost?

Westy fixed on Khe Sanh Combat Base. Isolated, that plateau in the mountainous northwestern corner of South Vietnam sat twenty kilometers south of the DMZ, fifteen east of the Laotian border, and seemed to COMUSMACV an attractive place to keep watch on the enemy, protect Route 9 (a vital east-west highway transversing Vietnam from Laos to Dong Ha), and a potential jumping-off place for expeditions against the Ho Chi Minh Trail along Laos's eastern border. In enemy hands, it would threaten the whole northwestern allied flank, perhaps all of I Corps. A plateau in mountainous country, it looked more like Dien Bien Phu than most exposed positions.

So at Khe Sanh, on ground he could claim suited his choosing, General Westmoreland decided to match and beat the enemy. Westy knew that a good many army and Marine officers thought Khe Sanh useless—too far from Laos to block incursion along Route 9, too remote to provide useful contact intelligence. Holding it seemed to some an absurdity.

MACV window-dressed his decision with a staff study of sieges throughout history and of Dien Bien Phu in particular. The verdict, rendered by a command historian to the MACV staff on February 11, 1968, was depressing. Most besieged places fall, so history said. At Dien Bien Phu, the attackers succeeded "primarily because the defenders lost all initiative." As he listened, Westy realized that there were no real similarities between Khe Sanh and the French outpost. "I knew that Khe Sanh was different, both because the tremendous air and artillery support available afforded us an effective tool for the initiative and because other American troops might be diverted [there] either by air or overland . . . if initiative became a matter of grave concern." But he noted, even as he totted his advantages, that his staff sat stunned at the list of historical losses. Speaking forcefully, COMUSMACV said, "We are not, repeat not, going to be defeated at Khe Sanh. I will tolerate no talking or even thinking to the contrary." Ramrod straight, he stalked out.[7]

Lyndon Johnson wondered, though. He sat in a welter of crises at the end of January. On the twenty-third he reported to the Tuesday lunch group that a U.S. unit had inadvertently intruded into Cambodia the day before, an act requiring apology; that day, too, North Korea captured the USS *Pueblo*, an ELINT ship working in what were thought to be international Pacific waters; a B-52, with atomic bombs aboard, had crashed near Thule, Greenland (experts were rushed to save it before it sank under the ice); assassins had been deflected in an attempt to kill the president of South Korea; and indications increased of North Vietnamese attacks around the great Lunar New Year celebration of Tet.

After LBJ tolled the list, McNamara joshed Clifford, his replacement: "Clark, this is what it is like on a typical day around here."

"May I leave now?" came Clifford's plaintive response.[8]

Things were, really, worse than usual that day, but Johnson capitalized on the avalanche to impress the Democratic leadership later that evening, pulling in Hubert Humphrey, Speaker McCormack, senators Mike Mansfield, Robert Byrd, and Russell Long, congressmen Hale Boggs and Carl Albert, Postmaster General Larry O'Brien, along with Joe Califano, Mike Manatos, and Tom Johnson. Those who watched and knew him could notice, as both meetings unfolded that day, something of the way Lyndon Johnson handled a mass of troubles—he focused on one above others. Focusing helped him balance puzzles in a personal priority. And Khe Sanh, that place of "his Marines," became his main concern.

The battle-scarred plateau became, for the President of the United States, a touchstone for heroism. To anyone touched by Texas history, Khe Sanh resembled the Alamo as much as France's forlorn fort. And LBJ's fascination led him to have a sand-table model of Khe Sanh erected in the Situation Room so he could watch the battle as it happened. The base looked small on any general map of South Vietnam, tiny, like Dien Bien Phu: on an east–west axis, about two thousand feet across and thirteen hundred from top to bottom, with a reconditioned airstrip that could handle huge C-130 cargo planes. But, as he looked at his sand table in his wandering hours before dawn, LBJ kept harking back to Dien Bien Phu. He asked Maxwell Taylor to assess the possibilities and got a disturbing opinion that there were, indeed, similarities between Khe Sanh and the French position.

That irked Westmoreland, who had convinced himself, the MACV staff, and the JCS that the similarities were more apparent than real—guns on the ground, air mobility, and heavy artillery in supporting distance made crucial differences. Westy had no qualms about Johnson's virtual order to the JCS, reportedly issued in Texanese: "I don't want any damn Dinbinphoo." Westmoreland could understand and accept the president's rumored demand for a written guarantee of Khe Sanh's sanctity from the JCS.[9] Khe Sanh would not be lost.

Westmoreland's certitude faded a bit when his faith in Marine leadership dimmed. He sent army units north to bolster I Corps and noted a lackadaisical attitude toward using them. He agreed that the 26th Marines Regiment should go to Khe Sanh but worried its men might hug their dugouts and lose the initiative. His old resentment about the Marines' resistance to lending their unused planes flared again, and he decided to move closer to the action and put a field army headquarters into I Corps for coordination of all ground and air actions.

None of this bothered LBJ; Khe Sanh's situation did. He liked what he heard of Khe Sanh's commanding officer, Col. David E. Lownds, who took his 26th Marines there to stay. The president appreciated Lownds's jaunty handlebar moustache, his tough optimism, and cool determination.

And when a North Vietnamese officer defected to Lownds's men on January 20, talked for hours, and revealed an enemy scheme for widespread attacks, Johnson felt better. Lieutenant La Than Tonc predicted an after-midnight Khe Sanh attack on January 21. Combining his information with enemy battle plans revealed in a document captured nearly a month earlier would have given U.S. intelligence officers more information than almost any army ever had about enemy intentions.[10] But too much detailed information is instantly suspect; documents filled with battle orders are usually taken for disinformation. Some skepticism greeted Tronc's warnings—until Marines beat off a highly disciplined, well-organized attack that began thirty minutes past midnight on the twenty-first. Then the defenders—true believers at last—settled down to a siege.

Johnson kept his nightly vigil at the sand table, thinking of Dien Bien Phu.[11] Still needing reassurance, he harassed his generals. Hear his questions at various meetings:

January 23:

Q.   Are we confident of our situation at Khe Sanh?

A.   [General Wheeler] Yes.

Q.   Have we given Westmoreland everything he needs?

A.   Yes.

January 25:

Q.   Does Westmoreland need B-52s?

A.   [Wheeler] "In recent cables he has asked for 120 B-52 mission capability per month. We are doing that. . . . He is about to have the most vicious battle of the Vietnam war."

January 29:

Q.   Are the JCS "completely in agreement that everything has been done to assure that General Westmoreland can take care of the expected enemy offensive against Khe Sanh?"

A.   Wheeler and the JCS agreed and thought all would go well.

February 7:

Q.   How do things look at Khe Sanh?

A.   [Wheeler] "We may have to move back that company on Hill 861."

Q.   Bob, are you worried?

A.   [McNamara] "I am not worried about a truly military defeat."

A.   [Wheeler] "Mr. President, this is not a situation to take lightly. This is of great military concern to us. I do think that Khe Sanh is an important position which can and should be defended. It is important to us tactically and it is very important to us psychologically. But the fighting will be very heavy, and the losses may be high."

February 10:

Q.   How do you feel about Khe Sanh?

A.   [McNamara] "There seems to be no alternative except to hold it and put in reinforcements."

Q.   What's causing delay in the enemy attack on Khe Sanh?

A.   [McNamara] "The bombing affected their schedule."

Q.   "Should we just sit and wait?"

A.   [McNamara] "I think so."

A.   [Rusk] "Westmoreland wants them to commit themselves before hitting them with our reinforcements. In that sense, Khe Sanh is bait."[12]

Johnson dealt with other problems. Apologies were made to Cambodia. The lost-bomber issue dwindled into nothing, but the *Pueblo* issue forced him to make a decision he hated. Since it seemed likely that North Korea was taunting the south into calling home its forces in South Vietnam, and that the Soviet Union had advance knowledge of the attack and perhaps had connived in it, LBJ agreed to a limited call-up of selected air force reserves and Air National Guard units and the dispatch of 350 planes to U.S. bases in South Korea—to equalize air disparities and discourage North Korean aggression. Vietnam made other deployments difficult and gave Johnson warnings of strategic overstretching.[13]

That looming possibility, plus his own innate sense of the fitness of things, disposed the president to agree with Rusk and others who urged against military action in favor of negotiations; but he worried that months would pass before the *Pueblo* crew was returned. Keeping the issue largely in his hands, LBJ knew that caution would bring some loud complaints of pussyfooting—and it did. But he assessed not only the military limits on reaction, but also the international limits—the treaties existing between North Korea, China, and the Soviet Union—against the need to save the lives of the crew. He also asked George Ball to leave civilian life for a bit to head a special committee to "try to find out how this incident could have occurred and what steps should be taken to prevent future events of the same kind." Ball reported verbally to the president: Details were not crystal clear on the ship's exact location; the whole action had been wretchedly planned, organized and directed. Quiet negotiations were urged lest details expose the government to acute embarrassment.[14]

Johnson continued his nightly trips to the Situation Room and read Khe Sanh's truths on the little sand hills and the flattened place of the mountain base, the metallic strip of the runway. People said he read little and, since even good friends could only cite one book, Barbara Ward's *The Rich Nations and the Poor Nations*, the indictment seemed to stand.[15] Certainly the often abstruse dicta of such as Carl von Clausewitz, Sun Tzu, Mao, and Giap eluded his attention. But he had the deep-struck logic of combat in him, which saw beyond surfaces into the heart of situations. That sand table spoke to him in ways beyond the ken of Walt Whitman Rostow, Bus Wheeler, H. K. Johnson, or the aide who dogged the Situation Room, Col. Robert Ginsburgh. That table rose from its limits to fill a president's mind with portents. Portents are rarely neutral; they are positive or negative—but Khe Sanh's hung uncertain for long and bloody weeks.

Johnson's sand table showed him a realistic skein of Khe Sanh right enough, but one sanitized into an effrontery of tidiness. He looked at a relief map, a clean rendition of a hellish blotch of earth. Laid out for his anxious eyes were the hills, the east–west running airstrip, the Rao Quan River east of the combat base, and the clear ribbon of Route 9 just below. He could see, too, the nearby Special Forces camp at Lang Vei, which was held by a dozen Green Berets and some five hundred CIDG defenders, including Montagnards and demoralized Laotian soldiers. Johnson knew that Lang Vei's commander, Capt. Frank C. Willoughby, could summon reinforcements and an awesome deluge of firepower. On the board it looked well prepared.

In truth, realities were varied in and around Khe Sanh. As January closed, numbers escalated until, at last, LBJ could see that nearly forty thousand North Vietnamese regulars, with some VC and others thrown in, were arrayed against a U.S. Marine, army and South Vietnamese ranger force of 6,053 (the 26th Marines in the majority), strung out over seven—some isolated—positions. The airstrip had to be lengthened, and that brought Seabees [navy construction troops] and their heavy equipment on the scene. This kind of U.S. activity did just what Westy hoped: it attracted thousands of the enemy into a great American mincing machine.[17] The Marines were nearly ready. A momentary glitch with the ARVN—which had been mindlessly left out of Westy's plans—marred preparations, but that smoothed when the 37th ARVN Ranger Battalion, made of 317 cocky troops in red berets, arrived and the defense took solid shape.[18]

The sand on Johnson's table told only externals, it could not show the nitty-gritty details of a burrowing existence that made life at Khe Sanh hard duty from the start. Consider local conditions.

First, there was the weather. Mists from a weather system named *crachin* by the French, hung heavy up on the protecting hills, often swayed bafflingly along the landing strip, and brought a chill that mingled with dread into a kind of bone-chilling cold.

Second, the whole place stank—simply and purely stank. The stench from burning garbage, petroleum, and a gagging mix of shit and diesel fuel "hangs, taking you full in the throat."[19] Old fought-over red mud oozed in the bunkers and trench lines, stayed wet most of the time, and, when it dried, stank and turned to stifling dust. Sand bags were hard to fill—and they were essential—and bunkers were dug deep, often lined with van bodies or drums or whatever else might hold off rounds from the long-range 130mm and 152mm guns firing from Co Roc Mountain in Laos and from a map bearing of 305 degrees, ten thousand meters west-northwest of the base. Defenders could hear the big ones coming. Someone would yell, "ARTY, ARTY, CO ROC," or "ARTY, ARTY, 305," and everyone dove for cover.[20]

Third, misery came from all the enemy ordnance, but a Russian-built 122mm rocket did "awesome and effective," damage, as did other long-range guns. The big stuff dug huge holes, plowed the runway, smashed hooches sometimes, and was beyond the range of most U.S. weapons. Small stuff, 60mm and 82mm mortars, was scattered around the perimeter some two thousand to three thousand meters out.

Fourth were the hills the Marines held—the surrounding hills were the key to Khe Sanh's defense, and the men on them took the brunt of things. Everyone on the base knew that if hills 558, 861, 861 Alpha, 881 South, and 950 (protecting the communications link to Dong Ha) were lost, all was lost.

Nothing seemed strong enough, close up. There was never enough cover; Marine artillery revetments were too flimsy; dugouts were scourged even by the duds from Co Roc, which drove four feet into the ground; water was always short; food was sometimes gone; yet artillery and small-arms ammunition was amazingly plentiful despite a blown ammo dump. Everything depended on the landing strip, which took repeated hits and had to be fixed all the time.

Isolated, Khe Sanh hung out on the end of Westy's I Corps string of strong points at the mercy of the enemy and the elements, and dependent on valor.

Details of that valor over seventy-seven searing days came to the White House slowly, almost in rationed bites of agony, and they touched deeply Johnson's faith in "his boys." They endured nearly constant shelling, probing attacks, and skirmishes, which they repulsed with rifles, machine guns, 105mm howitzers, 155mm guns, 4.2-inch mortars, six tanks, and one Ontos vehicle mounting six 106mm recoilless rifles. They were sustained by heroic resupply runs flown by C-130 and helicopter crews who devised unique ways to survive and deliver the goods, by more than three hundred tactical air strikes a day, and by 2,602 B-52 sorties that dropped over seventy-five thousand tons of bombs around the base. The B-52 raids were "an awesome display of firepower," Westy said, "one of the heaviest and most concentrated in the history of warfare."[21]

But no really overwhelming attack ever came; enemy saps ran toward the Marine lines, using an old NVA tactic, but no storming mass rush ever tested the defenses. There are several possible reasons why. Massive U.S. firepower may have dislocated enemy plans, forcing a change of objective. Then, too, the threat of a nuclear strike may have been a factor.

Westmoreland created a small, secret study group at MACV to consider whether nuclear weapons could be used effectively at Khe Sanh. The president himself, who loathed the thought of having to make a nuclear decision and feared hawks might pressure him into it, asked Wheeler to find out if Westmoreland might need tactical nuclear weapons.

In the end, Johnson made up his mind not to use weapons that would poison world opinion. At a White House meeting on February 10, he queried McNamara: "Is it true there are no nuclear weapons in Vietnam?"

"It is true there are none there," came the reassuring reply.[22]

Press leaks actually helped LBJ in this instance. Newspapers floated the possibility of nuclear ruin in Vietnam on February 9 and, following up on questions at a February 16 press conference, Johnson said, "No recommendation has been made to me. Beyond that, I think we ought to put an end to that discussion."[23]

There is some evidence that leakage of the nuclear possibility may have influenced General Giap to change his plans in early February about pressing the siege—on the tenth he began detaching troops to Hue.[24]

Speculation persists about Giap's purposes at Khe Sanh. Did he plan a large-scale diversion there to suck in U.S. strength and resources while he aimed his main blows at other objectives? So say many sources. Others suggest that he did intend to capture the combat base, but resistance and firepower changed his mind. At any rate, he later dismissed the analogy to Dien Bien Phu and said that "Khe Sanh wasn't that important to us. Or it was only to the extent that it was important to the Americans—in fact, at Khe Sanh their prestige was at stake."[25] It may be that Giap's assessment of importance shifted with his own decision to abandon the siege.

Finally it ended—without a major U.S. defeat. When the ragged, hollow-eyed Khe Sanh defenders were finally relieved by Operation Pegasus on April 8, they left a place they could scarcely recognize. Hills and trees were gone; the landscape had changed into a reddish, misshapen moonscape of scars, craters, stumps, bamboo splinters, bits of helmets, clothes, broken weapons, bones, and blood. What did all this destruction cost in lives? Enemy numbers vary; the NVA suffered terrible punishment, with best estimates ranging between 10,000 and 15,000 killed and wounded. Estimates of U.S. casualties are various, too, because they were counted by named operations. Only 205 Americans were reported killed at Khe Sanh, obviously too few. But none died unmourned or forgotten by their commander in chief.[26]

Those nightly visits to the Situation Room, the constant need for news from Khe Sanh, were symptoms to many of a quirky presidential obsession. Not so. Johnson used fixation to bring problems in perspective, as an oddly personal way of prioritizing. Tough to fool or intimidate, Johnson's common sense finally reassured him about Khe Sanh. Although he continually badgered advisors and commanders for Khe Sanh assessments, these were really the moves of a mind puzzling over fragments of a broadening crisis.

TET!

Lady Bird Johnson selected a red suit with navy trim; daughter Lynda put on the navy-blue dress with white buttons that her daddy had given her for Christmas. The president's lady looked at her guest list for the State of the Union address one more time, checked the seating chart, and, a bit past eight in the evening on Wednesday, January 17, 1968, went down to the White House library. She had mulled hard—"choosing the guests for the State of the Union is always important"[27]—and thought it would be a good occasion to honor some people who had helped implement important administration programs. Her smile flashed as she saw them all, but she worried that evening especially for Lyndon.

She knew he had wrestled over his upcoming address with more than usual zeal and that he would carry with him as he went to the joint session an addendum to his speech—crafted by George Christian—that would take her home to Texas or launch her once again on the tumults of politics. Would her husband take that paper from his pocket at the end of his speech and say, "And now I want to speak to you about a personal matter. . . ."? If he did, he would go on to say he would not run again. He had been wavering for days. He had talked often to her, days and nights, and with John and Nellie Connally. The Texas Governor had just decided not to run again; he and Nellie seemed serene and happy in the choice. John had been candid to the president: "You ought to run only if you look forward to being President again—only if you *want* to do it. You also ought not to run just to keep somebody else from being President."

More than others, she knew her husband's weariness, that "he feels older and more tired than . . . five years ago." What of the next five; would his health hold? Did he want to run? He worried questions on the edges: What would history say of him? What about his friends and supporters? The soldiers in Vietnam? Connally thought the State of the Union would be the best forum for LBJ to declare he would not run.

A scant hour and a half before she joined her guests, the president asked Lady Bird plaintively, "Well, what do you think? What shall I do?"

Knowing the urges pulling at him, she looked at him helplessly before saying, "Luci hopes you won't run. She wants you for herself and for Lyn and all of us. She does not want you to give up. Lynda hopes you *will* run. She told me so this afternoon, with a sort of terrible earnestness, because her husband is going to war and she thinks there will be a better chance of getting him back alive and the war settled if you are President."

Standing in the door between the Oval Office and the little side snuggery, he looked at her wistfully. So she said, "Me—I don't know. . . . I can't tell you what to do."

She realized that the poignancy of Vietnam touched everywhere. One of the guests, Lawrence Joel, a black Medal of Honor winner from Fort Bragg, greeted her, smiling. She remembered him for "one of the most touching [medal] citations I had ever read." He had been a medic who, "although twice wounded . . . had gone on and on and on to save life after life, crawling across the battlefield with his plasma and his medicines."

The lady in the red suit enjoyed the exciting protocol before the president's arrival, basked in the clear warmth of congressional affection. She liked the way he looked, some fifteen pounds lighter, hair a little longer and not "slicked down," and she liked his unexpected insertion of support for highway beautification and the fact that he spoke for only forty-nine minutes and garnered some fifty rounds of applause. He did not speak at length about the Vietnam War, but instead talked soberly of America's will being sorely tested there, mentioned South Vietnamese elections, and promised a forceful push for peace. He went on to offer a ringing declaration of war on crime, which won roaring approval. She waited and watched; he closed his binder, turned, and walked down the steps and out among his former colleagues.[28]

At the Speaker's office—a traditional stop after State of the Union addresses, she felt her initial enthusiasm draining. There were very few compliments or clusters of admirers. And yet she felt relieved—she had wondered during the talk if she really wanted him to read that addendum. Only later did she hear that he had forgotten the paper.[29] A Freudian slip?

Back in the traces, the president picked up his activity tempo. He had laid out an ambitious program of congressional action, but he knew that everything depended on money. He had been badgering Congress for months about a 10 percent tax surcharge but nothing had happened. Now a crisis threatened in the international gold market that might weaken the dollar. He had to work on that and on whatever loomed in Vietnam.

At Tuesday lunch on January 30, he mused over the coming agendas to Rusk, McNamara, Clifford, Helms, Rostow, Christian, Tom Johnson, and General Wheeler, touched on tensions between Israel and Egypt over the Suez Canal, and then centered on Vietnam.

As usual, LBJ wondered about Khe Sanh. Wheeler optimistically reported seven hundred enemy killed and only light U.S. casualties. But he added something surprising: There had been rocket and mortar attacks on Da Nang, with some action apparently within the city itself. Some two hundred men had attacked Pleiku, terrorized the city, and then moved out to the air base. He had his audience's full attention, and Wheeler added that the U.S. 4th Infantry Division had sustained an attack at both Nha Trang and Kontum. But Wheeler left something out—or did not have full information—when he briefed his luncheon colleagues: He failed to mention Ban Me Thuot, an important location in any Communist attempt to bisect Vietnam. Kontum had been attacked at 2:00 A.M., while Ban Me Thuot had suffered earlier, at 1:35.[30]

At 2:30 Walt Rostow returned to the dining room after taking a phone call. He interrupted the discussion in some excitement. "We have just been informed we are being heavily mortared in Saigon. The Presidential Palace, our BOQ's, the Embassy and the city itself have been hit."

For a moment silence hung in the room, echoing oddly off the wallpaper picture of Cornwallis's surrender.

Johnson stirred. "This could be very bad," he said quietly.

"Yes," Rusk agreed. "I hope it is not Ambassador Bunker's residence."

"What can we do to shake them from this?" asked Johnson. "This looks like where we came in. Remember it was at Pleiku that they hit our barracks and that we began to strike them in the north." After a moment, "What comes to mind in the way of retaliation?"

Thoughts circled around Saigon.

"In a city like Saigon," Wheeler philosophized, "people can infiltrate easily. They carry in rounds of ammunition and mortars. They fire and run." He went on in the same vein. "It is impossible to stop this in its entirety. This is about as tough to stop as it is to protect against an individual mugging in Washington, D.C."

With everyone's attention, he explained that "we have got to pacify all of this area and get rid of the Viet Cong infrastructure." Then, insight at last tying several things together, he added, "They are making a major effort to mount a series of these actions to make a big splurge at TET."

McNamara saw the Saigon attack as "a public relations problem not a military one." Conditions there hinged on keeping the strong police chief, he thought, and CIA director Helms agreed. "The answer to the mortar attacks," in McNamara's view, "is success at Khe Sanh. We must get our story across. . . . We are inflicting very heavy casualties on the enemy and we are not unprepared for the encounter."[31]

Johnson clung to such stray shreds of optimism as he could in the next hours as the media spewed forth increasingly outrageous accounts of massacres, bombs, fires, and attacks in Saigon and across Vietnam. He had always believed that a "man's judgment is no better than his information,"[32] but only sound information. Johnson desperately wanted to know what had happened in Vietnam. In the meantime, he kept a bold front and tried to reassure others.

Congressional leaders at a White House breakfast on January 31 got LBJ's latest data on the *Pueblo* and on the diplomatic blitz that the administration carried to ninety countries. Johnson told what he knew about Vietnam, tying the current attacks into the *Pueblo* incident as part of a large Communist effort.

Wheeler, at LBJ's request, took the floor. He had an infectious calmness that lent truth to his words. In mufti that morning, the general looked more scholar than soldier. He said that Westy had enough troops for the "wide attacks throughout South Vietnam . . . heavy attacks in Saigon" he had reported at 4:18 that morning. Everything had been sent that Westy requested; he had no doubts of repulsing all attacks. As for the North Vietnamese, Wheeler said they had lost heavily, perhaps 3,000 killed in the last two days, matched by only 300 allied dead—100 of them Americans.

Listening, Johnson's own confidence rose. "We still face a big challenge at Khe Sanh," he said, but he wanted the leadership to know that "we are going to stand up out there. We are not about to return to the enclave theories." He also sought to emphasize the skewed nature of news coming from the battle zone: "You won't hear much in the press about how bad the enemy's bombing of Saigon was last night. You won't hear many speeches about the North Korean's attempt to cut off President Park's head and to kill the American Ambassador. All we hear about is how bad our bombing is."[33]

As patches of intelligence built into a mosaic of the enemy's Tet offensive, Johnson's reactions shifted from watchful waiting to alarm to increased confidence to satisfaction. But the process took agonizing time. The worst of it was that Tet spilled luridly into most of America's living rooms—the president's included—as harrowing pictures of Vietnamese civilians, soldiers, towns, cities, and villages—battered, burned, and blasted—flashed across the screens in an awful montage of ruin.

Johnson watched and saw it, endured it with the stoicism he summoned in his hardest times. He watched the attack on the new, six-story chancery of the Saigon embassy in all its exploding confusion. He saw the attackers come and the defenders fight back, some of them falling as rockets smashed into walls and chattering machine guns dissolved the chancery entrance. He watched the attackers drop, one by one, as smoke and rubble built a twisted monument to their misspent energy and daring.

One VC team hit the embassy at 3 A.M. and caught it pretty much off guard. Tet's languor had affected the Americans, and only a skeleton staff pulled night duty. There were three Marines, five military policemen [MPs], three Vietnamese night watchmen, and six American civilians in the compound and chancery. Armed only with a few light weapons, they held out against varied attacks, threats, and explosions. George Jacobson, a retired army colonel, and retired master sergeant Robert L. Josephson held their residence on the grounds with one grenade and a coat hanger until an MP ran the gauntlet across the lawn and threw Jacobson a .45-caliber pistol (all on TV). The colonel shot an intruding VC, picked up his AK-47, and waited for more. None came.

When the shooting stopped after nearly six and a half hours, the embassy grounds looked like a battlefield; debris and wreckage of all kinds littered the lawn, with bodies strewn brokenly around. When a relief force arrived, most of the enemy were dead. United Press International's Kate Webb said the compound looked like "a butcher shop in Eden." Some sixteen VC reportedly died, along with five Americans.[34]

Oddly enough, although radio communication between defenders failed, telephone contact with the outside world continued—so the State Department and the White House Situation Room were close bystanders to the action. Local news media flashed increasingly lurid details. The *Washington News* headline read like a grocery store tabloid: "WAR HITS SAIGON." Television cameras managed bites of the action that reached some 14 million Americans watching 10 million screens for the January 30 evening news.[35] Commentators trying to keep up with the incredible footage got most of the story wrong—but their words were largely ignored by an audience mesmerized by the carnage.

Other parts of Saigon were hit—Independence Palace, the South Vietnamese navy headquarters, the government radio station. A VC battalion tried to free five thousand prisoners from Saigon's jail but got lost and waged an eerie life-and-death struggle in a graveyard. Two battalions hit the ARVN armored and artillery headquarters only to find the tanks gone and the breechblocks missing from the guns. Probably the most successful attack captured the Phu Tho racetrack; the aggressive captors had to be driven out of this important military enterprise.

Far more serious were the attacks at Tan Son Nhut Air Base and the nearby South Vietnamese Joint General Staff compound. These vital objectives were held by a makeshift force of airmen and airborne soldiers long enough to be relieved by a U.S. cavalry squadron.

Discipline often changes battles; it hurt the VC that night. They stuck too closely to their plan, could not adjust to changing situations, and paid a high price for this inflexibility.

Cholon[36] and some other residential suburbs became battlegrounds for several days. Westy finally intruded on the ARVN's assignment of protecting the capital and sent in U.S. troops to hasten mop-up operations before American TV swamped the war in bathos.[37]

General Westmoreland had a fair idea of Saigon's situation by the time he entered the crazed embassy grounds at 9:20 A.M. on the thirty-first. First he shook hands with the surviving Marine guard who held his chancery post throughout the ordeal. Then the general reported to Washington and to Ambassador Bunker. As he started out, the embassy's press chief suggested a quick meeting with clustering media representatives. Westy agreed. It sounded like a good opportunity to put the raid and all the other attacks in perspective. The MACV commander looked good—relaxed, uniform crisply pressed, ready. He emphasized that no VC had gotten inside the chancery, and, foreshadowing what Bunker would say when he arrived later, branded the enemy's countrywide offensive a costly failure: "The enemy's well-laid plans went afoul. Some superficial damage was done to the [chancery] building. All of the enemy that entered the compound so far as I can determine were killed." Overall, he analyzed enemy efforts as "very deceitfully" aimed at creating confusion, at turning attention from the big battle which he still expected at Khe Sanh. Then he boasted of allied reaction: "The enemy exposed himself by virtue of his strategy and he suffered great casualties. . . . American troops were on the offensive and pursued the enemy aggressively."[38]

Many nearby listeners had a momentary expectation of the Mad Hatter racing among them; corpses and debris lay strewn around him and Westy fairly brimmed with satisfaction. Had madness finally entombed them all?

William Childs Westmoreland had not gone mad. He had merely looked beyond chaos to its outcome. He had not expected attacks on the scale confronting him that morning. Still, MACV had not been utterly unready. Lieutenant Gen. Frederick C. Weyand, commanding II Field Force, a former intelligence man himself, had put together bits and pieces of evidence and noted that NVA and VC elements were moving away from the border toward southern population centers; he had urged Westy to get ready. Brigadier Gen. Phillip B. Davidson, Westy's chief intelligence officer, offered similar ideas and, on January 27, prophesied countrywide attacks aimed at cities, but guessed they would happen after Tet.[39]

Taking seriously these varied signals, Westy ordered Weyand to move a cavalry squadron close to Ton Son Nhut. Weyand did.[40] Since Tet loomed as such a large Vietnamese holiday, Westy guessed that ARVN leaves would be generous, especially since a truce had been announced by both sides. He asked President Thieu to curtail both leaves and the truce. Thieu agreed to cut the truce and promised that his forces would be at least at 50 percent strength. American units went on full alert several days before Tet.

As a result, Westy knew that the enemy could not possibly take and hold the cities they assaulted. But the general's optimism wore a bit thin during the first forty-eight hours of Tet. Beyond Saigon, attacks spread across South Vietnam from north to uttermost south. Viet Cong teams hit five of six major cities considered securely in government control—not just Nha Trang and Kontum, as Wheeler had reported earlier, but also Hoi An, Da Nang, and Qui Nhon on the coast—mortared the huge American base at Cam Ranh Bay, struck at Hue and at Pleiku, and broke an informal truce that had spared the resort city of Dalat. Provincial capitals were prime targets; thirty-six of forty-four were attacked—including My Tho in the Mekong Delta, where President Thieu had gone for Tet. Sixty-four district capitals were hit, along with fifty hamlets. American search and destroy plans were, for the nonce, destroyed. Initiative now with the enemy, the allies had to react. Westy was at his best in battle. A superior tactician, his mind tuned to the battlefield, he performed superbly as he took charge of counter-Tet operations.

Keeping an open mind, he settled into the intricate business of juggling forces to counter enemy attacks, of disengaging in less threatened areas to create reserves where needed, and reinforcing hard-pressed ARVN units. Attacking where he could, he showed himself a nimble gambler. He saw quickly that Giap had launched many offensives, that they were designed to reap military and political benefits, and that coordination had been spotty. Many of the attacks were unsupported and quickly smashed with heavy losses. Some VC cadres hung on with uncharacteristic fury; they had been ordered to hold out until reinforced, either by NVA forces or a massive uprising of the South Vietnamese people—who were expected to rally for freedom in the final phase of a People's War. When no uprising came, the stubborn attackers were sacrificed.

Westy's transformation from director to commander began on the night of February 7 with two frantic phone calls. Both came from the embattled Special Forces camp at Lang Vei, which suddenly found itself under enemy tank attack. This came as a shock, as the NVA had never before employed armor. Early in the morning, COMUSMACV picked up Brig. Gen. John Chaisson, a Marine serving as director of MACV's Combat Operations Center, and flew to Da Nang for conferences with his I Corps commanders.

Calm and deliberate, Westy listened for three hours to various general's reports. Chaisson watched him take charge. After each report, "Westmoreland gave emphatic orders: 'Get the roads open'—'Get troops between the enemy and Da Nang Air Base; time is of the essence; get a task force from Koster; get at it; we've got to take some risks'—'The Qua Viet [River] *must* be kept open; this is a *must*—and so on." As for the scattered groups of surviving defenders at Lang Vei, Westy wanted them extracted; assault the camp, he ordered, and authorized the use of cluster bomb units and high fragmentation bombs. "Go."

"One of Westy's best days," Chaisson wrote in his pocket journal.[41]

American and ARVN troops reacted quickly and fought extremely well; in fact, South Vietnamese soldiers fought better than ever in obvious battles for their homes. Clearly, the main North Vietnamese effort had been aimed at the ARVN. Prominent U.S. symbols, such as the embassy and Ton Son Nhut Airport, were targets, but ARVN units took the worst hits.

A VC order, captured during the first days, indicated the seriousness of their undertaking. They were urged "to liberate the 14 million people of South Viet-Nam . . . fulfill our revolutionary task." Their attacks would result in "the greatest battle in Vietnamese history," one that "will decide the fate and survival of the Fatherland," so they were expected "to achieve the final victory at all costs."[42] Hanoi realists did not expect total victory, but they did hope for enough defections from southern military and civilian ranks to change the balance of the war. With enough indications of southern decay, they could follow the old Communist plan of fighting while negotiating.

Hanoi also arranged one other matter: The North Vietnamese let the VC do most of the Tet fighting; NVA regulars fought in the northern I Corps area and in a few other places, but the VC were called on to bear the brunt of the offensive. They were mowed down, nearly exterminated. This led to some postwar speculation that North Vietnam used the Tet offensive as a way of tidying up its political future, of eliminating thousands of nationalist veterans who might have opposed a Communist regime after reunification.[43] A prominent southern Communist confided to Stanley Karnow in 1981 that "we lost our best people," and added that Tet, combined with attacks by the CIA's Phoenix program, uprooted the VC rural framework. Northerners were sent in to rebuild the southern apparatus and won few friends. Karnow heard a lamentation of things to come: "They behave as if they had conquered us."[44]

Although skirmishes flickered in many areas, in the suburbs of Saigon for instance, the crisis had passed in a week—save for Hue. Seventy-five hundred enemy troops attacked that ancient seat of the Kingdom of Annam at 3:30 A.M. on January 31. They took most of the city, held it for twenty-five days, and carried out a planned series of gruesome atrocities against southern or American sympathizers—sometimes against innocents—in a drenching of blood that took nearly three thousand civilian lives.

While the occupiers indulged their brutalities, a few Marines and ARVN troops, initially surprised, held on and were reinforced as vicious street fighting turned inexorably against the enemy. Bitter combat centered around the symbolic Citadel on the northern bank of the Perfume River. A Marine company commander remembered the intimacy of the slaughter: "We were both in a face-to-face, eyeball-to-eyeball confrontation. . . . After a while, survival was the name of the game as you sat there in the semidarkness, with the firing going on constantly. . . . And the horrible smell. You tasted it as you ate, as if you were eating death. . . . and still we weren't depressed. We were doing our job—successfully."[45]

When the three-week holocaust ended, nearly 50 percent of ancient Hue had been battered to bits. It struck some as hideous that it had to be ruined to be saved—a simile often used in Vietnam. The enemy attack failed, but at grievous cost. Graves sprang up everywhere as monuments to a war that turned against humanity itself and dimmed the souls of those who lived.

Fighters had searing losses to remember: The Marines lost 142 killed and 857 seriously wounded, the ARVN lost 384 killed and 1,800 wounded, and the North Vietnamese and VC lost 5,113 killed and 89 captured. An odd sense of participation touched the deeds in Hue. Television cameras brought the deadliness into homes in a kind of global clutch of combat.[46]

No powers of magic, mind, or will could hide the woeful, wandering flotsam of war that spread everywhere. In Saigon, 125,000 were homeless, and across the country 821,000 refugees survived to join 904,000 already dispossessed before Tet. Refugees amounted to 10 percent of South Vietnam's population.[47] In the final counting, Tet's worst costs were in lives lost and broken: 12,500 civilians killed, 22,000 wounded; U.S.-ARVN killed, about 6,000 (Westmoreland put U.S. killed at 1,001), wounded, uncertain; North Vietnamese and Viet Cong killed, nearly 40,000 of some 84,000 committed, wounded also uncertain.[48]

Tet ranks as one of the most decisive battles of the twentieth century and, in odd reflections of the fog of war, both sides won and lost.

Four conditions made Tet a decisive defeat for America: [1] devastating surprise; [2] confused, faltering, wearied leadership; [3] luridly slanted reporting by the media, especially television; and [4] the collapse of public belief in the administration and the war effort. North Vietnamese officers correctly assessed Tet as a major defeat for themselves, only to watch its uncanny metamorphosis.

JUDAS SQUARED

Lyndon Johnson had seen a good many happier days than the last ones of January, 1968. Usual American optimism fled, all save the military's; shock waves of Tet rippled through all the media and an uncommon cynicism swept the country. Johnson, still holding a core belief in success, felt America drifting slowly toward one of two conclusions: win the war or get out. Always he feared the right, but now he began to fear the left—the doves whose poison turned American determination flabby and remorseful. Converts wavered from side to side as opinions diverged, coalesced, and shifted. Two new nouns appeared in the language to describe this phenomenon: dawks and hoves. More than anything else, Johnson kept his eye on how he rated with the people—and that, too, began to scare him. A January Gallup Poll showed 47 percent disapproved of his war management and only 39 percent approved. How long would the country stay the course?[49]

He kept these concerns to himself, but the deep circles under his eyes and the slight stoop when he thought no one looked were plainly visible to observers. To the Tuesday group, whose daily contact modulated subtle changes, Johnson stayed his calm, concerned self.

The president liked the Tuesday luncheons; enjoyed that small group of trusted people working in a closed society, usually leakproof and, consequently, free-flowing, open, suited to his insecure proprieties. He did not close himself off, he kept his lines open to people of all shades of domestic and international opinion—to hawks, doves, hoves, and dawks on Vietnam. Still, there is comfort in the familiar. The luncheons were familiar, comfortable, and they came to be more: they came to be traps of a special kind—traps for the trusted to ensnare the truster. Consider that most of the Tuesday lunchers were products of a special time. They had grown up in the era of Hitler, Hirohito, Mussolini, of FDR, Churchill, de Gaulle, Truman, Marshall, MacArthur, and Eisenhower. They remembered that appeasement had ended in a horrifying world war.

Backgrounds loomed important, as did personal styles and agendas, in the months after Tet when the Tuesday lunches spawned two conspiracies with opposite goals, conspiracies that attacked Johnson's purposes and, in effect, sold him out.

Politics intruded heavily in February as various primaries approached. What would LBJ do? Who would the Republicans offer? Most pundits predicted it would be Richard Nixon. Tet's impact on the elections had to be assessed, and early surmises were damaging. Most media dove into Tet with a kind of macabre spasm of guilt, as though doomsayers saw themselves somehow redeemed. Big media names joined the funerary throng in assaulting the public conscience. As it happened, Walter Cronkite—he of the homey, discursive manner and well-worn pipe—who chatted with viewers five nights a week at 6:30 P.M. had an almost mystical hold on America's trust. Somehow, in his warm way, Walter Cronkite became everyman's American. He had seen his share of wars, had hit the beaches with the Allies in North Africa, dropped with the 101st Airborne Division into Holland, flew in the first B-17 raid over Germany, broke out of the Bastogne siege in the Battle of the Bulge, and pretty much agreed with anti-Communist programs.

In early February, 1968, Cronkite went to Vietnam to see what had happened. On the evening of February 27, he delivered a measured diatribe against U.S. policies there. Not victory but stalemate seemed the only outcome of so many anguished years. He concluded his devastating presentation with a pious declamation:

On the off chance that military and political analysts are right, in the next months we must test the enemy's intentions in case this is indeed his last big gasp before negotiations. But it is increasingly clear to this reporter that the only rational way out then will be to negotiate, not as victors but as an honorable people who lived up to their pledge to defend democracy, and did the best they could.[50]

Behind this calmly sensational statement were some dubious reportorial practices—reporters are not supposed to make the news, just report it. Cronkite's avuncular influence, though, had promoted him from reporter to commentator, and he expanded into the role with only moderate pomposity. In the case of Tet, Cronkite openly admitted that his comments were his personal views. Nevertheless he'd been to Hue, he said, had seen the masses of graves of the many purged by the VC and NVA, smelled death in the air, and would do everything he could to bring the war to an end. One observer felt this "a peculiar and reverse reaction to an enemy atrocity."[51]

The president felt betrayed; he had taken Cronkite into his confidence and kept him up on the war. Likeable and a power with the public, Cronkite could have been in the inner circle—but now he'd turned. Some people thought that his broadcast hit Johnson hard enough to nudge him closer toward negotiations. Some thought that wishfully enough to put words in George Christian's mouth: the post-Cronkite "shock waves rolled through the Government."[52] Johnson suffered, right enough, and he did tell Christian that "If I lost Cronkite, I probably lost the country." Still, he tried to take it as another defection to the doves.[53] Sad, indeed, but only part of a general anti-Tet media blitz.

Later, some commentators and reporters examined media coverage of Tet with chagrin. Howard K. Smith of the American Broadcasting Company recalled that "although Viet Cong casualties were one hundred times ours . . . we never told the public that. We just showed pictures day after day of Americans getting hell kicked out of them. That was enough to break America apart." Peter Braestrup, in his thorough examination of the media's Tet coverage, says that even after "the fog of war began to lift" and show allied success, TV executives would not listen. The National Broadcasting Corporation rejected a proposed late-1968 series depicting Tet as a major American victory because "Tet was already established 'in the public's mind as a defeat, and therefore it was an American defeat.'"[54]

Robert Elegant, who covered Vietnam for several years, berates his colleagues for distorting Tet and the war. "Never before Vietnam," he wrote, "had the collective policy of the media . . . sought by graphic and unremitting distortion—the victory of the enemies of the correspondents own side."[55]

Often enraged at the press and baffled by its persistent failure to present the American side, Johnson fulminated to insiders.[56] Cartoons especially irritated him, but now and then he found some of the jibes nearly funny. In the *Washington Post* of February 6, for instance, he read Art Buchwald's exclusive interview with General Custer at the Little Big Horn, who said the battle had "just turned the corner and he could now see the light at the end of the tunnel. 'We have the Sioux on the run,' Gen. Custer told me. 'Of course, we still have some cleaning up to do, but the Redskins are hurting badly and it will only be a matter of time before they give in.'"

Many whose critical minds should have saved them succumbed to the rhythm of the moment. Even Harry McPherson, a close White House aide and possessed of more than normal sense, confessed later that he believed that "the country had just about had it. I suppose that . . . it is particularly interesting that people like me—people who had some responsibility for expressing the presidential point of view—could be so affected by the media . . . while downstairs was that enormous panoply of intelligence-gathering devices."[57]

Tet probably damaged Johnson psychologically more than anyone guessed.[58] It quenched him, shrank his faith in himself, cast doubt on everything he had done or believed in, everything that ordered the fitness of things in his mind. Not that he showed it; somehow, in his worst moments, he raised up around himself an aura of strength. At the Tuesday lunches, to groups visiting in the White House, to reporters, Johnson hewed hard to his belief that "the time to keep your head is when everybody else loses theirs,"[59] and showed a calm, collected self to keep the confidence of his cabinet and his country.

Before Tet, he had sometimes gone with what his gut feeling told him was right—sometimes overriding advisors—but he stopped doing that, and instead turned away from certainty to the comforts of consensus. Understandable, of course, often wise in crises, but in the uncertainties following Tet the country needed the president to put the surprise attacks in perspective. And he wanted to, he wanted to talk about the *Pueblo* and Vietnam. Twice on February 6 he raised the issue in meetings, first in the morning with senior foreign policy advisors, then with the Tuesday lunchers. Rusk and Wheeler, during the morning session, thought it too soon for a presidential speech; Johnson doubted it but said, "I do accept your advice." At lunch Clifford said "the situation is so fluid now in Vietnam and Korea I don't feel it advisable for the President to have public comment. Any statement now will just augment public concern."

Obviously unhappy, LBJ grumped, "I believe somebody in government should say something. I do not share the view that many people have that we took a great defeat. Our version is not being put to the American people properly."[60] Again, on the ninth, he badgered his team: "I continue to think that somebody has to put this whole matter into perspective. We are letting the other side have the floor and saying nothing. . . . "[61] But, distrustful now of instincts, he did not speak.

Johnson's instincts had not failed him. He tried to follow them through halfway measures: First, he urged Bunker and Westmoreland to hold daily press briefings stressing success (they rejected the idea as a show of panic); second, he called a press conference early in February and read a statement pronouncing Tet a great enemy failure. He added that the situation remained uncertain and that he would keep the people informed. Unfortunately, he flunked the question-and-answer period. Reporters, worried like the rest of the country, probed for presidential admissions of surprise and reassurances of rebound. Johnson could not do it. He claimed the allies had not been surprised, then waffled on predictions of the outcome and gave an overall impression of defensive indecision.[62]

In the agony of the public doubting and deserting him, writing him increasingly stressful letters, he held outwardly firm and focused on priorities. At a meeting with the Joint Chiefs of Staff in the White House Cabinet Room on February 9, LBJ asked for an overview. Seeking honest answers, he looked at Bus Wheeler, who was ready with a response. The chairman—who came close to understanding enemy Tet strategy better than any other

U.S. officer save Oley Sharp[63]—had been on the phone with Westy, who told him he expected some new attacks to start on the tenth—which happened to be that very night, Washington time—but knew he'd crush them all. Wheeler happily added that Westy had reported proudly on the ARVN's Tet performance. Its units had fought well, experienced few defections, and surprised the enemy, who had obviously been fooled by U.S. news reports about the "puppet army." But, said Wheeler, there were doubts about whether the ARVN could handle another wave. Time would tell. Westy seemed confident; he'd moved troops to handle events north of Hue and was opening "MACV Forward," his advanced headquarters.

Johnson, hunched worriedly in his chair, brows knit, pencil wandering, wondered "are we doing all we can?"

Wheeler did not miss the opening. Westy, he said quietly, "needs reinforcements for several reasons. The reinforcements he has in mind are the 82d Airborne Division and [a regiment of Marines]. This would total 15 battalions." Why did he need them? One, to prevent the collapse of the ARVN, and two, to provide a ready reserve to greet any enemy initiative. A problem: The 82d Airborne and the Marine regiment could be sent only if the president removed restrictions on tour frequencies and length of service in Vietnam. McNamara objected; lengthening tours would hurt morale.

Wheeler calmly explained that there were deployment options and reinforced his plea with news that "based on my conversations with General Westmoreland, I believe [he] is now dictating a message to ask for early deployment of the units I have now mentioned." (True, and for reasons Wheeler did not reveal.)

When Johnson asked how many men, Wheeler said 25,000, plus supports. McNamara observed that meant a total of about 40,000 men.

Johnson, squirming, asked carefully, "How many men do we have there now?" Wheeler said 500,000. Johnson wondered if men already promised could be sent more quickly. General H. K. Johnson, army chief of staff, doubted it because of training time. McNamara then asked if some could be sent to "short training into rear areas."

"Mr. Secretary," General Johnson said in a flat voice, "there are no rear areas in Vietnam anymore."

McNamara fought hard against creating what he called "a massive force structure." At best he suggested new units be made up of short-timers. But Wheeler pressed his case. If the 82d Airborne went, he told LBJ, no deployable reserve would remain; "I do not think we should deploy these troops without reconstituting our strategic reserves in the United States."

The president, still slumped, brow knit into a question, said that he had been asking if Westy had what he needed and the JCS had said yes. "The second question was," Johnson reminded them, "'Can Westmoreland take care of the situation with what he has now?' The answer was yes. Tell me what has happened to change the situation between then and now."

Wheeler launched into a chart-supported discourse on new North Vietnamese battalions that altered the combat ratios of allied versus enemy units to about 1 to 1.

Johnson got the point quickly enough. "What you are saying is this. Since last week we have information we did not know about earlier. This is the addition of 15,000 North Vietnamese in the northern part of the country. Because of that, do we need 15 U.S. battalions?"

Wheeler said Westy would request those troops that night.

Finally Clark Clifford, mainly still a listener, spoke up:

> There is a very strange contradiction in what we are saying and doing. On one hand, we are saying that we have known of this build up. We now know the North Vietnamese and Viet Cong launched this type of effort in the cities. We have publicly told the American people that the communist offensive was: (a) not a victory. (b) produced no uprising among the Vietnamese in support of the enemy, and (c) cost the enemy between 20,000 and 25,000 of his combat troops. Now our reaction to all of that is to say that the situation is more dangerous today than it was before all of this. . . . I think we should give some very serious thought to how we explain saying on one hand the enemy did not take a victory and yet we are in need of many more troops and possibly an emergency call up.

LBJ tried a weak gambit: the enemy had changed tactics, "they are putting all of their stack in now." Wheeler agreed. Rusk, cool, impersonal, but intrigued, asked, "In the past, we have said the problem really was finding the enemy. Now the enemy has come to us. I am sure many will ask why aren't we doing better under these circumstances, now that we know where they are."[64]

Johnson quickly switched the subject.

THE FIRST CONSPIRACY

The president's reaction to this meeting could hardly have been happy. Clifford, lawyerlike, had put the obvious question. Johnson, no novice at the intrigue game, must have guessed things were running under the obvious currents.

There were. Bus Wheeler had become involved in a puzzling minuet with Westmoreland. The chairman of the JCS, worried about America's capacity to meet worldwide commitments, had endured Johnson's limited war reluctantly but loyally. His patience wore thin with Tet and with threats in Korea, the Middle East, with NATO's problems, and as Berlin got hotter. Tet changed him, as it did so many others. Frustrations piled on sublimated anger until at last Wheeler knew he had to maneuver the president into hardening the war by increased commitment in South Vietnam and by calling up the reserves. To do this, the general wrapped a campaign inside a conspiracy.

In increasingly frequent White House meetings Wheeler pushed for tougher actions. At a Tuesday lunch meeting on February 6, he urged removal of the five-mile bombing restrictions around both Hanoi and Haiphong.

McNamara, speaking for Rusk and others, argued against the idea. "Civilian casualties will be high," he warned LBJ, then added, ". . . the price is high and the gain is low. The military commanders will dispute all the points I have made except aircraft loss."

Wheeler nearly lost his temper. "I do not think," he said, edgily, "the effects on the civilian population will be that high. Frankly, this [business about civilian casualties] does not bother me when I compare it with the organized death and butchery by the North Vietnamese and the Viet Cong during [Tet]. . . . I am fed up to the teeth with the activities of the North Vietnamese and Viet Cong. We apply rigid restrictions to ourselves and try to operate in a humanitarian manner with concern for civilians at all times. They apply a double standard. . . . They place their munitions inside of populated areas because they think they are safe there. In fact they place their SAMS in civilian buildings to fire at our aircraft."[65] Wheeler struck the right note—he touched a warrior's urge running deep in Johnson's blood. Wheeler's dudgeon matched his own, and he lifted the five-mile limit, authorized fourteen new targets, and wondered about how many more men might have to go.

Wheeler maintained the pressure at a National Security Council meeting on February 7 by painting a pallid picture of political conditions in Saigon. Tet had dimmed confidence in both the South Vietnamese government and the United States's effort, he said, warning, too, that the enemy had acquired more MIGs, which might complicate allied resurgence.

McNamara, surprisingly, shared Wheeler's worries. "We do get the feeling that something big is ahead," he told the president. "We do not exactly know what it is, but our commanders are on alert."

Johnson looked hard at him, then swept the table with a harsh glare as he gave orders. "I want all of you," he growled, "to make whatever preparations are necessary. Let's know where we can get more people if we need to move additional ones in."

Johnson's emotional turmoil offered Wheeler the chance he sought. Relying on Westy's sense of nuance, Wheeler launched a devious campaign to get the reserves. He had cabled COMUSMACV on February 3 that "the President asked me if there is any reinforcement or help that we can give you." The day the chiefs met with Johnson, Westy had sent Wheeler an appreciation of his situation. Voicing expectations of continued enemy action, the MACV commander nonetheless sounded optimistic. Although conceding he had problems and could use reinforcements, he had no doubt of his ability to handle all enemy threats.[66]

Westy's sense of nuance needed work; he had not gotten the point. Confident that things were going his way, COMUSMACV said he needed another squadron of C-130 cargo carriers and additional helicopters. Looking ahead at the hope of operating in Laos, Westy said he would need another U.S. division later in the year. The "later in the year" reference showed COMUSMACV's general confidence, but Wheeler kept pestering. On February 8, the JCS chairman attacked Westy's optimism with a hint that came close to an order: "The United States Government is not prepared to accept a defeat in South Vietnam. In summary, if you need more troops, ask for them."[67]

Slowly Westmoreland began to feel that "for political reasons or otherwise, the president and the Joint Chiefs of Staff were anxious to send me reinforcements. . . . My first thought was not to ask for any, but the signals from Washington got stronger."[68]

On Friday, February 9, Westy advised his superiors that his concern centered in the north and, although he felt fairly optimistic, he would "welcome reinforcements any time they can be made available," to permit him to keep the initiative and strengthen I Corps positions.[69]

While these cables were crossing, President Johnson worried over what other surprises awaited him in Vietnam. To McNamara and Wheeler he gave cautionary guidance: "I want you to lay out for me what we should do in the minimum time to meet a crisis request from Vietnam if one comes. Let's assume we have to have more troops."[70] After Westy's mild request arrived, Johnson relaxed a little. If Westmoreland did not directly ask for troops, "I don't feel so worried," he said, despite McNamara's confession that he felt insecure about political instability in South Vietnam and lethargy in ARVN and RF/PF units. Still, LBJ thought "emergency augmentation" unnecessary.

On February 11, Wheeler tried one more time. Westy's cable, he said, had caused some uncertainty in the White House. He then recast Westy's request in an effort to get a more positive response: "You could use additional . . . troop units, but you are not expressing a firm demand for them; in sum, you do not fear defeat if are not reinforced. . . . Additional forces would give you increased capability to regain the initiative and go on the offensive at an appropriate time."[71]

Finally, Westy understood Wheeler's persistent points. Since he had mentioned losing the initiative before, he guessed the depth of Wheeler's concern. Moreover, he noted some criticism from Washington about him and his strategy. On Monday, February 12, a canny general preempted some of the strategy argument and a worried general suddenly saw threats combined in opportunities.

> Since last October, the enemy has launched a major campaign signaling a change of strategy from one of protracted war to one of quick military/political victory during the American election year. His first phase, designed to secure the border areas, has failed. The second phase, launched on the occasion of Tet and designed to initiate public uprising, to disrupt the machinery of government and command and control of the Vietnamese forces, and to isolate the cities, has also failed. Nevertheless, the enemy's third phase, which is designed to seize Quang Tri and Thua Thien provinces has just begun. This will be a maximum effort by the enemy. . . .
>
> If the enemy has changed his strategy, we must change ours. On the assumption that it is our national policy to prohibit the enemy from seizing and permanently occupying the two northern provinces, I intend to hold them at all cost. However, to do so I must reinforce from other areas and accept a major risk, unless I can get reinforcements, which I desperately need. . . . We are now in a new ball game where we face a determined, highly disciplined enemy, fully mobilized to achieve a quick victory . . . in the process of throwing in all his "military chips to go for broke." . . . I now have 500,000 U.S. troops and 60,981 Free World Military Assistance troops. . . . I have been promised 525,000 troops, which according to present programs will not materialize until 1969. I need these 525,000 troops now. . . . Time is of the essence. I must stress equally that we face a situation of great opportunity as well as heightened risk. . . . I don't see how the enemy can long sustain the heavy

losses. . . . Therefore, adequate reinforcement should permit me . . . to capitalize on his losses by seizing the initiative in other areas. Exploiting this opportunity could materially shorten the war.[72]

This bombshell started a confused textual argument among the president and his war advisors as soon as they received it.

Johnson, having just made a speech declaring the United States would stick in Vietnam, remarked in some testy puzzlement that "it doesn't look like the same person wrote the Westmoreland wire today and the one Friday." He wondered why the difference.

Dean Rusk, wearing his old soldier's hat, read the message fairly accurately as an expression of opportunities rather than "desperate" need. Westy, he thought, wanted to take advantage of the enemy at a time of weakness and shorten the war, "and that has a certain attractiveness to all of us."

McNamara disagreed sharply. "I read the Westmoreland cable differently from Dean. I read that he needs these six battalions in order to avoid defeat. . . ." If, on the off chance that Rusk were right, and Westy wanted more men "to take advantage of the opportunity to do more, I would also send them."

Clark Clifford sat quietly through most of the discussion, hands making a tent in front of him, lips slightly pursed. He nursed still some of the worries he'd expressed at a Friday discussion and earlier. Unruffled and deliberate, the defense secretary–designate observed that Westy's new cable "has a much greater sense of urgency in it. Why is that?"

Patiently dissimulating, Wheeler said that the general found his "earlier low-key approach was not proper based on a full assessment of his situation. . . . General Westmoreland has been conservative in his troop requests in the past. Now he finds that his campaign plan has been preempted by enemy action."

Clifford expressed surprise that Westy had no control over other allied forces. That gave McNamara a chance to urge a renewed push toward a combined allied command, which had been stalled by South Vietnamese political opposition. Johnson, sprawled in his chair, mused, "I would sure try to do this for maximum control of the South Koreans, the Australians, and the South Vietnamese." Then, sweeping the room, frowning in emphasis, the president said he wanted to get all the questions asked so that answers could come quickly. "I hope all of you see what has happened during the last two weeks. Westy said he *could* use troops one day last week. Today he comes in with an urgent request for them." Heavily, he added, "I want to look at all of these things now. I want to anticipate that more will happen to us than we had planned. . . . I have a mighty big stake in this. I am more unsure every day. . . . I want a crash program to get these men out there just as fast as they can."

The suggestion that some Air National Guardsmen would have to be called prompted another querulous "How many men?" from LBJ. Two to three thousand, McNamara replied. Nodding, Johnson said "Well, let's do it."

Wheeler, sensing a door opening, said the Joint Chiefs recommended a reserve call-up of some thirty thousand National Guardsmen if Westy got a brigade of the 82d Airborne; if some additional Marines went, the 4th Marine Reserve Division ought to be called.

Johnson wearily swiveled toward the JCS chairman and said, "Let's not decide that today." You and McNamara "go back and agree on what to call. We must move as soon as we can. I was ready Friday. The clock is ticking."

When Wheeler left the room to issue the orders for reinforcements, McNamara said he did not support the call-up of reserves. Wryly, Johnson said, "Well, if you cannot agree with the Joint Chiefs on what is needed, then submit . . . a minority viewpoint."

Johnson then listened to Walt Rostow's comment that President Thieu agreed with the proposed action. What about the extra sixty-five thousand men South Vietnam had promised? LBJ wondered. When Rostow replied that new draft laws had gone into effect to meet the need, the president mused that if the South Vietnamese could not go it alone "we will have to do it rather than let them all get defeated. I think Westmoreland is confronted with a defeat or a victory."

With that, LBJ wearily closed the meeting.[73]

At the next day's lunch meeting, Wheeler confirmed that the troops authorized for Westy were being readied—a Marine regiment and a brigade of the 82d Airborne Division. He also had some good news: "General Westmoreland indicated to me this morning that 'things are looking better all over.'" That might have been a slip, considering that he then raised the reserve issue again.

Considerable disagreement greeted that topic, and Johnson, looking sober and attentive, said to the general, "I sure want you and Bob McNamara to get together on one program." Then he recalled JFK's troubles with reserves. Why is a call-up needed, LBJ wondered? If needed, how large should it be? Could numbers be reduced with troops from Europe or South Korea? Could individual calls be avoided or postponed? Where would reserves go? How long would they serve? What would it cost? Would Congress have to authorize a call?[74]

Rusk weighed in with a negative response from Hanoi to a Rumanian peace feeler and suggested added air attacks to emphasize U.S. determination. Clifford agreed. Johnson detected no real enthusiasm, though, and delayed decision.

Wheeler still had not won. But Johnson, picking up on a McNamara idea, handed the chairman a golden opportunity: Go back to Vietnam for consultations with Westy, the president directed. Get the picture clearly and come back with an assessment of "what Westmoreland felt he had to have to meet present" and future needs.[75] Wheeler had hoped to go earlier, but LBJ kept him close while McNamara defended the Tonkin Gulf Resolution before Fulbright's rangers on the Hill.

These meetings typified the president's agenda for several weeks after Tet and during Khe Sanh's siege. And during these weeks he worried about the defenders there and especially about the men just ticketed for Vietnam. On the spur of the moment—his favorite timetable—LBJ announced a February 17 trip to Fort Bragg, North Carolina, home of the 82d Airborne, and then on to El Toro Marine Corps Air Station, California, to visit the departing Marines.

There are some who think those visits shaped much of Johnson's thinking over the next weeks.[76] Certainly, seeing the troops opened wounds in his heart that touched a compassion in him, a compassion stirred by the casualty lists that came every morning with his breakfast.[77]

Fort Bragg had been around awhile and ranked as a prime army base with all kinds of support functions, but the president's interest remained fixed on the men of the 82d Airborne who were about to leave. He met them in difficult circumstances. Some were Vietnam veterans. An effort had been made to screen them out, but some were volunteers and others were needed in the force structure. As he stood with them, shaking hands, many looked grim. The president looked strained, concerned, and nearly overwhelmed. They were marching to planes as he put out his hands, trying to say something comforting and felt heartbreak in return.

> These visits with brave men were among the most personally painful meetings of my Presidency. . . . I told them I regretted more than they would ever know the necessity of ordering them to Vietnam. . . . I remember vividly my conversation with one soldier. I asked him if he had been in Vietnam before. He said: "Yes, sir, three times." I asked if he was married. He said: "Yes, sir." Did he have any children? "Yes, sir, one." Boy or girl? "A boy, sir." How old is he? "He was born yesterday morning, sir," he said quietly. That was the last question I asked him. It

tore my heart out to send back to combat a man whose first son had just been born.[78]

At El Toro Johnson found the Marines, as he expected, ready to go, and yet he felt a deep hurt in sending them. Two of his closest White House staff, Horace Busby and Harry McPherson talked with a couple of dozen pilots just back from Vietnam. The president was in an adjoining stateroom and McPherson guessed he heard everything, since LBJ reported most of the feelings at the next Tuesday lunch meeting.

"It began conversationally," McPherson noted, senior officers extolling the deeds of their pilots. During a lull,

> a lieutenant with an Irish name broke in. "Permission to speak, sir."
> "Granted," said the commander. There followed a furious assault on the bombing program. Men were being asked to fly through the heaviest antiaircraft defenses ever seen, in order to bomb meaningless targets. "I've hit the same wooden bridge three times . . . for that I've flown through SAMS, flak, and automatic weapons fire. I've seen the goddamned Russian freighters sitting there, and the supplies stacked along the wharves. I can't hit them. 'It might start a wider war.' Well, the war is too wide for me right now.[79]

When Johnson stopped on the way back to Washington for a visit with General Eisenhower at Palm Desert, California, and a golf game at the El Dorado Country Club, he got some good news. Eisenhower, ever on the president's side, cautioned against second guessing people who "know the information. He spoke glowingly of General Wheeler and General Westmoreland." Back in the White House, Johnson wrote Ike a note of thanks that revealed more of his seared soul than he guessed: "The contrast between the beauties of El Dorado and the brutalities of Vietnam haunted me all day."[80]

Haunting thoughts disturbed LBJ's flight to Washington as he weighed proposals for more soldiers against the wages young men were paying. He knew, in his heart, that his country's duty would not be done until South Vietnam lived in freedom,[81] and he steeled himself to find the way.

Bus Wheeler, with Maj. Gen. William DePuy (special assistant to the JCS for counterinsurgency), Foreign Service Officer Philip Habib, and a few others in tow,[82] arrived in Saigon on February 23. Westmoreland, who met them, stared at his old friends in shock. They looked weary—Wheeler nearly exhausted—not just from the hours in the air, but from some wearing process that made them older, oddly distracted. It was soon clear that they were victims of "doomsday reporting." Wheeler, for his part, seemed rattled by Westy's optimism and good humor, surprised, too, by general appearances—debris had been cleared from Ton Son Nhut, and Saigon, though scarred, went on with business. He saw far better things than expected, and later confessed to Westy that "the newspapers had given him the impression that the Tet offensive was 'the worst calamity since Bull Run.'"[83]

Sped away to a briefing room, Wheeler greeted Westy's staff—and they, too, were stunned by the chief's appearance. One of them saw him as "haggard, gray, obviously tired, and most astounding of all, he had acquired a notable 'potbelly.'" Worries about him tensed the room.

Westmoreland opened the session with an upbeat overview of the war, a view that Ambassador Bunker later endorsed. General Phillip Davidson gave an intelligence estimate of the enemy situation, stressing the heavy casualties open attacks had cost the VC and NVA and their currently expanded problems of manpower and logistics. Wheeler and DePuy listened in surprise. In the discussion that followed, Davidson watched Westmoreland with growing admiration. At his articulate best, Westy displayed a firm grasp of the whole theater and spoke persuasively—but to a cold house. Wheeler, DePuy, and Habib either did not appreciate, or did not want to appreciate, the opportunities opened by allied success. Instead, huddled in his chair, Wheeler harped on possibilities of another round of attacks. All the staff thought that danger slight, but "by the end of the briefing, it was obvious that the efforts . . . had not lightened the gloomy view of the situation which General Wheeler and the Washington contingent had brought with them."[84] Subsequent talks with President Thieu and Vice President Ky, who spoke of rapid recovery across the country and of revived pacification efforts under Komer's frenetic leadership, failed to dent the visitors' rigid pessimism.

Why were they so resistant to progress? Did they come with prejudices in place? Did Wheeler's gloom ring true? Was he looking for disaster?

Next day, the two four-star generals talked for hours—during which Wheeler dangled a tantalizing plan before Westmoreland. Things were changing in Washington, he explained. McNamara, certainly to Wheeler's comfort, would depart the scene at the end of the month and his replacement, Clark Clifford, was an unabashed hawk. It seemed possible, at last, that a fresh voice would convince LBJ to lift some of the restrictions on operations in Laos and Cambodia, perhaps even permit a seaborne right hook north of the DMZ. Not that Wheeler promised this idyllic future—but he thought it should form part of a revised plan for expanded war.

Westy eagerly agreed, and the two decided to examine a number of scenarios—from a worst case with the ARVN ineffective, South Vietnam sundered, South Korean troops withdrawn for home defense, and a major infusion of North Vietnamese troops, to a best case that would give COMUSMACV enough men to finish the enemy. All of this, of course, depended on LBJ's willingness to abandon gradualism in favor of aggressive war.

Whether Wheeler really believed the president would change his cherished policy is questionable. He *had* believed it for a time, but the possibility had a charm of its own. Detailed planning began on force requirements for 1968. Plan big, Wheeler urged, with an eye to providing troops not only for Southeast Asia but also—here came Wheeler's hidden pitch—for a U.S. strategic reserve. Planning time would be short—Wheeler had to present his ideas to the president on February 28.

A frenzied staff designed three force packages totaling about 205,000 men—a figure Westy later denied knowing[85]—with the first one, consisting of 108,000 men, scheduled to reach Vietnam by May 1, 1968. The second and third packages were to be deployed in September and December if needed; if not, they would be the strategic reserve. Westmoreland had, he thought, a "clear understanding" with the chief that only the first package would definitely come to Vietnam—the rest would come if the war's scope widened or disaster struck MACV. Later Westy described the project as simply "a contingency plan based on the assumption of a decision." And he thought the whole discussion would remain secret until that decision came.[86]

Armed with exactly what he came for, Westy's force requirements, Wheeler left for Washington on February 25, with a stop for talks with Oley Sharp in Honolulu. By the time he reached CINCPAC headquarters, Wheeler had devised a plan of persuasion for the president and his advisors that hinged on bad news. He had told Westy that he worked on the idea of "one thing at a time" in dealing with the White House, and the one thing this time would be enough men to handle world contingencies. From Honolulu he sent McNamara and the president a summary of his report—which neither Westy nor Oley Sharp saw[87]—and Johnson read it with some irk at his Texas ranch.[88] Wheeler refined his presentation on the way across the Pacific.

While Wheeler crossed the ocean, McNamara convened a departmental group for quick assessment of the Wheeler-Westmoreland request; reactions were hostile. On Tuesday the twenty-seventh Walt Rostow teletyped the president a summary of a meeting held in Rusk's dining room, at which Rusk, McNamara, Clifford, Katzenbach, Bill Bundy, Rostow, Harry McPherson, and Joe Califano gathered to talk about a speech Johnson had determined to give on Vietnam. Their discussion had been disrupted by what they termed "the tentative proposals of General Westmoreland and General Wheeler for additional troops."[89] McNamara had talked of three options. One, to accept the Wheeler-Westmoreland proposal, said the lame-duck secretary of defense, would put about four hundred thousand men on the military muster rolls and cost something like $10 billion more in fiscal 1969. His second option centered on a military augmentation with a peace proposal, which brought Rusk in with the thought that such a proposal should be specific and he mentioned ending bombing of North Vietnam at the twentieth parallel, "or stop bombing altogether if Hanoi would withdraw military forces from . . . just below the DMZ."[90] McNamara's third option was to stick with the status quo on troops, but change strategy, protect populated areas, and curtail action in the backcountry of South Vietnam.

Clark Clifford, about to sit in McNamara's hot seat, expressed an old worry about keeping public support for the war. "Despite these optimistic reports, the American people and world opinion believe we have suffered a major setback. How do we gain support for major programs if we have told people that things are going well? How do we avoid creating the feeling that we are pounding troops down a rathole? What is our purpose?" He suggested another alternative, one he did not advocate but thought should be considered as a message of determination to the enemy: send in five hundred thousand to one million men and win. He really wanted a complete review of Vietnam.

McNamara wryly noted that either doing much more or little more "had the advantage of clarity." He did not, he emphasized, understand the logic of adding 205,000 men—which was certainly not enough to signal a determination to win or lose. Phil Habib reported division in Saigon, and said many there believed sending more troops would only encourage the South Vietnamese to excuse themselves further in favor of the United States. McNamara urged deliberation in decision making and noted that acceptance of the Wheeler-Westmoreland plan had large military and economic implications. When Rusk suggested a discussion about intensifying the bombing campaign, McNamara cracked.

Lips aquiver, words coming in bursts, he nearly screamed, "The goddamned Air Force, they're dropping more on North Vietnam than we dropped on Germany in the last year of World War II, and it's not doing anything!" Gasping through sobs, he looked plaintively at Clifford. "We simply have to end this thing. I just hope you can get hold of it. It is out of control."[91]

"Everyone in the room," Clifford noted, "understood what had happened: this proud, intelligent, and dedicated man was reaching the end of his strength on his last full day in office. He was leaving the Pentagon just in time."

Harry McPherson, sitting in as one of the speech drafters, wrote a personal note to himself at the end of that emotional gathering: "We are at the point of crisis. McNamara expressed grave doubts over military, economic, political, diplomatic, and moral consequences of a larger force buildup. . . . Question is whether these profound doubts will be presented to the President."

As he transmitted the minutes of this meeting to Johnson, Rostow made the neutral comment that the issues raised needed close study. He noted "the only firm agreement" that came from the meeting: "The troop issue raised many questions to which you ought to have clear answers before making a final decision." He urged that the president set up a team to investigate the alternatives and thought Clifford should chair an "intensive working group."[92]

Rain lashed Andrews Air Force Base as Wheeler's plane reached Washington a bit after six in the morning on the twenty-eighth.[93] The president, just returned from his ranch,[94] had scheduled an 8:30 A.M. meeting, so Wheeler rushed straight to the White House. Johnson sat at the head of the breakfast table, surrounded by the vice president, Rusk, McNamara, Clifford, Max Taylor, Paul Nitze, Dick Helms, Rostow, George Christian, and ubiquitous note-taker Tom Johnson. Wheeler joined them. To anyone with a sense of vibrations, several currents ran through the room.

Helms launched the meeting with a survey of CIA observations about Vietnam's momentary condition. Wheeler could scarcely have wished for a better introduction. The North Vietnamese, Helms said, were in "high gear," and might continue pushing for three or four months. Their objective was to wreck the southern government and its military forces; U.S. units would be gratuitous targets. The CIA saw the allies on the defensive, with some 50 percent of enemy forces intact and in the field. Although the ARVN had fought well, it suffered from post-trauma languor and might lose defectors to a victorious foe. If the enemy went flat out, Helms thought the ARVN would be ruined and that the Saigon government would collapse. Helms added that "the longer this thing is drawn out, the less likely I think negotiations are."[95]

Everything worked for Wheeler. Just back from a mind-sapping flight across the Pacific, after three days in Vietnam, he won empathy with deep fatigue. Old friends could see, in the slumping pose and the slow words, a weariness beyond mere travel—things seen and heard had drained him of soul energy and he seemed almost a messenger from Thermopylae.

Levelly, the general said he had talked with Bunker, Westmoreland, President Thieu, Vice President Ky, and senior U.S. commanders, and the things he had learned surprised him. Tet attackers hit powerfully, hit nationwide, largely against ARVN units and the South Vietnamese government, but with some focus on U.S. logistical and air bases and command-and-control centers. The enemy erred, Wheeler said, in following American press assessments of ARVN weakness and ran into stubborn resistance from the so-called puppets. Expected mass defections to the VC and NVA failed, but, still, Wheeler added, "the margin of victory was very thin in a number of battles." Pacification programs were at a standstill and "Bob Komer said the situation was not satisfactory anywhere." American forces were in good shape with air capability high. Helicopter losses were up, but adequate replacements were on the way. Still, equipment losses were measurable.

He had a matter-of-fact look to him, and his stolid calm, his dark-rimmed glasses accenting clear-eyed earnestness, rode over disbelief as his woeful tale unwound. This year, he prophesied, "will be a critical year in the war. There is heavy fighting ahead. The losses will be high in men. The losses will be high in equipment. The question is, can the ARVN withstand another wave of attacks? The government has many problems, among them are the refugees, many civilian casualties, and the continuing problem of morale."

He knew most of the men around the table worried about Westy, and he told them that COMUSMACV "must have a sufficient force in I Corps to hold securely those two northern provinces." Enemy options were several: They could attack Khe Sanh [a direct threat for the president], they could use Khe Sanh as a decoy and attack Quang Tri and Hue again, or they could attack Da Nang. Important to all of these options, Wheeler stressed, was the fact that Westy had no theater reserves with which to repulse invasion, destroy enemy bases, or exploit enemy defeats.

Wheeler confessed his surprise that U.S. forces had nearly lost Tan Son Nhut Air Base. "It was touch and go there. . . . Around Da Nang we had another close call." He concluded by saying that he and Westy suggested a theater reserve of two divisions.

A stunned silence filled the room. Clark Clifford felt that Wheeler's words were "so somber, so discouraging, to the point where it was really shocking."[96]

Finally LBJ asked, "What are the alternatives?"

Without the recommended reinforcements, Wheeler said, "we should be prepared to give up the two northern provinces of South Vietnam. This, of course, would be a political hazard. It would also give the North Vietnamese a strong position for negotiating." Quietly Wheeler added that "it would, I believe, cause the collapse of the ARVN."

A fast learner, Johnson wondered if opportunities offered Westy to take the offensive. "Is there anything we can do other than just sitting and waiting for them to attack?"

Wheeler confessed that "as far as new bombing efforts there is nothing new in the cards. We could plan an amphibious operation in the north, but we do not have the capacity to do it at this time."

Johnson picked through the maze. "So [Westmoreland] really has no initiative of his own other than to interrupt their road building and to patrol."

Sitting back, looking around the table, the president guessed that "we may get some dazzling and shocking surprises." Then, "it looks like the enemy can pick and choose his own time and place."[97]

Wheeler listened and waited. His performance had the beauty of truth partly told. His gambit centered on bad news triggering good. By excising Westy's optimism, by sidestepping the provisional nature of the whole program, he rested his case on imminent danger.

Reactions were varied. The most interesting of these came from Clifford, who heard the whole presentation with dismay and read into Wheeler's swords dimming respect for COMUSMACV. So bright had been reports from Saigon that the emergency request for more men made Westy look silly or incompetent.[98] "It was clear that although he avoided criticizing Westmoreland directly, he had lost some degree of confidence in his theater commander and no longer fully accepted Westmoreland's judgment of the war. . . . Wheeler still wanted to win, as the troop request in his report made clear, but his report damaged Westmoreland because in a disagreement between the two men, President Johnson would unquestionably give far greater weight to the views of Wheeler."[99]

Clearly Clifford gave greater weight to Wheeler and the reason is clear. "Wheeler had a modest and low-key style: he lacked Westmoreland's theatrical appearance and carefully avoided the blustery personal style many military men adopt when dealing with civilians."[100] He had the deference for trust.

Johnson's options were unattractive. If he agreed with Westmoreland's request, it would unleash outrage in Congress and the public, would continue to Americanize the war, cost millions, and lead to something like partial mobilization.

Interestingly enough, Wheeler himself admitted that no more than one hundred thousand men could be sent by May 1, but he nonetheless urged approval of the total program for long-range needs. He could afford to bide a little time—his conspiracy to build up a strategic reserve teetered on the edge of success.

Johnson, however, backed away from accepting anything at that meeting. He took Rostow's advice and asked Clifford to head a group study of the issue. Organize subgroups, said LBJ, break the problems down into workable proportions. "Give me the lesser of evils. Give me your recommendations."[101]

Trying for the lesser evil—that, for LBJ, was the nightmare of Vietnam and echoed a remorseless question: "I can't get out. I can't finish it. What the hell can I do?"

chapter
FOURTEEN

Command Decision

T here seemed too little time for much of anything but the "miserable war." Clark Clifford had rushed to his assignment and convened the first session of the "Clifford Group," and the president, reaching out as usual when crises ringed him in, asked Dean Acheson, on February 28, 1968, to come to the White House that evening.[1] Acheson came and Johnson sat him down for a talk about Vietnam. A study in contrasts they were: Johnson, informal, often earthy, the clear product of politics; Acheson, fastidious, formal, long face bumpered by a clipped moustache that fixed his self-assurance as a kingpin of the eastern establishment. Johnson respected the former secretary of state for his clear intellect and high attainments in Truman's troubled years, also for his support as one of the Wise Men, and he wanted that veteran diplomat's opinion on the war. Acheson had some contempt for Johnson and mocked him to friends as "Our Hero," a "real Centurion—part man, part horse's ass."[2]

Acheson found Johnson testy and distracted, surrounded by ringing phones and people, persisting in a windy monologue that finally bored his visitor. In the midst of all this, Acheson seems to have murmured some excuse and walked back to his office. Later he recalled his words to Rostow, who phoned quickly to find out what had happened, "You tell the President—and you tell him in precisely these words, that he can take Vietnam and stick it up his ass!"[3]

Johnson got on the phone and invited Acheson back. They finally did discuss Vietnam and the JCS's request for more men. This brought back memories of Truman's troubles with Douglas MacArthur and Acheson spoke plainly.

"With all due respect, Mr. President, the Joint Chiefs of Staff don't know what they're talking about." Johnson thought that a shocking remark and Acheson said "Then maybe you should be shocked." Johnson said he wanted Acheson's assessment of Vietnam options. He would have to get beyond "canned briefings," Acheson said—they gave only surface impressions. When LBJ offered to give him access to anyone and any kind of information available, Acheson accepted the assignment and left, this time politely.[4]

In the midst of all the Vietnam uncertainties, Johnson also consulted with Matthew Ridgway and Cabot Lodge. Interestingly enough, Ridgway, who had fought the Chinese, urged the president to pay attention to the strategic reserve situation because America's forces were stretched too thin for crises outside of Southeast Asia.[5] Lodge, always welcomed by LBJ, offered sobering thoughts on the search-and-destroy strategy. Drop it, he suggested, send no more troops, scale down fighting, impose press censorship on Vietnam news, hunker for the long haul. Not only an old Saigon hand but also one of the supportive Wise Men, Lodge's comments hit hard.[6]

Everything seemed to be closing in on the Oval Office. Vietnam loomed darker daily, and violence seemed about to burst again in the cities. And, in those troubled days, domestic politics broke through the war miasma at the White House with some cold realities of public opinion.

Back in November, Sen. Eugene McCarthy of Minnesota, a prominent liberal and Vietnam dove, announced he would run against Johnson in various Democratic primaries. New Hampshire scheduled the earliest of those primaries on March 13 and the signs were not good for the president. Media coverage began to bill the election as a referendum on the war and McCarthy did all he could to garner support from the disenchanted. Johnson worried about other indicators running against him. In February, presidential mail clerks reported a sharp upswing in letters criticizing the administration's Vietnam policy, and the Gallup organization showed more slippage in LBJ's approval ratings—only 35 percent approved of his war management.[7] Nothing could hide the massive defection of public support for Vietnam.

Too many handwringers and doomsayers dominated the news. Johnson worked constantly at press relations, but somehow the media seemed to him wrapped in a mysterious fog of doubt that turned them from the truth. Johnson persisted. Veteran columnist Max Lerner came for a private presidential visit on March 5, and the whole thing seemed to go wrong. Johnson launched into one of his lectures about the Communist failure in Vietnam, spouted statistics, and waved intelligence reports. Tet offered a "giant opportunity for the United States," the president claimed, but the longer and louder he lectured, the less Lerner believed. Lerner left the meeting with a sad image in mind. Johnson struck him as "a last-ditch fighter in a Western movie of the bad old days, surrounded by the savages, with his horse shot out from under him, embattled, unyielding, waiting for reinforcements to carry the day." Unconvinced by LBJ's performance, Lerner nonetheless responded to his personality, catching Johnson's fullness far better than he knew in an admiring exit line: "Above all, one must be impressed with the naked willpower of the man, as if he were exerting sheer will to hold everything together at once—the war, the nation and his own inner universe."[8]

Presidential options narrowed. A good deal depended on the administration's handling of the post-Tet situation and a lot on Clifford's study group. Johnson knew that Clifford, a canny stalker of the corridors of power, understood the politico-military situation. He had a tough assignment: review the troop requests in a general war context and do it in five days.

Clifford had some qualms. When he gathered his group for its first meeting on February 28, he recognized the challenges presented by the divergent views around him. Rusk he knew to be a steady hawk; Treasury Secretary Joe Fowler was a solid administration man; Nick Katzenbach, Rusk's undersecretary, might be ambivalent; Deputy Secretary of Defense Paul Nitze seemed to be a hard-liner but a thinker, a man who kept an iron code[9] by which he measured men; Dick Helms purveyed the official intelligence man's constant pessimism; Walt Rostow believed in winning; Max Taylor had a wise soldier's belief in power; and Bus Wheeler had his own agenda but might still be useful.

All the members realized that their chairman was concerned with more then Westy's troop request. Should another two hundred thousand men be sent to Vietnam? Should the present course of action be followed there? Could the war be won at all with any number of men? "The answers to these questions, the formulations of alternative courses open to the U.S., was to be the initial focus of the review. To that end, general assignments were made concerning papers to be written . . . for discussion among the group on Saturday, March 2."[10]

The group's nearly open brief put every member on a round-the-clock grind. "I hardly hit the bed in that period of time," Clifford recalled, and in grueling sessions he learned much about Vietnam, the members of his own task force, the Pentagon, the JCS, and America's military morass.[11]

Chief Justice Earl Warren swore Clifford in as the secretary of defense at noon on March 1. He came to office with some predilections, of course, but not those LBJ expected. Johnson knew his doubts about the mid-1965 infusion of troops to Vietnam, but Clifford had accepted the decision and been a growing hawk ever since. Tet stirred doubts, however, and undermined some of his perceptions of America's program in Vietnam. What the secretary learned in his early days produced a crisis of conviction and led him down a clouded path of conscience. Suppose the war could not be won, that the Vietnam venture had failed? Lyndon Johnson would not accept that brutal conclusion—too much of his heart and mind were embedded in Vietnam's bloody ground. How could this great engine of a man steaming on to victory be shunted to another track? With difficulty, especially because he often acted on the spur of the moment, sometimes made decisions on the road, and had a practiced gift of blindness. If he could be managed—many doubted the possibility[12]—he would have to be handy.

And he had just left town on a personal, sentimental journey. He would spend March's first weekend at Ramey Air Force Base in Puerto Rico, visiting his Vietnam-bound son-in-law, Pat Nugent. Too many things could happen in these untethered times. Something important did happen. Johnson basked in some great news in Puerto Rico.

The president had all along believed Tet to be a huge allied victory, and on the evening of March 3 he received the best kind of confirmation. Westmoreland cabled him that "throughout the country, we are moving to a general offensive. . . . I hope that the impact of these simultaneous major operations will convince the people in South Vietnam and in Washington that we are not waiting for either the VC to resume the initiative, or for someone to help us. The time is ripe to move out and we will do so."[13]

Clark Clifford pressed his workers. He noted that recent discussions had identified a few men who seemed to feel uncertainties like his own. Harry McPherson for one, whom he would finally regard as his "silent partner" in the White House,[14] perhaps Nick Katzenbach; in the Pentagon he found others who told him they thought America could not win a military victory.

Chief among his new allies was Paul Warnke, who had moved up to John McNaughton's post of assistant secretary of defense for international security affairs. Unknown to Clifford before he went to the Pentagon, Warnke, in the frank give-and-take of task force discussions, soon won his fullest trust. He, like Wheeler, struck Clifford as the right kind of man. "His self-deprecating manner and casual style made him easy to work with, but I learned quickly that behind that easygoing style lay an incisive mind that cut fearlessly through the circumlocutions and evasions of others in the government."[15] Not everyone shared this opinion, especially the JCS and other high brass, who considered Warnke "a noted dove."[16] With Clifford, though, Warnke's artful affability lent him suasion and he often won his wants with warmth.[17]

Clifford listened carefully during the maundering discussions of his early meetings. Since he came from the outside and had no old agendas, he could query with impunity. Questions all through the Pentagon brought bothersome answers.

During a meeting on March 2, his group talked with various Pentagon brass and the secretary, proper and precise, conducted what amounted to a court of inquiry. Would two hundred thousand men "do the job?" No one could tell. How many more would it take? Again, no precise answer. Can the enemy counter U.S. buildups? Yes. "Can bombing stop the war?" No—it would inflict human and material losses but not end the war. Will increased bombing decrease U.S. casualties? Probably not. How long must America keep on sending men and carrying the war? No one knew if the South Vietnamese would ever be ready to fend for themselves. What was the U.S. plan for victory? There was no such plan. That session left Clifford "appalled" and opposed to dispatching more troops.[18]

Everyone on the task force realized by March 3 that no real agreement could be reached on the troop issue. Other urges had crowded into the discussion, including a proposal for a bombing halt that charmed some of the conferees and irked others. That afternoon Clifford decided on compromise. He asked Warnke to prepare a Draft Presidential Memorandum (DPM), leaving out a bombing halt and adding recommendations for a reserve call-up and a small addition to MACV's troops. Clifford met Warnke's obvious dejection by arguing that the task force was not the right forum to resolve "the fundamental issues dividing the Administration."

On the fourth some order had come to the DPM. It had a tough tone and recommended twenty thousand more men for Vietnam and a reserve call-up "adequate to meet the balance of [Westmoreland's] request." To doubters Clifford could argue that behind the compromises necessary to get the document approved at all, he had hidden the real objective in the last paragraph, which might result in "slowing down the military push for reinforcements" while granting them something. "I suggested that the final decision on the troop request be contingent upon three factors: a week-by-week reexamination of the situation; improved performance by the Saigon government and the South Vietnamese Army; and a complete review of our political and strategic options in Vietnam."

In effect, the group's report played for time, attended to some minor necessities, and hinted at much more to come.

When the meeting with the president began at 5:30 P.M. in the Cabinet Room on Monday, March 4, Clifford felt the nervousness of ambiguity—he did not quite know the direction of things. For the first time he took his seat as secretary of defense and felt direct responsibility for what would be proposed. Johnson opened with a recapitulation of Clifford's assignment: Provide recommendations on how many troops would go immediately and where they would come from, determine what should be asked of the Saigon government, and analyze possible congressional and financial difficulties that might impact on these decisions.

Then, looking at Walt Rostow, the president said, "As I understand it, Clark Clifford, Secretary Rusk, and Rostow and others have been meeting on these questions in conjunction with the Joint Chiefs of Staff." Rostow agreed, and LBJ looked at Clifford, who began his statement by outlining the "central problem" Johnson faced: Will current and requested troop levels save South Vietnam? Contrasting views of Tet confused the picture, forcing the president to make a "watershed" decision: Does the United States want to continue sending more of everything while the enemy matches escalation? Clifford's group confessed uncertainty about continuing the present course. There were too many variables. Was the South Vietnamese government really trying to help itself, or merely leaving everything to the United States?

Playing for time, Clifford suggested sending only enough men to meet immediate needs—say twenty-two thousand. Johnson jumped on that small increment and Clifford played the reserve card, saying that a proposed call-up would provide men for Westy's future needs.

As for strategy, Clifford reported his group was unsure that "conventional victory" could be won. Maybe, he suggested, it was time for a different strategy.

A far more detailed study must be made before a clear course could be recommended on negotiations or increased war.

Johnson, listening intently, leaned toward Clifford and focused on that one thing of his. "Does this change the tour of duty?" If he meant that kind of ricochet question as a displacement maneuver, he got the right effect. Poised to defend the whole reappraisal thesis, everyone sank to details.

Sitting on LBJ's right, listening, thinking, Rusk had kept his customary private counsel. Now, looking in the president's eyes, the secretary of state surprised nearly everybody as he began to speak in an unusually serious voice. "Mr. President, without a doubt, this will be one of the most serious decisions you will have made since becoming President." Rusk said he felt it was imperative that South Vietnam do its full share and become strong enough to survive, and he urged a strategy shift from a geographical to a demographic approach. Sadly, he saw little hope for peace negotiations in the near future.

Johnson stuck to his point and asked why enlistment extensions had to be combined with a reserve call-up? Wheeler explained that extensions were the quickest way to build the strategic reserve—experienced men had to be kept.

Johnson mused that Congress might want the reserves first and added he understood the need for them. Talk ran the table about numbers in calls and in the draft and finally Treasury Secretary Fowler added his own chilling figures—he guessed sending all the men would cost an additional $2.5 billion for fiscal 1968 and $10 billion in 1969. More than that, "there would be an adverse balance of payments impact of $500 million." Credit controls and wage-price limits would be necessary.

Subdued, Johnson saw trouble in the Senate.

Wheeler, fairly dejected, saw the whole problem for the first time. "If we *could* provide Westy with the troops he wants I would recommend they be sent. They cannot be provided. This [twenty-two thousand] is what we can do by 15 June." But, and he picked up his own morale, "I find nothing wrong with going along with this track."

Rostow, who sat quietly through much that troubled him, watched LBJ and sensed some of his worries with the vagueness of Clifford's pitch. The national security advisor finally broke in to argue that "we should put aside the generalities about military solution vs. diplomatic solution; or population strategy vs. real estate protection." Sitting up, he spoke louder as he got into his concerns. "We need to look for a fresh summary of the reasons for mining Haiphong. There may be additional military steps to resolve the matter sooner."

Nitze argued for an increased ARVN role and then returned to the issue of reserves. "We must rebuild them." Then, to Clifford's surprise, he added, "We must get into negotiations soon . . . We must make up our own minds when we want to cease the bombings and see what happens."

Rusk sat placidly through all this and, when Nitze finished, he leaned forward with a suggestion that stunned Clifford and changed the whole thrust of the meeting. "We could stop the bombing during the rainy period in the North." Then, in explanation, "it would not cost us much militarily, since our air sorties are way down at that time anyway."

Johnson, who knew some of Rusk's recent thinking, jumped in strongly: "Really 'get on your horses' on that!"[19]

After some lingering discussion, the meeting ended at about 7:30 P.M. A number of participants emerged from it with changed perspectives.

Johnson came away both troubled and hopeful. He found in Clifford and some of his colleagues a deeper sense of pessimism than he thought Vietnam's facts sustained, and that irked him; Clifford's uncertainty, his failure to get hold of real details, his air of doom and distaste for military things, revealed a side of him Johnson neither expected nor liked.[20]

Recovery efforts in Vietnam had impressed LBJ, and he thought joint efforts by Thieu and Ky had produced results: RF/PF were up to 75 percent of pre-Tet strength, and 118 ARVN battalions were rated "combat effective."[21] Bunker's Saigon reports showed steady progress each week after Tet, even in the pacification area, and the veteran diplomat who saw only good things ahead ended his February 29 weekly report by saying, "If we stick with it I am confident we will come out all right in the end."[22] As LBJ thought about Westy's needs, he felt better; he believed Westy could handle things over there and might even change the outcome by himself.

Should there be a more detailed examination of everything about Vietnam? Probably. The president made no effort to take the bit from Clifford's teeth. But Rusk's doings were of real interest. He had come to LBJ with some ideas from a British group that suggested America might copy the Communist method of fighting while negotiating. What they proposed dovetailed nicely with Clifford's proposals: Announce a willingness to talk, name negotiators, stop bombing the north, appeal for world approval, and at the same time reinforce in the field and emphasize pacification.[23] Obviously the careful secretary of state thought new opportunities opened. So did the president; that meeting began shifting old priorities in a gravely troubled man.

By the time the Tuesday lunch group met at about 12:30 P.M. the next day, Johnson's ponderings had led him some distance in various directions. Would things have been better, Johnson wondered, if less gradual steps had been taken in Vietnam? Rusk guessed that if JFK had sent in a hundred thousand men in 1961 "it might have saved things."[24] All these might have beens were gambits to assuage a president's unease, an unease everyone could notice as he swung in his chair and speculated out loud about changes popping up in things people said. "It appears," he mused with deceptive calmness in his tone, "we are about to make a rather basic change in the strategy of this war if we tell the ARVN to do more fighting; we tell them we will give 20,000 men, no more; we tell them we will do no more until they do more; [and]

we tell them we will be *prepared* to make additional troop contributions but not unless they 'get with it.'"

Thinking aloud, he added, "I frankly doubt you get much out of them unless they have a good coach, the right plays, and the best equipment."[25]

Finally Johnson turned to the subject clearly uppermost in his mind that day. He asked Rusk about his suggestion of the day before. Rusk, who had ridden his horses fairly swiftly, replied that State had "come up with an idea that would put additional responsibility on Hanoi for not seeking peace."

Casually pulling a piece of paper from his breast pocket, Rusk read a paragraph he suggested for Johnson's promised speech on Vietnam: "After consultation with our allies, I have directed that U.S. bombing attacks on North Vietnam be limited to those areas which are integrally related to the battlefield. No responsible person could expect us to fail to provide maximum support to our men in combat. Whether this step I have taken can be a step toward peace is for Hanoi to determine."

Rusk explained that no major military sacrifice would follow and that if the enemy launched intensive attacks or failed to respond, bombing could resume. He thought two things were vital: Do not engage in a world campaign à la December, 1965–January, 1966; leave everything on the "de facto level of action," without "conditions or assumptions."[26]

To any who had listened long to Dean Rusk, this proposition reflected a paradigm shift. Always before he had wanted tit for tat, some kind of quid for quo. Now he suggested a "de facto" bombing halt and a wait for a "de facto" response. Not everyone recognized the amazing passage of the secretary of state. Clifford, for instance, heard him in "silent skepticism,"[27] and thought his suggestions covered a cynical "public relations move in order to justify an intensification of the war after its failure—the opposite of the direction I wanted to take." But, not one to miss possibilities, Clifford thought he might subsume Rusk's proposal.[28]

Of all who heard them, Johnson most attentively pondered Rusk's remarks. Sitting at the big cabinet table, looking around at his colleagues, Johnson heard one of the war's real hard-liners suggest a subtle softening for suasion. Tuned to Rusk, appreciative, LBJ had done some mental doodling during the discussion and conjured up a tantalizing scene: What would happen if he followed Rusk's suggestion and also announced his decision not to run for the presidency in 1968? Later that day LBJ told his staff not to enter a stand-in for him in the Massachusetts primary.

For the moment, Johnson and Rusk decided to keep the peace idea more or less secret. If it became too widely known it might be undercut. Flurries of peace were in the air and Johnson wanted to control that arena for just the right moment.[29]

Johnson stepped back from decision for a few days. He wanted a reading on how Congress felt about such things as reserve call-ups and enlistment extensions. He already had a pretty fair notion that old Hill chums would oppose sending two hundred thousand men to Vietnam, but he did ask Wheeler and Clifford to take soundings for him. Talk to Dick Russell, John Stennis, and others, he suggested. See what they could accept.

The answers were what the president expected: Mike Mansfield pretty well summarized congressional feelings in telling Clifford that the administration had "reached the end of the line on increases."[30] Wheeler passed the word to Westmoreland that he might well get no more men than the 10,500 already en route.

On March 8 Johnson made a firm decision. "I am not going to approve 205,000," he told his advisors. "All of you moderated my judgment in that Monday meeting [March 4]. . . . I was ready then to say that we should call up the reserves to strengthen the strategic reserves; to ask Congress for authority to call up selected reservists; to use this as a basis for a new position on the tax bill; and to ask for authority to extend enlistments. That Monday session did moderate my judgment some. I do think we should reevaluate our strategy."[31]

A private session with Clifford that morning may also have helped "moderate" LBJ's views. There is no doubt that it did confirm a suspicion building in Johnson's mind for several days—certainly since the big meeting on the fourth. The new secretary of defense had some old doubts returning. Awkwardly Clifford expressed his worries, tried to gloss them with uncertainty, and, faced with a quiet, level-eyed president, ended by expressing hope that Johnson would take his time making decisions and with the speech that now seemed essential for the national psyche.[32] The friendship between them survived but cooled.[33]

Johnson's own morale fluctuated pretty much with what he heard from Westy, the CIA, and the media. Westy buoyed him, Helms depressed him, and the media often outraged him; he watched public opinion closely.

Rumors reached a few cabinet members of an approaching New York Times scoop on Westy's troop request. Clifford picked up solid information about the coming story at the annual Gridiron Dinner on March 9. The executive editor of the Washington Post told him the Times would lead its Sunday, March 10, edition with a three-column headline: "Westmoreland Requests 206,000 More Men, Stirring Debate in Administration."

That ignited furies on campuses, in legislatures, in all the media, and

Capitol Hill erupted with the pent-up frustrations of Babel. Fulbright flayed Rusk during two rough days of hearings, March 11–12, and cautioned against any furtive escalation. The fact that the whole furor raged ex post facto most angered Johnson—he had already decided against more troops but he found himself in the predicament of not being able to deny it all without sounding defensive, especially in view of the New Hampshire primary on the twelfth.

There were compensations, though. The Sunday morning of the *Times* leak, LBJ won special kudos from a loving wife. She felt deep gloom as she read the papers, but saw none in her husband, whose "voice was hearty," and who had lively stories to tell when he stopped to talk with us. His work . . . ground on and on. I never took off my hat to him more, or felt more tender toward him." There were signs of pressure that she noted, however—"the sties are coming back." She knew that what bothered him most was the unity of the country. He felt he could not keep it together—"is there simply too much built-up antagonism, division, a general malaise, which may have the Presidency—or this President—irrevocably as its focal point?" She noted her husband was "serenely philosophic about politics."[34]

That serenity was shattered the day after the New Hampshire primary. Eugene McCarthy garnered 42 percent of the vote. Johnson, on a write-in ballot, led in the primary and won the state's delegates to the Democratic national convention, but by a bare 7 percent margin. Counting McCarthy's Republican write-ins put him only a few hundred votes behind the president. Doves erupted joyfully. Only later did it become clear that McCarthy benefitted from a good many hawks who voted for him in protest against the administration's limited war policy![35]

New Hampshire hit LBJ like another Tet; his coonskins were peeling off the wall.

While he assessed the damage, others were plotting more surprises. Bobby Kennedy met Clifford in odd circumstances on March 14. Bobby and his close friend Ted Sorenson had a proposal for the president: Kennedy would agree not to run for the Democratic nomination—now much up for grabs—if Johnson would change his Vietnam policy. Sorenson had already broached to LBJ the idea of a blue-ribbon panel to review the war. With Kennedy's obvious concurrence, Sorenson said that if the president would make a public admission of error in Vietnam and announce the appointment of a special review group, Kennedy would stay in the Senate.

Flabbergasted, Clifford said, "Ted, you know as well as I do that the President could not issue a statement saying that this country's policy was a failure."

Kennedy understood. The statement could say Johnson thought the time had come for a total reevaluation; that and the board appointment would be sufficient. When asked who he thought should be included in the group, Kennedy produced a list that was loaded with doves. Clifford tried to explain the futility of Kennedy's proposed deal, the political wreckage it would cause, and the damage a bitter campaign would do to Bobby himself. All to no avail. Clifford dutifully put the proposition to the president, and Johnson, who could never warm to Bobby, rejected the idea instantly. Clifford notified Sorenson, and Bobby entered the race on March 16.

Johnson felt more buffets than ever as March dragged on to the ides. Lady Bird felt that "his life sounded more and more like the tribulations of Job."[36] But he kept his outward calm midst crowding confusion.

Dean Acheson returned to the White House on the fourteenth to render his Vietnam report and found Johnson attentive, well informed, and reasonable. Blunt as ever, the former secretary of state said, "Mr. President, you are being led down the garden path." Send only emergency troops, he said, and then—apparently without prior knowledge of Ted Sorensen's proposition—suggested a high-level panel to look into America's future in Southeast Asia. He doubted the wisdom of military leaders; they wobbled between irrational pessimism and its opposite. Unlike Johnson, he did not think Hanoi would negotiate; the North Vietnamese wanted victory. Too much American blood and money had been wasted in Indochina. Turn the war over to the South Vietnamese, he urged, stop or reduce bombing and find a way out. Johnson listened respectfully to that negative voice.[37] More were murmuring in the wings.

Johnson thought increasingly about not running, even talked favorably of Bobby Kennedy as a possible president in a strangely detached conversation with Harry McPherson and Joe Califano later in the month. Califano predicted Johnson would win if he ran and got a heated response: "Win what? The way it is now we can't get the tax surcharge passed and Ho Chi Minh and Fulbright don't believe anything I say about ending the war."[38] Then Johnson pressed McPherson: "What would be so bad about my not running?"

"Because you're the only guy who can get anything done," the aide replied.

Johnson looked pensive as he said, "Others can get things done. The Congress and I are like an old married couple. We've lived together so long and we've been rubbing against each other night after night so often and we've asked so much of each other over the years we're tired of each other. They'd have a honeymoon. . . . I wouldn't have one."[39]

But he made no decisions and kept listening to anything he could hear about Vietnam; in fact, he asked the State Department to compile current proposals on the war by all kinds of American leaders—including Fulbright, Wayne Morse, and writers from *Time, Newsweek,* and other sources. An hour and a half with Norman Cousins gave him the viewpoint of a militant peace activist—to mix adjectives—and they both learned something from the exchange. Abe Fortas remained an unregenerate hawk. "Take the war to the North," he urged, unleash a massive air campaign, "without explanation or apology."[40] Arthur Goldberg, long on the fringes of power at the UN, finally broke his silence. On March 16 Johnson, at his ranch, read a memorandum from that old friend advocating a complete bombing halt. Stop, Goldberg said, "for the limited time necessary to determine whether Hanoi will negotiate in good faith." Talks in UN halls gave him a perspective different from Fortas or even Clifford, more in tune with Rusk. "No foreseeable time will be better for negotiations than the present and never has a serious move toward a political settlement been more necessary."

The president read Goldberg's proposal with typical care, noting that Rusk had no violent objections and that Rostow thought something like it might work in time. Johnson put Goldberg's memo on the agenda for early discussion. Although he did not intend to stop bombing altogether,[41] he saw it as a possible stalking horse. It might be a good subject for the Vietnam review panel he proposed to organize—LBJ had been impressed with Acheson's idea.[42]

Clark Clifford felt some serious qualms of conscience as his initiation continued. Senator Fulbright sent him a formal request to testify before the Foreign Relations Committee and that put Clifford in a vise—if he testified, the differences between him and Rusk would make world headlines and probably derail all current actions. If he testified, he knew he would lose his influence with LBJ. He had two choices: He could refuse to testify and alienate his old golfing pal, Fulbright, or he could go behind LBJ's back and involve Fulbright in his plot to change America's Vietnam policy. He went to see Fulbright.

"Bill, I must talk to you in absolute confidence. I cannot testify before your committee because I can no longer support, in good conscience, the President's policy. I hope you will let me off the hook, because I can do more good if you leave me alone for a while." Delighted that Clifford had "come around," the senator relented.[43] Clifford's comfort chilled quickly.

Johnson had again gotten away to the ranch. Frustration bubbled in him, resentment against being shoved, fenced in, and he indulged a feeling that things could work out in Vietnam, that the war might still be won. In this mood he had accepted invitations to speak on March 16 and 18 at conventions of the National Alliance for Businessmen in Washington and the National Farmers Union in Minneapolis. When he got worked up and let go, LBJ ranked among the nation's best extemporaneous speakers—in Washington he announced "we are going to win" the war and in Minneapolis he got really worked up.

"Your President," he thundered to a welcoming throng, "your President has come here to ask you people, and all the other people of this nation, to join us in a total national effort to win the war, to win the peace and to complete the job that must be done here at home. . . . We seek the right and we will—make no mistake about it—win." Recalling other wars, the sinking of the *Lusitania,* the heroes of Korea at the Pusan perimeter, the Berlin airlift, he announced "the time has come when we ought to stand up and be counted, when we ought to support our leaders, our government, our men, and our allies until aggression is stopped. . . . We are not doing enough to win it the way we are doing it now. . . . We don't plan to surrender . . . [or] let people influence us, pressure us, and force us to divide our Nation in a time of national peril."[44] The crowd's cheers warmed him, but some in the audience were unpersuaded. A national uproar brought a quick avalanche of mail—most of it hostile.

Jim Rowe, a good and trusted friend who headed Johnson's small reelection staff, asked LBJ on March 19 to tone down the hard-line rhetoric. "I am shocked," he told his boss, "by the number of calls I have received today in protest against your Minnesota speech." Rowe thought that Johnson still held the middle ground, but that most people had moved to the right or left. Then, going beyond his political turf, he suggested a bombing halt over North Vietnam and thought any troop infusion dangerous.[45]

Clark Clifford took Johnson's warlike words as a sobering personal alarm. "The speech . . . reminded me that we were engaged in a tense struggle for the soul and mind of Lyndon Johnson." An unbridgeable chasm apparently opened between LBJ and Clifford. "My God," he remembered thinking, "after only eighteen days in office, am I in such fundamental disagreement with the man who appointed me?" For the first time, the new defense secretary thought he might have to resign. Desperately he looked for ways to pull together some allies and redouble efforts to corral the president.[46]

Most of his allies shared his alarm. McPherson, who let Clifford see drafts of the president's upcoming Vietnam address, wallowed in worry about hard words Johnson inserted. Phrases such as "The American people . . . do not engage in craven retreats from responsibility, whatever the year" showed some of the Minneapolis syndrome alive and well. It might be that the

Clifford cabal was losing the battle for Johnson's mind. Still, final results depended on LBJ's response to the various ideas that inundated him.

Not long after Goldberg's bombing halt proposition surfaced, Chester Bowles, the U.S. ambassador to India, sent in a similar suggestion, and Johnson's longtime friend Drew Pearson, an influential Washington columnist, wrote to say he could no longer stick with present American policies in Vietnam. "I fear," he lamented, "you have been led astray by such short-sighted advisers as Rostow and the military, while some of your other advisers have not spoken up." Obviously Pearson had no hint of the struggles within the administration.[47]

When the Tuesday lunchers met on March 19, Johnson talked calmly of peace feelers—which proliferated—and asked about "the Goldberg-Bowles proposal." Rusk, who sent his own idea for a partial halt along with Goldberg's to Ambassador Bunker for Saigon's reaction, said that Goldberg believed unilateral acceptance of the San Antonio formula would "unify the country. I don't think it will affect the doves." Clifford, unimpressed with the Goldberg plan and increasingly desperate as he realized Johnson's drift to the right, offered another suggestion, one he thought might be the only avenue left to change Johnson's mind.

He knew the president had been toying with the idea of creating a Vietnam review panel and wondered if simply asking the Wise Men back would be a better idea. (In a sense, Clifford stacked his own deck with this suggestion—he had talked with some of these old hands and detected significant shifts of opinion.)[48] A quizzical silence greeted this idea. Johnson worried around it for a while as he saw some dangers: It might look like accepting Kennedy's demand; it might indicate administration doubts; public reaction might be negative since the old hands were known war supporters. Both Rusk and Fortas supported the idea, however, and Johnson finally told Rostow to arrange a meeting for March 25.[49]

Turning finally to his Vietnam speech, LBJ urged haste; he wanted a draft in two days—by the twenty-first. The timing frightened Clifford, who realized that the president still saw this address as a means to justify sending more men to Vietnam and calling up reserves. In none of the drafts McPherson shared was there any hint of a bombing halt. During recent weeks, people in the Pentagon, especially in Warnke's camp, had come to believe that Hanoi would accept the San Antonio formula if a path to talks could be found. A bombing halt would be a clear signal, a sign of good faith, a point Clifford now accepted firmly. Who would Johnson heed in these days of renewed confidence in Vietnam and gruff assertions of his own power? Probably Dean Rusk. Clifford thought Rusk's bombing halt plan cynical (it would last during bad weather) and designed to fail, but he needed help and Rusk's views on building up the ARVN and forcing Saigon to take the war seriously closely approached his own. Somehow he would forge a collaboration.

To anyone who listened closely and watched body language, there were undercurrents of suspicion between Rusk and Clifford—both were jockeying for a presidential decision, and Rusk had a tinge of jealousy that sprang from seniority. Some of Clifford's helpers sensed troubles for their champion, probably stemming from the way he presented things to Johnson: he spoke in generalities, sometimes lofty ones, and lacked Rusk's down-to-earth directness. Johnson sometimes seemed to tune him out, excluding him from some meetings with that estranging crossness of his.[50] But Clifford persisted. His presentations lacked precision because his own thinking had not crystallized. His perception of Johnson's thinking confused him.

The subject of Clifford's machinations pursued a typically baffling course. Old Johnson hands were neither surprised nor comforted by the president's shifts of emphases, his failure to make clear-cut decisions. Always he pushed decisions ahead of him, as Mac Bundy had seen, not only because he had not made up his mind but also because he needed to be flexible and courted secrecy.[51] Bitter experience taught LBJ that almost anything a president contemplates somehow leaks out—often forcing unintended decisions. Then, too, Johnson hated being predictable. Predictability parted the veil of presidential mystery, so much a part of power.

As March waned, Johnson made it clear that he would make the Vietnam speech at the end of the month. President Thieu made an important speech of his own, calling for much harder war efforts. It seemed South Vietnam would soon go to semimobilization.[52] That made LBJ feel even better about the situation there.

Harry McPherson struggled with various pieces of a draft and took what he had to the Cabinet Room for an evening meeting on the twentieth. As everyone gathered, McPherson noted some fresh faces. Mac Bundy, in Washington on business, had been invited, as had William Jorden, former newsman and NSC Far East specialist, Abe Fortas, and Ambassador Goldberg. All of them had come to discuss Johnson's speech, and he gave them a pep talk about what he wanted: "a well-thought-out, well-balanced statement. If . . . nothing new is said, people really will think we are stale." Four areas should receive emphasis, Johnson said, "military strength; economic strength; diplomatic strength; peace." With much feeling, he added, "I want war like I want polio, [but] what you want and what your image is are two different things."

Going around the table, Johnson asked for ideas. Responses wandered from person to prejudice about as expected. Dean Rusk, who had talked with LBJ privately and knew better than most what ideas chased his musings, cited risks and negative signs from Hanoi. Then he read a draft statement proposing highly restricted bombing as possible speech material but received no comment. (Actually, Johnson had no quarrel with it save for some phrasing, but he kept quiet.)[53] Rusk concluded with a realist's assessment: "Unless we are prepared to do something on bombing, there is no real proposal for us to make."

Clifford floundered in real puzzlement. He could not decide which way Johnson leaned. That morning a presidential phone call had confounded his confusion. Johnson, in talking about the speech, said it should indicate a two-handed approach to the North Vietnamese. A military offensive would press the war, while and at the same time, with the other hand, "we had to offer a peace proposal." Johnson wanted him to "come up with something."[54]

Well into the meeting, however, Clifford noted no real presidential enthusiasm for peace proposals. Rusk's effort had generated nothing, and even Walt Rostow's feeling that "we need to turn war to the ballot box" failed to raise an eyelid. Clifford concentrated on Johnson's charge to the group and said the speech should reiterate the importance of Vietnam for the United States as a reason for sending more troops, stress the upcoming months as critical, and reassure the nation of Saigon's increased efforts. It should also review past peace offers and their results.

Although he wanted an end to bombing, Clifford, hoping to win Rusk's support, suggested Johnson might open with an offer to halt all bombing north of the twentieth parallel; if the enemy stopped attacks along the DMZ, the halt would be permanent. "This," he said, sweetening the president's pot, "takes the edge off 'war candidate' vs. peace candidate." For the hawks he added a cynical guess that his plan's effect would be largely psychological, that Hanoi would probably reject the whole thing.

As he looked around he saw general sympathy. Mac Bundy said bombing the whole north did little good and the president observed, sourly, "it brings fury and violence from abroad." Bundy spotted a weakness since "our campaign friends will say we have the President running," but added he advocated an unconditional halt. Rusk agreed and observed that Ambassador Bunker did not like either kind of cessation but thought South Vietnam could accept a partial one.

Arthur Goldberg, slumped behind his thick glasses, listening in growing frustration, finally sat up and broke in emphatically on the side of a complete stoppage. "Our problem is profoundly serious. I am going to talk frankly. . . . Let's don't go with a proposition which will not be acceptable. . . . [The] only thing Hanoi wants is [a] suspension of bombing. . . . Hanoi sees it as a possibility for starting talks. I think we should do that."

Bundy agreed with full suspension and an excited Goldberg explained too much. Finally Johnson asked, "Would I combine this with talk on reserves?"

Goldberg said he thought not, then offered an interesting idea: "I would make [a] peace proposal or a *support of war* speech. I would not combine the two. . . . It won't be seen in good faith if you couple it with troops."

Clifford wondered if Goldberg thought full stoppage would bring Hanoi to talks. The ambassador thought so and Rusk observed, wryly, "Why shouldn't they talk? They get talks and put in men and a sanctuary [in Laos]."

Johnson, looking seriously at Goldberg, expressed a worry that had nagged him before: "You have another Panmunjom."

Goldberg handled that adroitly. "Suppose you continued with no Panmunjom? How many men would you have lost?" he asked.

At that, Abe Fortas, who had listened, frowning, keeping a difficult silence, finally presented his ideas for the speech: it should give a reason for a reserve call-up and avoid any peace offer as a sign of weakness.

Johnson adjourned the meeting after asking for separate proposals on peace and war and saying that he wanted all peace suggestions carefully studied to determine if any of them would expose the men in Vietnam to increased risks.

As he left the Cabinet Room he leaned toward Rusk's ideas; after all, that old Georgia boy understood "the way I wished to move."[55]

Shortly after most of his advisors left, Johnson called a press conference and began tidying things up, doing what needed doing while he still had the full powers of the presidency. Although the timing seemed dreadful in the wake of Tet and all the raucous aftermath, Johnson told reporters he had decided to make General Westmoreland army chief of staff effective in July. Appointing and reassigning commanders stood among the higher callings of the commander in chief and fortunately Johnson had not been faced with Abraham Lincoln's parade of field commanders. Westy's reassignment was timed to coincide with several others. Bus Wheeler's term as chairman of the JCS had been extended an extra year; Adm. U. S. Grant Sharp's tour would end, with his successor to be appointed later, and Gen. Creigton Abrams likely would be the new COMUSMACV, but no announcement came.

Still, no window dressing or media hype could make it seem like anything but kicking Westy upstairs. Even redoubtable Ellsworth Bunker saw Westy's "elevation" as being political.[56] Johnson knew how long the change had been in the works, knew that McNamara had recommended Westy for the post and wanted it to happen. And for Johnson the timing had importance. He would do Westy the kind of justice he thought that loyal and good soldier deserved and, at the same time, send a signal along with his speech of basic changes in American conditions.

That signal would be blurred. Did he want to flag a new strategy along with peace feelers, a conservative strategy of protection not unlike General Navarre's? Or did he want to tell the North Vietnamese that America's resolve would be carried by new men and new ideas? On March 12, LBJ cabled Westy the reasons for his reassignment, saying that McNamara had first recommended it and that Clifford fully concurred. "I cannot find language strong enough," he concluded, "to express the confidence we feel in you; our gratitude for the unique service you have rendered your nation and the cause of freedom in Vietnam; and our satisfaction that you will be joining the team in Washington, where you will be my strong right arm."[57]

Would it not be better, Clifford wondered, if Wheeler met with Westy, explained the reassignment business and got some kind of agreement on lesser troop needs?[58] A consensus on numbers would soothe ruffled congressional feathers and, perhaps, comfort parents with boys in Vietnam.

Wheeler met Westy at Clark Air Base in the Philippines on Sunday morning, March 24. There must have been some tension when the two met. If COMUSMACV felt badly used, he had justification. The chairman had not been honest in reporting their Saigon session. But the two old friends got down to business and talked far into the night. Wheeler had no encouraging words. "The President says very bluntly that he does not have the horses to change our strategy," he said. In case Westy had not already read the tea leaves, Wheeler explained that the war had become mired in politics and that America's determination ebbed. Even old-line hawks like senators Russell and Stennis had turned and the prospects of a reserve call-up appeared dubious. Johnson regretted it all, but hoped his field commander would understand.

Westy chafed, but did understand, and stuck up for his position—the men had been requested for future possibilities. Since he faced no emergency, he could live with the 13,500 proposed, could, in fact, continue his offensive. As consolation, Wheeler told Westy he could keep the 82d Airborne Division brigade, he would get adequate support troops, and he could hire 13,500 civilians to fill some military slots.[59] For the field commander the portents were clear—the limited war would continue in a steady stain of blood.

Two generals returned from the Philippines—Creighton Abrams flew in with Wheeler for "consultations" that might have been a kind of presidential vetting of Westy's heir apparent. Abrams impressed people. A soldier's soldier, blunt often to fault, he suffered fools badly and had bruises in proof. At a meeting with the president on the morning of March 26, Abrams offered encouragement on ARVN progress. Liking what he heard, LBJ invited the generals to brief the Wise Men, saying, "We don't want an inspirational talk or a gloom talk. Just give them the factual, cold, honest picture as you see it."

On Sunday evening, March 25, the Wise Men met for dinner at the big State Department dining room with a fairly impressive government delegation that included Rusk, Clifford, Averell Harriman, Rostow, Helms, General Wheeler, Paul Nitze, Nicholas Katzenbach, and Bill Bundy from State.[60]

Questions from the visitors ranged the whole Vietnam scene—operational conditions after Tet, pacification's progress, and especially the current state of the South Vietnamese government. Dinner done, the whole party moved to the State Department's operations center. Maps of Vietnam were set up and everything ready for the formal briefings by a trio recently assigned the task. Wheeler had been billed for one of the briefings but his Philippine trip left him no time to prepare, so Maj. Gen. William DePuy got the job. Protocol then selected other briefers of similar rank, which had some effect on the briefing's impact.

Philip Habib, Bill Bundy's deputy, a tough Brooklynite with a pungent tongue, described post-Tet conditions in South Vietnam, touched on corruption, a burgeoning refugee problem, and, warming to his gloom, said that Tet had exposed unexpected weaknesses in the Vietnamese government. George Carver, a bland, rotund CIA man with the air of a field agent, gave a mildly dyspeptic assessment of the enemy. General DePuy then presented a report of solid military progress: an impending American offensive, remarkably good efforts by the ARVN, terrible enemy casualties not only during Tet but during the follow-up attacks, which failed miserably.

Questions peppered the briefers; Carver and DePuy, not accustomed to public quizzing, failed the test. Habib, asked by Clifford if he believed military victory was possible, gave a forthright no. Douglas Dillon remembered the optimistic feeling at the November meeting; he felt then that the war could be ended in a year. How long now? he pressed, and sat stunned by the answer: "Maybe five, maybe ten years."

Arthur Goldberg, his lawyer's antennae twirling, hoisted DePuy on his own arithmetic. The general said the enemy had 230,000 men in the field, and had lost 80,000 men in Tet. That baffled Goldberg. "I am not a great mathematician but with 80,000 killed and [even] with a [scaled back] wounded ratio of three to one, or 240,000 wounded, for a total of 320,000, who the hell are we fighting?"[61]

Discussion continued on into the late evening and clear shifts of feeling emerged. Tet's ghost played around the room.[62]

Meeting again in the morning, the group heard Clifford's views on options open to the United States: expand the war into Laos, Cambodia, maybe even into North Vietnam; put in a few thousand more men and rock along with no changes in direction; or try a "reduced strategy" of curtailed bombing, withdrawal from the empty countryside, and protection of population enclaves while the South Vietnamese government gradually took over the war.

After lunch the Wise Men met the president, who introduced them to Wheeler and Abrams. Westy's deputy showed well as a plainspoken, tough officer but without belligerence. He seemed unawed by so much civilian brass and, at the president's invitation, gave a positive report about Vietnam.

When he finished, the questions began to fly. What did he expect in the next weeks? Pressure on Saigon, Abrams replied. "[The enemy] will try to keep up the pressure. He may try at Hue. I don't believe he has the strength to do that."

Serious, the president asked, "What do you see this year?"

Hard fighting and continued attrition of the enemy, considerable improvement of the ARVN and RF/PF units, Abrams answered, emphasizing that the "enemy is making this year an all-out effort."

Goldberg asked if more Tets might happen and Abrams said no. Dillon, obviously worried, asked if a refurbished ARVN could carry more of the fighting. Abrams, directly and emphatically, said, "Yes. I would have to quit if I didn't believe that." Everyone listened carefully.

When Abrams was finished, Mac Bundy straightened up, looked at his notes, and began a summary of what the Wise Men thought. A sea change had swept them, he said, and a majority no longer felt America could achieve a military victory. A majority urged a negotiated solution. Johnson, holding baby grandson Lyn Nugent on his lap, polled the table. Bundy confessed a fundamental change in himself. "I must tell you," that old-line hawk said firmly, "what I thought I would never say, that I now agree with George Ball." Cabot Lodge opted for a strategy of population protection to cut casualties. Dillon, still shaken from the previous night's session, opposed more bombing and more men.

A lot hinged on Acheson, whose presence gave him leadership of the group. Johnson already knew what he thought, but had never before heard it expressed so forcefully. America's world interests demanded rapid disengagement in Vietnam, Acheson said, and added wryly, "The old slogan that success is just around the corner won't work." He castigated the South Vietnamese government as spurious and without support, and condemned American efforts to force victory. When Wheeler objected to that, Acheson erupted, "Then what in the name of God have we got five hundred thousand troops out there for—chasing girls? This is not a semantic game, General. You know damned well that's what we're trying to do—to force the enemy to sue for peace. It won't happen—at least not in any time the American people will permit."[63]

That outburst released some tension, but the polling ran inexorably against the war. George Ball agreed with Acheson. "I have felt that way since 1961—that our objectives are not attainable." He voted to stop the bombing. Cy Vance, to Johnson's surprise, sided with Ball and Bundy.

Some hawks were left. Fortas vehemently advised sticking it out. General Bradley agreed with troop limitation but wanted no cession of American will. Bob Murphy, shaken by what he had just heard, rejected what he called a "giveaway" policy. Max Taylor said he had been reading Vietnam materials for years and had a far different view than the majority's. "Let's not concede the home front; let's do something about it." General Ridgway took a special position, wanting to give Saigon two years to take over the war.

Everyone present worried about the divisions rending the country.

Johnson counted noses. He saw six favoring some kind of disengagement, four opposed, one in between. Mac Bundy wasn't sure things were that clearcut and advocated waiting to see what might result from a bombing halt and increased South Vietnamese responsibility.[64]

Thanking them all, wondering who had "poisoned the well,"[65] LBJ closed the meeting.

Walking with Humphrey back to the Oval Office, Johnson weighed what he had heard. Not all of it had been a surprise; he had known what George Ball thought, Acheson and Ridgway, too. Bundy and Vance had changed, so had Dillon and Arthur Dean. The president pondered what those shifts in thinking told about the country. If Tet had influenced those able, intelligent men so deeply, "what must the average citizen in the country be thinking?"

As if he heard LBJ's thoughts, Humphrey muttered quietly, "Tet really set us back."

Agreeing, Johnson thought the worst damage had been done at home. "We were defeating ourselves."[66]

No one really knew what the president would say, yet. And he had doubts himself. He shared most of the recent lamentations and yet knew that the

United States could not simply turn its back on a bad deal and leave South Vietnam to some unguided fate.

March 28 may have been the day that a lot of thoughts coagulated in the White House. By then everyone around the president realized that changing "the speech" looked to be the only way to change Johnson's Vietnam view. That realization resulted in an unexpected alliance between two polite opponents and in an amusing boast by both of them.

Clifford, Harry McPherson, Rostow, and Bill Bundy gathered in Rusk's office at about 11:00 A.M. Behind the paper shufflings and greetings lurked a sense of urgency. Anyone who looked at Clark Clifford would have noted his nervous anxiety. He had read McPherson's latest draft of Johnson's March 31 speech and wallowed in gloom. Warlike phrases prickled through it, still: "Our will is being challenged. . . . We shall not quit." Clifford had rummaged in vain for any mention of a bombing halt or pause and felt, instead, a blooming bellicosity, although troop numbers remained small. He thought the speech as drafted would hurt Johnson immensely and inflame the country.[67]

With that thought in mind, he opened the meeting bluntly: "I have a fundamental problem with this speech," he said to Rusk. "It is still about war. What the President needs is a speech about peace. We must change it. . . . I believe the first step should be an announcement that we have unilaterally restricted our bombing of the North to the area north of the DMZ. Not that we have paused, but that we have *stopped* bombing north of the 20th parallel. If there is a favorable response from the other side, we should be prepared to take other steps."

Later, Clifford professed surprise when neither Rusk nor Rostow opposed him and instead began a deliberate analysis of what the speech ought to accomplish. All through lunch Clifford schemed to avoid forcing Rusk to a decision. "Finally," he remembers, "I had an idea: let McPherson draft a substitute, a softer speech, and let the President choose between the two. Rusk agreed. . . . Rusk suggested language for the new version of the speech on a partial bombing halt, to which I agreed immediately."

Rusk's recollections ran differently. That the draft lacked a way to peace he knew, that Clifford had grudgingly accepted the idea of partial halt he surely noted. "As we reviewed it, Clark Clifford expressed strong misgivings about its tone and substance. He wanted to soften the language and stress negotiations. Halfway through the meeting, following vigorous discussion of options . . . , I suggested that a second draft be prepared, incorporating many of Clifford's ideas. I also inserted a paragraph outlining a bombing halt . . . which I had intended to add quite apart from Clifford's views."[68]

Both deserve credit for moving toward each other. As Rusk noted, they both realized the collapse of war support and "simply came together on what we must do."[69]

McPherson rushed off to try two versions and Rusk asked Bill Bundy to draft a cable telling Bunker the president had approved a partial bombing halt—just in case the president agreed.

McPherson's second draft had a much different beginning. The first one opened with "I speak to you tonight in a time of grave challenge to our country." The new one began, "Tonight I want to speak to you of the prospects of peace in Vietnam."

Rusk saw Johnson that evening and advised him to use the second draft. The president read both drafts and came, finally, to Rusk's passage in the second:

> Beginning immediately, and without waiting for any signal from Hanoi, we will confine our air and naval attacks in North Vietnam to the military targets south of the 20th parallel. . . . North Vietnam's military reaction to this change in our bombing programs will determine both our willingness to confine it—and the reasonableness of our assumption that they would not take advantage of a complete bombing halt during the course of negotiations.[70]

Johnson liked it, had decided it "needed to be done," but made no flat acceptance. He feared another leak that might weaken his speech—and also might rob him of a moment of a surprise. Rusk, though, could see the coming presidential mindset, especially when Johnson approved the cable to Bunker. Johnson thought the cable too pessimistic—it stressed expectations of enemy rejection—but he knew he had an unexpected card to play, one that might tilt the pot toward peace.

CONSPIRACIES' RESULT

Nobody knew for sure. Even those close to the White House were uncertain. Lady Bird had ideas, had agonized with her husband for days about whether he would run for reelection; she had read several drafts of his speech as well as several versions of a paragraph he might add at the end. But she knew him well, knew that even he did not know; seething deep within him were signals to fight for his job, stay for the war and others to "rise above" politics to a statesman's role of peacemaker. She suffered with him.

Lynda came in on a "red-eye" flight from California at seven in the morning on Sunday, March 31. Her parents greeted her at the entrance to the

Diplomatic Reception Room and were shocked by her appearance. Her mother thought she looked like a ghost. Lynda had come from Camp Pendleton after seeing her husband off to Vietnam, had taken a sedative on the plane, and that probably made her look wraithlike and withdrawn. Why, she cried to her father, was Chuck going away to fight, perhaps die, "for people who did not even want to be protected?"[71] After this outburst, her mother put her to bed and then joined her husband.

"When I went back into Lyndon's room," Lady Bird recalled, "his face was sagging and there was such pain in his eyes as I had not seen since his mother died."

Later in the morning the president and Lady Bird talked with houseguests Arthur and Mathilde Krim and he read them a paragraph he said would end his speech that night. They had heard him talk of bowing out of the race, often wondered if he should, had counseled and disbelieved and slowly thought he might. But after he finished reading the statement, all four were oddly quiet. "Maybe," thought the First Lady, "maybe it was the calm finality in Lyndon's voice, and maybe we believed him for the first time."[72] When he told Muriel and Hubert Humphrey, that good and faithful man expressed the hope LBJ would not do it.

All of it had been said, thought over, and suffered about. Now Lyndon Johnson faced the moment of decision. What he would say would chart history, he hoped, in ways to save the young men of all the warring sides, save the national mind from a paranoia of itself. That it must be done he knew, had known, and had worked out his own acceptance in his heart. And yet it seemed, as the time approached, altogether too hard a thing to ask of him, to go before the world and turn away from all he'd worked to win for four abrading years. How could he tell the parents of the dead and serving that the crusade somehow had become a broken dream that blood itself could not mend? Those thoughts were surely in him and doubts were hard to stifle; and yet it would not be a confession of defeat. He would not dishonor or neglect America's pledge to South Vietnam but would keep that faith in different ways.

Good news from Vietnam lifted LBJ's heart; bad news from J. Edgar Hoover about possible race troubles at home smothered it again. Luci and Pat Nugent went with Johnson to mass at Saint Dominic's later that day, and the president felt some comfort coming from the sere spires and ceremony.

In the White House that afternoon, secretaries worked on pieces of the speech. Harry McPherson was ecstatic; LBJ had asked him to massage the softer speech! Horace Busby knew; in the Lincoln Room he worked on a final paragraph with George Christian's occasional help. Juanita Roberts, that marvelous organizer of Oval Office business, knew; so did Marie

Fehmer, loyal personal secretary. Marvin Watson, guardian of the presidential calendar, knew and resisted. Rusk had some hints but no certainty.

The media all guessed wrong—again. Tom Wicker summed up the erroneous bias in a late-1967 *New York Times* piece: "It is as likely that Lyndon Johnson will get out of the White House and go back to Texas as it is that Dean Rusk will turn dove, Dick Nixon will stop running, or J. Edgar Hoover will retire."[73]

Nervousness stalked the White House, too, with Lady Bird thinking she "ought to do *something* . . . but what?" She kept looking at the clock circling so slowly toward nine.[74]

People began coming around eight; Marvin Watson, Arthur Krim to plead against withdrawal, then Walt and Elspeth Rostow, Clark and Marny Clifford. The president pulled Clifford into his bedroom and showed him the new ending. Stunned, the defense secretary asked, "You've made up your mind?"

"Yes," LBJ replied, "I've made up my mind totally."

Sententious ever in momentous moments, Clifford said, "I understand your decision, Mr. President, but that does not keep me from deeply regretting it. If this is your decision, then it becomes my decision."[75]

In a later afterthought, Clifford observed that Johnson should have told his close advisors that he would not run—it would have changed the tone of the speech they were writing. Still, he continued to wonder if LBJ really knew himself before the moment the words were spoken. The secretary felt the two subjects—peace and recusal—should not have been combined in one speech. Separate statements would have made withdrawal look less a Tet result and "perhaps strengthened him for the remainder of his term." But Johnson's vulnerability might be revetted as Clifford moved from counsel to consul.[76]

At about 8:45, Lady Bird, Clifford, Busby, and a distraught Lynda—who thought her father alone could stop the war—went to the Oval Office. "What a stage setting," Lady Bird thought as she tiptoed across cables, around and under TV lights, to the big desk where her husband sat quietly, his face deeply lined but in a "marvelous sort of repose." She leaned over him, whispering, "Remember—pacing and drama." She thought the speech was "great" and wanted it to be his personal best.

Flashbulbs popped, the producer checked sound and lighting, and then the red light came. The president, looking directly into the camera, launched into his speech:

Good evening, my fellow Americans:
Tonight I want to speak to you of peace in Vietnam and Southeast

Asia. No other question so preoccupies our people. No other dream so absorbs the 250 million human beings who live in that part of the world. No other goal motivates American policy in Southeast Asia.

Then he rehearsed the many failed peace ventures and gave a positive review of Tet while warning that more attacks might come as the war went on. "There is no need for this to be so." he said. In hope of peace talks, he announced a halt to bombing North Vietnam, save for a strategic area just north of the DMZ. If Hanoi responded favorably, all bombing would stop. Brandishing his olive branch, LBJ announced the appointment of Averell Harriman as his personal negotiator, with help from Ambassador Llewellyn Thompson. They would go to Geneva or any other place to talk with Hanoi's representatives. He added an important point:

> Some weeks ago—to help meet the enemy's new offensive—we sent to Vietnam about 11,000 additional Marine and airborne troops. They were deployed by air in 48 hours, and other units that were needed to work with and support these infantry troops in combat could not accompany them on that short notice.
>
> In order that these forces may reach maximum combat effectiveness, the Joint Chiefs of Staff have recommended to me that we should prepare to send—during the next five months—support troops totalling approximately 13,500 men.

The president could not promise results from what he had started that night, but he expressed "fervent hope" that North Vietnam would move toward negotiations. With special emphasis he said:

> There is division in the American house now. There is divisiveness among us all tonight. And holding the trust that is mine, as President of all the people, I cannot disregard the peril to the progress of the American people and the hope and prospect of peace for all peoples. . . .
>
> Fifty-two months and ten days ago, in a moment of tragedy and trauma, the duties of this office fell upon me. I asked then for your help and God's, that we might continue America on its course, binding up our wounds, healing our history, moving forward in a new unity, to clear the American agenda and to keep the American commitment for all of our people. . . .
>
> Through all time to come, I think America will be a stronger nation, a more just society, and a land of greater opportunity and fulfillment

because of what we have all done together in these years of unparalleled achievement. . . .

What we won when all of our people united just must not now be lost in suspicion, distrust, selfishness, and politics among any of our people.

A momentary pause, while all the friends around him wondered, then:

Believing this as I do, I have concluded that I should not permit the Presidency to become involved in the partisan divisions that are developing in this political year.

With America's sons in the fields far away, with America's future under challenge right here at home, with our hopes and the world's hopes for peace in the balance every day, I do not believe that I should devote an hour or a day of my time to any personal partisan causes or to any duties other than the awesome duties of this—the Presidency of your country.

Accordingly, I shall not seek, and I will not accept, the nomination of my Party for another term as your President.

And let men everywhere know, however, that a strong, a confident, and a vigilant America stands ready tonight to seek an honorable peace —and stands ready tonight to defend an honored cause—whatever the price, whatever the burden, whatever the sacrifices that duty may require.

Thank you for listening.

Good night and God bless all of you.[77]

It was over. An air of stunned relief permeated the Oval Office and the president arose and began walking around, talking to people and relishing the bewilderment he had caused. Luci threw her arms around her father, Lynda kissed him, Pat Nugent shook his hand. Amidst the clatter of ringing telephones, LBJ finished talking to some friends, then walked with Clifford back toward the family wing and said, "I never felt so right about any decision in my life." Clifford watched energy flowing back in that great bulking human who had again taken charge.

Lady Bird's heart glowed and sorrowed for him. Her hopes were gratified; he had given a great speech. "Those who love him must have loved him more," his wife believed, and "those who hate him at least have thought: 'Here is a man.'" The Rostows were subdued. An ebullient commander in chief looked ahead. "I have 525,000 men whose very lives depend on what I do, and I can't afford to worry about the primaries. Now I will be working full time for those men out there. The only guys that won't be back here by the time my term ends are the guys that are left in the last day or two of my term."[78]

The clogged White House switchboard and the swamped mail room recorded oceans of messages from friends, enemies, and unknown folks from everywhere. "They were messages wishing me well," that touched LBJ's deep need for love, "from people who simply wanted me to know they were thinking of me . . . but they left their names and something of themselves that I will remember to the end of my life. There was a steady refrain: 'Just tell him my prayers are with him.'"[79]

The president's announcement struck sober notes in Saigon, where the country team worried lest the enemy take advantage. Two thoughts raced through the streets of that war-swept capital: LBJ had pulled a political trick to insure reelection; LBJ meant it and America would soon quit South Vietnam under the obvious successor, Bobby Kennedy. A Communist official boasted to the troops that LBJ's decisions were forced by the sacrifices and travails of the People's Liberation Army. Bill Fulbright told the Senate on April 2 that nothing had changed; LBJ's grandstanding offered no real hope for positive peacemaking efforts, which sparked heated reaction from some old and some newfound friends in the Senate.

And how did the conspirators feel? Wheeler got few reserves but had a heavy hand in pushing Johnson away from the war, and so, in a sense, damaged his own cause. Clifford thought he had been the one that changed America's course in history and basked in his own reflections.

On Wednesday morning, April 3, while the president entertained his grandson and Sen. and Mrs. Henry Jackson and their two children, Tom Johnson ran into the Oval Office waving a piece of ticker tape. A bulletin from Singapore said, in effect, that Hanoi was ready to talk. A long statement from the government of North Vietnam followed, filled with expected rhetoric but stating its willingness to meet. Johnson showed Scoop Jackson the message and said, "It looks like it's turning out the way we hoped it would."[80]

chapter

Requiem
for a Tortured Soul

uphoria lasted briefly, like all moods in Washington. Early in April, 1968, black leader Martin Luther King was shot dead in Memphis and America suddenly teetered on fiery chaos. King's aura lingered in the smoky air of 110 burning cities—his dream of justice, even for an end to Vietnam, eddied dimly in the hateful air. Lyndon Johnson, who shared much of King's hope, felt a harder blow than Tet to the things he cherished most. Would the Great Society rend in racial division?[1]

On June 4, 1968, America took another blow to democracy. Robert F. Kennedy—JFK's brother, former attorney general, U.S. senator, and presidential candidate—was shot dead in Los Angeles after winning the California primary.

Somehow, there seemed an odd logic in the senselessness—that the country kept attacking itself from behind, that some kind of anger chopped at progress for peace, for justice, for honor, for humanity. Johnson appointed a commission to consider American violence[2] and wondered, in the midst of tragedy, why he and Bobby had never been close. There was dysfunctional chemistry between them, dysfunctional history, and an occluding dual ambition. But Bobby's death soon faded into a wallow of deaths and disasters. The U.S. ambassador to Guatemala was shot, Russian troops invaded

Czechoslovakia on August 21 (short-circuiting missile talks about to be held with the United States). That week, too, students, dissidents, and police disrupted the Democratic National Convention in Chicago, where Hubert Humphrey accepted the nomination and to which LBJ received no invitation. Scenes of savage fighting spilled across the national news.

Saddened, horrified, LBJ watched and knew that the North Vietnamese watched as well and gloated. Wearily he kept the power tokens and held the government together. Expecting Richard Nixon to be nominated by the Republicans, LBJ tried to keep all the candidates (including George Wallace) informed of presidential actions, and especially aware of the peace process in Paris. And the process dragged alarmingly. Haggling over a North Vietnamese demand for a total bombing halt as a basis for further discussion ground up weeks of time. Ambassador Harriman and Cyrus Vance, representing the United States, stressed three counterpoints: "prompt and serious" talks including representatives of South Vietnam must follow a full bombing halt; Hanoi must not violate the DMZ in any way; and continued attacks against major South Vietnamese cities must cease. American representatives kept asking for evidence of "reciprocity"—what would North Vietnam give in return for an end to the bombing? Slowly, agonizingly, there were bits and pieces of progress. America, true to its word, stopped the bombing at the nineteenth parallel, but North Vietnamese attacks continued against Saigon and other large cities in the south. Casualties mounted.

More skeptical than most about the negotiations, LBJ kept badgering his delegation. In mid-September, Johnson had a long talk with Harriman about Paris. That veteran negotiator thought the North Vietnamese representatives were serious, but doubted that they would ever give open assurances of reciprocity because their political situation precluded this concession.

A crack came in October when North Vietnamese representatives asked privately if including South Vietnam in the talks (representatives of the National Liberation Front would be present) would end the bombing. Johnson, hopeful, reacted carefully. An apparent thaw deserved analysis and the president asked Ambassador Bunker and General Abrams if a halt under the three U.S. conditions would be acceptable. The answer was yes. Bunker thought that "Hanoi is ready for a tactical shift from the battlefield to the conference table." Abrams and Bus Wheeler, even Clark Clifford, believed that North Vietnam considered the war lost and wanted a face-saving way out.[3] Military optimism aroused Johnson's deep-struck urge to victory and he nursed it by believing that bombing could resume if U.S. conditions were not met; nevertheless, LBJ pushed the negotiations.[4] He knew that a bombing halt would appear to be motivated by domestic politics—it would look like an effort to help Humphrey—but he kept the candidates informed and supportive.

At last, on October 27, Hanoi told the U.S. delegation that, in return for a bombing cessation, "expanded" talks based on the three U.S. conditions could start on November 2. There would be a joint Washington-Saigon-Hanoi-NLF announcement on October 31. Suddenly, Saigon backed out. Intense conversations between Bunker and President Thieu had first indicated South Vietnamese agreement, but the presence of the NLF in Paris eroded Thieu's domestic political support in the National Assembly and he raised new worries. Saigon wanted more time, assurances that South Vietnamese negotiators would deal only with the North Vietnamese.

Anger and frustration clouded presidential conferences through a hectic three days. What had gone wrong? South Vietnam's sudden balk shook LBJ. "I thought we would have known about Thieu's problems," he carped, and listened as his advisors reported on Thieu's fears of a coup and suspicions of a possible U.S. sellout.[5] Washington could not force Saigon to agree—despite some sentiment in that direction. Rusk ruefully said that if talks proceeded without Saigon they would be a debacle—but "that's why we have diplomats. We are the department of debacles."[6]

Still, Rusk urged patience and told the Tuesday lunchers on October 29:

President Kennedy said we would make a battle . . . to save South Vietnam. That set us on course. We lost 29,000 men and invested $75 billion to keep South Vietnam from being overrun. We must be careful not to flush this down the drain. But we do have a right to expect cooperation from the South Vietnamese. Thieu and Ky agreed to this. . . . If the problem in Saigon is only a matter of timing, we should set a time convenient to them.[7]

Gradually through the discussion came wafting suggestions that U.S. politics played an important role in Saigon's hesitations. As the election campaign escalated, Humphrey and Nixon took divergent views on the war, with Nixon staking a strong position on getting out and Humphrey hesitantly trying to sidle away from LBJ's policies. Public reaction showed the confusion of the situation, but gradually plumped on Nixon's side. He had, he said, patting his coat pocket, a secret plan to end the war.

Secrets there were, deep ones that traced back to Richard Nixon's New York apartment and to a renegade strain in American politics. Constitutionally, presidents are supposed to be in charge of U.S. foreign policy but they often receive unwelcome help, not only from Congress but also from individuals—and the individuals can do real mischief. Two people, acting in a kind of semiofficial role through Nixon's campaign organization, confused and nearly wrecked the Paris peace talks: South Vietnam's Washington ambassador, Bui Diem, and Anna Soong Chennault, sister of Madame Chiang Kai-shek, widow of famed Flying Tigers leader, Maj. Gen. Claire Chennault, and chair of the Republican Women for Nixon. Early in 1969 she apparently introduced Diem to Nixon, who asked him to work with Campaign chairman John Mitchell. Rumors and hints chaff through the murk of what happened, but it is clear that President Thieu got the distinct impression Nixon would offer Saigon a better deal than lame-duck Johnson. A bombing halt might elect Humphrey, and that would spell trouble for Saigon at the peace talks.

Intelligence reports came to the White House about Chennault, Mitchell, Nixon, and Diem. Republican interference in the peace process struck Clifford as "potentially illegal."[8] It was certainly a direct interference in foreign policy. Johnson fumed—he wanted to blow the lid and make the whole thing public, but there were too many questions and uncertainties. No evidence pinned responsibility directly on Nixon, and a revelation of outside interference would erode confidence in whoever was elected president. So Johnson kept quiet. It was a decision that Rusk supported and that Clifford viewed as a slap at Humphrey.[9]

Johnson found himself in a tortured dilemma. Too much pressure on Thieu might topple his government, which would ruin the whole American effort in Vietnam. At the same time, the recalcitrant ally could not dictate the outcome of the November election. Despite feeling that the South Vietnamese leaders "had let me down,"[10] Johnson had some sympathy for them— South Vietnam's aims were different from America's. War created and American aid sustained that nation—sudden peace could fragment the country, especially a peace that seemed somehow to recognized the NLF.

There were other considerations, of course, at this crisis time. How did the Joint Chiefs and General Abrams feel about a complete bombing halt? Would too much military momentum be lost? Johnson called Abrams to Washington and grilled him before the Vietnam group in an after-midnight session on October 29. Abrams approved fully and said the military situation was steadily improving. The president listened, fidgeted, and waxed optimistic and depressed. Without Thieu's agreement, aware of the political pressures at home, Johnson, at 8 P.M. on October 31, 1968, told the world that "I have now ordered that all air, naval and artillery bombardment of North Vietnam cease as of 8 A.M., Washington time, Friday morning."[11] He also announced new Paris talks on November 6, and said South Vietnamese representatives "are free to participate." They came, at last, on December 8 —after Richard Nixon became President-elect of the United States.

By January 18, 1969, arrangements were completed to start the next round of peace talks—two days before LBJ left the White House. Good news, of course, but somehow sad, the kind of news that begs questions of decisions, successes, and failures. Johnson "regretted more than anyone could possibly know that I was leaving . . . without having achieved a just, an honorable, and a lasting peace in Vietnam," but took some comfort in "turning over to my successor a situation more promising and manageable than it had been for years."[12]

Last days are nostalgic, lonely ones, days to worry the past. A great pageant passed across Johnson's mind, a pageant of the Great Society, crippled as it was by Vietnam, but still a shining promise of what America could achieve in its heart and in its strength. Vietnam seemed hardly a pageant, and yet there were good things about promises fulfilled, of Communism for a time corralled, of valor for what seemed right.

To the lonely man in the White House making ready to return to Texas, the last days and hours of his presidency had deep, disturbing poignance. There were snubs that hurt—his party shunned him, public opinion shifted, and the trappings fell away. He had done the things that made the pageants, yet there was so much more he wanted to do. Always, it seemed, he wanted something, some talisman of love beyond the gift of family and friends, a talisman beyond the daily carpings of office and of things done right and wrong.

What could this flawed giant want beyond his awesome reach? As a politician he knew the short memory of democracy; as a realist he knew the fickleness of fame; as a man he knew what he had done. In the days after the White House, the few years at the ranch, what was it that Lyndon Johnson wanted, still? Of fame, friendship, and hatred he had had more than most mortals. He had taken on JFK's battles and fought them doggedly, he had an American vision that achieved things for blacks and the poor and downtrodden beyond any president's boast. Yet he realized that whatever he wanted would be blurred by Vietnam prejudices, because Vietnam shrouded him like Lady Bird's black cloud. What did he want?

He feared what he wanted with a fear that quenched him some and gave, too, a kind of hope. He wanted something he could not guarantee—he wanted well of history. The hope was that his record would weigh for him, the fear was of the man that others saw.

There was, in Lyndon Johnson, much of America's own self. Big, powerful, full of hope for the future, and determined to protect democracy, he struck many as a colossus without conscience, and yet one that somehow touched the hope of millions in the world.

notes

CHAPTER 1

1. Lyndon B. Johnson, *The Vantage Point: Perspectives on the Presidency, 1963–1969*, 17.

2. *The World Book Encyclopedia*, 1995 ed., s.v. "Lyndon Baines Johnson"; Robert Dallek, *Lone Star Rising: Lyndon Johnson and His Times, 1908–1960*.

3. Lady Bird Johnson, *A White House Diary*, 16.

4. Jack Valenti, *A Very Human President*, 39.

5. Johnson, *Vantage Point*, 15, 19.

6. Ibid., 20.

7. Ibid., 41.

8. Ibid., 29–30.

9. The phrase "inheriting a shambles" is from Phillip B. Davidson, *Vietnam at War: The History, 1946–1975*, 303.

10. See John P. Glennon and Edward C. Keefer, eds., *Vietnam August–December, 1963*, volume 4 of *Foreign Relations of the United States, 1961–1963* series, 536–37.

11. Johnson, *Vantage Point*, 43–44; John A. McCone Oral History, August 19, 1970, Lyndon Baines Johnson Library, Austin, Texas.

12. Author's interview with Mrs. Lyndon B. Johnson, June 18, 1990.

13. Stanley Karnow, *Vietnam: A History*, 213.

14. Ibid., 214.

15. Johnson, *Vantage Point*, 44.

16. Author's interview with McGeorge Bundy, December 8, 1988.

17. Ibid.

18. Johnson, *Vantage Point*, 45. This NSAM was issued on November 26, 1963.

19. LBJ, *Vantage Point*, 44–45.; author's interview with McGeorge Bundy, December 8, 1988; Neil Sheehan et al., *The Pentagon Papers as Published by the New York Times*, 232–33.

20. Johnson, *Vantage Point*, 24.

21. Ibid.

22. *Public Papers of the Presidents of the United States, Lyndon B. Johnson, 1963–1969*, vol. 1, 8.

23. Johnson, *Vantage Point*, 42.

24. Mike Gravel, ed., *The Pentagon Papers: The Defense Department History of United States Decisionmaking in Vietnam*, vol. 3, 494.

25. Gravel, *Pentagon Papers*, vol. 3, 496.

26. Author's interview with McGeorge Bundy, April 15, 1991.

27. Karnow, *Vietnam*, 395.

CHAPTER 2

1. Valenti, *Very Human President*, 159.

2. Davidson, *Vietnam at War*, 290.

3. Davidson, *Vietnam at War*, 312; Gravel, *Pentagon Papers*, vol. 3, 502.

4. *Karnow,* Vietnam, 338.

5. Ibid., 334.

6. Author's interviews with McGeorge Bundy, November 12, 1990, and April 15, 1991; Davidson, *Vietnam at War,* 304.

7. Memorandum, McNamara to the President, March 16, 1964, in Gravel, *Pentagon Papers,* vol. 3, 499–500.

8. Johnson, *Vantage Point,* 575.

9. Ibid., 180–87.

10. Author's interview with McGeorge Bundy, November 12, 1990.

11. Ibid., February 7, 1990.

12. Author's interviews with Jack Valenti, June 27, 1991; McGeorge Bundy, November 12, 1990; George Ball, December 7, 1988; Paul Nitze, July 26, 1990.

13. Author's interview with William Bundy, December 7, 1988.

14. For a clear description of the De Soto program, see Eugene Windchy, *Tonkin Gulf,* chap. 4.

15. Gravel, *Pentagon Papers,* vol. 3, 508.

16. Ibid. See also Johnson, *Vantage Point,* 66–67.

17. Davidson, *Vietnam at War,* 317.

18. Johnson, *Vantage Point,* 67.

19. Windchy, *Tonkin Gulf,* 54–70.

20. Ibid., 117.

21. Ibid., chap. 4–7; Karnow, *Vietnam,* 366–69; Johnson, *Vantage Point,* 112–13; author's interview with Adm. Thomas Moorer, December 7, 1989; Davidson, *Vietnam at War,* 317–21; Wilbur H. Morrison, *The Elephant and the Tiger: The Full Story of the Vietnam War,* 138–41; Dean Rusk, *As I Saw It,* 144.

22. Johnson, *Vantage Point,* 112–13.

23. Ibid., 114–15.

24. Author's interview with McGeorge Bundy, February 7, 1990.

25. Ibid.; Adm. U. S. G. Sharp, *Strategy for Defeat: Vietnam in Retrospect,* 42–44.

26. Gravel, *Pentagon Papers,* vol. 3, 184–86; Karnow, *Vietnam,* 371.

27. Author's interviews with Adm. U. S. G. Sharp, December 17, 1988; Adm. Thomas Moorer, December 7, 1989; Comd. Gordon Jones, December 20, 1988.

28. Author's telephone interview with William Bundy, August 24, 1992.

29. Karnow, *Vietnam,* 371.

30. Johnson, *Vantage Point,* 115–16.

31. Ibid., 116–17; Rusk, *As I Saw It,* 444–45.

32. Morrison, *Elephant and Tiger,* 141; Guenter Lewy, *America in Vietnam,* 32–36. Windchy, *Tonkin Gulf,* 224–25, discusses the timing confusion which found Johnson announcing action one and one-half hours before it happened.

33. The complete text of the resolution is in Windchy, *Tonkin Gulf,* 19–20.

34. Lewy, *America in Vietnam,* 35.

35. Rusk, *As I Saw It,* 445.

36. Johnson, *Vantage Point,* 110; Richard Goodwin, *Remembering America: A Voice from the Sixties,* 303–305.

37. Valenti, *Very Human President,* 118.

38. Author's interview with Alec Douglas, Lord Home, October 29, 1988. For some official details of the prime minister's visit, February 12, 1964, see *Public Papers,* 1963–64, 293–95.

39. See Karnow, *Vietnam,* 412; Davidson, *Vietnam at War,* 335–36.

40. See Karnow, *Vietnam,* 404–10; Johnson, *Vantage Point,* 120–21; Herbert Y. Schandler, *The Unmaking of a President: Lyndon Johnson and Vietnam,* 8–11.

41. As quoted in Johnson, *Vantage Point,* 122.

42. Lyndon B. Johnson, *The Choices We Face,* 24. See also Schandler, *Unmaking of President,* 7–17; Karnow, *Vietnam,* 397–400, 404–11; Gravel, *Pentagon Papers,* vol. 3, 275–79, 293–98, 302–306; Douglas Kinnard, "The Soldier as Ambassador: Maxwell Taylor in Saigon, 1964–65," *Parameters: US Army War College Quarterly* 21 (Spring, 1991): 34–38. See also author's interview with John B. Connally, September 17, 1991; William P. Bundy's Oral History, May 29, 1969, LBJ Library.

43. Gravel, *Pentagon Papers,* vol. 3, 134.

44. Ibid., 137–39; Karnow, *Vietnam,* 410; Johnson, *Vantage Point,* 121–22.

45. George Ball, *The Past Has Another Pattern: Memoirs,* 382; George Ball's Oral History, July 8, 1971, LBJ Library, for the "once you get one of those things" quotation.

46. Johnson, *Vantage Point,* 122.

47. Gravel, *Pentagon Papers,* vol. 3, 303.

48. Ibid.

49. Karnow, *Vietnam,* 413.

50. Ball, *Past,* 390.

51. Ibid.

52. For the Johnson quotation see *Vantage Point,* 125. For the treatment of Humphrey, see Ball, *Past,* 390, and Karnow, *Vietnam,* 413.

53. Details of the air strikes vary with the sources. See, for example, Neil Sheehan et al., *Pentagon Papers, NYT,* 343; Gravel, *Pentagon Papers,* vol. 3, 302–303; Davidson, *Vietnam at War,* 336; Johnson, *Vantage Point,* 125; and Karnow, *Vietnam,* 413.

54. Johnson, *Vantage Point,* 125; *Public Papers,* 1965, vol. 1, 153–54.

55. Gravel, *Pentagon Papers,* vol. 3, 306.

56. Ibid., 273; Davidson, *Vietnam at War,* 336; Johnson, *Vantage Point,* 130.

57. Davidson, *Vietnam at War,* 342.

58. Johnson, *Vantage Point,* 42.

59. Karnow, *Vietnam,* 415–16; Schandler, *Unmaking of President,* 19–20.

60. Karnow, *Vietnam,* 417.

61. Ball, *Past,* 392.

62. See George Ball, "Vietnam Papers," a collection of his memoranda to LBJ on peace options, in author's possession.

63. See Johnson, *Vantage Point,* 68. On the impact of "losing China," see Brian VanDeMark, *Into the Quagmire: Lyndon Johnson and the Escalation of the Vietnam War,* xiv; Davidson, *Vietnam at War,* 335; Doris Kearns, *Lyndon Johnson and the American Dream,* 253.

64. Author's interviews with Jack Valenti, June 27, 1991, and Walt Rostow, April 12, 1990.

65. Ibid., with Walt Rostow, April 12, 1990; Dean Rusk, October 12, 1988; and Jack Valenti, June 27, 1991; U. Alexis Johnson's oral history, June 14, 1969, LBJ Library; author's telephone interview with McGeorge Bundy, October 14, 1991.

66. See Valenti, *Very Human President,* 108; author's interviews with Valenti, June 27, 1991; McGeorge Bundy, April 15, 1991; and Mrs. Lyndon Johnson, June 18, 1990; Ball, *Past,* 393–94.

67. Author's interview with William Bundy, December 7, 1988.

68. See George Herring's suggestion that LBJ "brought to the White House the Southern populist's suspicion of the military," in "'Cold Blood': LBJ's Conduct of Limited War in Vietnam," *Harmon Memorial Lectures in Military History,* no. 23

(1990): 3. See also author's interviews with Jack Valenti, June 27, 1991; Richard Helms, October 17, 1988; and Cyrus Vance, February 5, 1990.

69. See author's interview with McGeorge Bundy, April 15, 1991.

70. For the Bundy working group report and reactions to it, see Gravel, *Pentagon Papers,* vol. 3, 210–51. See also Johnson, *Vantage Point,* 122–27.

71. Johnson, *Vantage Point,* 126.

72. Ibid., 127; Gravel, *Pentagon Papers,* vol. 3, 312. Emphasis in the original.

73. Johnson, *Vantage Point,* 128.

74. Ibid., 128–29.

75. Taylor would recall that "I soon sensed that, having crossed the Rubicon on February 7 [the Pleiku bombing decision] he [LBJ] was now off to Rome on the double." See Maxwell Taylor, *Swords and Ploughshares,* 121.

76. See George Ball's Oral History, July 8, 1971, LBJ Library.

CHAPTER 3

1. Johnson, *Diary,* 6.

2. Valenti, *Very Human President,* 60; Johnson, *Diary,* 523, 763. This account of the Johnson White House relies heavily on Emmette S. Redford and Richard T. McCulley, *White House Operations: The Johnson Presidency.*

3. See Juanita Roberts oral history, August 29, 1969, LBJ Library, for a detailed account of White House routine.

4. Valenti, *Very Human President,* 60.

5. For the secretarial roles and early staff, see Valenti, *Very Human President,* 46–81; Joseph A. Califano, Jr., *The Triumph and the Tragedy of Lyndon Johnson: The White House Years,* 20, 22, 26, 29, 60, 93, 143; Liz Carpenter, *Ruffles and Flourishes: The Warm and Tender Story of a Simple Girl Who Found Adventure in the White House,* 1–31. Lady Bird Johnson's *Diary* is a rich mine of information on daily White House activities.

6. Johnson, *Vantage Point,* 74–75.

7. See Robert Dallek, *Lone Star Rising: Lyndon Johnson and His Times, 1908–1960,* chap. 2.

8. Johnson, *Vantage Point,* 69–72. Johnson realized he had an advantage in that most people saw him as a "populist," which he knew to be an eastern translation of "southern progressive."

9. Ibid., xi.

10. Ibid., 69–72.

11. For the planning and early history of the War on Poverty, see Johnson, *Vantage Point,* 76–81; for Larry O'Brien, see Valenti, *Very Human President,* 52, 62.

12. For the O'Neill quote, see Thomas O'Neill with William Novak, *Man of the House: The Life and Political Memoirs of Speaker Tip O'Neill,* 207.

13. Valenti, *Very Human President,* 62.

14. The survey of Johnson's domestic team relies heavily on Califano's *Triumph and Tragedy,* as well as on Valenti's *Very Human President.* For Clifford's views on Moyers, see Clark Clifford, *Counsel to the President: A Memoir,* 430.

15. Valenti, *Very Human President,* 54.

16. See Califano, *Triumph and Tragedy,* 17–18.

17. Valenti, *Very Human President,* 63.

18. Ibid., 64.

19. For Jenkins, see ibid., 69; Califano, *Triumph and Tragedy,* 19–20; Clifford, *Counsel to President,* 399–402.

20. Quoted in Dallek, *Lone Star Rising,* 352.

21. Author's interview with Dean Rusk, November 12, 1988; Rusk, *As I Saw It,* 328.

22. For Ball's quote, see Ball, *Past,* 161. For his career, see ibid.; David Halberstam, *The Best and the Brightest,* 491–99; and author's interview with George Ball, December 7, 1988.

23. Author's interview with George Ball, December 7, 1988.

24. Valenti, *Very Human President,* 108.

25. See Halberstam, *Best and Brightest,* 213–40.

26. Halberstam, in ibid., argues that a kind of eastern establishment elite, embracing old school ties from Groton, Harvard, Yale, and a few smaller but similarly prestigious colleges and universities, emerged under JFK, and that this "old boy network" of the best and the brightest blood and brains ran the country.

27. For McNamara, see Halberstam, ibid., 213–50; Ball, *Past,* 173–74; Larry Berman, *Lyndon Johnson's War: The Road to Stalemate in Vietnam,* passim; Johnson, *Vantage Point,* 20; Rusk, *As I Saw It,* 207, 521–22. One of the latest biographies is the best, albeit devotedly unsympathetic: Deborah Shapley, *Promise and Power: the Life and Times of Robert McNamara.*

28. For Vance's career, see *Who's Who in America,* as well as Halberstam, *Best and Brightest,* 224. See also Cyrus Vance, *Hard Choices: Critical Years in America's Foreign Policy.*

29. Halberstam, *Best and Brightest,* 152–54.

30. Ibid., 48.

CHAPTER 4

1. Author's interview with William Colby, October 17, 1988.

2. Ibid.; author's interview with McGeorge Bundy, November 12, 1990. See also David M. Barrett, *Uncertain Warriors: Lyndon Johnson and His Vietnam Advisers,* 1–13.

3. William Bundy oral history, May 26, 1988, LBJ Library.

4. See Karnow, *Vietnam,* 442–43.

5. Ibid.

6. Gravel, *Pentagon Papers,* vol. 3, 494.

7. See Colby, *Lost Victory,* 161–62.

8. Gravel, *Pentagon Papers,* vol. 3, 495.

9. Ibid.

10. Colby, *Lost Victory,* 158.

11. Gravel, *Pentagon Papers,* vol. 3, 494.

12. Ibid., 495–96.

13. Ibid., 494.

14. Tran, *Our Endless War,* 121.

15. Colby, *Lost Victory,* 171.

16. Karnow, *Vietnam,* 338.

17. Ted Gittinger of the LBJ Library reported to the author in a telephone conversation, May 4, 1993, that he learned that General Taylor wrote Harkins's orders in an interview with Taylor. See Halberstam, *Best and Brightest,* 183.

18. President Kennedy doubted that so conventional a soldier could handle the unconventional warfare expected in Vietnam. "After he met Harkins in Palm Beach, where the President was resting, Kennedy was asked what he thought of the new commander for Vietnam. He answered, somewhat less than enthusiastically, 'Well, that's what they're offering me'" (Halberstam, *Best and Brightest,* 180).

19. See General Bruce Palmer, *The Twenty-five Year War: America's Military Role in Vietnam,* 11.

20. Quoted in Karnow, *Vietnam,* 258.

21. Halberstam, *Best and Brightest,* 186. For Halberstam's full indictment of Harkins, see Karnow, *Vietnam,* 183–88.

22. See George Herring, *America's Longest War: The United States and Vietnam, 1950–1975,* 82–83.

23. See Halberstam's careful assessment of Taylor's emergence as part of the Vietnam cast in *Best and Brightest,* 162–72.

24. See Herring, *Longest War,* 86–87.

25. See Don, *Our Endless War,* 148–50.

26. Sources for the action at Ap Bac are scattered but substantial. Touched on in Herring, *America's Longest War,* 88, Ap Bac receives somewhat longer treatment in Andrew F. Krepinevich, Jr., *The Army and Vietnam,* 78–79. Karnow covers it well in *Vietnam,* 259–62 (the quote from Vann is on p. 262). Halberstam uses Ap Bac to make points about the poor conduct of the U.S. war in Vietnam (*Best and Brightest,* 202–205). A full and graphically detailed recounting of the battle is in Neil Sheehan, *A Bright, Shining Lie: John Paul Vann and America in Vietnam,* 203–65. Important to any evaluation of the effects of Ap Bac is William M. Hammond's volume in the U.S. Army in Vietnam series titled *Public Affairs: The Military and the Media, 1962–1968,* 29–38. For a particularly shrewd military analysis, see Dave R. Palmer, *Summons of the Trumpet: U.S.-Vietnam in Perspective,* 27–38.

27. Karnow, *Vietnam,* 262.

28. Hammond, *Public Affairs,* 37. Hammond adds that "as time passed the enmity between the two groups became emotional. At one point David Halberstam is reported to have driven past General Harkins' Saigon quarters, shaking his fist and vowing, 'I'll get you, Paul Harkins.'"

29. See Sheehan, *Bright, Shining Lie,* 383–86. Sheehan concludes that Vann's resignation capped a large disinformation campaign to hide a stain on his record that would bar him from general's stars, but that his fight to get the truth told in Vietnam stemmed from rare professional integrity. It seems possible that two factors explain Vann's resignation: one, he had accepted the impossibility of future promotion and couched his departure in terms to help blast Harkins out of MACV and make Diem put more vigor in the war; two, he became fed up with deceit at all levels in the U.S. Army and, ignoring his own situation, left the army urgently to call attention to the quagmire in Vietnam. Considering the labyrinth of Vann's personality, both issues may well have melded in his mind. See Halberstam, *Best and Brightest,* 203–205. Most of the army accepted the idea that Vann's sacrifice reflected his personal and professional honor and respected him for it. See, for example, Palmer, *Twenty-five Year War,* 21–23.

30. See author's interview with William Colby, March 28, 1990. Colby added, "With all due respect for John . . . I think we overreacted a bit to the Ap Bac thing."

31. See Dennis J. Duncanson, *Government and Revolution in Vietnam,* 326–27; Leslie H. Gelb with Richard K. Betts, *The Irony of Vietnam: The System Worked,* 81.

32. See Ball, *Past,* 183–84.

33. Ibid., 184; Halberstam, *Best and Brightest,* 152.

34. Edward Doyle, Samuel Lipsman, and editors of the Boston Publishing Company, *America Takes Over* in the Vietnam Experience series, 84.

35. See Henry F. Graff, *The Tuesday Cabinet: Deliberation and Decision on Peace and War under Lyndon B. Johnson,* 35–36.

36. See Colby's apt summary of the whole affair in *Lost Victory,* 148–49.

37. Karnow, *Vietnam,* 345.

CHAPTER 5

1. Details of the day are traced from Johnson, *Vantage Point,* 187, and White House Daily Diary, April 24, 1965, LBJ Library.

2. Johnson, *Vantage Point,* 188–89.

3. Rusk, *As I Saw It,* 369, 372–73.

4. This account summarizes Ball, *Past,* 327–28; Rusk, *As I Saw It,* 369–71; and Johnson, *Vantage Point,* 191–92.

5. Johnson, *Vantage Point,* 193.

6. See Daily Diary, April 27, 1965, entry for 10:40 to 11:30 A.M.

7. Quoted in Johnson, *Vantage Point,* 194. See also Ball, *Past,* 328.

8. Daily Diary, Wednesday, April 28, 1965.

9. Philip Geyelin, *Lyndon B. Johnson and the World,* 237.

10. Johnson, *Vantage Point,* 195–96. Congressional leaders present at the meeting included Senators Mansfield, Dirksen, Fulbright, Hickenlooper, Kuchel, Long, Saltonstall, and Smathers, along with Speaker McCormack and several other House members.

11. Ibid.

12. Valenti, *Very Human President,* 216.

13. Rusk, *As I Saw It,* 374.

14. Ibid., 373–74.

15. Johnson, *Vantage Point,* 197.

16. Daily Diary, April 28, 1965.

17. Rusk, *As I Saw It,* 373–74; Ball, *Past,* 329.

18. Papers of George W. Ball, LBJ Library, Dominican Republic [4/29/65–6/26/65] Note #4, Telcon/President/Ball, 4/29/65, 2:25 P.M., 1.

19. Rusk, *As I Saw It,* 372; Johnson, *Vantage Point,* 199.

20. See Daily Diary, April 29, 1965; Papers of Ball, Dominican Republic [4/29/65–6/26/65] Note #4, 4/29/65, and Note #5, Telcon Ball to Cyrus Vance, 4/29/65, 2:30 P.M.

21. Author's interview with William Colby, October 18, 1988.

22. Ball, *Past,* 329.

23. See George Ball's comment in his memoirs, *Past,* 329: "At [LBJ's] instructions, key members of the Administration engaged in a great deal of to-ing and fro-ing." Ball had a high opinion of Fortas; his throw-away phrase merely reflected an old State Department chill toward out-of-channels negotiation.

24. Johnson, *Vantage Point,* 200.

25. See Ball, *Past,* 329–30.

26. Author's interview with Jack Valenti, June 27, 1991.

27. Johnson, *Vantage Point,* 201.

28. Ball, *Past,* 329; Laura Kalman, *Abe Fortas: A Biography,* 235.

29. General Bruce Palmer Oral History, May 28, 1982, LBJ Library.

30. See Kalman, *Fortas,* 234–35.

31. Rusk, *As I Saw It,* 375.

32. Author's interview with McGeorge Bundy, February 7, 1990.

33. Rusk, *As I Saw It,* 375.

34. Palmer, *Twenty-five Year War,* 190–91.

35. Author's interview with McGeorge Bundy, February 7, 1990.

36. See William C. Gibbons, *The U.S. Government and the Vietnam War: Execu-*

tive and Legislative Roles and Relationships, pt. 4, 38–39. The other critical senator is quoted in ibid., 42. See also R. B. Woods, *Fulbright: A Biography,* 376–92.

37. Rusk, *As I Saw It,* 377.

38. Ball, *Past,* 331.

39. Graff, *Tuesday Cabinet,* 55. For a short, nearly contemporaneous, summary of the Dominican crisis, see Geyelin, *Johnson and World,* 236–58.

40. Daily Diary, April 12, 1967.

CHAPTER 6

1. See Karnow, *Vietnam,* 416 and photo facing p. 386. See also Johnson, *Vantage Point,* 138; Doyle, Lipsman, et al., *America Takes Over,* 6.

2. Numbers are difficult to pinpoint. Johnson says in *Vantage Point,* 138, that "the numbers of advisers had been increased to nearly 23,000 by the end of 1964." He then explains that as 1965 began, "the situation in Vietnam was as different from 1963 as 1961 had been from 1959" because of the continuous intrusion of North Vietnamese regulars.

3. See Karnow, *Vietnam,* 399; Shapely, *Promise and Power,* 310; Robert S. McNamara with Brian VanDemark, *In Retrospect: The Tragedy and Lessons of Vietnam,* 153, 208. Dates for the games are given variously.

4. McNamara, *In Retrospect,* 207–15.

5. Sharp, *Strategy for Defeat,* chap. 5.

6. See Ball, *Past,* 385.

7. For Ball's entire memorandum, see Ball, "Papers." McNamara laments in *In Retrospect,* 156–58, that neither he nor others gave the memo the serious attention or respect it deserved.

8. Karnow, *Vietnam,* 380.

9. See photograph of Ky and his wife in ibid., 355.

10. Ibid., 381–82.

11. Author's interview with Jack Valenti, June 27, 1991. See also Kinnard, "Soldier as Ambassador," 34–33, and Gravel, *Pentagon Papers,* vol. 3, 240–41.

12. See Karnow, *Vietnam,* 382; Don, *Endless War,* 138.

13. Karnow, *Vietnam,* 382.

14. Don, *Endless War,* 138.

15. Karnow, *Vietnam,* 382.

16. This confusing period is well summarized in Karnow, *Vietnam,* 381–86.

17. Gravel, *Pentagon Papers,* vol. 3, 293. The American official was William P. Bundy. For some details of the Binh Gia operations, see Karnow, *Vietnam,* 407–408; Davidson, *Vietnam at War,* 333–34; Morrison, *Elephant and Tiger,* 155–56; Sheehan, *Bright, Shining Lie,* 382.

18. Karnow, *Vietnam,* 397, quotes Taylor: "We should not get involved militarily with North Vietnam and possibly with Red China if our base in South Vietnam is insecure and Khanh's army is tied down everywhere by the Vietcong insurgency."

19. Ibid., 397–98.

20. Quoted in Thomas M. Coffey, *Iron Eagle: The Turbulent Life of General Curtis LeMay,* 427–28.

21. Karnow, *Vietnam,* 383.

22. See Gravel, *Pentagon Papers,* vol. 3, 668, where Taylor says: "The ability of the Viet Cong continuously to rebuild their units and to make good their losses is one of the mysteries of this guerrilla war. We are aware of the recruiting methods by which local boys are induced or compelled to join the Viet Cong ranks and have some general appreciation of the amount of infiltration of personnel from the out-

side. Yet taking both of these sources into account, we still can find no plausible explanation of the continued strength of the Viet Cong if our data on Viet Cong losses are even approximately correct . . . the Viet Cong units have the recuperative powers of the phoenix."

23. See Geyelin, *Johnson and World*, 214.

24. Philip Geyelin, quoted in Gravel, *Pentagon Papers*, vol. 3, 307.

25. Clifford, *Counsel to President*, 405, asserts that "in none of the discussions leading up to Rolling Thunder was the President told, either by the Joint Chiefs of Staff or his Secretary of Defense, that once bombing of the North began, the military would require, and demand, American combat troops, first to protect the American air bases from which the bombing was launched, and, then, inevitably, to begin offensive operations." Clifford indicts the US military for "failing to tell their Commander in Chief that the bombing of the North would inevitably lead to requests for ground troops."

26. Geyelin, *Johnson and World*, 203–209; Johnson, *Vantage Point*, 67, 579; Rusk, *As I Saw It*, 461–62; Karnow, *Vietnam*, 348, 376–77.

27. Author's interview with McGeorge Bundy, December 8, 1988.

28. Quoted in Karnow, *Vietnam*, 418–19.

29. See *Public Papers*, 1965, vol. 1, 394–99; Johnson, *Vantage Point*, 133–34; Herring, *America's Longest War*, 134; Schandler, *Unmaking of President*, 18–19; U.S. Department of Defense, *United States–Vietnam Relations, 1945–1967*, IVC(3), 95–98, 106–30.

30. Herring, *America's Longest War*, 134–35.

31. Geyelin, *Johnson and World*, 204–205.

32. Rusk, *As I Saw It*, 462; Karnow, *Vietnam*, 419.

33. Johnson, *Vantage Point*, 138–39. LBJ commented on assassinations: "It is obvious what that kind of slaughter means to a small, young nation and its people. A man thinks twice about becoming chief of his village or a district official if two or three of his predecessors have been murdered in their beds or disemboweled in the village square. Even in Saigon it was easier, and safer, to remain in private life rather than work for the government."

34. Quoted in Kearns, *Johnson and American Dream*, 263.

35. Karnow, *Vietnam*, 416–17; Shapley, *Promise and Power*, 334; William C. Westmoreland, *A Soldier Reports*, 125.

36. Westmoreland, *A Soldier Reports*, 126.

37. Krepinevich, *Army and Vietnam*, 140.

38. Westmoreland, *A Soldier Reports*, 126.

39. See an analysis of the decision to approve combat roles for marines in Halberstam, *Best and Brightest*, 566–87. See also Shapley, *Promise and Power*, 334.

40. Author's interview, McGeorge Bundy, December 8, 1988.

41. Rusk, *As I Saw It*, 450; Graff, *Tuesday Cabinet*, 40.

42. Shapley, *Promise and Power*, 334.

43. Johnson, *Vantage Point*, 139.

44. Ball, *Past*, 387. See Halberstam's excellent summary of Taylor's worries in *Best and Brightest*, 566.

45. Taylor's enclave strategy is discussed clearly in Halberstam, *Best and Brightest*, 566–69; Lewy, *America in Vietnam*, 42–49; and Krepinevich, *Army and Vietnam*, 140–43.

46. See Westmoreland, *A Soldier Reports*, 156.

47. Lewy, *America in Vietnam*, 43–45.

48. Krepinevich, *Army and Vietnam,* 146–47. See also Karnow, *Vietnam,* 419–20; Schandler, *Unmaking of President,* 23–24.

49. *US–Vietnam Relations,* IVC(5), 74; Karnow, *Vietnam,* 419; Maxwell Taylor, *Swords and Ploughshares,* 341–42.

50. See Krepinevich, *Army and Vietnam,* 148.

51. Schandler, *Unmaking of President,* 23.

52. Krepinevich, *Army and Vietnam,* 148.

53. Numbers are various. Shapley in *Promise and Power,* 335, says the agreed upon addition "would raise the number of American troops to 75,000." Halberstam in *Best and Brightest,* 577, sets the number at 82,000 "in country," plus four Third Country battalions and 7,250 men. Schandler in *Unmaking of President,* 24, accepts the 82,000 figure. Gibbons, *U.S. Government and Vietnam War,* pt. 3, 231, cites the 82,000 figure.

54. Krepinevich, *Army and Vietnam,* 150.

55. Shapley, *Promise and Power,* 335. See also Gelb, *Irony of Vietnam,* 134n, where the definition of victory is discussed.

56. Sharp, *Strategy for Defeat,* 80.

57. Gibbons, *U.S. Government and Vietnam War,* pt. 3, 224–25.

58. Ibid., pt. 3, 265–72. For discussion of various facets of student protest movements, see Seymour Martin Lipset and Philip G. Altbach, eds., *Students in Revolt,* and Terry Anderson, *The Movement and the Sixties.*

59. Ball, *Past,* 393.

60. Ibid.

61. George Ball, "Memorandum for the President," April 21[20?], 1965, in Ball, Papers.

62. Ball, *Past,* 394.

63. The north's four points were: (1) Recognition of the national rights of the Vietnamese people: peace, independence, sovereignty, unity, territorial integrity. Under the Geneva Agreements (unsigned by the United States), America must withdraw all troops, military personnel, and weapons from South Vietnam, dismantle all military bases, cancel its alliance with the South Vietnamese, and stop acts of war against the north. (2) Pending peaceful reunification, with Vietnam still temporarily divided, military provisions of the 1954 Geneva Accords must be strictly enforced; the two Vietnams must avoid entangling military alliances with any foreign countries. (3) The internal affairs of South Vietnam must be settled by South Vietnamese people. (4) The peaceful reunification of Vietnam to be settled by the people in both zones, without foreign interference. See "Memorandum for the President," April 21[20?], 1965, Ball, Papers.

64. This dialogue is derived from Gibbons, *U.S. Government and Vietnam War,* pt. 3, 233–34, and 233n.

65. *New York Times,* April 21, 1965.

66. On acceptance of North Vietnam's four points as a negotiating base, see Gibbons, *U.S. Government and Vietnam War,* pt. 3, 257n.

67. Ball, *Past,* 395.

68. Author's interview with George Ball, December 7, 1988. See also Shapley, *Promise and Power,* 328–29; McNamara, *In Retrospect,* 156–58.

69. See Halberstam, *Best and Brightest,* 581. He summarizes the troubles between Ball and McNamara this way: McNamara perhaps had doubts, but they were "reconciled when he was in those meetings; then they were never evident, and he was brilliant and forceful in obliterating others." When Ball suggested that massive escalation was coming, McNamara shot back things like: "It's dirty pool; for

Christ's sake, George, we're not talking about anything like that, no one's talking about that many people, we're talking about a dozen, maybe a few more maneuver battalions."

70. See Westmoreland, *A Soldier Reports*, 136; Schandler, *Unmaking of President*, 25–26; Krepinevich, *Army and Vietnam*, 151–52; Gibbons, *U.S. Government and Vietnam War*, pt. 3, 274–75.

CHAPTER 7

1. Quoted in Arthur Schlesinger, Jr., *A Thousand Days*, 547. The chapter's title comes from Johnson, *Choices We Face*, 24.

2. Gibbons, *U.S. Government and Vietnam War*, pt. 3, 240–59.

3. *Public Papers, 1965*, 484–92.

4. Ibid., 506; Johnson, *Vantage Point*, 142.

5. Leonard Meeker, legal adviser to the State Department, considered the supplemental appropriation another indication of congressional support for administration war policies. See Gibbons, *U.S. Government and Vietnam War*, pt. 3, 249 and 249n.

6. Kearns, *Johnson and Dream*, 327.

7. Gibbons, *U.S. Government and Vietnam War*, pt. 3, 255–56.

8. Ibid., 257.

9. Karnow, *Vietnam*, 421.

10. Ibid.

11. The meeting is summarized in Gibbons, *U.S. Government and Vietnam War*, pt. 3, 256–57, based on meeting notes taken by Jack Valenti in Meeting Notes File, LBJ Library.

12. Quoted in Ball, *Past*, 387.

13. Author's interview with Mrs. Lyndon B. Johnson, June 18, 1990. Kearns in *Johnson and Dream*, chap. 11, weaves a web of fantasy around LBJ's psyche. She describes a "siege psychosis" situation growing in the White House as the president's hopes dwindled, praise faded, and critics became enemies—all of which made him an increasingly isolated, megalomanic personality. The resulting picture of Johnson shutting his ears to bad news and clutching sycophants to him seems overdrawn.

14. Clifford, *Counsel to President*, 409–10.

15. The definition of "maneuver battalions" in the text follows Gibbons, *U.S. Government and Vietnam War*, pt. 3, 277. There is some dispute of the definition— many veterans of Vietnam recall maneuver battalions as something like "light infantry." According to General Westmoreland, they were battalions "that can be maneuvered . . . as opposed to a supporting battalion such as artillery, engineers, or aviation." *A Soldier Reports*, 155.

16. Gravel, *Pentagon Papers*, vol. 3, 440.

17. Gibbons, *U.S. Government and Vietnam War*, pt. 3, 277–78; Westmoreland, *A Soldier Reports*, 139–41.

18. Gibbons, *U.S. Government and Vietnam War*, pt. 3, 277–78; Gravel, *Pentagon Papers*, vol. 3, 462.

19. Sheehan, *Bright, Shining Lie*, 568.

20. This meeting is oddly neglected in many standard sources. Johnson in *Vantage Point* does not mention it, nor do Ball in *Past*, Rusk in *As I See It*, Shapley in *Promise and Power*, or Karnow in *Vietnam*. It is well covered in Gibbons, *U.S. Government and Vietnam War*, vol. 3, 347–50, and in Walter Isaacson and Evan Thomas, *The Wise Men: Six Friends and the World They Made—Acheson, Bohlen, Harriman, Kennan, Lovett, McCloy*. For the Acheson quote, see Isaacson and Thomas, 652.

21. See Shapley, *Promise and Power,* 340.

22. See Westmoreland, *A Soldier Reports,* 142–43.

23. Quoted in Shapley, *Promise and Power,* 344. McNamara's visit is well covered on pp. 343–44. Some controversy clouds the Vance cable. Early accounts by editors of the *Pentagon Papers* (Gravel, *Pentagon Papers,* vol. 3, 475, and vol. 4, 299) mention it but do not copy it and use it as proof that LBJ had already made up his mind to commit troops. This is clearly untrue. See Barrett, *Uncertain Warriors,* 41–42, 214–25. Vance's cable is extracted in Shapley, *Promise and Power,* 344.

24. McNamara, *In Retrospect,* 204.

25. Valenti, *Very Human President,* 259. Valenti took notes at these key White House meetings, and they are the best source for all the discussions. See his Part IV, entitled "The War." Originals are in Jack Valenti's Notes, Office of the President Files, LBJ Library.

26. Ball, *Past,* 400–401. Valenti covers these two meetings in *Very Human President,* 254–70.

27. Shapley, *Promise and Power,* 345–46. McNamara understood LBJ's dilemma: "subterfuge versus the twin dangers of escalatory pressures and the loss of his social programs." But the secretary deplored a widening of LBJ's "credibility gap." In *Retrospect,* 206, 205.

28. Clifford, *Counsel to President,* 411–16.

29. Ball, *Past,* 395.

30. See Clifford, *Counsel to President,* 416–17.

31. Ibid.

32. This discussion of the Camp David gathering is based largely on ibid., 418–22.

33. Ibid., 421n. Clifford observes that LBJ in *Vantage Point* indicates that he made his final decision after NSC meetings on July 26–27, "but almost everyone else involved in the process believed that the decision was made over the weekend." Johnson, in *Vantage Point,* 149, says that when he presented various alternatives to the NSC, he had already decided to "give our commanders in the field the men and supplies they say they need." Interesting insights into the whole business of Johnson's decision to send more troops are contained in Gibbons, *U.S. Government and Vietnam,* pt. 4, 1–38.

34. Johnson's dissembling stemmed from the pressures McNamara grasped, fear of escalation and fear for Great Society programs (McNamara, *In Retrospect,* 205–206), and did widen the credibility gap.

35. Johnson, *Vantage Point,* 153, and "Statement of the President at His Press Conference: The White House, July 28, 1965," copy in the Carl Albert Congressional Research and Studies Center Congressional Archives, University of Oklahoma, Norman, Oklahoma. See also *Public Papers, 1965,* vol. 2, 794–803.

CHAPTER 8

1. Valenti, *Very Human President,* 261–62.

2. Halberstam, *Best and Brightest,* 605–606.

3. Shapley, *Promise and Power,* 368–69. McNamara explained the idea to Johnson, who endorsed it, as a way to convince the Joint Chiefs that they could not expect to "receive one nickel without a plan" (Kearns, *Johnson and Dream,* 312).

4. Shapley, *Promise and Power,* 373.

5. Ibid., 372, 655 (citing a letter from Krock to Pat Munroe, July 11, 1972).

6. Ibid., 356.

7. Halberstam, *Best and Brightest,* 607.

8. Shapley, *Promise and Power,* 350.

9. Ibid., 350–51; *New York Times,* August 10, 12, 1965.

10. See Halberstam, *Best and Brightest,* 362–69, for a general assessment.

11. See Palmer, *Summons of Trumpet,* 157.

12. Shapley, *Promise and Power,* 352.

13. Author's interview with George Ball, December 7, 1988. Ball observed that he used to argue with colleagues pushing the domino theory: "Look, you've not demonstrated this. You've asserted it, and there's a difference as far as I'm concerned. I don't believe that. You tell me this but how do you expect me to believe it?"

14. Ball, *Past,* 386 and 504n, quotes Jonathon Schell's *The Time of Illusion,* 9–10, where Schell explains the shifting views by arguing that "according to the psychological domino theory, the ill effects of a nation's fall would not necessarily be on neighboring nations, but would be on nations all over the world which, by merely watching the spectacle, would lose confidence in the power of the United States." Note LBJ's somewhat similar thinking about handling the crisis in the Dominican Republic, though in that case he thought more about power projection than the domino theory.

15. Ball, *Past,* 404.

16. Karnow, *Vietnam,* 423.

17. Palmer, *Summons of Trumpet,* 155–56.

18. See Don, *Endless War,* 168–69.

19. Sheehan, *Bright, Shining Lie,* 512.

20. See Lewy, *America in Vietnam,* 51. Lewy's figure is 184,314. See also Johnson, *Vantage Point,* 233, and Krepinevich, *Army and Vietnam,* 168.

21. Lt. Gen. Harold G. Moore (Ret.) and Joseph L. Galloway, *We Were Soldiers Once . . . and Young. Ia Drang: The Battle That Changed the War in Vietnam,* 12, 42 (this splendid book hereafter cited as *Soldiers Once*). For a synopsis of Giap's plans, see Palmer, *Summons of Trumpet,* 91–92.

22. See Davidson, *Vietnam at War,* 360.

23. Palmer, *Summons of Trumpet,* 92.

24. This mountain formation is generally referred to as "Chu Pong" in the battle literature, but a *National Geographic* map of 1967 labels it "Chu Prong," a name also used in Sheehan, *Bright, Shining Lie,* 572.

25. See Davidson, *Vietnam at War,* 360; Palmer, *Summons of Trumpet,* 93–94; Moore and Galloway, *Soldiers Once,* 14–15.

26. See Palmer, *Summons of Trumpet,* 93–94, where Man's strategy is outlined clearly. See also Doyle et. al., *Vietnam Experience,* 66.

27. Halberstam, *Best and Brightest,* 614–15.

28. Shapley, *Promise and Power,* 355–56; Gravel, *Pentagon Papers,* vol. 4, 303. McNamara's depressing memo may have triggered the violent interview LBJ had with the JCS "one . . . day in early November 1965," which Lt. Gen. Charles G. Cooper, USMC, recalls in "The Day It Became the Longest War," U.S. Naval Institute *Proceedings* (May, 1966): 77–80. Then aide-de-camp to Adm. David McDonald, CNO, Cooper does not give the exact day, but "early November" ties in with McNamara's memo. The chiefs had been granted a "private audience" with the president. Admitting that McNamara did not agree with them but thought the president should hear their views, they proposed plans to mine and blockade Haiphong harbor and to launch a "B-52 bombing offensive on Hanoi." Johnson listened carefully, then exploded. "He screamed obscenities, he cursed them personally, he ridiculed them for coming to his office with their 'military advice.' Noting that it was he who was carrying the weight of the free world on his shoulders, he called them filthy names—sh——heads, dumbsh——s, pompous assh——s—and used the

'F-word' as an adjective more freely than a Marine at boot camp. He then accused them of trying to pass the buck for World War III to him" (p. 80). Cooper remembers the whole thing as "unnerving" and "degrading." After asking them to put themselves in his place, and hearing sympathetic comments, he resumed his bullying by saying he was not "going to let some military idiots talk him into World War III." Then he told them to get out of his office. I have not found this meeting mentioned in other sources.

29. Gravel, *Pentagon Papers,* vol. 4, 306. For more of Westmoreland's views on numbers, see Halberstam, *Best and Brightest,* 613–15.

30. Inclusive dates for the campaign vary in various accounts. The text follows Shelby Stanton, *Vietnam Order of Battle,* 9. See also John Schlight, *The War in South Vietnam: The Years of the Offensive, 1965–1968,* 103, where November 1 is given as the starting date for Silver Bayonet. Palmer, *Summons of Trumpet,* 93, gives inclusive dates of October 23 to November 26 for the campaign. Operation Silver Bayonet may have been the second part of a joint operation. In General Westmoreland's historical files in the Lyndon Baines Johnson Presidential Library is the following notation: "24 October 1965 [—] 1st Cav Div began operations in area west of Plei Me (Op[eratio]n Long Reach, 24 Oct–9 Nov; Op[eratio]n Silver Bayonet 9–28 Nov)." See "Important Events August 1964–Present date 9 Dec 1965," in Document # 56, Folder # 2, History File, 25 Oct.–20 Dec. 1965, Box 7, Papers of William Westmoreland, LBJ Library.

31. Numbers are difficult to confirm for the confused October–November fighting. The U.S. totals in the text are taken from Moore and Galloway, *Soldiers Once,* 322, and the NVA totals from Doyle et al., *Vietnam Experience,* 70. McNamara, *In Retrospect,* 221, reports 300 U.S. dead.

32. Moore and Galloway, *Soldiers Once,* 319.

33. Schlight, *War in South Vietnam,* 105.

34. Moore and Galloway, *Soldiers Once.*

35. For these statistics, see ibid., 199; Palmer, *Summons of Trumpet,* 102.

36. Quoted in Moore and Galloway, *Soldiers Once,* 277.

37. See entries for Thursday, November 18, and Monday, November 29, 1965, in General William Westmoreland's History File, 28 Nov–4 Dec 1965, Folders # 22 and 46, Box 7, Papers of William Westmoreland, LBJ Library.

38. Moore and Galloway, *Soldiers Once,* 199.

39. Ibid., 198; Sheehan's account of the fighting at X-Ray is succinct and graphic in *Bright, Shining Lie,* 573–78.

40. Halberstam, *Best and Brightest,* 615–16.

41. Entry for Monday, 29 November, Document # 46, Folder # 22, Box 7, Westmoreland's History File, 28 Nov–4 Dec 1965, in Papers of William Westmoreland, LBJ Library.

42. See Shapley, *Promise and Power,* 357; Nguyen Cao Ky, *Twenty Years and Twenty Days,* 80.

43. Quoted in Shapley, *Promise and Power,* 358. George Herring, in a Vietnam Symposium at the LBJ Library in October, 1993, suggested that the Ia Drang fighting stunned McNamara and marked the beginning of "his schizophrenic efforts to win the war and pull out"; at the same time he pushed harder for bombing halts and for more effective pacification efforts. McNamara's narrative in *In Retrospect,* 221–26, tends to confirm Herring's suggestion.

44. Shapley, *Promise and Power,* 357–59.

45. Westmoreland, *A Soldier Reports,* 186, 192.

46. Sharp, *Strategy for Defeat,* 105; McNamara, *In Retrospect,* 221–24.

47. Halberstam, *Best and Brightest*, 616. See also McNamara, *In Retrospect*, 225.

48. Sharp, *Strategy for Defeat*, 107.

49. See Halberstam, *Best and Brightest*, 621; Rusk, *As I Saw It*, 459–74.

50. The first Valenti quote is from the author's interview with Mr. Valenti, June 27, 1991; the second is from Karnow, *Vietnam*, 479.

51. Shapley, *Promise and Power*, 362–63.

52. Rusk, *As I Saw It*, 464–65. Ho Chi Minh insisted on unconditional halting of all acts of war against North Vietnam before talks could begin. The main sticking point for the United States, whenever Hanoi's Four Points were mentioned, was the recognition of the NLF of South Vietnam (the VC) as part of any new South Vietnamese government. Vice President Hubert Humphrey said that allowing the VC in a government would be "like putting 'a fox in a chicken coop.'" See Graff, *Tuesday Cabinet*, 67.

53. Johnson, *Vantage Point*, 235.

54. Kalman, *Fortas*, 295, 464n. 12.

55. Valenti, *Very Human President*, 174–76.

56. Ibid., 176–77.

57. Ibid., 177–80.

58. Ibid., 187–88.

59. The scene is described in Johnson, *Vantage Point*, 235–37; Shapley, *Promise and Power*, 364, 654n. 35; Karnow, *Vietnam*, 482; Clifford, *Counsel to President*, 434–36; Kalman, *Fortas*, 295–96; and in detail in Valenti, *Very Human President*, 173–90. See Gibbons's excellent survey of the bombing halt in *U.S. Government and Vietnam War*, pt. 4, 113–35. See also McNamara, *In Retrospect*, 224–25.

CHAPTER 9

1. Speech to a Joint Session of Congress, November 27, 1963, *Public Papers*, 1963, 8.

2. Rusk, *As I Saw It*, 464–65.

3. The term is from ibid., 465.

4. Ball, *Past*, 404.

5. Shapley, *Promise and Power*, 364.

6. Ball, *Past*, 404–405.

7. W. Averell Harriman Oral History, June 16, 1969, LBJ Library.

8. Ibid.

9. Johnson, *Diary*, 347.

10. Johnson, *Vantage Point*, 237–38. The quotation is on p. 238.

11. Ball, *Past*, 405.

12. Johnson, *Vantage Point*, 237–38.

13. Ibid., 238–39.

14. Johnson, *Diary*, 351.

15. Rusk said that the United States contacted 145 countries (*As I Saw It*, 465).

16. Johnson, *Vantage Point*, 239. See also Califano, *Triumph and Tragedy*, 117–19. For the full text of the speech, see *Public Papers*, 1966, 3–12.

17. Quoted in Johnson, *Vantage Point*, 239.

18. Document # 3, Jan. 25, 1966, recounting the meeting in the Cabinet Room, 5:30–7:40 P.M., Box 13, "Notes Taken during Various Meetings 1965 and 1966," Jack Valenti's Notes, Office of the President Files, LBJ Library.

19. The quotes from the meeting are from Documents # 1, 3, 4, 5, 7, ibid. The last quote is from Document # 7, recounting a second White House meeting for January 29, 1966.

20. Johnson, *Diary,* 347.

21. Ball, *Past,* 405.

22. Ball, "Papers."

23. Ball, "Papers," Memoranda, Jan. 5, 19, 20, 25, 1966; Ball, *Past,* 405–406.

24. Ball, *Past,* 406, admits that he "overestimated" the chances of China entering the war, but said, candidly, that "President Johnson was deeply preoccupied with the China menace and the more I emphasized it, the stronger was my case for cutting our losses." On January 25, Ball sent an almost desperate eighteen-page memo to LBJ urging the dangers of China coming into the war; he cited the Korean precedents and offered sobering estimates of possible Chinese troop strengths.

25. Valenti, *Very Human President,* 190–91.

26. Johnson, *Vantage Point,* 242.

27. Johnson, *Diary,* 358–59; Westmoreland, *A Soldier Reports,* 193.

28. Karnow, *Vietnam,* 444.

29. Ky, *Twenty Years,* 80–81; Johnson, *Vantage Point,* 243.

30. Ky, *Twenty Years,* 81.

31. Johnson, *Vantage Point,* 243.

32. Quoted in Karnow, *Vietnam,* 444. Karnow says that Ky's American advisers wrote the speech. Probably true; but Ky at least accepted the ideas as his own.

33. Ky, *Twenty Years,* 81–82.

34. Johnson, *Vantage Point,* 243–45.

35. Westmoreland, *A Soldier Reports,* 194.

36. Johnson, *Vantage Point,* 243–44.

37. Ibid., 244. The "open arms," or *Chieu Hoi,* program offered amnesty and economic incentives to any VC or NVA who joined.

38. Ky, *Twenty Years,* 83–84.

39. Ibid., 84.

40. Charles L. Garrettson III, *Hubert H. Humphrey: The Politics of Joy,* 188.

41. Halberstam, *Best and Brightest,* 535, casts this assignment in an entirely anti-Johnson light: "In 1966 he [Humphrey] was assigned a trip to Asia (again in a particularly humiliating way. It was a two-and-a-half week trip and he was given twenty-four hours' notice, no chance to prepare, barely a chance to get his various vaccinations). Jack Valenti was sent along . . . to keep an eye on the Vice-President, to call Johnson every day and to bring the President's instructions to Humphrey. . . ." (Garrettson, *Humphrey,* 189–90, quoting Humphrey, *The Education of a Public Man,* 329–30).

42. Westmoreland, *A Soldier Reports,* 192–93.

43. Ibid., 193.

44. Ibid., 193–94.

45. Clifford, *Counsel to President,* 451.

46. Item # 9 "Vice President's report on his Asian trip, February 24, 1966," Box 13, Jack Valenti's Notes, Office of the President Files, LBJ Library. Present at the meeting were the president and vice president, Speaker McCormack, Carl Albert, Gerald R. Ford, Everett Dirksen, Thomas H. Kuchel, Leslie C. Arends, Russell Long, and Hale Boggs.

47. Westmoreland, *A Soldier Reports,* 195.

48. Valenti, *Very Human President,* 192.

49. Johnson, *Diary,* 362.

50. Ibid., 247; author's interview with Mrs. Lyndon B. Johnson, August 23, 1989.

51. Author's interview with McGeorge Bundy, December 8, 1988.

52. Author's interview with Robert Komer, March 17, 1989.

53. Johnson, *Vantage Point,* 240n, says that Walt W. Rostow assumed Bundy's old post on April 1, 1966.

54. Larry Cable, *Unholy Grail: The U.S. and the Wars in Vietnam, 1965–8,* 127–29.

55. See, especially, Orville Freeman to Robert McNamara, February 21, 1966. Freeman, reporting on his visit to Vietnam, said he had reports of little real coordination between military and civil authorities. Freeman felt the opportunity for an effective, coordinated program ought to be used and added that, as he told LBJ, "I see little hope for effective agricultural assistance or even for military success unless military-civil assistance is planned at the highest military levels and operations are similarly coordinated at all subordinate levels in Viet-Nam." In folder "Agriculture [1]," Komer-Leonhardt File (1966–68), Box 1, National Security Files, LBJ Library.

56. The conversation is from author's interview with Robert Komer, March 17, 1989. The wording of Komer's question is his own in the interview.

57. The whole scene is from ibid.

58. Valenti, *Very Human President,* 201–202; Johnson, *Vantage Point,* 245.

59. Author's interview with Robert Komer, March 17, 1989.

60. See "Memorandum for Mr. Komer; Subject: Talking Points for Secretary Freeman, August 8, 1966," Komer-Leonhardt File (1966–68), Box 1, National Security Files, LBJ Library, in which Freeman reports efforts to prod AID to focus Saigon's attention on follow-ups in the field. Status reports indicated "positive actions in most fields with generally spotted performance."

61. Stanton, *Order of Battle,* 59–60.

62. Westmoreland, *A Soldier Reports,* 98. The discussion of Hop Tac continues through page 102.

63. Ibid., 99.

64. Colby, *Lost Victory,* 90–91.

65. All that follows involving Captain James Floyd Ray and his subdistrict assignment in Vietnam is based on his letters to his wife, Charlotte Walters Ray, and his Vietnam diary. His letters and diary were given to me by his wife, now Charlotte Rhodes, of Dripping Springs, Texas. There are not words to thank her for her confidence. Ray's letters and diary constitute an important Vietnam source; they are in the author's possession.

66. Ray, Vietnam diary, August 29, 1964.

67. Ibid., October 6, 1964.

68. Ray, Letter to Charlotte, January 8, 1965.

69. Ray, Vietnam diary, December 5, 1964.

70. Exactly how Ray died is in dispute. His Bronze Star citation described his death as follows:

Captain Ray distinguished himself by heroic action on 9 January 1965, in the Republic of Vietnam. On this date Captain Ray was serving as advisor to a Vietnamese patrol, which was preparing an ambush for any Viet Cong forces that might be in the area. At approximately 1730 hours the patrol moved out of the base camp toward the ambush area. At approximately 2100 hours, the patrol stopped in order that Captain Ray and his Vietnamese counterpart could reconnoiter the local area. With two Vietnamese sergeants, Captain Ray and the Vietnamese commander moved toward a house that was suspected of being a Viet Cong stronghold. One of the sergeants moved around one side of the house while the other men moved toward its front. Captain Ray and his companions heard a shot from the other side of the house, and with complete disregard for his own safety, Captain Ray advanced to aid the

Vietnamese sergeant. Arriving to within three meters of a haystack, Captain Ray assisted in providing cover for the sergeant, when without warning, four Viet Cong appeared from the haystack and opened fire, hitting Captain Ray. Despite being mortally wounded, Captain Ray still continued to provide cover for the Vietnamese sergeant, who was able to withdraw to a safe position. Captain Ray's outstanding devotion to duty and personal courage were in keeping with the highest traditions of the United States Army and reflected great credit upon himself and the military service.

Charlotte Ray copied this citation, and added, "UNOFFICIAL INFORMATION GIVEN ME A YEAR LATER—MARCH, 1966: Captain Ray, while on a night patrol, was shot in the back by his Vietnamese counterpart, Capt. Trac, a VC infiltrator in the ARVN." She subsequently crossed out this note and added—in August, 1968—the following clarification: "Above statement's truth is not proved." True or not, Jim Ray's special flair and his undeniable success as a subdistrict advisor made him just the kind of target most sought by the VC. They wanted to do away with the best ones.

71. For a general survey of advisors in Vietnam, see Jeffrey J. Clarke, *Advice and Support: The Final Years, 1965–1973*, 49–78.

72. Westmoreland, *A Soldier Reports*, 200.

73. Victor H. Krulak, *First to Fight: An Inside View of the U.S. Marine Corps*, 185–86.

74. Ibid., 186.

75. Ibid., 185.

76. Ibid., 187–89; Westmoreland, *A Soldier Reports*, 202; Clarke, *Advice and Support*, 180–81.

77. Introduction by LBJ in Lewis W. Walt, *Strange War, Strange Strategy: A General's Report on Vietnam*, x–xi.

CHAPTER 10

1. Author's telephone interview with Luci Johnson, October 20, 1992.

2. Nancy Zaroulis and Gerald Sullivan, *Who Spoke Up? American Protest against the War in Vietnam, 1963–1975*, 85–86.

3. This whole story is admirably summarized in Zaroulis and Sullivan, *Who Spoke Up?*, 66–69. See also Anderson, *Movement and Sixties*.

4. Quoted in Morrison, *Elephant and Tiger*, 217. An alliance with the SNCC would have had good and bad potential. Carmichael became increasingly violent and had no sympathy for a war for South Vietnamese freedom, when freedom for America's blacks went unachieved.

5. The Dirksen quote is from ibid., 202; the Kearns quote is in *Johnson and Dream*, 342.

6. Kearns, *Johnson and Dream*, 327.

7. Quoted in Morrison, *Elephant and Tiger*, 203.

8. This account of the antiwar movement relies heavily on Zaroulis and Sullivan, *Who Spoke Up?*; Lipset and Altbach, *Students in Revolt*; and Morrison, *Elephant and Tiger*, 201–204, 216–17.

9. See Dallek, *Lone Star Rising*, 420–21; author's interview with J. William Fulbright, October 17, 1988. For the section on Fulbright's offensive, see also William C. Berman, *William Fulbright and the Vietnam War: The Dissent of a Political Realist*; Tristam Coffin, *Senator Fulbright: Portrait of a Political Philosopher*; and Randall B. Woods, *Fulbright: A Biography*.

10. Confidential Name File, J. William Fulbright, May 27, 1966, LBJ Library.

11. Califano, *Triumph and Tragedy*, 336–37.

12. Fulbright felt, too, that Johnson went back on his 1964 campaign pledge not to send American boys to fight in Asia. See author's interview with Fulbright, October 17, 1988.

13. See the deft description in Shapley, *Promise and Power*, 453–54.

14. Gravel, *Pentagon Papers*, vol. 4, 640–44.

15. Johnson, *Diary*, 360.

16. See Dallek, *Lone Star Rising*, 384; Karnow, *Vietnam*, 507.

17. This entire section about the ranch meeting relies heavily on Califano, *Triumph and Tragedy*, 114–17.

18. *Public Papers, 1966*, vol. 1, 4.

19. See Harry Middleton, *LBJ: The White House Years*, 251; and Califano's dedication, *Triumph and Tragedy*.

20. Ky, *Twenty Years*, 89.

21. Westmoreland, *A Soldier Reports*, 207; Karnow, *Vietnam*, 445. Karnow's account seems to miss the depth of Westmoreland's understanding of Ky's motives and his problems.

22. Ibid., 205–206.

23. Memorandum for the record, Subject: Meetings with Generals Chuan and Thieu, March 18, 19, 1966," in Document 6, Folder 5 History File, 13 Mar–23 April 1966; Box 8, Papers of William Westmoreland, LBJ. Thieu's remarks to Westy are unusually candid, but he does not admit that the military directorate had an unusual arrangement with the corps commanders. They had, in effect, the autonomy of satraps in their areas, controlled a web of influence and treasure trading, and shared diffusion of national power. Instead of creating a strong central government, Ky and his men had removed most of the power from Saigon "so that the very stability of the Ky regime was no more than a function of its weakness" (Frances FitzGerald, *Fire in the Lake: The Vietnamese and the Americans in Vietnam*, 349). Ky explained to a *Time* reporter: "Governing a country like South Vietnam is a very delicate matter, requiring balance. The way we work is that my colleagues [in the directorate] and I decide what we want done, and then I try to carry it out," (Ky, *Twenty Years*, 89–90).

24. Ky, *Twenty Years*, 90.

25. Johnson, *Vantage Point*, 247.

26. See the humorous account in FitzGerald, *Fire in Lake*, 347–48.

27. Quoted in Karnow, *Vietnam*, 446.

28. For the conflicts, see Westmoreland, *A Soldier Reports*, 207; FitzGerald, *Fire in Lake*, 352–53. Karnow, *Vietnam*, 446, says that Lodge provided planes and pilots to Ky. Two secret messages from Westmoreland to General Walt in Da Nang, on April 3 and 4, 1966 ("MAC 2650" and "MAC 2667," Papers of William Westmoreland, LBJ Library), indicate that the general's memory failed him when he wrote his memoirs. In the first message COMUSMACV speculates to Walt that no U.S. planes will be used: "I suspect that Vietnamese Marines will be flown into Danang by Air Vietnam and VNAF C-47's, thence deployed by VNAF helicopters." The second message, sent on the April 4, changes the story: "The Prime Minister has requested an airlift . . . and the Ambassador has agreed." In some pique Westy told the South Vietnamese "that they should plan to make local moves by their own helicopters. . . . I did not want to chance the involvement of American troops or confrontation by Americans with demonstrators and mobs." There is an argument, too, about the number of men Ky took with him. Numbers in the text follow Westmoreland (above), who said the force comprised three South Vietnamese Ma-

rine battalions (about 3,000); but Karnow (above) puts the number at 4,000 South Vietnamese soldiers. In his secret message to Walt on April 4, 1966, Westy reported the troops Ky dispatched: "I have just talked with Generals Co and Vien and learned the following: A state of siege will be declared in the whole country. Two Vietnamese Marine battalions, field police and military security elements, psywar teams, and a command group will move to Da Nang under cover of darkness this evening." The total of 3,000 men seems close. Interestingly enough, Ky manages to dodge this first expedition by mixing parts of it with the second in his book, *Twenty Years.*

29. FitzGerald, *Fire in Lake,* 354.

30. This point is well covered in ibid., 354–56.

31. Ky, *Twenty Years,* 91. Some sentiment floated in Washington to use the Buddhist crisis as an excuse to get out of Vietnam.

32. Westmoreland, *A Soldier Reports,* 208–209. Troop numbers are again in dispute. FitzGerald, *Fire in Lake,* 360, says Ky sent in one thousand marines, while Karnow, *Vietnam,* 447, puts the number at two thousand. Since Ky, *Twenty Years,* 94, says that the forces combined paratroops, marines, and armor, the larger number seems correct.

33. Ky, *Twenty Years,* 95.

34. Karnow, *Vietnam,* 446. For more details on Ky's civil war, see Clarke, *Advice and Support,* 127–44. Gibbons, *U.S. Government and Vietnam War,* pt. 4, 267–303, covers the Buddhist uprising in superb detail.

35. Johnson, *Vantage Point,* 247. The entire Buddhist episode is well covered in the FitzGerald, Gibbons, Johnson, Karnow, Ky, and Westmoreland books cited above.

36. The quote is from Karnow, *Vietnam,* 451. For summaries of the election see Johnson, *Vantage Point,* 247–48; Westmoreland, *A Soldier Reports,* 228–29. FitzGerald covers it with an important, though slightly cynical, perspective, in *Fire in Lake,* chap. 11.

37. Westmoreland, *A Soldier Reports,* 228.

38. Quoted in Johnson, *Vantage Point,* 247–48.

CHAPTER 11

1. Author's interview with Mrs. Lyndon B. Johnson, August 23, 1989.

2. Valenti, *Very Human President,* 73–74.

3. Barrett, *Uncertain Warriors,* 186–88.

4. Valenti, *Very Human President,* 201–203.

5. Ibid., 203–204.

6. See the photo of Cam Ranh Bay in Joel D. Myerson, *Images of a Lengthy War,* 125.

7. For McNamara's report and his quotations, see Gravel, *Pentagon Papers,* vol. 4, 348–54. Italics are in the original. See also McNamara, *In Retrospect,* 262–63. McNamara dated his report October 14, 1966.

8. Johnson, *Vantage Point,* 359.

9. Quotes are from Hugh Sidey, *A Very Personal Presidency: Lyndon Johnson and the White House,* 136–37.

10. Johnson, *Diary,* 430. Mrs. Johnson quotes New Zealand newspapers on the crowds greeting LBJ: "The staid city of Wellington gave him the warmest, most boisterous welcome in memory that a foreign head of state has received in New Zealand. . . . Authorities said the crowd was bigger than that which turned out for Queen Elizabeth when she visited Wellington three years ago." There are opposing views about the Johnson welcome in Wellington and in Melbourne. Berman,

Johnson's War, 17, says that "the president's arrival in Manila was preceded by a visit to Australia where hostile demonstrations in Melbourne and Sydney against U.S. foreign policy overshadowed festivities planned by Australian leaders waiting to greet the president." Mrs. Johnson, *White House Diary*, 431–32, offers a different view, as does another eye witness, Sidey, *Personal Presidency*, 141–44.

11. Johnson, *Diary*, 432; Sidey, *Personal Presidency*, 143.

12. Johnson, *Vantage Point*, 361.

13. Sidey, *Personal Presidency*, 144.

14. Johnson, *Diary*, 434–35.

15. Sidey, *Personal Presidency*, 146–47.

16. Westmoreland, *A Soldier Reports*, 231. See, especially, General Westmoreland's Historical Briefing, 6 November 1966, Document #2, Box 9, Papers of William Westmoreland, LBJ Library. Westmoreland received hints from McNamara and Henry Kissinger that he might be given wider duties.

17. Westmoreland, *A Soldier Reports*, 146–47. Westmoreland dictated his memo to Walt Rostow at LJB's request. See MEMORANDUM FOR: Mr. Walter W. Rostow SUBJECT: COMUSMACV'S Comments on Rolling Thunder, October 25, 1966, Box 9, Papers of William Westmoreland, LBJ Library. In this summary Westmoreland made an important comment: "To stop the bombing campaign to the North would adversely affect the war in the South." See also Gravel, *Pentagon Papers*, vol. 7, 359–61.

18. General William Westmoreland's Historical Briefing, 6 November 1966, p. 11, Document #2, Box 9, Papers of William Westmoreland, LBJ Library.

19. Johnson, *Vantage Point*, 363.

20. For the reconstruction of the Thailand, Malaysia, and Korea visits, see Johnson, *Diary*, 436–53; Sidey, *Personal Presidency*, 151–54; Johnson, *Vantage Point*, 363; Middleton, *LBJ*, 148–53.

21. Johnson, *Vantage Point*, 363.

22. Sidey, *Personal Presidency*, 139–40, 154–55.

23. Johnson, *Vantage Point*, 364; Johnson, *Diary*, 453.

24. Valenti, *Very Human President*, 120.

25. Gravel, *Pentagon Papers*, vol. 4, 356–65.

26. Analysts differ on the scope of the Democratic defeat. Ibid., 363, refers to the Republican gains as "minor." Richard N. Goodwin, *Remembering America: A Voice from the Sixties*, 469, says "the Democrats lost . . . more than they had gained in the 1964 landslide. The liberal majority, which had made it possible to enact Johnson's program, was gone."

27. Gravel, *Pentagon Papers*, vol. 4, 362.

28. Ibid., 359–60.

29. Ibid., 369n.

30. Shapley, *Promise and Power*, 414. Shapley, 413–14, shows Enthoven's reluctance to become involved with Vietnam.

31. Ibid., 413.

32. Gravel, *Pentagon Papers*, vol. 4, 368–69.

33. For a comparison of Salisbury's articles and some North Vietnamese pamphlets, see Phil G. Goulding, *Confirm or Deny: Informing the People on National Security*, 89–90; Lewy, *America in Vietnam*, 400–404.

34. Quoted in Shapley, *Promise and Power*, 412; Goulding, *Confirm or Deny*, 89–90.

35. Author's interview with Jack Valenti, June 27, 1991.

36. Johnson, *Vantage Point*, 240.

37. See ibid., 578, 584–85.

38. Author's interview with Adm. U. S. G. Sharp, December 17, 1988. See also Sharp, *Strategy for Defeat,* 122–23.

39. Johnson, *Vantage Point,* 258.

40. Ibid., 259.

41. See Barrett, *Uncertain Warriors,* 223n. 44.

42. Westmoreland, *A Soldier Reports,* 259.

43. Barrett, *Uncertain Warriors,* 74–75. Lilienthal's description of the "treatment" is classic: "The President's whirlwind manner I had seen before; still, I wasn't prepared at all for the tumultuous, almost visible emanations of vitality, exuberance, a sense of power . . . a flow of ideas, words, emotions, facial expressions that would tax an accomplished actor. . . . It was as prodigious an exhibition of energy and the pulling out of all the stops as I have ever seen, or expect to see" (ibid., 75).

44. FitzGerald, *Fire in Lake,* 410; Johnson, *Vantage Point,* 259–60.

45. Quoted in Barrett, *Uncertain Warriors,* 77.

46. See the photo in Westmoreland, *A Soldier Reports,* in a gallery between pp. 326 and 327.

47. Quoted in Barrett, *Uncertain Warriors,* 77.

48. For the letters, see Johnson, *Vantage Point,* 592–95; Gravel, *Pentagon Papers,* vol. 4, 9.

49. Westmoreland, *A Soldier Reports,* 261–62.

50. Author's interview with Robert Komer, March 17, 1989.

51. See a succinct summary of the arrangement in Clarke, *Advice and Support,* 210–12.

52. The Bunker sketch is based on Westmoreland, *A Soldier Reports,* 264; Palmer, *Twenty-five Year War,* 47–49; Sheehan, *Bright, Shining Lie,* 669–71; Douglas Pike, ed., *The Bunker Papers: Reports to the President from Vietnam, 1967–1973,* ix–xvii.

53. For the full text of the message, see *Public Papers, 1967,* 2–14.

54. *Gallup Opinion Index,* April, 1968, 3, showed that in January, 1967, 38 percent of the American public approved of Johnson's handling of the Vietnam War, while 43 percent disapproved, and 19 percent were uncertain.

55. Westmoreland, *A Soldier Reports,* 272.

56. Gravel, *Pentagon Papers,* vol. 4, 442.

57. See Walt W. Rostow, *The Diffusion of Power: An Essay in Recent History,* 513; Westmoreland, *A Soldier Reports,* 276; History File, March 27–April 30, 1967, folder 15, Box 11, Papers of William Westmoreland, LBJ Library.

58. Westmoreland, *A Soldier Reports,* 276. Westy ruminated on p. 277 that his second prediction proved accurate, "for it was almost exactly my minimum force that the President eventually was to approve, and five years later all American troops were destined to be out of Vietnam."

59. Gravel, *Pentagon Papers,* vol. 4, 442. Johnson wanted to be sure that the ARVN did its share. See ibid., 443.

60. Westmoreland, *A Soldier Reports,* 277–78.

61. For the text, see *Ramparts* (May, 1967), 5:11. The size of the New York crowd is disputed. See Barrett, *Uncertain Warriors,* 225n. 70. Barrett points out that on the same day as King's speech, some fifty thousand protesters turned out in San Francisco.

62. See Lewy, *America in Vietnam,* 444–47. Lewy makes a careful assessment of responsibility for civilian casualties and his tables are revealing.

CHAPTER 12

1. Johnson, *Diary,* 520; the title of this chapter is from a quote on page 274.
2. Author's interview with Mrs. Lyndon B. Johnson, June 18, 1990.
3. Johnson, *Diary,* 522.
4. Johnson, *Vantage Point,* 287–98. The quote is on p. 287.
5. Quoted in many places. See, for example, Johnson, *Vantage Point,* 299; Califano, *Triumph and Tragedy,* 204.
6. See Kalman, *Fortas,* 301–302, 466n. 51.
7. Ibid., 466n. 57; Califano, *Triumph and Tragedy,* 205.
8. Daily Diary, June 7, 1967, LBJ Library, notes an 8:40 P.M. phone call that mentions the offending memo. Johnson's telephone comments were mild.
9. Ibid., June 5, 1967.
10. Ball, *Past,* 434.
11. Daily Diary, June 5, 1967, 5, 14.
12. Rusk, *As I Saw It,* 387.
13. Daily Diary, June 5, 1967.
14. Ibid., June 6, 1967, 2.
15. Ibid., 13; *Public Papers, 1967,* vol. 1, 253.
16. Daily Diary, June 7, 1967; Johnson, *Vantage Point,* 300.
17. Daily Diary, June 8, 1967; Rusk, *As I Saw It,* 388; Califano, *Triumph and Tragedy,* 205–206; LBJ, *Vantage Point,* 300–301; Clifford, *Counsel to President,* 445–47.
18. Quoted in Rusk, *As I Saw It,* 388.
19. Ibid.
20. Clifford, *Counsel to President,* 446–47.
21. Johnson, *Vantage Point,* 301; Califano, *Triumph and Tragedy,* 205–206.
22. Johnson, *Vantage Point,* 302. The timing of Hot Line messages is disputable. The account in the text is an attempt to reconcile the White House Daily Diary with Johnson, *Vantage Point,* and other sources.
23. Author's interview with Jack Valenti, June 27, 1991.
24. Gravel, *Pentagon Papers,* vol. 4, 478.
25. Ibid., 419. For McNamara's memorandum, see ibid., 418–21, 600–601, quoting the text in the LBJ Library as declassified for Gen. William C. Westmoreland v. CBS, Inc. Portions of this memo appeared in Gravel, *Pentagon Papers,* vol. 4, 477–89, and Johnson, *Vantage Point,* 369–70. See also McNamara, *In Retrospect,* 273–77.
26. Shapley, *Promise and Power,* 419.
27. Ibid., 420.
28. See Pike, *Bunker Papers,* vol. 1, 7, 13, 15, 71–72, dispatches covering May–July, 1967. In his weekly telegram to the president, July 5, 1967, Bunker said, "I believe we are gradually achieving our aim in Viet-Nam. If we stick with it long enough—and this is not a short term proposition—and reinforce the success already achieved, I am confident that we shall achieve our objective" (Ibid., 71–72).
29. Johnson, *Vantage Point,* 366–67.
30. Ibid.; Gravel, *Pentagon Papers,* vol. 4, 474.
31. See Clifford's assessment of why he thought about the war as he did in *Counsel to President,* 425–26. In an interview with the author on March 29, 1990, Clifford said:

This is what happened to me. . . . I had made my all-out pitch for the policy that I thought he should follow. He had chosen another policy. . . . Now. . . .

I could have said, "Mr. President, in view of your making this other decision, I will no longer be available as an advisor"; that really did not occur to me. . . . He made the other decision and I went right along. I continued to attend the meetings, and because he had set the policy, I supported the policy. And . . . in 1967 I supported it and if anything a little more strongly. And the reason was, because of the reports we were getting. . . . And the reports coming from Vietnam were quite encouraging.

See also Barrett, *Uncertain Warriors,* 100.

32. Author's interview with Mrs. Lyndon B. Johnson, June 18, 1990.

33. Jack Valenti commented on Johnson's concern about the civilian casualties in an interview with the author on June 27, 1991:

He was very careful about civilian expenditure of life which is why he picked out the bomb sites. . . . He was careful. Now, that speaks well for him as a humanitarian, but that's not the way to run a war. War is, by its very nature, the outer limits of brutality and inhumanity. . . . He was very, very careful about putting to hazard the future of the country with another war on his hands. He used to say "now these things take on a life of their own; sink the Russian ship and then they're going to sink one of ours. Then we got to sink one of theirs, and all of a sudden, we're at war." He didn't know what the Chinese were going to do. He remembered the Yalu River. . . . At the time those decisions were taken, I think those were reasonable . . . worries, anxieties, on the part of the President. I did not find it unworthy of him to worry about where these bombs were going to drop.

See also Rusk, *As I Saw It,* 457.

34. Rusk, *As I Saw It,* 349, gives a lively description of the problems involved in moving the U.S. president around.

35. Author's interview with Mrs. Lyndon B. Johnson, June 18, 1990.

36. Johnson, *Diary,* 535–36.

37. Shapley, *Promise and Power,* 393–94.

38. Johnson, *Vantage Point,* 256. The Vietnam discussion is well covered in Lloyd C. Gardner, *Pay Any Price: Lyndon Johnson and the Wars for Vietnam,* 372–74.

39. Johnson, *Vantage Point,* 256–57; Rusk, *As I Saw It,* 471.

40. Johnson, *Diary,* 535–42, covers the Glassboro summit. In an interview on June 18, 1990, Mrs. Johnson spoke of Glassboro at length, with essentially the same points, but looked back in perspective: "I do remember a lot about Glassboro which in retrospect loomed very small on the horizon."

41. Sharp, *Strategy for Defeat,* 177–79.

42. Author's interview with Robert Komer, March 17, 1989.

43. Sharp, *Strategy for Defeat,* 179–80, 184.

44. Shapley, *Promise and Power,* 423–24.

45. See Westmoreland, *A Soldier Reports,* 280, where his later reaction is less cordial. For his original comments, see History File, July 12, 1967, p. 5, Box 12, Papers of William Westmoreland, LBJ Library.

46. See Shapley, *Promise and Power,* 661n. 42.

47. In Tom Johnson's notes (Meeting with McNamara, Katzenbach, Wheeler, Clifford, Rostow, July 14, 1967, Box 1, Tom Johnson's Notes, LBJ Library), Johnson said, "We are going to send Westmoreland the troops he needs. I told him that. That has been our policy and will continue to be." He added that "the details on the numbers of troops must be worked out."

48. Gravel, *Pentagon Papers,* vol. 4, 526–27. Johnson, in *Vantage Point,* 263, says he made an announcement on August 3 that he had approved sending forty-

five thousand to fifty thousand men. He did. See *Public Papers,* 1967, vol. 2, 736, 741, 744.

49. See Shapley, *Promise and Power,* 425, 661n. 43.

50. White House Meeting July 14, 1967, Box 1, Tom Johnson's Notes, LBJ Library.

51. Clifford, *Counsel to President,* 448.

52. Pike, *Bunker Papers,* 92, 98 (telegram of July 26, 1967); Clifford, *Counsel to President,* 449; White House Meeting July 14, 1967, Box 1, Tom Johnson's Notes, LBJ Library.

53. See Barrett, *Uncertain Warriors,* 102.

54. Clifford, *Counsel to President,* 451.

55. See Berman, *Johnson's War,* 60.

56. Johnson, *Vantage Point,* 266–67; McNamara, *In Retrospect,* 295–302.

57. McNamara, *In Retrospect,* 302.

58. See Johnson, *Vantage Point,* 266–67; Berman, *Johnson's War,* 83–84; Clifford, *Counsel to President,* 452–54.

59. Tuesday Lunch Meeting, August 8, 1967, Box 1, Tom Johnson's Notes, LBJ Library. McNamara rebutted Rostow's numbers by saying other estimates showed infiltration had been slowed by only 1 percent.

60. Meeting with Democratic Congressmen, State Dining Room, 9:02 A.M. to 10:40 A.M., Box 1, Tom Johnson's Notes, LBJ Library.

61. Tuesday Lunch Meeting, August 8, 1967, ibid.

62. Quoted in Shapley, *Promise and Power,* 431–32. See also *William C. Westmoreland v. CBS Inc et al.,* U.S. District Court, Southern District of New York, deposition taken on December 6, 1984, pp. 4982–94, LBJ Library.

63. Gravel, *Pentagon Papers,* vol. 4, 13; Sharp, *Strategy for Defeat,* 198.

64. See the summary in Shapley, *Promise and Power,* 432–33.

65. Meeting at White House, August 16, 1967, Box 1, Tom Johnson's Notes, LBJ Library.

66. Tuesday Lunch Meeting, August 8, 1967, ibid.

67. Berman, *Johnson's War,* 113. See also Kowet, *Matter of Honor,* which covers the Westmoreland vs. CBS case.

68. See the assessment in Barrett, *Uncertain Warriors,* 106–108.

69. See Paul Hendrickson, "McNamara, Specters of Vietnam," *Washington Post,* May 10, 1984. For McNamara's quote, see Shapley, *Promise and Power,* 435–36. McNamara repeated his opinion in *In Retrospect,* 303–305.

70. That this occurred at the Tuesday Lunch meeting is confirmed by Clifford, *Counsel to President,* 457, and Tom Johnson's Notes, LBJ Library. See Clark Clifford's summary of the meeting in *Counsel to President,* 454–55. Details of the various opinions are in Berman, *Johnson's War,* 104–109.

71. This highly secret memo is reprinted in McNamara, *In Retrospect,* 292–93. McNamara says he never saw the memo and that it has "only recently been declassified." He believes Johnson "never showed it to anyone else" (ibid., 293).

72. Berman, *Johnson's War,* 101–103. Details of the Wise Men's gathering and McNamara's November 1 memo are given in Gibbons, U.S. Government and Vietnam War, vol. 4, 872–93.

73. Johnson, *Vantage Point,* 372–78, 600–601.

74. Berman, *Johnson's War,* 115.

75. Westmoreland, *A Soldier Reports,* 280–85.

76. Quoted in Berman, *Johnson's War,* 116.

77. Johnson, *Diary,* 591–93; author's interview with Mrs. Lyndon B. Johnson, August 23, 1989. Commenting on McNamara's departure, Mrs. Johnson said,

"Lyndon respected him and just loved him. I think in the end . . . there came a point where McNamara was physically about to crack up. . . . [Lyndon] thought he was sort of saving him from just cracking up." McNamara denies illness in *In Retrospect*, 313.

78. Author's interview with Mrs. Lyndon B. Johnson, August 23, 1989.

79. See Califano, *Triumph and Tragedy*, 249, and Johnson, *Diary*, 592.

80. Califano, *Triumph and Tragedy*, 249.

81. See Shapley's cogent assessment in *Promise and Power*, 437–39. See also McNamara, *In Retrospect*, 311–14.

82. Johnson, *Diary*, 592.

83. Shapley, *Promise and Power*, 440.

84. Kearns, *Johnson and Dream*, 336.

85. Author's interview with Mrs. Lyndon B. Johnson, August 23, 1989.

86. Valenti, *Very Human President*, 222–32.

87. Johnson, *Vantage Point*, 379.

88. Valenti, *Very Human President*, 227–32; transcript of meeting with the Pope, December 23, 1967, Jack Valenti's Notes, Office of the President Files, LBJ Library.

89. Quoted in Berman, *Johnson's War*, 137.

90. See Cable, *Unholy Grail*, 212–13. Cable condemns Johnson for continuing the bombing campaign against North Vietnam. "The . . . President is open to a more damning indictment with regard to the air war. Here the Administration knew how to know if the United States was winning. It was clear from all the intelligence assessments that the air war over the North was a counterproductive failure which should be terminated. There were good pragmatic reasons for its ending and a real possibility that the benefits would accrue from stopping the bombing. The President chose to reject or ignore excellent counsel and intelligence and authorize a continuation of an aerial campaign which had all too obviously failed."

91. Meeting, November 15, 21, 1967, Box 1, Tom Johnson's Notes, LBJ Library.

92. Meeting, December 5, 1967, ibid.

93. Meeting, November 15, 1967, ibid.

CHAPTER 13

1. The chapter title comes from the author's interview with Mrs. Lyndon B. Johnson, August 23, 1989, in which Mrs. Johnson quoted her husband as saying: "I can't get out. I can't finish it. What the hell can I do?"

2. Robert Pisor, *The End of the Line: The Siege of Khe Sanh*, 161–62. For a more recent study of Khe Sanh, see John Prados, *Valley of Decision: The Siege of Khe Sanh*.

3. Pisor, *End of Line*, 162. The one-year rotation policy was forced on U.S. troops when reserves were not called up and enlistments were not "for the duration."

4. Karnow, *Vietnam*, 541.

5. See Westmoreland, *A Soldier Reports*, 379. Johnson in *Vantage Point* offers a somewhat different version of all this (see pp. 395–432). Rusk covers these nascent negotiations in *As I Saw It*, 459–74.

6. Palmer, *Summons of Trumpet*, 169.

7. Westmoreland, *A Soldier Reports*, 410–11. See also Karnow, *Vietnam*, 540. See "Analysis of Khe Sanh Situation in Light of Previous Sieges," March 3, 1968, referencing "Dien Bien Phu Briefing presented on 11 Feb 68," History File [II], March 1–31, 1968, Folder 30, Box 16, Papers of William Westmoreland, LBJ Library.

8. See "President's National Security Meeting, January 23, 1968," Box 2, Tom

Johnson's Notes, LBJ Library; Clifford, *Counsel to President,* 465. There are slight differences in the McNamara and Clifford quotes, which I have tried to reconcile by using both sources.

9. Pisor, *End of Line,* 134–38. There is doubt about Johnson's terminology and demand for a written guarantee, "signed in blood," about Khe Sanh. See his denial of both in Tom Johnson's Notes of the President's Meeting with John Steele, Bureau Chief, *Time* magazine, February 8, 1968, Box 1, Tom Johnson's Meeting Notes, LBJ Library: "I did say we do not want another Dien Bien Phu. General Westmoreland, not all of the Joint Chiefs, did write me a letter saying Khe Sanh should and could be defended. But I never said 'we don't want another damned Dien Bien Phu.'" Don Oberdorfer, *Tet!,* 171, accepts the idea that Johnson "insisted on a formal paper from the Joint Chiefs, 'signed in blood,' . . . that Khe Sanh could be held." Johnson asked Tom Johnson to look over meeting notes to find if he had demanded a letter from all the JCS and had used "damn" in speaking of another Dien Bien Phu. Tom Johnson replied: "I have reviewed all of the notes . . . [and] searched my memory thoroughly. . . . At no time do my notes show, or my memory recall, an incident when the President said: 'I do not want any Damn Dien Bien Phu.'" Johnson did tell a congressional leadership group on January 30, 1968, that he had "it in writing" that the JCS were prepared at Khe Sanh (January 30, 1968, Meeting, Box 2, Tom Johnson's Notes, LBJ Library). See Berman, *Johnson's War,* 142–43, 213.

10. For La Than Tronc's revelations, see Pisor, *End of Line,* 108–12; for the North Vietnamese battle order, see Oberdorfer, *Tet!,* 119–20.

11. See Tuesday Lunch Meeting, January 23, 1968, Box 1, Tom Johnson's Notes, LBJ Library; Clifford, *Counsel to President,* 467; Westmoreland, *A Soldier Reports,* 408–409.

12. See Tom Johnson's Notes, LBJ Library, for meetings on respective dates.

13. Johnson, *Vantage Point,* 535.

14. President's Meeting with John Steele, Bureau Chief, *Time* magazine, February 9, 1968, Box 2, Tom Johnson's Notes, LBJ Library; Ball, *Past,* 436; Clifford, *Counsel to President,* 465–67. For a clear view of administration concerns about the *Pueblo,* see Meeting of the National Security Council, January 24, 1968, Box 1, Tom Johnson's Notes, LBJ Library.

15. See Sidey, *Personal Presidency,* 216.

16. Rudyard Kipling, "The Young British Soldier."

17. See Oriana Fallaci, *Nothing and So Be It,* 226.

18. Pisor, *End of Line,* 137.

19. Ibid., 203–204.

20. See Moyers S. Shore II, *The Battle for Khe Sanh* 57–58; Pisor, *End of Line,* 184–90, for a Lang Vei vignette.

21. Westmoreland, *A Soldier Reports,* 413. See also p. 411, for ordnance at Khe Sanh.

22. President's Meeting with the Senior Foreign Policy Affairs Advisory Council, February 10, 1968, Box 2, Tom Johnson's Notes, LBJ Library.

23. *Public Papers,* 1968–69, vol. 1, 234. Westy's nuclear study group dissolved quickly—against his better judgment. See Westmoreland, *A Soldier Reports,* 411.

24. See Davidson, *Vietnam at War,* 564–66. Davidson says that "the loss of Khe Sanh and its 6,000 man garrison would have sparked within the United States a political and psychological explosion of massive proportions. President Johnson knew this, and for this reason in 1968 the fate of Khe Sanh became and remained his primary concern." Davidson also suggests that the nuclear idea may well have

seemed plausible to Giap, who recalled talk about using nuclear weapons to help the French at Dien Bien Phu (Ibid., 565).

25. Quoted in Pisor, *End of Line*, 266. Lieutenant Gen. Victor Krulak suggests in *First to Fight*, 217–19, that Giap's action at Khe Sanh conformed to Westy's hopes of creating a killing ground. Once Giap saw the strength the Americans would commit, he left enough men at the combat base to freeze U.S. commitment and shifted men to other phases of Tet. "In the end," Krulak asserts, "Giap, having milked as much out of the Khe Sanh operation as he could, simply caused his forces to melt away. . . . Their only investment was blood, to which they assigned a low importance" (Ibid., 219).

26. For the casualty problem, see Pisor, *End of Line*, 258–63. Westmoreland, *A Soldier Reports*, 422, gives the numbers in the text.

27. Johnson, *Diary*, 618.

28. For the full text of the message, see *Public Papers, 1968*, 25–33. See Johnson, *Diary*, 611–18, for the resignation issue.

29. Johnson, *Diary*, 617–19; Johnson, *Vantage Point*, 430.

30. For a remarkably clear and detailed account of the entire Tet offensive, see Oberdorfer, *Tet!*; for the early attacks, see pp. 122–24. See also James J. Wirtz, *The Tet Offensive: Intelligence Failure in War*; Clarke, *Advice and Support*.

31. Tuesday Lunch Meeting, January 30, 1968, Box 2, Tom Johnson's Notes, LBJ Library.

32. Breakfast Meeting with Congressional Leaders and Policy Advisors, January 31, 1968, ibid.

33. Ibid.

34. For the Embassy attack see Oberdorfer, *Tet!*, 2–40; I accept the casualty figures in Meyerson, *Images of War*, 166.

35. The number of people watching is in dispute. Oberdorfer, *Tet!*, 28, 354, citing national Nielsen ratings, gives the number cited in the text. Karnow, *Vietnam*, 526, says 50 million watched the embassy action.

36. NSC Meeting, February 7, 1968, Box 2, Tom Johnson's Notes, LBJ Library.

37. See Westmoreland, *A Soldier Reports*, 396–99.

38. Quoted in Oberdorfer, Tet!, 34. See also Westmoreland, *A Soldier Reports*, 385.

39. Westmoreland, *A Soldier Reports*, 386–90.

40. Ibid., 390.

41. This whole episode is covered in various sources. See Pisor, *End of Line*, 189–98; Davidson, *Vietnam at War*, 493–94; Oberdorfer, *Tet!*, 187–90.

42. Pike, *Bunker Papers*, vol. 2, 327–28, weekly telegram dated February 8, 1968.

43. This is the theme of Cable's *Unholy Grail*, in which he makes an intriguing, if not entirely convincing, case for the thesis.

44. Quoted in Karnow, *Vietnam*, 534.

45. Ibid., 533.

46. Oberdorfer, *Tet!*, 198–235, covers Hue especially well. See also Herring, *America's Longest War*, 190, for a fine condensation. See also Karnow, *Vietnam*, 529–34; Westmoreland, *A Soldier Reports*, 399–402. For more information on casualties in Hue, see Lewy, *America in Vietnam*, 274–75.

47. See Oberdorfer, *Tet!*, 179.

48. Casualty figures vary. Oddly enough, Oberdorfer, *Tet!*, presents no real compilations of losses. Westmoreland, *A Soldier Reports*, 404, offers apparently low estimates, which Herring, *America's Longest War*, 191, largely accepts. Lewy, *America in Vietnam*, 127, 134, 146–47, offers some clarification. I found Clarke, *Advice and Support*, 327–28, helpful.

49. See *Gallup Opinion Poll Index,* April, 1968, 3.

50. Quoted in Oberdorfer, *Tet!,* 250–51.

51. See Davidson, *Vietnam at War,* 486.

52. This comment received wide quotation. See Schandler, *Unmaking of President,* 198.

53. Johnson is alleged to have said to George Christian, while watching Cronkite's program, "If I've lost Cronkite, I've lost middle America." (Quoted in Davidson, *Vietnam at War,* 486, quoting, in turn, David Culbert, "Television's Vietnam: The Impact of Visual Images," [TV documentary as reported in *The Monitor,* McAllen, Texas, March 20, 1981]). George Christian, in a telephone interview, June 2, 1994, gave the author the quote used in the text.

54. Peter Braestrup, *Big Story: How the American Press and Television Reported and Interpreted the Crisis of Tet, 1968, in Vietnam and Washington,* 509; Davidson, *Vietnam at War,* 486.

55. Quoted in Davidson, *Vietnam at War,* 487.

56. Kearns, *Johnson and Dream,* 317.

57. Quoted in Davidson, *Vietnam at War,* 492.

58. Author's telephone interview with George Christian, June 2, 1994.

59. Meeting (2C), April 3, 1968, Box 3, Tom Johnson's Notes, LBJ Library.

60. Meetings on February 6, 1968, Box 2, ibid.

61. Meeting, February 9, 1968, Box 2, ibid.

62. Braestrup, Big Story, 469–71. Ronnie E. Ford argues in *Tet 1968: Understanding the Surprise,* that the Tet offensive achieved exactly what the North Vietnamese intended—a shift in U.S. opinion.

63. Wheeler suggested to Westmoreland and Oley Sharp on February 9, 1968, that "over-all enemy strategy might be to attack and attrit the ARVN thereby destroying them and ultimately gaining acceptance by the people of a coalition government. Massive Khe Sanh buildup would be an alternative threat to force a syphoning off of troops from the south thereby reducing security and affording the enemy opportunities to destroy ARVN units." Sharp, in relaying this thesis to Westy, carried it further, saying the Khe Sanh buildup might be a diversion to "weaken U.S. and ARVN as much as possible to facilitate an attack on Saigon" (Document 93, History File, February 1–29, 1968, Box 16, Papers of William Westmoreland, LBJ Library). This message triggered Westy's own analysis of enemy strategy which touched Wheeler's at some points but preserved COMUSMACV's certainty about massive I Corps battles and a Khe Sanh attack. See Document 95, Westmoreland to JCS and CINCPAC, ibid. See also Schandler, *Unmaking of President,* 94–95.

64. Meeting with JCS, February 9, 1968, Box 2, Tom Johnson's Notes, LBJ Library.

65. Tuesday Lunch Meeting, February 6, 1968, ibid.

66. See Document 95, February 9, 1968, Folder 29, History File, February 1–29, 1968, Box 16, Papers of William Westmoreland, LBJ Library.

67. Quoted in Schandler, *Unmaking of President,* 95.

68. Quoted in ibid., 97.

69. Document 95, Westmoreland to Wheeler and Sharp, February 9, 1968, Folder 29, History File, February 1–29, 1968, Box 16, Papers of William Westmoreland, LBJ Library.

70. Meeting, February 9, 1968, Box 2, Tom Johnson's Notes, LBJ Library.

71. Document 105, Wheeler to Westmoreland, February 12, 1968, Folder 29, History File [1] February 1–19, 1968, Box 16, Papers of William Westmoreland, LBJ Library.

72. Document 107, Westmoreland to Sharp and Wheeler, February 12, 1968, ibid.

73. Meeting, February 12, 1968, Box 2, Tom Johnson's Notes, LBJ Library.

74. Tuesday Lunch Meeting, February 13, 1968, ibid.

75. Quoted in Schandler, *Unmaking of President,* 105.

76. See ibid., 104; Davidson, *Vietnam at War,* 498–99.

77. Author's interview with Tom Johnson, December 16, 1988. Johnson spoke eloquently of LBJ's deep sensitivity. "The pain that I know he felt as he would drive along . . . with young people standing at the sides of the road with banners, yelling 'Hey, Hey, LBJ, How many kids did you kill today?' . . . He felt to his last days . . . that he was trying to provide a shield behind which the people of Vietnam could live at peace . . . that these people, who did not want to be overtaken by the aggression from the North had a right to live free and particularly free of Communist agression, and it was sort of fundamental for him." Senator Everett Dirksen commented on LBJ's feelings with unusual empathy: "Lyndon B. Johnson is one of the most sensitive men I ever knew" (Neil McNeil, *Dirksen,* 328).

78. Johnson, *Vantage Point,* 387–88.

79. Quoted in Barrett, *Uncertain Warriors,* 122–23.

80. Quoted in ibid., 123.

81. Author's interview with Tom Johnson, December 16, 1988.

82. Johnson, *Vantage Point,* 390.

83. Westmoreland, *A Soldier Reports,* 429–30.

84. Davidson, *Vietnam at War,* 501.

85. Westmoreland, *A Soldier Reports,* 435. General Westmoreland's denial seems incredible. The three packages were carefully structured: the first, 108,000; the second, 42,000; the third, 55,000.

86. Karnow, *Vietnam,* 551. Davidson, *Vietnam at War,* 503, discusses the "clear understanding." See Westmoreland, *A Soldier Reports,* 435.

87. Sharp, in *Strategy for Defeat,* 216, says that he "was bypassed in this particular instance, most likely because of the perception of urgency generated by both the Tet offensive and the . . . siege of Khe Sanh, but I was, as always, in favor of giving the field commander what he needed to do his job." Westmoreland, in *A Soldier Reports,* 433, says he did not see the report either.

88. See Barrett, *Uncertain Warriors,* 125.

89. Johnson, *Vantage Point,* 388.

90. Ibid., 389–90. This suggestion seems to have been ignored in later meetings.

91. Quoted in Clifford, *Counsel to President,* 485.

92. See Johnson, *Vantage Point,* 389–90. The McPherson quote is in Clifford, *Counsel to President,* 485.

93. Oberdorfer, *Tet!,* 281.

94. Johnson, *Vantage Point,* 388.

95. President's Meeting to Discuss General Wheeler's Trip to Vietnam, February 28, 1968, Box 2, Tom Johnson's Notes, LBJ Library.

96. Karnow, *Vietnam,* 551.

97. President's Meeting to Discuss General Wheeler's Trip to Vietnam, February 28, 1968, Box 2, Tom Johnson's Notes, LBJ Library.

98. Whether Wheeler meant to damage Westmoreland's reputation is unclear. Westy never accused him of it, but others suggest the possibility. See Davidson, *Vietnam at War,* 504–509, whose bias may cause some discounting. Karnow, *Vietnam,* 551, accepts Westmoreland's later complaint that Wheeler had "conned" him. See also Schandler, *Unmaking of President,* 105–20. Clifford, *Counsel to President,* 479–83, offers a strident and inconclusive defense of Wheeler. Bruce Palmer, in *Twenty-five Year War,* 80, says "regrettably General Wheeler, who engineered and in reality was

responsible for Westmoreland's abortive request, did little to set the record straight."

99. Clifford, *Counsel to President*, 480.

100. Ibid., 479–80.

101. Johnson, *Vantage Point*, 393; Clifford, *Counsel to President*, 486.

CHAPTER 14

1. There is no mention of Acheson coming to the White House on February 28 in the White House Diary, LBJ Library.

2. Barrett, *Uncertain Warriors*, 128, mentions the summons to Acheson and the date.

3. Quoted in ibid., 129, that Rostow "remembers no such colorful language."

4. Ibid., 128–29.

5. Ibid., 128.

6. Johnson, *Vantage Point*, 389.

7. See Barrett, *Uncertain Warriors*, 114. See *Gallup Opinion Index*, April, 1969, 3.

8. Oberdorfer, *Tet!*, 292–93.

9. Author's interview with Paul Nitze, July 26, 1990. Nitze believed that a department head owed first loyalty to his department at all times.

10. Johnson, *Vantage Point*, 394.

11. Author's interview with Clark Clifford, March 29, 1990.

12. Author's interview with McGeorge Bundy, November 12, 1990: "Well, you don't manage him."

13. Johnson, *Vantage Point*, 396.

14. Schandler, *Unmaking of President*, 247, quotes McPherson as saying that Clifford counted on him as his "eyes and ears in the White House."

15. Clifford, *Counsel to President*, 490–91.

16. Sharp, *Strategy for Defeat*, 203.

17. Author's interview with Paul Warnke, March 29, 1990.

18. Clifford, *Counsel to President*, 493–94. General Davidson, in *Vietnam at War*, 515, suggests that the military did have a war plan: "The JCS had formulated plans to win the war, and so had Admiral Sharp and General Westmoreland. These plans provided for shifting from strategic defensive to strategic offensive by executing one or a combination of the following operations: a 'right hook,' airborne-amphibious landing north of the DMZ, Laos or Cambodia; and finally, bombing vital targets in Haiphong and Hanoi." Admiral Sharp gave his and the JCS's plan in *Strategy for Defeat*, 203.

19. See President's Meeting with Senior Foreign Policy Advisers, March 4, 1968, Box 2, Tom Johnson's Notes, LBJ Library. Clifford, *Counsel to President*, 494–95, offers a shortened, somewhat different account of the proceedings. Lyndon Johnson's account, *Vantage Point*, 397–99, offers extra insights of importance.

20. Schandler, *Unmaking of President*, 243, where Rostow is quoted as saying, "Clifford was very vague. He lectured us on the impossibility of military victory, but he did not advocate anything operational. . . . What shocked President Johnson was that he didn't know what Clifford wanted. . . . Clifford was at cross purposes with the president, not in specific acts of policy but in not stating lucid operational alternatives."

21. Johnson, *Vantage Point*, 397.

22. See ibid.; Pike, *Bunker Papers*, vol. 2, 316–61.

23. Johnson, *Vantage Point*, 399. Rusk, in *As I Saw It*, 479, truncates his account of the bombing suggestion.

24. Johnson, *Vantage Point*, 399; Tuesday Lunch Meeting, March 5, 1968, Box 2, Tom Johnson's Notes, LBJ Library.

25. Tuesday Lunch Meeting, March 5, 1968, Box 2, Tom Johnson's Notes, LBJ Library.

26. Johnson, *Vantage Point*, 399–400.

27. Clifford, *Counsel to President*, 497.

28. Ibid.

29. Barrett, *Uncertain Warriors*, 134.

30. Clifford, *Counsel to President*, 499.

31. Tuesday Lunch Meeting, March 12, 1968, Box 2, Tom Johnson's Notes, LBJ Library.

32. See Barrett's careful reconstruction of this meeting in *Uncertain Warriors*, 136, 242–43.

33. Clifford, *Counsel to President*, 489.

34. Johnson, *Diary*, 637–38.

35. See Karnow, *Vietnam*, 558–59. Schandler, in *Unmaking of President*, 223, says that "studies have shown that of those who favored McCarthy before the Democratic convention but who had switched to some other candidate by November, a plurality switched to [George] Wallace," a hard-line anti-Communist.

36. Johnson, *Diary*, 638.

37. Barrett, *Uncertain Warriors*, 137, 243; Oberdorfer, *Tet!*, 295.

38. Califano, *Triumph and Tragedy*, 268.

39. Ibid., 266.

40. Barrett, *Uncertain Warriors*, 140. See Bruce Allen Murphy, *Fortas: The Rise and Ruin of a Supreme Court Justice*, 257–59, where Murphy overemphasizes Johnson's hawkishness; Kalman, *Fortas*, 304–306, where Fortas's hawkishness is put in fair perspective.

41. Schandler, *Unmaking of President*, 242.

42. Barrett, *Uncertain Warriors*, 140–41; Oberdorfer, *Tet!*, 295–96.

43. Clifford, *Counsel to President*, 506. The "can no longer support" phrase may have been a later convenient "recollection."

44. See Oberdorfer, *Tet!*, 298–99; Clifford, *Counsel to President*, 507; Schandler, *Unmaking of President*, 248–49. For the Washington speech, see *Public Papers, 1968*, 402–405; for the Minneapolis speech, see ibid., 406–13. Success in Vietnam ran through almost all of Johnson's public remarks through February and March, and he pressed the need for protection of South Vietnam during any peace negotiations.

45. See Barrett, *Uncertain Warriors*, 139.

46. Clifford, *Counsel to President*, 507.

47. Barrett, *Uncertain Warriors*, 141; Davidson, *Vietnam at War*, 523.

48. Clifford, *Counsel to President*, 507.

49. Johnson, *Vantage Point*, 409; Schandler, *Unmaking of President*, 255; Clifford, *Counsel to President*, 508–509.

50. Schandler, *Unmaking of President*, 245.

51. Johnson, *Vantage Point*, 424.

52. Ibid., 413–14.

53. Ibid., 411.

54. Ibid., 410. Clifford, *Counsel to President*, 508–10, in discussing March 20, does not mention any conversation with Johnson about a peace proposal.

55. See Meeting, March 20, 1968, Box 2, Tom Johnson's Notes, LBJ Library.

56. See Sheehan, *Bright, Shining Lie*, 720, who cites an interview with Bunker as his source.

57. Document 84, History File, March 1–31, 1968, Box 16, Papers of William Westmoreland, LBJ Library.

58. Clifford, *Counsel to President*, 511.

59. Westmoreland, *A Soldier Reports*, 436.

60. The cast is in various sources. See Schandler, *Unmaking of President*, 259.

61. Ibid., 260–61; Oberdorfer, *Tet!*, 309–31; Clifford, *Counsel to President*, 511–19.

62. See Karnow, *Vietnam*, 561–62.

63. Acheson's statement is in Karnow, *Vietnam*, 562.

64. Foreign Policy Advisors Luncheon—Regulars plus Added Group—Vietnam, March 26, 1968, Box 2, Tom Johnson's Notes, LBJ Library.

65. Suspicious that the official briefings had overdrawn the situation, Johnson had two of them repeated for him and decided other factors changed the Wise Men's minds. See Barrett, *Uncertain Warriors*, 151.

66. Johnson, *Vantage Point*, 418.

67. Clifford, *Counsel to President*, 519.

68. For these dual claims, see Clifford, *Counsel to President*, 519–20; Rusk, *As I Saw It*, 481.

69. Rusk, *As I Saw It*, 482.

70. Johnson, *Vantage Point*, 420.

71. Ibid., 431.

72. Johnson, *Diary*, 642–43.

73. Quoted in Johnson, *Vantage Point*, 433.

74. Johnson, *Diary*, 644–45.

75. See Clifford, *Counsel to President*, 522–23; Johnson, *Vantage Point*, 434.

76. Clifford, *Counsel to President*, 525.

77. *Public Papers*, 1968–1969, vol. 1, 469–76. Clifford, *Counsel to President*, 524; Johnson, *Vantage Point*, 435–36.

78. Daily Diary, April 1, 1968; Califano, *Triumph and Tragedy*, 270–71.

79. Johnson, *Vantage Point*, 495–96.

80. Ibid.

CHAPTER 15

1. For an indication of growing civil disorder during the summer of 1968, see charts, Attacks on Police and Other Public Officials, June 30, 1968–August 5, 1969, and August 6, 1968–September 2, 1968, in Personal Papers of Warren Christopher, Box 8, LBJ Library.

2. See *Public Papers*, 1968–69, vol. 1, 692. The commission "will look into the causes, the occurrence, and the control of physical violence across this Nation, from assassination that is motivated by prejudice and by ideology, and by politics and by insanity, to violence in our cities' streets and even in our homes."

3. Johnson, *Vantage Point*, 51; Notes of President's Meeting of Foreign Policy Advisors, October 14, 1968, Box 4, Tom Johnson's Notes, LBJ Library.

4. Various uncertainties surrounded the issue of resumed bombing. Lieutenant Gen. Bruce Palmer cautioned Johnson's foreign policy advisors on October 14 that once bombing stopped it would be difficult to resume. General Wheeler, on September 25, 1968, said that "we can't resume bombing easily once we stop it," but on October 14, he had changed his mind. Clifford thought bombing could be resumed and George Ball feared it diplomatically. See National Security Council Notes, September 25, 1968, and Notes of President's Meeting with Foreign Policy Advisors, October 14, 1968, Box 4, Tom Johnson's Notes, LBJ Library.

5. Notes of Tuesday Lunch Meeting, November 20, 1968, Box 4, Tom Johnson's Notes, LBJ Library.

6. Notes on President's Meeting with Foreign Policy Advisors, October 14, 1968, Box 4, Tom Johnson's Notes, LBJ Library.

7. The quotation is an amalgam of Rusk's remarks as recorded in Notes of a Tuesday Lunch Meeting with Foreign Policy Advisors, October 29, 1968, Box 4, Tom Johnson's Notes, LBJ Library, and his remarks in *As I Saw It*, 489. The Thieu and Ky comment is not quoted in Rusk's book.

8. Clifford, *Counsel*, 583.

9. Ibid., 584.

10. Johnson, *Vantage Point*, 524.

11. *Public Papers*, 1968–69, vol. 2, 572.

12. Johnson, *Vantage Point*, 529.

bibliography

The author interviewed a number of people in pursuit of this book. Individual interviews are cited in the endnotes. Copies are in the author's possession. In addition to personal interviews, the oral history interviews collected at the Lyndon Baines Johnson Library, Austin, Texas, have been invaluable. They, too, are cited in the endnotes, as are the various collections of personal papers consulted (most of these are in the LBJ Library). Regrettably, a large collection of tapes of White House phone conversations began to be released too late for use in this book. A quick look at some of the tapes seems to sustain the arguments presented here.

PUBLISHED SOURCES

Altshuler, Bruce. *LBJ and the Polls*. Gainesville: University of Florida Press, 1990.

Anderson, James. "President Johnson's Use of the Cabinet as an Instrument of Executive Action." *Journal of Politics* 48, no. 3 (1986).

Anderson, Terry. *The Movement and the Sixties*. New York: Oxford University Press, 1995.

Arnold, James R. *The First Domino: Eisenhower, the Military, and America's Intervention in Vietnam*. New York: William Morrow, 1991.

Ball, George. *The Past Has Another Pattern: Memoirs*. New York: Norton, 1982.

Barrett, David M. "The Mythology Surrounding Lyndon Johnson, His Advisers, and the 1965 Decision to Escalate the Vietnam War." *Political Science Quarterly* 103, no. 4 (1988–89).

———. *Uncertain Warriors: Lyndon Johnson and His Vietnam Advisers*. Lawrence: University Press of Kansas, 1993.

Berman, Larry. *Lyndon Johnson's War: The Road to Stalemate in Vietnam*. New York: Norton, 1989.

———. *Planning a Tragedy: The Americanization of the Vietnam War*. New York: Norton, 1982.

Berman, William. *William Fulbright and the Vietnam War*. Kent, Ohio: Kent State University Press.

Bornet, Vaughn D. *The Presidency of Lyndon B. Johnson*. Lawrence: University Press of Kansas, 1983.

Braestrup, Peter. *Big Story: How the American Press and Television Reported and Interpreted the Crisis of Tet 1968 in Vietnam and Washington*. Abridged ed. New Haven: Yale University Press, 1983.

Burke, John P., and Fred I. Greenstein, with the collaboration of Larry Berman and Richard Immerman. *How Presidents Test Reality: Decisions on Vietnam, 1954 and 1965*. New York: Russell Sage Foundation, 1989.

Cable, Larry. *Unholy Grail: The U.S. and the Wars in Vietnam, 1965–1968*. London and New York: Routledge, 1991.

Califano, Joseph A., Jr. *The Triumph and Tragedy of Lyndon Johnson: The White House Years*. New York: Simon and Schuster, 1991.

Carpenter, Liz. *Ruffles and Flourishes: The Warm and Tender Story of a Simple Girl Who Found Adventure in the White House*. New York: Doubleday, 1970. Reprint, College Station: Texas A&M University Press, 1992.

Chennault, Anna. *The Education of Anna*. New York: Times Books, 1980.

Christian, George. *The President Steps Down: A Personal Memoir of the Transfer of Power*. New York: Macmillan, 1970.

Clarke, Jeffrey J. *Advice and Support: The Final Years, 1965–1973*. U.S. Army in Vietnam Series. Washington, D.C.: U.S. Army Center of Military History, 1988.

Clifford, Clark, with Richard Holbrooke. *Counsel to the President: A Memoir*. New York: Random House, 1991.

Coffey, Thomas M. *The Iron Eagle: The Turbulent Life of General Curtis LeMay*. New York: Crown, 1986.

Coffin, Tristram. *Senator Fulbright: Portrait of a Public Philosopher*. New York: Dutton, 1966.

Colby, William, with James McCarger. *Lost Victory: A Firsthand Account of America's Sixteen-Year Involvement in Vietnam*. Chicago and New York: Contemporary Books, 1989.

Congressional Quarterly Almanac, 1965–68.

Cooper, Charles G. "The Day It Became the Longest War." U.S. Naval Institute *Proceedings*, May, 1966.

Cooper, Chester. *The Lost Crusade: America in Vietnam*. New York: Dodd, Mead, 1970.

Dallek, Robert. *Lone Star Rising: Lyndon Johnson and His Times, 1908–1960*. New York and Oxford: Oxford University Press, 1991.

Davidson, Phillip B. *Vietnam at War. The History: 1946–1975*. Novato, Calif.: Presidio, 1988.

Divine, Robert A. *Exploring the Johnson Years*. Austin: University of Texas Press, 1981.

Duncanson, Dennis J. *Government and Revolution in Vietnam*. New York and Oxford: Oxford University Press, 1968.

Don, Tran Van. *Our Endless War: Inside Vietnam*. Novato, Calif.: Presidio, 1978.

Doyle, Edward, Samuel Lipsman, and the editors of Boston Publishing Company. *The Vietnam Experience: America Takes Over, 1965–67*. Boston: Boston Publishing Co., 1982.

Duiker, William J. *Historical Dictionary of Vietnam*. Metuchen, N.J.: Scarecrow Press, 1989.

Ellsberg, Daniel. *Papers on the War*. New York: Simon and Schuster, 1972.

Fall, Bernard. *Hell in a Very Small Place: The Siege of Dien Bien Phu*. New York: Lippincott, 1967.

———. *Street without Joy*. Harrisburg, Penn.: Stackpole, 1967.

Firestone, Bernard J., and Robert C. Vogt, eds. *Lyndon Baines Johnson and the Uses of Power*. New York: Greenwood, 1988.

FitzGerald, Frances. *Fire in the Lake: The Vietnamese and the Americans in Vietnam*. New York: Vintage, 1989.

Ford, Ronnie E. *Tet 1968: Understanding the Surprise*. London: Frank Cass, 1995.

Fulbright, William. *The Arrogance of Power*. New York: Vintage, 1966.

Gaiduk, Ilya V. *The Soviet Union and the Vietnam War*. Chicago: Ivan R. Dee, 1996.

Gardner, Lloyd C. *Pay Any Price: Lyndon Johnson and the Wars for Vietnam*. Chicago: Ivan R. Dee, 1995.

Garrettson, Charles L., III. *Hubert H. Humphrey: The Politics of Joy.* New Brunswick, N.J.: Transaction, 1993.

Gelb, Leslie H., and Richard K. Betts. *The Irony of Vietnam: The System Worked.* Washington, D.C.: Brookings Institution, 1979.

Geyelin, Philip. *Lyndon B. Johnson and the World.* New York: Praeger, 1966.

Gibbons, William C. *The U.S. Government and the Vietnam War: Executive and Legislative Roles and Relationships.* Washington, D.C.: U.S. Government Printing Office, pt. 1, 1984; pt. 3, 1988; pt. 4, 1994.

Gittinger, Ted, ed. *The Johnson Years: A Vietnam Roundtable.* Austin: Lyndon B. Johnson Library, 1993.

Glennon, John P., ed. in chief, and Edward C. Keefer, ed. *Foreign Relations of the United States, 1961–1963.* Washington, D.C.: U.S. Government Printing Office, 1991, vol. 4, *Vietnam August–December, 1963.*

Goldman, Eric. *The Tragedy of Lyndon Johnson.* New York: Knopf, 1969.

Goodwin, Richard N. *Remembering America: A Voice from the Sixties.* Boston: Little, Brown, 1988.

Goulding, Phil G. *Confirm or Deny: Informing the People on National Security.* New York: Harper and Row, 1970.

Graff, Henry F. *The Tuesday Cabinet: Deliberation and Decision on Peace and War under Lyndon B. Johnson.* Englewood Cliffs, N.J.: Prentice-Hall, 1970.

Gravel, Mike, ed. *The Pentagon Papers: The Defense Department History of United States Decisionmaking in Vietnam.* 5 vols. Boston: Beacon, 1971.

Halberstam, David. *The Best and the Brightest.* New York: Random House, 1972.

Hammond, William M. *Public Affairs: the Military and the Media, 1962–1968.* U.S. Army in Vietnam. Washington, D.C.: U. S. Army Center of Military History, 1988.

Hendrickson, Paul. "McNamara, Specters of Vietnam." *Washington Post,* May 10, 1984.

Herring, George C. *America's Longest War: The United States and Vietnam, 1950–1975.* New York: Knopf, 1979.

———. "'Cold Blood': LBJ's Conduct of Limited War in Vietnam." *The Harmon Memorial Lectures in Military History.* No. 23. U.S. Air Force Academy, Colo., 1990.

———. *LBJ and Vietnam: A Different Kind of War.* Austin: University of Texas Press, 1994.

———. *The Secret Diplomacy of the Vietnam War: The "Negotiating Volumes" of the Pentagon Papers.* Austin: University of Texas Press, 1983.

Hoopes, Townsend. *The Limits of Intervention: An Inside Account of How the Johnson Policy of Escalation in Vietnam Was Reversed.* New York: McKay, 1969.

Hoxie, R. Gordon. *Command Decision and the Presidency: A Study in National Security Policy and Organization.* New York: Reader's Digest Press, 1977.

Humphrey, Hubert H. *The Education of a Public Man; My Life and Politics.* Garden City, N.Y.: Doubleday, 1976.

Hunt, Michael H. *Lyndon Johnson's War: America's Cold War Crusade in Vietnam.* New York: Simon and Schuster, 1987.

Isaacson, Walter, and Evan Thomas. *The Wise Men: Six Friends and the World They Made.* New York: Simon and Schuster, 1987.

Johnson, Lady Bird. *A White House Diary.* New York: Holt, Rinehart, and Winston, 1970.

Johnson, Lyndon B. *The Choices We Face.* New York: Bantam, 1969.

———. *Statement of the President at His Press Conference: The White House, July 28, 1965.*

———. *The Vantage Point: Perspectives on the Presidency, 1963–1969.* New York: Holt, Rinehart, and Winston, 1971.

Kalman, Laura. *Abe Fortas: A Biography.* London and New Haven: Yale University Press, 1990.

Karnow, Stanley. *Vietnam: A History.* New York: Viking, 1983.

Kaslow, David, and Stuart H. Loory. *The Secret Search for Peace in Vietnam.* New York: Random House, 1968.

Kearns, Doris. *Lyndon Johnson and the American Dream.* New York: New American Library, 1976. Paperback ed.

King, Martin Luther. "Declaration of Independence from the War in Vietnam." *Ramparts* 5, no. 11 (May, 1967).

Kinnard, Douglas. "The Soldier as Ambassador: Maxwell Taylor in Saigon, 1964–65." *Parameters: U.S. Army War College Quarterly* 21, no. 1 (Spring, 1991).

Kissinger, Henry. *White House Years.* Boston: Little, Brown, 1979.

Komer, Robert. *Bureaucracy at War.* Boulder, Colo.: Westview, 1986.

Kowet, Don. *A Matter of Honor.* New York: Macmillan, 1984.

Krepinevich, Andrew F., Jr. *The Army and Vietnam.* London and Baltimore: Johns Hopkins University Press, 1986. Paperback ed., 1988.

Krulak, Gen. Victor H. *First to Fight: An Inside View of the U.S. Marine Corps.* Annapolis, Md.: Naval Institute Press, 1984.

Ky, Nguyen Cao. *Twenty Years and Twenty Days.* New York: Stein and Day, 1976.

Lewy, Guenter. *America in Vietnam.* New York and Oxford: Oxford University Press, 1978.

Lipset, Seymour M., and Philip G. Altbach, eds. *Students in Revolt.* Boston: Houghton-Mifflin, 1969.

Marks, Leonard. "Johnson and Leadership," in *The Johnson Presidency: Twenty Intimate Perspectives of Lyndon B. Johnson.* Ed. Kenneth Thompson. Lanham, Md.: University Press of America, 1986.

Marolda, Edward J. *Carrier Operations.* Illustrated History of the Vietnam War. New York: Bantam, 1987.

McNamara, Robert S., with Brian VanDeMark. *In Retrospect: The Tragedy and Lessons of Vietnam.* New York: Times Books, Random House, 1995.

McNeil, Neil. *Dirksen.* New York: World, 1970.

McPherson, Harry C., Jr. *A Political Education.* Boston: Little, Brown, 1971.

Metzner, Edward P. *More Than a Soldier's War: Pacification in Vietnam.* College Station: Texas A&M University Press, 1995.

Meyerson, Joel D. *Images of a Lengthy War.* U.S. Army in Vietnam. Washington, D.C.: U.S. Army Center of Military History, 1986.

Middleton, Harry. *LBJ: The White House Years.* New York: Harry N. Abrams, 1990.

Miller, Merle. *Lyndon: An Oral Biography.* New York: G. P. Putnam, 1980.

Millett, Allan R., ed. *A Short History of the Vietnam War.* Bloomington: Indiana University Press, 1978. Paperback ed.

Moore, Lt. Gen. Harold G., and Joseph L. Galloway. *We Were Soldiers Once . . . and Young. Ia Drang: The Battle that Changed the War in Vietnam.* New York: Random House, 1992.

Morrison, Wilbur H. *The Elephant and the Tiger: The Full Story of the Vietnam War.* New York: Hippocrene Books, 1990.

Nitze, Paul H., with Ann M. Smith and Steven L. Rearden. *From Hiroshima to Glasnost: At the Center of Decision, A Memoir.* New York: Grove Weidenfeld, 1989.

Oberdorfer, Don. *Tet!* Garden City, N.Y.: Doubleday, 1971. Reprint, New York: DaCapo, 1984.

O'Brien, Tim. *If I Die in a Combat Zone: Box Me Up and Ship Me Home.* New York: Delacorte, 1973.

O'Neill, Tip, with William Novak. *Man of the House: The Life and Political Memoirs of Speaker Tip O'Neill.* New York: St. Martin's, 1988.

Palmer, Dave R. *Summons of the Trumpet: U.S.–Vietnam in Perspective.* San Rafael, Calif.: Presidio, 1978.

Palmer, Lt. Gen. Bruce. *The Twenty-five Year War: America's Military Role in Vietnam.* Lexington: University of Kentucky Press, 1984.

Patterson, Bradley H. *The Ring of Power: The White House Staff and Its Expanding Role in Government.* New York: Basic, 1988.

Perry, Mark. *Four Stars: The Inside Story of the Forty-Year Battle Between the Joint Chiefs of Staff and America's Civilian Leaders.* Boston: Houghton-Mifflin, 1989.

Pike, Douglas, ed. *The Bunker Papers: Reports to the President from Vietnam, 1967–1973.* Indochina Research Monograph No. 5. Berkeley, Calif.: Institute of East Asian Studies, 1990.

Pisor, Robert. *The End of the Line: The Siege of Khe Sanh.* New York: Norton, 1982.

Porter, Gareth. *A Peace Denied: The United States, Vietnam, and the Paris Agreement.* Bloomington: Indiana University Press, 1976.

Public Papers of the Presidents of the United States: Lyndon B. Johnson, 1963–1969. 9 vols. Washington, D.C.: U.S. Government Printing Office, 1965–70.

Race, Jeffrey. *War Comes to Long An.* Berkeley: University of California Press, 1972.

Redford, Emmette, and Richard T. McCulley. *White House Operations: The Johnson Presidency.* Austin: University of Texas Press, 1986.

Reedy, George. *Lyndon B. Johnson: A Memoir.* New York: Andrews and McMeel, 1982.

———. *The Twilight of the Presidency.* New York: World, 1970.

Rostow, Walt W. *The Diffusion of Power: An Essay in Recent History.* New York: Macmillan, 1972.

———. *The United States and the Regional Organization of Asia and the Pacific, 1965–1985.* Austin: University of Texas Press, 1986.

Rulon, Philip R. *The Compassionate Samaritan: The Life of Lyndon Baines Johnson.* Chicago: Nelson Hall, 1981.

Rusk, Dean, as told to Richard Rusk. *As I Saw It.* New York: W. W. Norton, 1990.

Schandler, Herbert Y. *The Unmaking of a President: Lyndon Johnson and Vietnam.* Princeton, N.J.: Princeton University Press, 1977.

Schlesinger, Arthur, Jr. *A Thousand Days.* Boston: Houghton-Mifflin, 1965.

———. *Robert Kennedy and His Times.* Boston: Houghton-Mifflin, 1978.

Schlight, John. *The War in South Vietnam: The Years of the Offensive, 1965–1968.* The United States Air Force in Southeast Asia. Washington, D.C.: Office of Air Force History, U.S. Air Force, 1988.

Shapley, Deborah. *Promise and Power: The Life and Times of Robert McNamara.* Boston: Little, Brown, 1993.

Sharp, Adm. U. S. G. *Strategy for Defeat: Vietnam in Retrospect.* Novato, Calif.: Presidio, 1978.

———, and William C. Westmoreland. *Report on the War in Vietnam, 1964–1968.* Washington, D.C.: U.S. Government Printing Office, 1968.

Sheehan, Neil. *A Bright Shining Lie.* New York: Random House, 1988.

————, et al. *The Pentagon Papers as Published by the New York Times.* New York: Bantam, 1971.

Shore, Moyers S., II. *The Battle for Khe Sanh.* Washington, D.C.: History and Museums Division, Headquarters, U.S. Marine Corps, 1969. Reprint, 1977.

Shulimson, Jack. *U.S. Marines in Vietnam: An Expanding War, 1966.* Washington, D.C.: History and Museums Division, Headquarters, USMC, 1982.

————, and Charles M. Johnson. *U.S. Marines in Vietnam: The Landing and Buildup, 1965.* Washington, D.C.: History and Museums Division, Headquarters, USMC, 1978.

Sidey, Hugh. *A Very Personal Presidency: Lyndon Johnson in the White House.* New York: Athenaeum, 1968.

Small, Melvin. *Johnson, Nixon, and the Doves.* New Brunswick, N.J.: Rutgers University Press, 1988.

Stanton, Shelby L. *Vietnam Order of Battle.* New York: Exeter, 1987.

Summers, Harry G. *On Strategy: The Vietnam War in Context.* Carlisle Barracks, Penn.: Strategic Studies Institute, U.S. Army War College, 1981.

Taylor, Maxwell. *Swords and Plowshares.* New York: Norton, 1972.

Tilford, Earl H. *Search and Rescue in Southeast Asia, 1961–1975.* Washington, D.C.: Office of Air Force History, 1980.

Tuchman, Barbara. *The March of Folly.* New York: Knopf, 1984.

Tuso, Joseph F. *Singing the Vietnam Blues: Songs of the Air Force in Southeast Asia.* College Station: Texas A&M University Press, 1990.

U.S. Department of Defense. *United States–Vietnam Relations, 1945–1967.* 12 vols. Washington, D.C.: U.S. Government Printing Office, 1971.

U.S. Department of State. *Foreign Relations of the United States, 1961–1963*, vol. 1, *Vietnam, 1961.* Washington, D.C.: U.S. Government Printing Office, 1988.

————. *Foreign Relations of the United States, 1961–1963*, vol. 2, *Vietnam, 1962.* [1990]

————. *Foreign Relations of the United States, 1961–1963*, vol. 3, *Vietnam, January–August, 1963.* [1991]

————. *Foreign Relations of the United States, 1961–1963*, vol. 4, *Vietnam, August–December, 1963.* [1991]

————. *Foreign Relations of the United States, 1964–1968*, vol. 1, *Vietnam, 1964.* [1992]

United States Naval Aviation, 1910–1980. Navy publication NAVAIR 00-80P-1. Washington, D.C.: U.S. Government Printing Office, 1981.

Valenti, Jack. *A Very Human President.* New York: Pocket Books, 1977. Paperback ed.

Vance, Cyrus R. *Hard Choices: Critical Years in America's Foreign Policy.* New York: Simon and Schuster, 1983.

VanDeMark, Brian. *Into the Quagmire: Lyndon Johnson and the Escalation of the Vietnam War.* New York and Oxford: Oxford University Press, 1991.

Vandiver, Frank E. "Lyndon Johnson: A Reluctant Hawk," in *Commanders in Chief: Presidential Leadership in Modern Wars.* Ed. Charles G. Dawson. Lawrence: University Press of Kansas, 1993.

Vietnam Hearings. Introduction by J. William Fulbright. New York: Vintage, 1966.

Walt, Gen. Lewis W. *Strange War, Strange Strategy: A General's Report on Vietnam.* New York: Funk and Wagnalls, 1970.

Weigley, Russell F. *The American Way of War: A History of United States Military Strategy and Policy.* Bloomington: Indiana University Press, 1973, 1977.

Werrell, Kenneth P. "Air War Victorious: The Gulf War vs. Vietnam." *Parameters: U.S. Army War College Quarterly* 22, no. 1 (Summer, 1992).

Westmoreland, William C. *A Soldier Reports.* Garden City, N.Y.: Doubleday, 1976.

Wicker, Tom. *JFK and LBJ: The Influence of Personality upon Politics.* New York: Morrow, 1968.

Windchy, Eugene. *Tonkin Gulf.* Garden City, N.Y.: Doubleday, 1971.

Wirtz, James J. *The Tet Offensive: Intelligence Failure in War.* Ithaca, N.Y.: Cornell University Press, 1991.

Woods, Randall B. *Fulbright: A Biography.* New York and Cambridge: Cambridge University Press, 1995.

Young, Stephen, interviewing Bui Tin. "How North Vietnam Won the War." *Wall Street Journal,* August 3, 1995.

Zaroulis, Nancy, and Gerald Sullivan. *Who Spoke Up? American Protest against the War in Vietnam, 1963–1975.* New York: Holt, Rinehart, and Winston, 1984.

Zaffiri, Samuel. *Westmoreland: A Biography of General William C. Westmoreland.* New York: Morrow, 1994.

Ziemke, Caroline. "Senator Richard B. Russell and the 'Lost Cause' in Vietnam, 1954–1968." *Georgia Historical Quarterly* 72, no. 1 (1988).

index

against all-out war, 128–29; and Ball, 125, 126, 127; bombing halts and, 153–54, 261, 314, 320–21; on bombing resumption, 163; at Camp David meeting, 127–29; disagreement of, with LBJ, 318, 319–20, 321, 371n. 20; doubts of, 116–17, 315, 318; Draft Presidential Memorandum of, 311–12; Fulbright and, 318; on McNamara, 127–28; as McNamara's successor, 270; maneuvering by, 318, 320, 321; at Manila summit, 217; and 1968 election, 316–17; and 1968 Vietnam speech, 322, 328; at 1965 Vietnam review, 125, 126–27; and 1964 election, 27; opposition of, to McCone, 116–17; predilections of, 309; recruitment trip of, 251–53; as secretary of defense, 264, 309; and Six-Day War, 240, 242; and South Vietnamese elections, 252; study group of, 305, 306, 308–12; on Tet, 291; troop requests and, 291, 295, 301, 304; on USS *Liberty* incident, 242; on Vietnam speech, 322, 328, 331, 333; and Wheeler-Westmoreland proposal, 301–302, 303, 304; and Wise Men, 259, 325, 326
Clifford, Marny, 331
Clifton, Chester V., 3
coalition government, 268
Colby, William, 63, 69; on Diem, 8; on Johnson, 58
Collins, James Lawton, 178
combat missions, 100–101
Combined Action Program (CAP), 188
Communism, 77, 78–79, 81
Congress, 112, 315; and war financing, 132
congressional leaders, 3, 25, 347n. 10; on ending bombing pause, 162–63; and Six-Day War, 241; on tax increase, 132. *See also* Johnson, Lyndon Baines: and Congress
congressional relations: in Johnson administration, 18, 24–25; on Vietnam, 24. *See also* Johnson, Lyndon Baines: and Congress
Connally, John, 277
Con Thien, siege of, 266

Cooper, Chester, 217
corruption, 60
counterinsurgency, 66
country team, U.S.: in Vietnam, 62, 66, 70
coup: in Dominican Republic, 72–73, 75; South Vietnamese, 62, 63, 90, 135
Cousins, Norman, 318
covert action, 11, 19
Cowles, John, 119, 120
credibility gap, 219, 226, 257, 258, 352n. 27
Cronkite, Walter, 287, 369n. 53
crossover point, 229, 234, 245
Crumm, William, 228
Cuba, 17
Cutler, Lloyd, 109

Dak To, 91, 266
Dalat, attack at, 283
Da Nang, 203–204, 278–79; troops at, 33, 84
dau tranh, 15
Davidson, Phillip B., 282, 299
Dean, Arthur, 119, 120, 259, 327
decision making: Johnson's style of, 33–37, 58, 82–83
Declaration of Honolulu, 169
"Declaration of Independence from the War in Vietnam," 235
"Declaration of the Goals of Freedom," 216, 220
de Gaulle, Charles, 11
Demilitarized Zone (DMZ), 32
Democratic National Convention (1968), 336
DePuy, William E., 118–19, 298, 299, 325
De Soto patrols, 19, 21, 30
Dien Bien Phu, 269–70, 271
Dillon, Douglas, 23, 31, 36, 259, 325, 327
diplomatic posturing, 115
Dirksen, Everett M., 7, 113, 162, 192; and Dominican Republic, 78; and Pleiku attacks, 36
disengagement, policy of, 30
dissent, 173, 358n. 4; Vietnamese, 201. *See also* protesters; teach-ins
Dobrynin, Anatoly, 156, 248

22; at Ap Bac, 67–68; assassinations by, 97; attacks by, 29, 32, 91, 97, 111, 280–81; compared with South Vietnamese forces, 118; desertions from, 227; inflexibility of, 281; numbers of, 91, 212; objectives of, 284; offensives by, 17; propaganda of, 269; rumored coalition with, 268; sacrificed, 283; tactics of, 118; weapons of, 16, 67

Vietnam: and American politics, 15, 22; central highlands of, 137; doubts about, 132–36; escalation in, 12, 29, 87–93, 130; and Great Society, 34, 197; information about, 57; LBJ's first visit to, 5–6; U.S. objectives in, 16–17, 36–37, 130, 139, 245; U.S. policy toward, 32; winnability of, 227–28. *See also* escalation; North Vietnam; South Vietnam

Vietnam review of 1965, 123–27

Vietnam review panel (1968), 316–17, 318, 320, 325–27

Vietnam speech: drafts of, 320; preparations for, 330–31; proposals for, 321–23, 328–29; reactions to, 333–34; text of, 331–33

Vo Nguyen Giap, 15, 16; and Khe Sanh, 276; long war strategy of, 267; and 1965 offensive, 137; troops of, 91–92; on U.S. errors, 267–68

Wadsworth, James J., 119

Wallace, George, 336

Walt, Lewis W., 187, 188, 203–204, 206–207

Walters, Charlotte, 179

war financing, 131–32

war games, 85

Warnke, Paul, 254, 309–10

War on Poverty, 28, 43–44; cabinet for, 39–40; Heller and, 43

Wasserman, Lew, 239

Watson, Marvin, 47–48, 331

weapons: at Khe Sanh, 275; North Vietnamese, 283; South Vietnamese, 67; Viet Cong, 16, 67

Webb, Kate, 281

Weisl, Ed, 239

Western capability, 125

Westmoreland, Katherine Stevens (Kitsy), 90, 166, 216, 233

Westmoreland, William Childs (Westy), 251, 265; address of, to Congress, 234; appointment of, as MACV commander, 70; as army chief of staff, 323; at Asian conference on Vietnam, 216–18; on bombing halt, 261; and CBS, 258; declining optimism of, 145; Dong Xuan offensive and, 137–38; duties of, 230; on enclaves, 102; and enemy numbers, 257–58; and escalation, 115; force ratios of, 121; and Guam conference, 230; and H. K. Johnson, 98–99; at Honolulu meetings, 103, 167, 168, 172; Khe Sanh and, 269–70, 271, 274; and Komer, 231; LBJ's Vietnam visit (1966) and, 218; lobbying of, 233–34, 249; and McNamara, 251; at Manila summit, 216–18; on Marines, 187, 271; and military initiative, 212; optimism of, 262, 298; pacification and, 178; and Pleiku attacks, 31; and post-Tet offensive, 309; public relations of, 232–33, 261–62; public reports of, 232–33, 234–35, 261–62; at ranch talks, 216, 221; reassignment of, 323–24; on Rolling Thunder, 217; and Saigon attack, 282; and "search and destroy missions," 102; security concerns of, 84–85, 91–92; strategy of, 117–19; as tactician, 283; and Taylor, 90; Tet and, 282, 283–84, 290, 293–95; Tri Quang's uprising and, 201, 205; troop requests by, 33, 99, 100, 117–18, 124, 135, 140–41, 172, 222, 233–34, 290–91, 293–95; and war financing, 132; and Wheeler's maneuvering, 298–300, 324; Wise Men on, 260

Weyand, Frederick C., 282

Wheeler, Earle G. (Bus), 109, 336; actions advocated by, 87, 103, 251, 292–93, 302–305; and attempts to maneuver Johnson, 292–97, 298, 300–305; on bombing resumption, 163; and bombing targets, 225; as chairman of JCS, 22, 53–54, 323; and Clifford's study group, 308; and Dominican Republic, 78, 79; and escalation, 115, 122; and Guam